The Business of iPhone and iPad App Development

Making and Marketing Apps That Succeed

Second Edition

Dave Wooldridge
with Michael Schneider

Apress®

The Business of iPhone and iPad App Development: Making and Marketing Apps That Succeed, Second Edition

ISBN-13 (pbk): 978-1-4302-3300-8

ISBN-13 (electronic): 978-1-4302-3301-5

Printed and bound in the United States of America 9 8 7 6 5 4 3 2 1

President and Publisher: Paul Manning
Lead Editor: Dominic Shakeshaft
Development Editor: Douglas Pundick
Technical Reviewer: Joe Kissell
Editorial Board: Steve Anglin, Mark Beckner, Ewan Buckingham, Gary Cornell, Jonathan Gennick, Jonathan Hassell, Michelle Lowman, Matthew Moodie, Jeff Olson, Jeffrey Pepper, Frank Pohlmann, Douglas Pundick, Ben Renow-Clarke, Dominic Shakeshaft, Matt Wade, Tom Welsh
Coordinating Editor: Kelly Moritz
Copy Editor: Marilyn Smith
Compositor: MacPS, LLC
Indexer: BIM Indexing & Proofreading Services
Artist: April Milne
Cover Designer: Anna Ishchenko

Distributed to the book trade worldwide by Springer Science+Business Media, LLC., 233 Spring Street, 6th Floor, New York, NY 10013. Phone 1-800-SPRINGER, fax (201) 348-4505, e-mail orders-ny@springer-sbm.com, or visit www.springeronline.com.

For information on translations, please e-mail rights@apress.com, or visit www.apress.com.

Apress and friends of ED books may be purchased in bulk for academic, corporate, or promotional use. eBook versions and licenses are also available for most titles. For more information, reference our Special Bulk Sales–eBook Licensing web page at www.apress.com/info/bulksales.

The source code for this book is available to readers at www.apress.com and www.iphonebusinessbook.com.

Contents at a Glance

Contents

About the Authors

Dave Wooldridge As the founder of Electric Butterfly, Dave Wooldridge has been developing award-winning web sites and software since 1995. When he's not creating Mac and iOS apps, he can be found writing. Dave is the author of *The Developer Sketchbook* series and a co-author of *Beginning iPad* Development for iPhone Developers (Apress), and he has written numerous articles for leading tech publications, including a monthly software marketing column for *MacTech Magazine*. Follow Dave at Twitter.com/ebutterfly.

Michael Schneider At the beginning of 2009, Michael Schneider left Silicon Valley technology firm Wilson Sonsini Goodrich & Rosati to found HiveBrain Software. HiveBrain publishes a variety of applications on the iTunes App Store, the most notable of which, TouchType, peaked at #13 in the U.S. App Store. Michael continues to practice law under the name Bitwise Legal, focusing on software and interactive media clients. Notable clients include Bungie and Innerfence. Follow Michael at Twitter.com/hivebrain.

About the Technical Reviewer

**Joe Kissell** is the senior editor of TidBITS, a web site and weekly e-mail newsletter about Apple and the Internet and is the author of numerous print and electronic books, including *Mac Security Bible* and *Take Control of Working with Your iPad*. He is also a senior contributor to *Macworld*, was the winner of a 2009 Neal Award for Best How-to Article, and has appeared on the MacTech 25 list (the 25 people voted most influential in the Macintosh community) since 2007. Joe has worked in the Mac software industry since the early 1990s and previously managed software development for Nisus Software and Kensington Technology Group. He currently lives in Paris, France, with his wife, Morgen Jahnke; their son, Soren; and their cat, Zora.

Acknowledgments

Dave and Michael would like to thank Dominic Shakeshaft and the entire Apress family for believing in this book. None of this would have been possible without the many amazing people who were involved in this project. The talented Douglas Pundick provided invaluable guidance. The wonderful Kelly Moritz not only kept us on track, but her positive spirit was a great motivator. The brilliant Joe Kissell contributed essential technical feedback and patiently tested all of the book's example code. The copyediting wizardry of Marilyn Smith truly made us better writers. The production team's usual magic ensured our humble words looked good in print, and the marketing and sales staff worked hard to deliver those words to readers everywhere. Thank you! We greatly appreciate all your efforts and dedication!

Dave would like to personally thank his good friends, Clay Andres and Dave Mark, for inviting him into the Apress gang. And a very special thanks to my supportive family. I certainly wouldn't be an author today without the writing skills I learned from my mother long ago. Thanks, Mom! Finally, I am eternally grateful for the immense love and support from my wife, Madeline, throughout this long journey. You are my rock and soul mate!

Michael would like to personally thank Clay Andres for involving him in this project, and Mark Johnson for making the introductions that got everything started. Many thanks to my parents, Mark and Nancy, for nurturing my interest in learning, and to my wife, Stacy, for supporting me in my contribution to this book and in my decision to leave corporate life and pursue my dreams.

Preface

First and foremost, I'd like to thank everyone who picked up a copy of the first edition, making it the best-selling business and app marketing book in publication for iOS developers. I truly appreciate all of the wonderful comments and feedback that we've received from app designers, programmers, and project managers who found the book beneficial. But even if you've already read the first edition, you'll quickly discover the wealth of new material within the pages of this second edition.

It has been only one year since the publication of the first edition, and yet there have been so many exciting new developments in the mobile arena that the book definitely warranted this well-deserved update. Within that short time, Apple changed the iPhone OS name to iOS for targeting app development on multiple platforms, released the instantly popular iPad tablet and iPhone 4, launched its own iAd in-app advertising network, unveiled the impressive new Xcode 4, rolled out Game Center, continued to evolve and improve iTunes Connect and the App Store, and the list goes on…

Some newcomers have the unrealistic belief that if you build a good app, people will buy it, so they feel an entire book on app marketing may be overkill. That couldn't be further from the truth! As any experienced developer currently selling apps in the App Store would attest, you should be doing anything and everything possible to help increase exposure and sales for your app. With more than 300,000 apps available in the already overcrowded App Store (and that number continues to grow exponentially every year), it's now more important than ever to learn how to successfully promote your app to stand out from the vast sea of competitors.

This newly revised and expanded second edition is packed with winning marketing solutions and effective business strategies on the very latest opportunities in the iOS world, including extensive new coverage of iPhone and iPad app marketing, universal applications, iAd, In-App Purchase updates, recent App Store submission policy changes, in-app cross-promotion, social media and sharing, and much more!

Enjoy! And may your app become the next big seller in the App Store.

Best Regards,
Dave Wooldridge

Chapter 1

Seeing the Big Picture in a Crowded App Store Marketplace

Living in Los Angeles, there's no shortage of Hollywood clichés. There was a time when it seemed like everyone I met—no matter their profession—was working on a screenplay.

Now they're all working on their own iOS apps!

And who can blame them? It's a testament to the soaring popularity of the iPhone, iPod touch, and iPad. There's money to be made in the App Store, and everyone wants in on the action.

We've all read about the success story of indie developer Steve Demeter. His Trism game, along with many of the 500 other apps that were included in the initial July 2008 launch of the App Store, experienced an overwhelming explosion in sales. With some price tags as low as 99 cents, iPhone and iPod touch owners were impulsively downloading these inexpensive apps at a feverish pace. In the months that followed, several of the most popular apps were already netting their creators hundreds of thousands of dollars, allowing programmers like Steve Demeter to quit his day job to focus full time on this lucrative opportunity.

The media quickly proclaimed the seemingly overnight sensation of the App Store as a "gold rush" for developers. With the lure of potential riches, inspired entrepreneurs from all over the world have downloaded the iOS SDK, racing to learn Objective-C and Cocoa Touch in the hopes of cashing in on this software phenomenon.

Fast-forward two years to July 2010. Apple has since introduced the iOS-powered iPad, selling more than 3 million in only the first 80 days. Combine that with the massive army of iPhone and iPod touch users for a staggering total of more than 120 million iOS devices sold and 7 billion app downloads from the App Store. You would think that with stats like that, it would be easier than ever to make money in the App Store, right? Think again....

Why a Business Book for iOS Developers?

With more than 300,000 applications in the App Store and developer interest continuing to grow at a stunning rate, industry analysts predict that number will likely double before the end of 2012.

Think about that for a moment. When browsing through the App Store, how many new apps do you stumble upon weekly or even monthly? 25? 50? According to Apple, approximately 15,000 new apps and updates are submitted each week to its app review team!

In such a crowded marketplace, it's becoming increasingly difficult for new apps to get noticed. Without the necessary exposure, your app may simply get lost in the endless stream of new software that floods the App Store on a daily basis. Gone are the days when you could quickly cobble together a simple app, throw it into the App Store, and then sit back and wait for the large royalty checks to roll in.

The media hype machine is so good at celebrating the underdog stories of a few indie developers who found instant wealth in the App Store that newcomers often assume that if they build an app, the sales will come. When the anticipated avalanche of profit turns out to be nothing more than a trickle, surprised developers quickly discover that a *Field of Dreams* philosophy is no longer enough in this highly competitive market.

"Ah, but what if I've just created the next killer app?" you ask. "Surely Apple will want to showcase it as a featured app in the App Store."

Having a great product is certainly the underlying key in this equation, but it won't be enough. It's true that being listed as a "Featured App," "New and Noteworthy," or a "Staff Favorite" can instantly propel your sales into the stratosphere, but unfortunately, those high-profile spotlights are not purchasable advertising spaces. Apple chooses only a select few apps every month for those coveted spots. With thousands of new apps vying for attention every week, your chances of getting that life-altering call from Apple are pretty slim. In fact, you may have better odds of winning the lottery.

But don't despair. Your killer app can certainly make a lot of money without being featured by Apple. Like anything else in life, finding success in the current App Store environment will require some hard work and planning, but who says the journey can't be fun along the way?

Tackling the New World of Mobile Marketing

If you have the benefit of working for a large software company with deep pockets, it probably has a dedicated department to handle all of the marketing for the products you create. But if you're an independent developer who is responsible for managing every aspect of your own business, then you're all too familiar with the haunting questions that arise when wondering how to implement effective marketing strategies to increase app sales.

And you aren't alone. Just take a look online at the various iOS-related developer forums and mailing lists, and you'll quickly see countless posts (some with generous amounts of cursing) from frustrated programmers, all asking similar questions:

- How do I promote my app?

- My app just got approved in the App Store. Now what?

- How do I get reviews for my app?

- Yikes! My 99-cent app is selling only a few units a week. What do I do?

- Is there anything I can do to avoid one-star customer reviews?

Although this all may look quite daunting, trust me—it's really not as overwhelming as it might appear. My goal here is to provide answers to those questions and much more. A lot of innovative marketing tactics, tools, and resources are available to iOS developers. Just as you wouldn't want to bring a knife to a gunfight, the key to success is in choosing the right weapon for the task at hand. This book's primary objective is to arm you with the ammunition you need, humbly serving as your definitive reference guide to the business of iPhone, iPod touch, and iPad app development.

Rest Easy—This Is Not Your Typical Business Book

If just the thought of reading yet another stale book on overgeneralized marketing concepts causes your eyes to roll back in your head, then don't worry! This is not your run-of-the-mill business book. You do not need a Harvard MBA to grok this material.

Like all Apress books, this one was written by developers for developers, taking you step by step through marketing solutions that have proven successful for professional iOS app creators. I won't just tell you what you need to do; I'll also show you how to do it.

This is not about expensive advertising campaigns. This is about cost-effective marketing alternatives that can help you sell more apps! In fact, most of the business strategies described in this book cost little to no money—perfect for all of us indie developers on shoestring budgets. All you need is some dedicated time, patience, a little creativity, and of course, this book.

Planning Your Own Success Story

I know what you're thinking. This all sounds very time-consuming, and free time is something you simply don't have to give. As a full-time developer myself, I understand this all too well. Whether I'm feeling the pressure from self-imposed work deadlines or racing to finish a project for a client, time often feels like the enemy. But I just want to spend any free time I do manage to salvage programming the next killer app. I don't want to be bothered with marketing concerns, at least not until my app is finished. Unfortunately, that would be too late.

Without a solid game plan in place, you'll find that one solitary publicity push when your app is released may not be enough to generate substantial sales. Once upon a time, sending out a press release, landing a few magazine reviews, and listing your product updates on the popular online software directories worked fine to promote traditional desktop applications. But many of those old shareware techniques don't apply here. In the unique world of the App Store, you would most likely see a momentary sales bump on launch day that quickly plummeted in the week that followed (see Figure 1–1). Then you would end up spending a lot of extra time that you had not originally allocated in desperate scrambling to figure out how to improve sales.

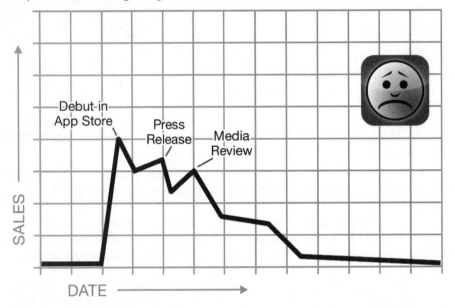

Figure 1–1. *Without a long-term marketing plan in place, you risk drastically shortening the life span and profitability of your iOS app.*

If no one knows about your app, it won't matter how many cool new features you add in the future. Did you build an app that consumers will want, satisfying an existing need in the marketplace? Did you do anything to create prerelease interest in your app? And what about your app's longevity in the App Store? Have you thought about how to sustain and grow your sales beyond the initial release? Wouldn't you prefer your sales to look more like the graph in Figure 1–2?

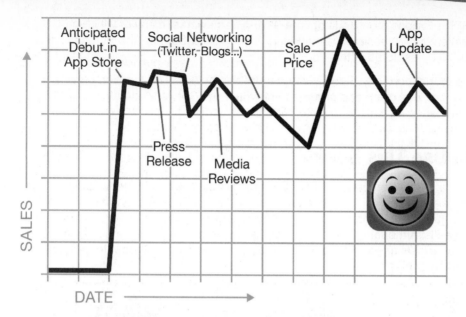

Figure 1–2. *Wouldn't you prefer your sales graph to look more like this?*

The reality is that if done right, your marketing efforts should actually help save you time in the long run. It's not just about time management. Sure, carving out a few hours every week to focus on promoting your app is important, but that's only part of the solution.

Think like a marketer. Think big picture.

It's not just about what to do after your app is available in the App Store. Did you know that as a developer, you can integrate several elements directly into your app that can encourage sales, produce additional revenue streams, help users spread the word via built-in social marketing, and improve customer support and reviews? Your app itself is one of your most powerful promotional tools, but to take advantage of these valuable tactics (and many others), you should start planning your marketing strategy before you've even written a single line of code.

In fact, this is such an important point that I feel obligated to say it again: start planning your marketing strategy before writing a single line of code. By incorporating marketing and business savvy into every aspect of the development process, you're giving your app the best possible chance of succeeding in the App Store.

Now just to be clear, I'm not suggesting that you turn your app's interface into a walking billboard—that's a task better suited for your App Store description, your web site, and publicity materials (which are also covered extensively in this book). What I'm talking about here are essential components that can be integrated into your app's functionality and user interface (UI) design that will help promote your app in very subtle ways that your users will perceive only as convenient, quality-enhancing features.

The iOS SDK provides thousands of time-saving frameworks, many of which can actually make your job easier as a marketer. For example, both In-App Purchase and In-App Email will be explored in this book.

Yes, you read that correctly. Several chapters of this book will be focused on what you love doing most: designing and programming your app! Got your attention now? And you thought marketing wasn't going to be fun!

How to Use This Book

The sequence of chapters takes a very systematic linear approach, working step by step through the planning, development, and release of an iOS app. Along the way, important business solutions will be presented in each phase of the process to help you produce an app that sells! Although you may be tempted to jump around, reading only the chapters that appeal to you, I recommend reading the chapters in order to benefit from this strategic, organized workflow (see Figure 1–3).

Figure 1–3. *For best results, follow the linear workflow of this book.*

- *Chapter 2, Doing Your Homework: Analyzing iOS App Ideas and Performing Competitive Research*: So you think you've got a great idea for a mobile app? Learn how to identify untapped markets and refine your app concept to be unique and highly marketable, setting it apart from your competition. You'll discover the immense value of doing some good old-fashioned detective work by analyzing what your competitors are doing right and wrong. We'll also explore the advantages of targeting multiple iOS devices beyond just the iPhone and the business challenges of universal applications.

■ *Chapter 3, Protecting Your Intellectual Property*: This just might be one of the most important chapters in the book! Although we probably all hate dealing with legal matters, it's crucial to the long-term health and success of your business not only to protect yourself, but also to protect the intellectual property of your original concepts and code. Michael Schneider, an expert lawyer turned app developer, will walk you through everything you need to know to safeguard your software business.

■ *Chapter 4, Your iOS App Is Your Most Powerful Marketing Tool*: Your app icon and screenshots are often the first visual elements users see in the App Store when evaluating your app. Bad first impressions can cost you sales and invite negative reviews, so fine-tuning your app's design is a critical component to success. Chapter 4 includes useful tips on prototyping, creating eye-catching app icons, crafting intuitive user interfaces, and designing for multiple iOS device targets.

■ *Chapter 5, Social Inception: Promoting Your Apps Within Apps*: Building upon Chapter 4's quest to transform your app into its own marketing powerhouse, this chapter will take you one step further by integrating convenient sharing and social media elements such as In-App Email, Twitter, and Facebook. Gracefully encourage App Store user reviews within your app, build synergy with in-app cross-promotion and third-party social gaming platforms, and learn how to implement these various ingredients for effective results.

■ *Chapter 6, Money for Nothing: When It Pays to Be Free*: Unlike the traditional desktop software world, the App Store does not currently allow time-limited or feature-crippled trial versions. To work around this restriction, many developers offer an In-App Purchase–supported "freemium" model or a free "lite" version of their apps, hoping users will buy in-app content or the separate paid edition to gain access to premium features. Learn the benefit of free to promote paid versions, plus the additional revenue opportunities of affiliate programs.

■ *Chapter 7, Monetizing Free Apps with iAd and Other In-App Advertising Opportunties*: Free apps can still make money on their own, even without paid content. Learn how to tap into alternative revenue streams with in-app advertising, sponsorships, and product-placement deals. The world of in-app advertising is thoroughly examined, educating you on the mobile ad networks available for iOS apps and the value of tracking usage through in-app analytics. Chapter 7 also includes a step-by-step guide to implementing Apple's iAd framework in your app.

■ *Chapter 8, Exploring the Freemium Model with In-App Purchase*: With In-App Purchase, developers can construct new business models within their applications, such as offering subscriptions, selling add-on content and services, and unlocking premium features. Interested in supplying additional value to your users while financially supporting your continued development efforts? This chapter provides in-depth instructions on when and how to use In-App Purchase and its related Store Kit framework in your iOS apps.

■ *Chapter 9, Testing and Usability: Putting Your Best Foot Forward*: Did you know that many of the one-star customer reviews in the App Store are caused by user frustration with hard-to-use app interfaces or buggy features? Low customer ratings can really hurt your app's perception and sales, so avoiding those situations when possible should be your top priority. Chapter 9 is all about the value of providing built-in help, provisioning apps for on-device testing, and conducting thorough beta tests.

■ *Chapter 10, Get the Party Started! Creating Prerelease Buzz*: Your app is finished, but before you submit it to the App Store, it's time to start generating some prerelease buzz for it. Chapter 10 will show you the best way to stir up some excitement and anticipation for your app by promoting it on your web site, blogs, Twitter, and other social networks, as well as by getting basically anyone you can to review or talk about your app.

■ *Chapter 11. Keys to the Kingdom: The App Store Submission Process*: Your product page in the App Store is the world's gateway to your app, so its presentation is essential in properly communicating the value of your app. This chapter will walk you through the app submission process in iTunes Connect, helping you optimize your app's text description, keywords, rating, screenshots, and other required elements, as well as discuss how to set the price to maximize your sales potential.

■ *Chapter 12, Increasing Awareness for Your iOS App*: Once you're in the App Store, it's time to rev up the publicity engine to increase consumer awareness of your app's availability. Even if your prerelease marketing efforts resulted in an initial sales surge, there's still vital work to be done. It's your job to ensure that your iOS application does not get buried amidst the thousands of new apps flooding into the App Store. Chapter 12 reveals how to craft effective press releases, utilize promo codes, gain exposure through interviews, and sustain momentum in the App Store with promotions, giveaways, and carefully timed sales events.

This book assumes that you're already familiar with Objective-C, Cocoa Touch, and iOS application programming. If you're looking for in-depth guidance beyond the documentation and tutorials available from the Apple Developer site, I highly recommend the following Apress books:

- *Learn Objective-C on the Mac* by Mark Dalrymple and Scott Knaster (http://www.apress.com/book/view/9781430218159)

- *Beginning iPhone 4 Development: Exploring the iOS SDK* by Jack Nutting, Dave Mark, and Jeff LaMarche (http://www.apress.com/book/view/9781430230243)

- *Beginning iPad Development for iPhone Developers: Mastering the IPad SDK* by Jack Nutting, Dave Wooldridge, and Dave Mark (http://www.apress.com/book/view/9781430230212)

- *More iPhone 4 Development: Further Explorations of the iOS SDK* by Jack Nutting, Dave Mark, and Jeff LaMarche (http://www.apress.com/book/view/9781430232520)

Getting Started with Your First iOS App

We have a lot of ground to cover here, so before we get too far along, make sure that you've already downloaded and installed the latest Xcode tools and iOS SDK (4.0 or higher). If not, make your way over to the Apple Developer web site at http://developer.apple.com/.

If you're not yet a registered Apple Developer, then sign up (it's free) so that you'll have access to the latest SDKs, tools, documentation, tutorials, and sample code at the iOS Dev Center (http://developer.apple.com/devcenter/ios/).

While you're there, take the time to apply for the required iOS Developer Program. Do not wait to do this when your app is ready to be submitted to the App Store, since it can take weeks to receive acceptance into the iOS Developer Program, which would delay your progress unnecessarily. After being accepted, pay the applicable fee to complete your registration. After your payment has been processed, when you're logged into the iOS Dev Center, you'll see an iOS Developer Program column on the right side of the browser screen. Click the iTunes Connect button listed there.

On the main page of iTunes Connect, be sure to visit the Contracts, Tax, & Banking Information section to view the contracts you currently have in effect. By default, you should have the Free Applications contract, which allows you to submit free apps to the App Store, already activated. But if you want to submit paid apps to the App Store, you'll need to request a Paid Applications contract. Apple needs your bank and tax information so that it can pay you when you've accrued revenue from app sales. Since Apple transfers money via secure electronic deposits, you'll need to provide your bank's ABA routing number, name, and address, as well as your account number, so make sure your bank supports electronic transactions with third-party vendors. If you plan on selling your app in several regional App Stores, in order to receive international payments, Apple may also require your bank's SWIFT code. Although most large national banks support the SWIFT system, some smaller independent banks and credit unions do not, so make sure your bank can supply a SWIFT code.

Until you complete the required steps (see Figure 1–4), Apple will hold any money it owes you in trust. And since this can also be a fairly lengthy process, I highly recommend completing the Paid Applications contract long before submitting your app to the App Store.

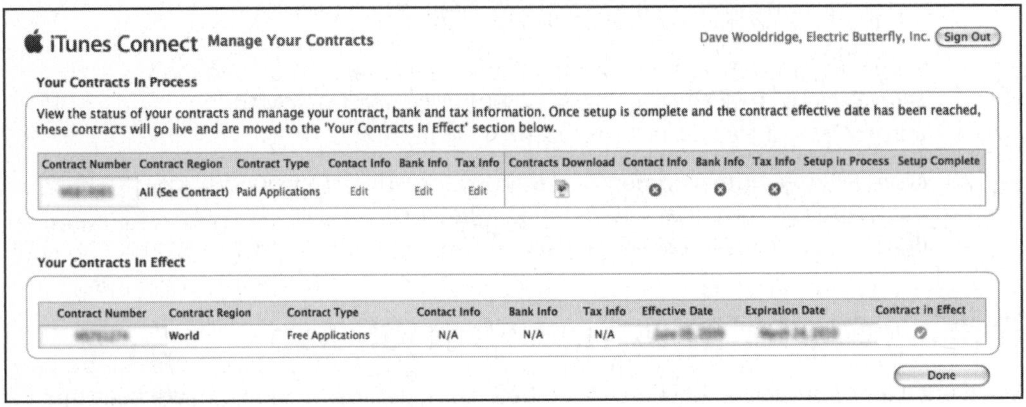

Figure 1–4. *In order to get paid for your App Store sales, make sure you complete Apple's required Paid Applications contract in the iTunes Connect online portal.*

Already in the App Store? It's Never Too Late to Boost Sales

Even if you're a veteran iOS developer with one or more apps currently available in the App Store, you can still do a lot to increase exposure and sales for those apps. You've already invested valuable development time and money to get to this point, so it would be a shame to give up now!

But don't make the mistake of skipping ahead to the postrelease chapters in this book. Many of the solutions presented in earlier chapters can be utilized with great effect, especially when planning new versions and updates for your existing apps.

Take the time to work through all the chapters in the order they're presented. You may be surprised by the tips you pick up along the way that can help even older apps that have been stagnating for months in the App Store.

Developing iOS Apps for Clients

This book can benefit not only the people who want to sell their own apps in the App Store, but also consultants who develop apps for third-party companies. You're being hired for your expertise, so anything you can do to help your clients succeed in the App Store will serve to strengthen your worth to them.

What better way to secure a consulting contract than by offering a full turnkey service, guiding your clients from app concept to launch, providing both code and marketing support? By adding an optional marketing/publicity package to your list of iPhone development services, you're also establishing new income opportunities for yourself!

The success of your clients directly affects the success of your relationship with them. Add this book's business solutions to your existing toolbox so that you can prove to be an indispensable superhero for all your clients' mobile app needs.

Ready to Dive In?

Now that we've taken a broad look at the current state of the App Store, it's apparent that several challenges await all iOS developers as they navigate their way along the road to success. As programmers, problem solving is what we all do on a daily basis, so I'm confident you'll enjoy each step in this process. And just think, put together the right puzzle pieces, and you may just find that elusive pot of gold at the end of the road. Mmmm, app sales!

First, shake off all that Objective-C code bouncing around in your brain. You'll want a clear head for the next two chapters. Don't worry—you'll be diving into design and development issues soon enough. But before you do that, you need to do a little competitive research and business planning. So, roll up your sleeves, put on your detective hat, and let's get started.

Doing Your Homework: Analyzing iOS App Ideas and Performing Competitive Research

So, you think you have a good idea for an iPhone or iPad app? Make sure it's a *great* idea. No amount of marketing will help sell a bad app. Sure, you may have excellent coding skills with the ability to produce a performance-optimized, high-quality application, but if it's based on a poorly conceived concept, it won't stand a chance in today's crowded App Store.

In this chapter, you'll learn how some good old-fashioned detective work can help test the validity and marketability of your app concept. Analyzing what your competition is doing right *and* wrong will give you the insight needed to truly refine and improve your ideas into a unique app that stands apart from the rest.

Even if the thought of doing a little competitive research seems elementary to you, keep reading. You may be pleasantly surprised to learn some new tricks here. We'll also explore the advantages of targeting multiple iOS devices beyond just the iPhone and the business challenges of universal applications.

Fulfilling a Need

People buy software to solve a problem or satisfy a need. To-do lists keep us organized. Weather and news apps keep us informed. Games feed into our desire to be entertained. Even silly novelty apps serve our basic need for acceptance by enabling people to bond over a few shared laughs. Although these general examples may be easy to recognize and understand, what about more specific needs?

If you're thinking of building something other than a game, such as a productivity or utility app, here are a few factors to consider:

- Does it focus on a need or issue that is currently not being addressed by existing apps?

- Does your app fulfill that need in a way that makes the mobile experience significantly easier than performing the same tasks on a desktop computer?

- If your app is similar to other existing apps, what feature(s) can you add that would solve the needs not currently addressed by your competitors?

Discovering Untapped Markets

Thousands of iPhone apps have very few users. Back in 2009, before Apple changed their policy on third-party app analytics (more on that in Chapter 7), the popular mobile advertising network AdMob reported that of the iPhone apps that actively displayed embedded AdMob ads, a whopping 54 percent of them had fewer than 1,000 users each. Granted, the few thousand apps included in that 2009 AdMob report represent a small sample compared to the sheer size of the App Store (then and now), but it's still a shocking wake-up call nonetheless, especially when you consider that most of the apps in AdMob's network are free.

Even if an app is free, it does not guarantee that people will use it. And if you expect people to pay for your app, it's that much more important that you provide a desperately desired service, feature, or experience—something users will feel compelled to download.

Although mobile apps are inexpensive compared to traditional desktop software prices, they are no longer considered impulse buys, as they were in the early days of the App Store. In the past year, users have packed their iPhones, iPads, and iPod touches with so many apps that they've gradually become much more selective about which apps they choose to download.

Just think about your own decision-making process when purchasing a new app. You may not think twice about spending $12 for a movie ticket, but for some curious reason, you more than likely contemplate at great length whether to spend a mere $2.99 on an iPhone game. I'm guilty of doing the same thing, even though as a programmer, I'm fully aware of how much hard work goes into creating an iOS application.

Part of the problem is that with so many apps priced at only 99 cents in an attempt to boost volume sales and rank higher on the App Store charts, users now have a distorted perception of app worth. Unfortunately, this has conditioned users to expect a lot of value for very little money. To cut through this purchase barrier, your app *must* be special, providing a unique experience and/or satisfying an existing need.

With more than 300,000 apps in the App Store, at first glance, it might appear that all the original ideas have already been taken. When Apple says, "There's an app for that," the company is not kidding, or so it would seem. But then, every so often, a pioneer comes along with a new app that causes developers worldwide to slap their own foreheads while shouting, "Why didn't I think of that?"

Sometimes the coolest ideas are the simplest concepts, hiding right under our noses. As developers, we're so captivated by (and envious of) the success stories of our peers that one of the first instincts to strike us is often the most fatal: how to take advantage of current trends by riding the coattails of what's popular. When iFart Mobile became a runaway hit in 2008, a flood of copycat fart apps bombarded the App Store, hoping to cash in on the popular novelty. Jumping on the bandwagon, the first handful of copycat apps probably generated enough sales to justify their development, but at a certain point, the App Store became oversaturated. With more than 500 fart-related apps currently available, the odds of consumers finding and purchasing your new fart app are pretty low. When needing to choose from such a large assortment, it's simply too overwhelming to look at them all, so consumers will more than likely settle for the most popular apps currently residing near the top of the charts.

Wouldn't you much rather be the visionary who develops *that* app—the one that hundreds of developers rush to emulate? Of course, we all would. So, how does one go about finding new, untapped ideas?

First, take a look at your own needs and interests. Sure, you're a developer, but first and foremost, you're also a user. Is there some missing functionality that you would love to see added to the iPhone? If so, do any existing apps already provide that functionality? No? Well, if it's a feature you want, then odds are that others out there are wishing for the same thing, and maybe even willing to pay for it—bingo!

It's worth noting that some wish-list items might make great features but not great apps. For example, the heavily requested copy-and-paste feature was finally added to iOS 3, but it doesn't really make sense as its own stand-alone app.

What interests do you have outside of technology? There are successful apps for bird-watchers, comic book collectors, sports fans, and so on. If you're passionate about a specific hobby and have not found any related apps, that might be a great space to fill. Just remember that the more niche it is (underwater basket weaving, anyone?), the smaller your potential customer base will be. If you develop a journal log for the small yet dedicated group of arctic nude swimmers, you could make a few shivering, blue-lipped individuals happy, but you may not make much money doing it. By broadening that idea to encompass all water sports (including custom log templates for surfers, boaters, swimmers, and scuba divers), your journal app dramatically expands its potential customer base, making it a much more viable app concept.

If you're feeling particularly void of any original ideas, try turning to your friends and family. See what specific needs and interests they have that might be well suited for a mobile app. But whatever you do, please do not solicit for app ideas on your blog, on your Facebook page, or via Twitter. Although your followers may provide some great suggestions, accepting their feedback leaves you legally vulnerable. If your app becomes successful, you run the risk of a stranger suing you for stealing his idea without providing adequate credit or compensation for it, producing evidence in the form of an archived tweet or blog comment he posted to you. You're better off limiting your inquiries to only your trusted friends and family.

Another great source for original ideas is your local newsstand. Although that may seem a little "old school," don't discount the ease of flipping through the pages of the latest magazines. The Internet is a vast treasure chest of data, but you need to know what you're searching for in order to find anything of relevance. At a newsstand, you can quickly browse through dozens of popular magazine genres. Print is expensive, so if there's a monthly magazine dedicated to a topic, the odds are good that enough people are interested in it to justify further exploration. The real question then lies in figuring out whether a decent percentage of those readers are tech-savvy and either plan to own or already own an iOS device. If the magazine has a web site, that's a good place to start. Check to see whether it has an active online forum, an RSS feed, podcasts, or a Twitter account. By just taking a few minutes to read some of the posts there, you can get a good feel for that magazine's reader base.

Also look to see whether any of the magazine advertisers are promoting computer- or mobile-related solutions. For example, writing magazines include several ads for software tools that assist authors with various elements of the writing business and the story-building process. The App Store already has several mobile writing tools to help authors organize their notes and story ideas, but what about giving freelance writers the ability to track the status of submitted queries to potential publishers?

Now that you have a general idea of what to search for, it's time to take your investigation to the Internet. Back in 2009 when I wrote the first edition of this book, there were several desktop software programs and subscription-based web sites that offered that query-tracking service, but there weren't any iPhone apps that handled that particular task. At the time, it looked like the market was wide open for this mobile app concept.

As fate would have it, several months later, Andrew Nicolle released his iPhone and iPad app, Story Tracker, to fill that demand. The vital point here is that if you do stumble upon an untapped market, it's best to start developing your app quickly. If you discovered a new niche, I can guarantee there are *at least* a dozen other developers thinking about similar app concepts. Time is of the essence. Just remember this famous (and very relevant) saying: "There's no such thing as an original idea. It's who does it first that counts."

When fulfilling an existing demand, you're selling to a known target audience. But if you introduce an entirely new product concept that is unlike anything else in the App Store, be aware that your marketing efforts will require educating consumers on why they should buy an app they do not yet know they need or want.

You can't sell people a solution for an issue that they aren't aware they have. That's why your marketing focus must illustrate the inadequacies of the current options available (or the lack thereof). Show how your app addresses that void and can save them time, improve their workflow, provide happiness, or whatever it does that would enhance their daily lives (as all software should strive to achieve). For an entirely new app category, you sell the solution by showcasing the problem.

Enhancing the Mobile Experience

When building an app for a mobile device such as the iPhone, iPod touch, or iPad, keep in mind that whatever features your app provides, it should do so in the most streamlined and convenient manner possible. Consumers may be using your app with only one hand (or a single thumb) while on the go. Take advantage of the unique mobile frameworks that Apple provides. Think about how you could simplify your app's features and usability by directly accessing built-in technologies such as the accelerometer, location awareness, Wi-Fi, and the cellular network, as well as the phone, mail, and calendar support.

A basic example of this is an app that searches for local businesses. Instead of forcing users to always type a ZIP code or address (which can often be very inconvenient in a mobile environment), enable an option to easily discover their current location using Apple's location-awareness frameworks. Just be sure to have the app first ask their permission. For privacy reasons, some consumers may not want to reveal their current location.

A large-scale example of a product that enhances the mobile experience is Bump, a free iPhone app that makes swapping contact information (as well as pictures, calendar events, and other data) as easy as bumping hands with another Bump user (see Figure 2–1). Exchanging contact information is not a new concept in smartphones. For years, numerous mobile apps have tried to streamline this process in handheld devices, but they typically involve too many button clicks with complicated methods of "beaming" vCard-formatted data. Some of them are even limited to sending vCards via e-mail, which adds more steps. The developers of Bump took advantage of built-in iOS technologies to simplify this need into a single action, which swaps contact information instantly and securely.

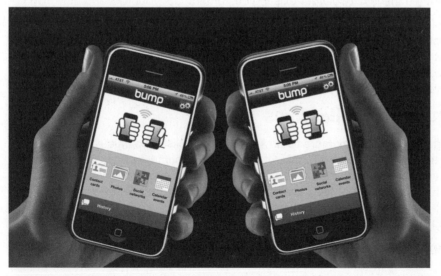

Figure 2–1. *Bump enhances the mobile experience by greatly simplifying the exchange of contact information between two people.*

"Our primary goal when designing Bump was to create a simple, fun, and intuitive way to connect two phones," says David Lieb, cofounder and president of Bump Technologies, Inc. "The accelerometer and location services allow us to do that. Bump monitors the output of the accelerometers and sends the output of the accelerometers up to the global Bump servers whenever a physical bump is felt. The servers then match up any pair of phones that felt the same bump at the same time in the same location. This allows connections to be made between any two phones with just a simple bump of the hands."

Lieb adds, "The idea for Bump came out of a moment of frustration (well, actually, two moments). Back in 2005, I was working as an engineer, and it really bothered me that in order to get some simple data like names and phone numbers from one phone to another one not 12 inches away from it, I had to ask someone to read out their information, and I had to type it in. I wanted to be able to just touch the phones together and transfer the information—but the phones of 2005 didn't have what it takes to make that work. Fast-forward to 2008, when I went to business school and found myself typing in the phone numbers of dozens of new classmates. Same frustration, but this time, I noticed everyone was carrying smartphones, many of which had accelerometers and location awareness. So we decided to build Bump."

Even though the app's idea stemmed from the needs of its own developers, it appears to be fulfilling a common need that many people have. In 2010, Bump surpassed 10 million downloads in the App Store.

The same logic of simplifying mobile tasks also applies for those developers who want to port their own Mac or Windows software apps into companion iOS versions. Don't just repackage the same features in an iPhone or iPad interface. By designing your app to be easier to use for the often one-handed, fast-paced world of mobile users, not only will you strengthen the loyalty of your existing customers, but your iOS app may also attract new users to your desktop versions.

Some people have even been known to switch from another mobile device (such as BlackBerry or Windows Mobile) to an iPhone just so they can use a specific app that's not available on any other mobile platform.

Competing with Similar Apps

Does the world really need any more to-do lists, shopping lists, tip calculators, music jukebox quizzes, or fart apps? If you think it does, then it must be because you've identified some new feature that none of the other apps has tapped into—a feature that people want and need. If not, trying to compete with the hundreds of existing tip calculators, to-do lists, and so on, may be futile, especially if really good ones have already captured that particular niche market.

Perform an App Store search for *tip*, and you'll discover that there are currently more than 100 tip calculator apps in the App Store. True, it's a great idea for a mobile app, but how do you find an audience for your new app when competing with so many existing tip calculators, especially when some of them are very well done and have been heavily featured in the media? One of the most popular ones, Tipulator, was even showcased in an Apple iPhone ad.

Sure, it might be a lot easier to quickly churn out a tip calculator app than to develop a complicated 3D game, but looking at such heavy competition in this space, would even such a simple app be worth developing if you couldn't sell that app? It's difficult to justify putting any amount of time into a venture—no matter how small—if it turns out to be a bad investment. If you can't offer a fresh approach or new features that would motivate users to choose your app over the hundreds of other similar apps, you may want to try another app idea.

Ah, but if you do know how to build a better mousetrap, then that knowledge, along with some creative marketing, may be enough to gain a toehold in the market. Just look at how many Twitter client apps there are, yet new ones pop up all the time with bigger and better features or a more intuitive mobile interface, causing users to switch.

If you think you have a winning concept and do decide to tackle a specific niche that's already saturated with similar apps, just know that you'll have your work cut out for you. It will be an upward battle to grow your customer base when users have so many choices vying for their attention. We'll take a more in-depth look at how to analyze and outmaneuver your competition a little later in this chapter.

If after releasing your app you find that competing in such a crowded space is too difficult and choose to abandon the app to develop a different product in a less crowded category, you run the risk of tarnishing your reputation and the future of any new apps you release. Why would any users buy any other apps from you if they can't trust that you'll continue to support them with updates and new features?

The App Store is littered with dozens of apps that have been abandoned by their developers from lack of sales. Their product pages are full of angry customer reviews. Although it may sound petty to make a big deal about losing 99 cents, these complaints are not really about the money, but about the principle. You must be passionate about your app, with a commitment to continue maintaining it for the long haul, in order to preserve the relationship with your customers.

When to Avoid Oversaturated Categories

When it comes time to submit your app to the App Store, you'll be asked to select an appropriate category to place it in. Sometimes the most obvious choice is not always the best choice.

When researching similar apps in the App Store, take a good look at which categories they're located in and how well they are faring in those categories. Just this bit of detective work alone can help you choose the best category that will give your app the greatest chance for exposure in the App Store.

A good example of this is DistinctDev's best-selling novelty app, The Moron Test. Even though the app includes several levels of game play, the developers made a conscious decision to avoid the massive Games category, opting instead to place it in the smaller

Entertainment category. This turned out to be a smart move. The Moron Test quickly rose to the top paid app in Entertainment. That exposure fueled even more sales, which in turn elevated its position to the top of the US App Store's Top 25. Would The Moron Test have sold as well if it had been in the Games category? Maybe not. Even though the main Games category is divided into 19 subcategories (such as Action, Arcade, and Board Games), it still would have proven difficult to compete against the immersive, high-action 3D games that dominate the overall Top Games chart.

But be careful. Depending on the kind of app you have, sometimes this strategy can work against you. Obviously, having the right keywords in your app name is vital so that you're included in related App Store searches, but people also like to browse their favorite categories to find new apps. With this in mind, don't pick a category just because it's smaller. Choose the category where most people will think to look for your type of app. So, even though DistinctDev bypassed the Games category, the smaller Entertainment category is still a very appropriate and intuitive location for The Moron Test.

For apps that would fit well in several different categories, the decision may not be so obvious. When this happens, it's best to investigate the categories that similar apps have chosen, especially the apps that are selling well. For example, dozens of note-taking apps are available, but should that kind of app be best placed in Utilities, Productivity, or Business? Do a quick App Store search for *notes* to see where most of those apps reside.

It's highly recommended that you use the desktop iTunes for all your competitive research because it displays much more information than the mobile App Store on iOS devices. For example, if you select an app from the search results, the app's category is not displayed in the mobile App Store listing, but it does appear in the desktop version of iTunes (see Figure 2–2).

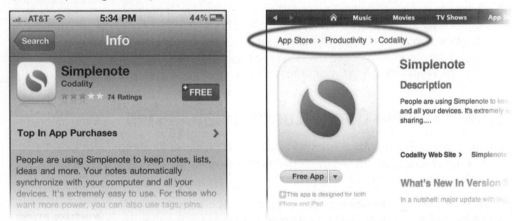

Figure 2–2. *If accessed from search results, an app's category is not listed in the iPhone's mobile App Store (left), but it is listed in the desktop version of the App Store in iTunes (right).*

When I shop for writing software, my goal is to find writing tools that will help me be more productive as an author, so instinctively, the Productivity category is the first place

I look. And apparently, I'm not alone in that thinking. Although some note-taking apps are located in Utilities and Business, the majority resides in Productivity.

Sometimes, a particular category can limit your potential audience. In the case of Bump, the contact-swapping app mentioned earlier in this chapter, the developers wanted the app to appeal to more than just business users. Although similar apps are rooted firmly in the Business category, the simplicity of Bump made it an easy data-sharing solution for anyone, so the decision was made to place it in the Social Networking category.

"At its core, Bump is much more than contact information exchange; it is a technology that lets two devices intuitively interact. We didn't want to pigeonhole Bump as a business app, nor did we want to position it as an iPhone-only utility," says Lieb. "By choosing the Social Networking category, we positioned Bump as a tool for connecting with the people around you. Also, we knew that if we were successful, being in the Social Networking category would put us right next to world-class brands like Facebook, MySpace, LinkedIn, AIM, Yahoo, and Loopt."

So when in doubt, check out your competition's category choices and the possible advantages they may gain from those locations.

Assessing the Competition

If your app idea faces some existing competition, don't rely on investigating only the competitors you know about. You'll need to do the legwork of finding all your major competitors in the App Store. After doing some initial searches, you may already have a rough idea of how many similar apps exist, but now you'll want to start compiling a list of them for later reference. And every time a new one pops up in the App Store, you should add it to your list.

Staying on top of what your competitors are doing is one of your primary jobs as a developer. The only way to grow your customer base and prevent users from switching to the other side is to make sure you're staying one step ahead of your competitors, and that requires keeping an eye on their updates. Believe me, if your app is a contender, your competitors are watching your every move, too.

You'll want to perform several searches using different keywords and phrase variations in order to find any similar apps that exist. It's worth taking the time to create a list of keywords that you, as a user, might try in order to find these kinds of apps. Also, use a dictionary and thesaurus to discover additional related words. There's no telling what keywords people may search for, so it's best to be thorough.

For example, let's say you're looking to build an app that helps people locate where they've parked their car. Since forgetting where the car is parked after a sporting event or a long day of shopping seems to happen to the best of us, it's actually a fitting concept for a mobile app—one that is the basis for at least 40 different apps currently available in the App Store.

To find all of these parked-car finder apps, let's run through a few searches in the App Store. The search results for keywords like *car* and *park* include too many unrelated apps, so let's narrow our search to a phrase. Here are the number of relevant apps that were listed in the top 20 search results for the following keyword phrases: *car park* (14), *find car* (13), *car locator* (9), *car finder* (8), and *parked car* (8). Interestingly enough, *car park* delivered the best results (see Figure 2–3), although you might expect *car locator* or *car finder* to be the better keyword combinations. That just goes to show how subjective search terms can be, so try everything!

Figure 2–3. *Searching the App Store for* car park *found 14 related apps within the first 20 listed items.*

This example demonstrates another important point. Did you notice that a select few apps, such as G-Park, come up in almost all the related searches? It's no coincidence that at the time of this search, G-Park is ranked higher in Top Paid Navigation Apps than any of the others.

Sure, G-Park has a slick interface and has benefited from publicity outside the App Store—such as being featured in Apple's International iPhone commercial, *USA Today*, *Los Angeles Times*, and *New York Times* —so in regard to G-Park sales, there's more at work here than just keywords.

But for those other frequently listed apps to outperform their competition and consistently show up in most of the relevant searches—and in the first 20 results, no less—proves they're utilizing important keywords and strategic app names to help achieve this.

When most consumers search for a type of app, they usually won't read past the first few screens of results, so it's important that you study the descriptions and names of your major competitors' apps to figure out which keywords are crucial for you to include.

Although descriptions are no longer searchable in the App Store, they do often include eye-catching text phrases that could prove valuable in your keyword quest. Getting placement in the first screen of related search results will provide much needed exposure for your app, which ultimately can also help boost sales.

Another tip for hunting down your competition is to read the customer reviews for the apps you already found. Often, customers will compare apps in their reviews, recommending one over the other. Make sure to add any new mentions to your growing list of competitive apps and also take a close look at them. Were the reviewers correct in their comparison of the apps and their features?

Using Alternative App Directories for Competitive Research

You'll perform most of your searches within your regional App Store in iTunes, but don't forget about competitive apps that may be available only in other countries. This is especially important if you plan on eventually offering your app in several country-specific App Stores outside your own.

Several web-based, third-party app directories are worth exploring. Many of these sites also post app reviews. You'll find a listing of these useful sites in this book's appendix.

Analyzing App Ranking Statistics

After getting a handle on how much competition is out there for your particular niche, it's also important to find out how your competitors are faring in the App Store. Are they ranked high in the App Store charts? Have any of them broken out of their primary categories to rank well in overall downloads? Do those apps perform better in some countries than in others? This information can also help you determine whether a particular niche is popular or profitable enough to warrant your own development investment in it.

Your iTunes Connect account limits you to viewing only your own app statistics, but thankfully, some amazing alternatives can assist in your competitive research quest:

- *Mobclix* (http://www.mobclix.com/appstore/): Beyond offering a compelling platform of iPhone services, ranging from embedded mobile advertising to sophisticated app analytics, Mobclix also provides comprehensive app rankings for the US App Store. Want to investigate the charting trends of your competition or even your own apps? You can find a wealth of valuable information here. The Mobclix web site should be a required destination for all iOS developers.

- *MajicRank* (http://majicjungle.com/majicrank.html): Majic Jungle Software's David Frampton has created a handy Mac OS X application that allows you to easily track iOS app ranking statistics across several regional App Stores. David has put a lot of work into this free software tool, so if you find it useful, consider buying one of his other apps as your way of saying thanks.

■ *APPlyzer (*`http://www.applyzer.com/`*)*: APPlyzer is a popular web-based source for free and paid app ranking statistics. This site provides an extensive amount of information for both regional App Stores and overall worldwide stats, so even though its free Standard membership offers a lot, it's well worth the small fee to upgrade to Pro membership.

■ *Top App Charts (*`http://www.topappcharts.com/`*)*: Top App Charts offers a unique spin on app ranking statistics by charting the big movers and shakers on the lists. Similar to APPlyzer, this free site uses visual markers for big debuts, jumps, and drops to reveal the actual movement of apps through the ranks.

■ *PositionApp (*`http://positionapp.com/`*)*: Want a mobile solution for checking App Store rankings? PositionApp by ustwo is a powerful iPhone application that enables you to track the historical chart movements of the top 300 apps in all App Store regions.

■ *App Store Metrics (*`http://148apps.biz/app-store-metrics/`*)*: This is a great web site, chock-full of iPhone and iPad development news and business insights. But beyond all of its wonderful content, 148Apps.biz may be best known for its comprehensive App Store metrics, which include statistics on active app count, submissions, approvals, app prices, and distribution of apps across the various categories.

■ *App Store Stats (*`http://www.yappler.com/Apple-iPhone-App-Store-Stats/`*)*: Even though Yappler is primarily an online directory for finding and sharing apps, it also provides some interesting App Store statistics that are worth checking out.

■ *AppTrends (*`http://appsfire.com/apptrends`*)*: Instead of tracking the App Store ranking of the top apps, Appsfire's AppTrends represents a ranking of which apps are most popular on Twitter and Facebook. This is a valuable site to monitor to see which kinds of apps are being talked about the most via social media word of mouth.

Although several other app analytics services, web sites, software tools, and even a few cool iPhone apps (such as AppFigures and AppViz) track App Store ranking, they're more focused on analyzing your own app's statistics and collecting data from your iTunes Connect account's sales logs. So, even though these resources may fall beyond the scope of competitive research, don't worry—they are profiled in later chapters.

Finding Inspiration in Your Competitors' Customer Reviews

Let's continue with the competitive research example of parked-car finder apps. Now that you've compiled a list of all similar apps, it's time to take a closer look at their individual feature sets and their customer reviews. All of these apps use the iPhone's built-in GPS location awareness to first store your parked-car location and then again to determine your current location to help you map a route back to your parked car, displaying an embedded map framework, such as MapKit. Some of the apps don't offer much more than that basic functionality. Others offer some additional features such as saving a text note, voice memo, and/or photo of your parked location for logging the actual row, level, spot number, and so on (perfect for multilevel parking garages). A select few also include the ability to log your arrival time, and if you parked at a meter, they can track the amount of time remaining on your meter so you can return to your car before it expires.

The interesting thing about comparing these apps is that they all deliver similar features in vastly different interfaces. And based on the posted customer reviews, you can quickly determine which interfaces have proven to be easy to use and which are less intuitive, causing user frustration.

Now, I'm not going to direct any criticism toward any specific apps here. Nor am I going to reveal which apps received negative customer reviews. The goal of this book is to help developers make more money with their apps, so I don't want to unintentionally make it any harder for them by pointing out their weaknesses. You can easily see for yourself which apps are receiving poor ratings in the App Store. So, for the purpose of this example, I'll give you a general look at customer reviews as a gauge of what some of these apps are doing right and wrong without naming any names. Let's dive in.

Learning from the Mistakes of Others

For those apps that log the remaining time left on your parking meter, some customers posted negative reviews, wondering why a particular app does not notify them with an alert, reminding them when their meter is about to expire. For example, one reviewer gave a low two-star rating, citing "needs a timer for meters that can alert you when the app is closed." As developers, we see this type of comment as a feature request, but disappointed consumers tend to view them as missing features. Unfortunately, their "feature requests" are posted as negative ratings, which hurt the overall perception of the app and can impact sales. The goal is learn from the mistakes of your competitors in the hopes of avoiding (as much as humanly possible) those kinds of reviews.

Most, if not all, of these apps also fall prey to a ton of negative reviews that complain about slow GPS performance and inaccurate GPS results. More often than not, these problems aren't caused by faulty programming, but are due to the user's current signal strength and the GPS shortcomings of older iPhone models. Most people (especially nontech users) don't understand the limitations of their mobile devices, so they simply blame the app for these issues.

To work around those GPS-related complaints, most of the developers have stated in very clear language in their App Store descriptions that for best results, they highly recommend using an iPhone 3G, 3GS, or iPhone 4, which offers much improved GPS location accuracy. But it would appear that many users are not taking the time to read the disclaimers in the App Store descriptions, and then they get upset when the app does not perform well on their iPod touch devices (which lack true GPS).

These developers also warn that if you're located deep within an underground multifloor parking structure, the thick concrete obstructions above you may prevent the app from pinpointing your exact location. The GPS built in to a user's car loses its signal nderground, but somehow the iPhone app's GPS is expected to still work flawlessly? It's not always about logic, but you do need to anticipate user expectations.

The apps that have fewer GPS-related complaints have successfully attacked the problem from within. Instead of relying solely on their App Store descriptions, these select few developers have taken a proactive approach by also integrating status indicators into their apps' interfaces. These UI indicators range from showing users the progress of retrieving the GPS location data (for impatiently dealing with slow signals) to location accuracy ratings (for notifying users if the retrieved GPS data is weak). A couple of these apps have even taken it one step further by enabling the user to manually adjust the location position on the map screen when the retrieved GPS results prove inaccurate. This also helps prevent frustration from iPod touch and first-gen iPhone users (the ones who missed the developer's text disclaimer).

From just our little example of parked-car finder apps, you can see that customer reviews can teach you a lot about what users expect in this kind of app. By monitoring their likes and dislikes with similar apps, you can better plan the features you need to build in to your own app to be competitive in this space. Anything less, and you'll be receiving the same feedback from your customers.

Going Beyond the App Store's Customer Reviews

Although the App Store's customer reviews are helpful in the course of doing competitive research, keep in mind that for a long time, Apple's implementation of ratings was somewhat flawed. Prior to iOS 4, when deleting an app from your iOS device, Apple asked whether you would like to rate the app first. Obviously, if you're deleting an app, either you didn't like it or you no longer have any use for it, so this automatically invited negative ratings. If you want to leave a positive rating for an app you love (and plan on using indefinitely), you need to go out of your way to find the app in the App Store to post your review. So, with this in mind, don't assume that the App Store's customer reviews are always a fair representation of an app's quality and value. (Thankfully, Apple removed that "rate upon deletion" prompt in iOS 4, so it will no longer be a concern moving forward.)

You should also take a look at the many web sites and blogs that offer extensive app reviews. Many of them also post video walk-throughs of the apps with audio commentary. Along with the app directories listing, you can find an extensive list of app review sites in this book's appendix.

Taking Your Competition for a Test-Drive

So, you've spent hours reading the reviews, but have you tried the apps yourself? Don't just take their word for it. Nothing beats firsthand knowledge. Download your competitors' apps, and kick the tires a little.

I know you're probably hesitant to put money in the pockets of your competitors, but with app prices hovering between 99 cents to a few dollars, you don't need to worry about them getting rich off your small purchase. Besides, it's in your best interest to play with the interfaces and functionality to see how well the apps accomplish their task. It's a good way to learn which UI pieces work and which elements feel awkward or nonintuitive—something you may not be able to properly evaluate by just viewing screenshots.

Even if lite/free versions of the apps are available, it's important to also download the paid versions in order to try the premium features that aren't available in the free editions.

The good news is that with app prices being as low as they are, even developers on a tight, shoestring budget can typically afford this, since purchasing a dozen iPhone or iPad apps probably won't cost you more than a night out at the movie theater.

Defining Your Differentiator

Mimicking the same features as similar apps won't propel your sales ahead of the pack. You need to offer something more—something better than the existing solutions.

What can your app do that makes it better than the rest of your competition? If you're building a parked-car finder app, what makes your app different from the others? You need to define one or more unique differentiators that make your app stand a cut above similar apps.

Upon reading customer reviews, you've discovered that some of the apps that track the remaining time left on a parking meter do not (yet) support the ability to notify the user with a reminder alert before their meter expires. If none of the other apps offer this functionality, then parking meter time notifications would be a nice differentiator to add to your own app, especially since many customers have already requested this feature.

Say you're meeting your friends at the mall and you want to let them know your exact location without needing to call or text them all individually. If your competitors are not addressing this potential convenience, then enabling your app to broadcast your current map location to your friends via Twitter, Foursquare, Facebook, or Short Message Service (SMS) with a single button click could prove to be a great differentiator.

Basically, your differentiators should be exciting enough that when promoting your app, these unique features make the purchase decision very easy for people who are evaluating your app along with several other similar apps. If users want that differentiating feature and no one else has it, then buying your app becomes a no-brainer.

But you can't stop there. Sooner or later (usually sooner than you would like), your competition will add those same features to their apps. And they will probably "one-up" you with a few new features of their own, forcing you to come up with some new differentiators in subsequent updates to ensure that people remain interested in your app.

Having multiple differentiators defined, along with a loose road map of new features you plan on adding to future versions, will help keep your app relevant and competitive. For example, earlier versions of iOS did not support a landscape keyboard in Mail, Notes, and Messages. To satisfy the demand for easier two-thumb typing, a slew of wide keyboard apps flooded the App Store, offering the ability to type e-mail messages and notes in landscape mode. Many of those iPhone apps were one-trick ponies, with the landscape keyboard being their only key selling point. When iOS 3 added landscape keyboard support to Mail, Notes, and other built-in Apple apps, it instantly invalidated the usefulness of many of those one-function apps. The ones that survived were the apps that still had something unique to offer, such as synchronizing notes with Google Docs, organizing notes into groups, posting notes to Twitter, and so on.

Just keep in mind that the more features you add, the more streamlined and intuitive your interface design needs to be, especially on a small mobile screen. After several updates, if your app begins to feel bloated and cluttered, then it is failing its primary objective, which is to provide an easy-to-use mobile experience. Take a look at the official Twitter app (formerly known as Tweetie). The developer, Loren Brichter, continues to add dozens of new features with every release, while spending a great deal of time simplifying the UI design so that additional features never interfere with enjoying the app's core Twitter functionality. Each new feature he implements serves to further empower the user without diminishing the app's usability.

Targeting Multiple iOS Devices

Unless your game or app requires a hardware or iOS system feature that's exclusive to a specific device, it's in your best interest to make your application available to as many users and devices as possible. It's simple sales logic, really. A larger target audience equals a larger number of potential customers. Although making your app available on multiple devices does require some extra development effort on your part, it's a great way to increase the return on your investment (of time and money). Why target only several million iPad users if your app could be designed for compatibility with all of the 120 million iOS devices out there? Your potential audience should continue to expand with every new iOS device that Apple releases.

Since a large percentage of users are still running iOS 3 on older iPhones and iPod touches, some developers take the lazy approach by simply producing apps for that lowest common denominator. They know that an iOS 3-compiled app will probably run fine on iOS 4 and even on iPads. Such an app is simple to code and compatible with a broad range of iOS devices, but that's hardly optimal. In following that path, you're doing a major disservice to your business's future in the App Store.

Users of the iPhone 4 and the very latest iPod touch want apps that take advantage of the Retina display's enhanced resolution. If your competitors offer a stunning Retina display-optimized UI, while your app still utilizes an old, pixelized iOS 3 interface, your competitors' apps are going to be much more visually appealing to iPhone 4 and new iPod touch customers. And that could result in lost sales. With a little extra graphics work, your app can—and *should* be—crafted so that its UI is optimized for both the Retina display and older lower-resolution screens. Chapter 4 discusses the design requirements for targeting both displays.

The same holds true for the iPad. Although your iPhone app may run fine on Apple's popular tablet, don't settle for an inferior user experience. Sure, the iPad includes a "2x" button for super-sizing iPhone apps to full screen, but this enlarged effect is very pixelized and rather ugly compared to the beautiful native iPad apps of your competitors.

Since iOS features some unique UI components exclusive to the iPad, some iPhone developers may not want to maintain two separate Xcode projects for essentially the same product in order to properly support both targets. To solve this problem, Apple introduced a new universal application format that runs on both iPhone and iPad devices. Depending on the device running the universal application, the appropriate version of the app is launched. That way, you can maintain one Xcode project with shared source code, but design separate UIs specifically tailored for each device target. For example, your iPhone app may use a navigation controller for organizing content, yet on an iPad, you would most likely want to display a split view controller instead. Both versions use the same data, but present it in different ways that best suit the chosen device.

For developers targeting both iPhones and iPads, Apple highly recommends building universal applications. Managing and updating only one application in the App Store makes it much easier for customers who use your app on both their iPhone and iPad (and even iPod touch). But if your iPad version is radically different from your iPhone app, with dozens of new features that require a fairly hefty code rewrite, a universal application may not be the ideal choice. If the two versions don't share much in the way of code, it may make more sense to build them as two stand-alone products: one for the iPhone and one for the iPad. Business and marketing factors also come into play in deciding whether to create a universal application.

Universal Applications from a Business Perspective

From a development standpoint, creating a universal application has many advantages, but is it the right choice for you? If your app is free, then your goal is to provide the most convenient, user-friendly access to it. A universal application makes it easy for users to download your app across all of their Apple mobile devices. But paid apps are a different story. Putting aside the technical benefits for a moment, let's look at the business factors involved.

When you create a universal application, existing owners of your iPhone app will be able to access the iPad version for free, since there's no official upgrade mechanism supported in universal applications. If your iPad app represents an enhanced edition, offering dozens of exclusive new features that are not available in your iPhone version, it may make more sense to release the app as a separate, stand-alone iPad version.

By selling the iPad app as a separate product, you have the opportunity to recoup your development costs. And if it provides additional value above and beyond your iPhone edition, most customers won't have a problem with paying for it, even after they've already purchased the iPhone version. I say "most" because there will always be a select few users protesting that they should receive all app versions for all applicable iOS devices for free. Ironically, the loudest complaints usually come from people who paid only 99 cents for your original iPhone app. But don't cut off a potential revenue stream that could help support your continued development just because you're worried about keeping everyone happy. Here's a little secret: it's not possible to please everyone. Just build the best features and user experience possible. If you provide your customers with additional value, most of them will be more than happy to pay for the enhanced iPad version.

On the other hand, if your iPad app does not offer anything new beyond an iPad-optimized interface slapped on top of the same iPhone feature set, you may want to consider a universal application. If you can't justify the iPad app price with additional iPad-exclusive functionality, selling it as a separate product will definitely attract an angry mob of customers, wielding pitchforks and writing negative App Store reviews! And Apple may just agree with them. Apple has been known to reject stand-alone iPad apps that don't add any significant value beyond what's available from their iPhone counterparts. In these situations, Apple usually advises the developer to convert it into a universal application before resubmitting it to the App Store.

Another major issue to consider is the file size of your app. A universal application combines the incremental code and separate *.xib* files and image resources for both the iPhone and iPad versions into one package, which means it can often be nearly double the file size of a single target app. Although Apple recently raised the cellular 3G download limit from 10MB to 20MB to help accommodate universal applications, some content-heavy games may still exceed that file size. If your universal application is larger than 20MB, that drastically reduces your app's potential audience to only people within Wi-Fi range. Whether your app is free or a paid product, this factor alone may persuade you to release separate iPhone and iPad versions to ensure that your app can be downloaded by both Wi-Fi and cellular 3G connections.

What's in an App Name?

While researching the competition, you undoubtedly performed a countless number of searches within the App Store. Along the way, you discovered that the words used in an app's name and related keywords can affect its placement in App Store searches. Chapter 11 discusses how to refine your App Store display name, keywords, and description; for now, let's focus on your app name. In the App Store, you're able to add short captions to your app's display name to help ensure inclusion in relevant search results, but we won't worry about those long App Store names just yet.

Your app name is the one you will use to promote your app everywhere, both inside and outside the App Store. Coupled with its icon, your app name is a brand—one that you hope to build into a recognizable name that is both symbolic of its core function and appealing enough to be memorable. If people can't easily remember your app's name, they can't recommend it to others.

There is also the application's bundle display name that is assigned in your Xcode project's property list (plist) file. This is the name listed in the very small space under your app icon on an iPhone or iPad home screen. You have approximately 12 characters to play with. Anything longer than that, and you risk your name being truncated (with …). For example, Rebisoft's Jack Nutting developed a stellar retro shooter game called Diabolotros, which makes great use of the iPhone's accelerometer. Having grown up in the 1980s, I spent a fair amount of time in the arcades playing Space Invaders, so I quickly downloaded the free Diabolotros Lite to check it out. It's an addictive, fun game, and I soon purchased the full version. I noticed that Diabolotros, at 11 characters long, displays quite nicely under the app icon on my iPhone home screen. DiabolotrosLite, however, is too long, so in order for it to fit, the name is automatically truncated to "Diabol…sLite" (see Figure 2–4).

Figure 2–4. *Try to keep your app name to 12 characters or less to avoid a truncated display on the iPhone's home screen.*

Since adding the word *lite* or *free* would put most app names over the 12-character maximum, many developers have inserted a lite or free badge into their app icon as a visual marker for users to easily distinguish it from the full version. This alleviates the need to clutter your app name with those words.

In comparison, Digital Chocolate's 3D Rollercoaster Rush has quite a long name in the App Store, but its actual bundle display name is shortened to 3D Coaster to ensure that it fits under the app icon on an iPhone home screen. Luckily, users recognize the shortened *coaster* as meaning *rollercoaster*. And for the free version, Digital Chocolate simply modified its app icon with a "FREE!" badge (shown in Figure 2–4).

If you do use an abbreviated name for your application bundle display name, take great care that it is not radically different from its App Store name. If the two names don't appear related in the eyes of Apple's app review team, it can be grounds for rejection from the App Store. Chapter 11 explores app name conventions as they relate to App Store submissions, but you do need to think about these issues in advance. When you're deciding on your app name, take extra care not to use long words that can't be broken down into nicknames or abbreviations. *Supercalifragilistic* is a memorable word but impossible to trim into a 12-character app name.

So now that you've figured out your length limitation, what would make a good name? Finding the perfect name can be very challenging, but it's worth spending the time to get the name right. In previous App Store searches, app names that included relevant keywords ranked well in the search results, but don't get too caught up with trying to integrate keywords into your app name. Remember that your app's name in the App Store can be much longer with a keyword-laden caption, so you should concentrate primarily on creating a name that's unique and memorable.

Although a name like Parked Car Locator is very descriptive, is rich with keywords, and can be easily shortened to the 11-character Car Locator when needed, it's probably too generic to be registered as a trademark. Since US trademark law prevents the trademark ownership of common words that describe a service or function—common words that other companies need to be able to use to describe similar things—legally protecting a name like Parked Car Locator would be difficult.

Instead, try coming up with something a little more creative. To prevent getting lost in the forest, travelers would often place markers on branches or leave a trail of breadcrumbs so that they could find their way back home. Since finding your way back to your parked car involves a similar strategy, you might want to play around with a cute app name like Breadcrumbs, which is only 11 characters. To ensure placement in relevant search results within the App Store, you could pack your app submission with important keywords and even expand your App Store name to Breadcrumbs—Parked Car Locator.

If another iOS app is using a similar name, you'll definitely want to come up with a different name. Even if you've locked in on a name that no one else is using in the App Store, you can't stop there. You should also search the Internet and all major software directories—the Mac App Store, Google.com, Android Marketplace, MacUpdate.com, and Download.com to name a few—to check for any possible conflicts on other software platforms.

You'll also want to search the US Patent and Trademark Office's Trademark Electronic Search System (TESS) database, at http://www.uspto.gov/trademarks/, for any filed trademarks on that name. Searching TESS in no way obligates you to file a trademark. That's something you can do later when you're ready. For now, you merely want to make sure the name is not already trademarked by another party.

> **NOTE:** If you're planning on making your app available in multiple regional App Stores beyond your own, you'll also want to check for registered trademarks and any usage of that name in those respective countries. For guidance on securing and protecting your application name rights internationally, you may want to consult a trademark attorney.

Why would it matter if an Android, a Mac, or a Windows software product is already using that name if you plan on using it only for your iOS mobile app? Well, it causes brand confusion for consumers who might incorrectly assume your app is the iOS version of the Android, Mac, or Windows application of the same name. If another software company was using that name first and can prove prior art (prior public use of the name and logo), especially if that company has already registered the trademark, you'll find yourself legally vulnerable. You don't want to spend months developing your app only to receive a cease-and-desist letter from the company's attorneys. Even worse, if your app has become a successful best-seller in the App Store, you don't want the company to sue you for trademark infringement and a percentage of your app royalties.

My intent is not to scare you, but simply to make you aware of the potential land mines to watch out for when picking a unique name for your iOS app. This is the kind of legal safeguarding that you'll want to do for your original app name, icon, and logo, so check out the section in Chapter 3 where Michael Schneider explains the benefits and process of registering a trademark.

One last thought on app names regards the distinction between different iOS device targets. If you're developing separate versions of your app for the iPhone and iPad (instead of a single universal application), you'll need to identify them accordingly.

When the iPad was first launched, iPhone developers released iPad-only versions with the identifying *HD* name suffix as a clever nod to the tablet's larger high-definition screen size. A quick browse through the App Store will reveal quite a few iPad apps and games using this naming convention, such as Real Racing HD, Harbor Master HD, and Flick Fishing HD. Unfortunately, in the months that followed, Apple unveiled the new iPhone 4 with its Retina display, a *true* high-definition screen. For those iPad apps that were already well established with their HD names, it wasn't worth the hassle to undergo a name change. But in a post-iPhone 4 world, new iPad developers are leaning away from the HD identifier, since there's no telling which iOS devices may get Retina displays in future models. Many recent app releases simply differentiate their App Store names by device, such as GoodReader for iPhone and GoodReader for iPad—a strategy I highly recommend.

Registering Web Site Domain Names

Now that you've decided on an app name, you'll want to snatch up a domain name for it before someone else does. Having a dedicated web site for your iOS app is critical to its success. The site is a central place for promoting your app and providing customer support. Don't worry about the design and structure of it yet. I'll discuss methods for shaping your web site into a thriving promotional tool and support center in Chapter 10.

The important task at hand is to secure a good domain name for your app. To find out whether the domains you want are taken (and if so, who is using them), search the WHOIS database. Here are a few sites where you can do this:

- DomainTools WHOIS Lookup (http://whois.domaintools.com/)
- WHOIS Domain Search (http://www.whois.net)
- Network Solutions WHOIS Search (http://www.networksolutions.com/whois/)

Just searching for domain names at a domain name registrar will tell you only whether a domain is already taken. A WHOIS search will often provide detailed information about the owners of taken domains.

If you're having trouble finding an available domain name that matches your app name, try adding the word *app* or *game* (if it's a game) to the end of it. For example, for the popular app Simplenote, the domain Simplenote.com was already taken, so the developers registered SimplenoteApp.com.

Register.com and NetworkSolutions.com are popular domain registrars. Personally, I prefer GoDaddy.com. Plenty of alternatives exist, with many of them offering cheaper registration prices. Do a little shopping online first to find a domain name registrar that offers the features you need at a price that fits your budget.

If you currently maintain your own blog or web site, you don't need to create a stand-alone site for your iOS app. You can add a directory to your existing site for your iOS app-related web pages and then redirect your app URL to that new directory in your site. Why have a unique app URL if your existing web site or blog already has a custom URL? It just looks a lot more professional to point consumers to `http://www.breadcrumbsapp.com/`, rather than to `http://www.mywebsite.com/software/iphone/breadcrumbs/`.

In addition, a short, dedicated app URL is a lot easier for people to remember. And most domain name registrars offer web-forwarding services so that you can easily set your unique app URL to redirect to wherever you want. Driving traffic to your existing web site is also a great strategy for cross-promoting other apps and services you offer.

> **NOTE:** When shopping for a domain name registrar, be sure to check which services require additional fees. For example, GoDaddy.com includes free web-forwarding with domain name registration, while other registrars may charge an extra annual fee for web forwarding.

Building a Unique Identity for Your iOS App

With all your competitive research done, you've had the opportunity to see the app icons that you'll be competing against.

It's important to have an app icon that's unique yet still reflective of your app's core function and UI design. This may sound obvious, but it's always surprising to me how many developers design an app icon in their own isolated vacuum without regard to the icons their competition are already using. Because of this, many similar apps unintentionally have similar icons. When doing a search in the App Store for a particular kind of app, the results are often a page full of app icons that look very much the same, which makes the entire group appear rather generic on the surface.

If you're building a writing app and all the similar apps utilize notebook-themed icons, try coming up with a clever visual that's different yet still communicates writing. If most of your competitors are using blue icons, think about using a contrasting color for your app icon (such as red or orange). You're attempting to package your app as a brand, and in order for this to succeed, the brand identity you're pitching must be unique and eye-catching.

Since you have your list of competing apps sitting in front of you, your app icon design is merely something to think about between now and Chapter 4 (which covers effective app icon design), especially since the next chapter includes helpful facts about filing a trademark for your app name and icon. So percolate on it.

Making Progress

You covered a lot of ground in this chapter, so take a moment to breathe. The next chapter is an important one. Yes, it tackles all of that daunting legal stuff that programmers would rather not deal with, but this is vital knowledge for safeguarding your business. Michael Schneider, an expert lawyer turned app developer, will walk you through the essentials of protecting both yourself and your intellectual property.

Chapter 3

Protecting Your Intellectual Property

This chapter was contributed by Michael Schneider, a technology transactions attorney and iPhone developer. As an attorney, Michael works with clients on intellectual property and technology-related contracts, helping them build, monetize, and protect their products. As an iPhone developer, Michael has published a number of successful apps, including TouchType, Private-I, and the Andrew Johnson series of self-help apps.

When you build an iOS app, you are creating intellectual property. Unlike traditional businesses, software companies typically are not valued based on physical assets. As you grow your business, you probably won't build factories or buy fleets of trucks. The value of your business won't be in real estate or equipment; it will be built on the intangible assets that you create. Your products and your ownership of them will be your company's core assets, so it is important to understand how to identify and protect the intellectual property that will become the basis of that ownership and your company's value.

In addition to being something that you can sell or license to other people, intellectual property rights are a way that you can prevent competitors from stealing your work. Even if you have no intention of monetizing your intellectual property beyond selling your app to end users, understanding your rights can help you fend off copycats.

Similarly, as an app developer, you will want to avoid infringing the intellectual property rights of others. Understanding the strengths and limitations of various types of intellectual property will help you understand what is and isn't permissible under the law. Armed with this knowledge, you can build apps more confidently, and fend off those who try to bully you with trumped-up claims. Knowing where the lines are helps you get closer to those lines without going over and violating someone else's rights.

In this chapter, you will learn about how to obtain the different types of intellectual property protection available to you and consider which types make the most sense in the context of app development. You will also explore some of the common pitfalls that can hurt your intellectual property rights and the value of your business.

To give you a sense of where this chapter is coming from, before venturing into iPhone development, I worked as a lawyer for technology companies helping to build, protect, and monetize products. As a disclaimer, even among iOS developers, every person's legal needs are different. Although I will try to explain in general terms some of the legal issues surrounding iOS application development and sales, this chapter should not be taken as legal advice. My hope is that you will become aware of some of the legal issues to watch out for, and use that information to engage in a meaningful way with a legal professional.

What Is Intellectual Property?

I talk to a lot of developers who have heard about intellectual property and understand that it is something that they should care about, but they are unclear exactly what it is.

Intellectual property (IP) refers to the intangible rights that you or your company can possess in your creative work. In our case, this creative work will likely be an iOS app, but it could also be components of that app, such as music or graphics.

The primary benefit that intellectual property provides you is the right to exclude others from using your protected work. If a competitor or another company takes something that you have properly protected (for example, your icon, your graphics, or your idea), intellectual property rights give you the ability to sue to stop them and possibly recover damages (that is, money).

Each type of intellectual property protects content in a different way:

- **Copyright**: In the case of a copyright, the authors are granted the right to dictate who can copy, distribute, publicly perform, modify, or create derivative works from their original work of authorship.

- **Patent**: In the case of a patent, the inventor is granted the right to stop other people from using, making, or exporting the subject of the invention.

- **Trademark**: Trademarks are intended to keep others from confusing your customers into thinking that the other company is you (or somehow affiliated with you).

Determining Your Intellectual Property Strategy

As you read this chapter, consider which types of intellectual property make sense in the context of your business and the apps that you are creating. The decision about which types of protection to pursue, and why, are your company's intellectual property strategy. Like making a business plan, defining and understanding your company's intellectual property strategy will help you make better decisions and avoid pitfalls that could jeopardize the intellectual property assets you are trying to build.

Although every company has its own factors to consider when determining which types of intellectual property protection to seek, some of these factors are specific to iOS apps. In this chapter, I will focus on the issues that are common to most iOS app developers.

iOS Apps Are Different

Although iOS apps share common origins with desktop software, certain differences influence the types of intellectual property that are worth pursuing. These differences will be the basis for determining which approaches are most appropriate.

One factor to consider is that our apps typically have a rapid time to market, and the barriers to market entry are extremely low. iOS apps are typically less expensive than their desktop counterparts, with most apps in the iTunes App Store priced at less than $5.

The iOS platform is an unprecedented opportunity for one- or two-person teams to make apps that can compete against apps from giant, well-funded companies. A developer account with Apple costs only $99, and the tools you need to build apps are bundled with every new Mac. From a technology standpoint, Apple has built an incredibly robust framework for creating compelling UIs, which takes much of the work out of otherwise complex features such as animation.

On mobile devices, simple programs are often more valuable to users than more feature-rich applications. Where the best desktop application is typically determined based on the extent of its features and capabilities, the best iOS apps often focus on doing one thing very well, intentionally keeping features limited.

The simplicity and ease of development fostered by Apple's tools mean that apps can move from concept to publication extremely quickly. Development of iOS apps is typically measured in weeks and months, as opposed to years, and many successful apps have been created in as short as a weekend.

For these reasons, independent developers dominate the iOS app marketplace. Some of the biggest hits on the iPhone have been fairly simple independently developed apps. My original TouchType app took less than a week to make and was among the most popular apps in the App Store for about a month. Other simple apps, such as The Moron Test, currently top the charts. As I look through the Top Apps list in the App Store, 15 out of the current top 25 apps in the App Store are developed by independent developers, with no preexisting brand. This new landscape requires a slightly different approach to intellectual property.

Developing an iOS App-Specific Game Plan

As a developer of iOS apps, a traditional intellectual property strategy may not fit your business. The speed with which apps can be developed and published makes some forms of intellectual property less useful in the iOS app context. You may have limited financial resources to pursue protection.

The strategies described in this chapter are based on some assumptions that are tied to the nature of the App Store. These won't apply to everyone, but they should serve as a backdrop for your analysis.

- **Speed:** If your app is simple in nature, the competitors will appear almost instantly, so you may want to focus your efforts on intellectual property protection that can be established fairly quickly. Rights that take years to establish are probably not well suited to the platform. Although you probably hope that your app will still be selling years from now in some form or another, there is a good chance mobile devices and apps will look very different in five years. With exceptions for app developers working on long-term business plans, developers should focus their energy on obtaining rights that can be protected immediately, such as copyright.

- **Cost**: The vast majority of apps fail commercially. As of the publication of this book, there are more than 300,000 apps in the App Store. When you combine the list of Top 100 Paid Apps overall, together with the Top 100 Paid Apps in each of the 40 categories (including the subcategories in Games), there are fewer than 4,000 apps represented in those Top App lists at any one time. I estimate that 98 percent of iOS apps published today haven't made more than $5,000. This means, depending on how ambitious your app is, you may want to focus on low-cost intellectual property protection. Depending on your goals, it also may make sense to wait and see whether you achieve a degree of success before spending money pursuing protectable rights in your work.

- **Geography**: You should also consider the worldwide nature of the App Store and whether you are going to focus your intellectual property strategy solely in the United States or in other countries as well. This chapter is focused primarily on US intellectual property law, but most other countries have some form of copyright, trademark, or patent protection available. Each additional country adds a layer of expense, and it would likely be impractical to pursue protection in all 90 countries that the App Store targets. Identify the jurisdictions that you care most about from a business standpoint, and then prioritize where you will spend your money.

Most developers see the vast majority of their sales generated from the US App Store, so protecting your interests in the United States is a good place to start. If you are developing your app outside the United States, you should be sure to do a trademark search in the United States to determine whether anyone else is using the mark already. You can run a simple trademark search yourself using Google. However, for a more thorough search, including searching records at the US Patent and Trademark Office, you can pay to use a trademark search service. Whether to pay for a comprehensive search will depend primarily on how much you are investing in your new mark. If changing the name of your company or app would be workable, you might just rely on your Google search to determine whether anyone is using a similar mark. On the other hand, if you were about to embark on an expensive advertising or public relations campaign to establish your brand, it would make sense to have a more thorough search performed before investing in the brand.

Copyrighting Your App

The concept of *copyrighting* an app is a little misleading because it implies that obtaining copyright protection for your work requires you to take proactive measures to have protection. In fact, in the United States and most other countries that follow the Berne Convention, some degree of copyright protection is established automatically the moment you put pen to paper (or start working in Photoshop or Xcode), assuming the thing you are creating is original to you.

Copyright protects original works of authorship. This includes literary, dramatic, musical, and artistic works, such as poetry, novels, movies, songs, computer software, and architecture. In the case of iOS apps, copyright can provide protection for things like your app's source code, graphics, and sound effects; the text of your instructions; the text of your app description; and creative video or audio content that you bundle with your app. Copyright does not protect facts, ideas, systems, or methods of operation, but if those facts, ideas, systems, or methods of operation are implemented in a creative/artistic way, copyright might provide some protection for the way these things are expressed.

How to Obtain a Copyright

A copyright automatically comes into existence when you create a work of authorship and fix it in a tangible medium. In app development terms, this means it starts when you type a line of code, draw some graphics, record sounds, or write your app's description. Assuming the work is creative and recorded somewhere (for example, on your hard drive or printed to a page), there is a copyright coming into existence.

Copyright protection is very affordable. A base level of protection exists at the time of creation without the need to pay lawyers or file a copyright application. That said, filing with the US Copyright Office provides some important additional benefits. Registered works, for instance, may be eligible for statutory damages and attorney fees if you decide to sue an infringer. This means that although you can protect an unregistered copyright, you might not be able to win as much in the lawsuit as you would if it were registered. Fortunately, copyright applications are relatively inexpensive compared to patent or trademark filings.

The current filing fee for a copyright application in the United States is $65, and it can be as low as $35 if you file online. It is fairly common for authors and software developers to pay an attorney to handle their copyright registrations for them, but if you are comfortable with legal concepts and willing to ask questions when needed, filing a copyright application on your own behalf is an option that the US Copyright Office supports. The place to start is `http://www.copyright.gov/eco/`. The electronic Copyright Office (eCO) has done a nice job of making the application process fast and easy through its site. If you are interested in filing a copyright on your own behalf, the eCO has a detailed tutorial posted at `http://www.copyright.gov/eco/eco-tutorial.pdf`.

Limitations of Copyright Protection

A copyright is a strong and affordable means of protecting your app's content and code, but copyrights protect creative expression of ideas; they don't protect the ideas themselves.

For instance, if you have an idea for an app that recommends new music to users based on the contents of their music library on their iPhone, a copyright could provide protection for your creative graphics or the text of your instructions. Copyright, however, would not provide protection for the concept of the app. In the context of iOS apps, this is a huge limitation.

Filing Trademarks for App Icons and Logos

I believe trademark represents an iOS developers' most affordable and effective means of fending off competitors. In the previous section, I discussed the limitations of copyright protection. An important one is that copyright does not protect ideas, so your app idea or concept will not have protection under copyright law. Patents can provide protection for concepts and ideas, but obtaining a patent is relatively expensive and time-consuming when compared with going through the copyright or trademark process.

Trademark doesn't protect concepts or ideas, but it can protect the logo or name that you give your app, if that logo or name is distinctive enough. Trademarks are a way to keep other developers from exploiting the goodwill you establish with your app or concept.

Let's say that you have created the first credit card processing app for the iPhone. You want to protect yourself. One option is to file a patent on the idea, but it would be years before you were issued a patent, assuming that your idea met the criteria for patent protection.

Without a patent, you don't have much protection for the concept, but you do have the advantage of being first to market. Your app, as the first of its kind, is likely to get media attention, and could even be featured by Apple. Once your app has achieved a degree of success, the competitors are likely to start making similar apps. Without a patent, you may not be able to prevent this from happening, but you can stop your competitors from tricking customers into thinking that they are you.

Similarly, Apple's approval process does not provide any filter for copycat apps, so you can't assume that the approval process or Apple will be doing anything to stop knockoffs from hitting the store. By creating an icon, name, and interface that people associate specifically with your company, you can establish trademark rights. These trademark rights give you a tool that you can use to prevent other people from using confusingly similar branding on their app.

If a competitor copies your app in a way that is likely to cause customers to be confused as to whether the app came from the competitor or from you, your trademark rights should give you a means to stop the competitor. But all names and logos are not equally protectable. This section describes the basics of trademark protection and how to choose a protectable trademark to identify your company and apps.

How to Get a Trademark

As with copyright, you can obtain some trademark rights automatically by simply using a name or symbol as an identifier of the source of your app. These "common-law" trademarks are fairly limited, though, and there are significant benefits to filing a trademark registration with the US Patent and Trademark Office.

A federal trademark registration provides notice to the public that you are claiming ownership of the mark. The registration also creates a legal presumption of your ownership of the mark and your exclusive right to use the mark nationwide in connection with the types of goods and services listed in your registration. Most important, a federal trademark registration is a prerequisite to bringing an action concerning the trademark to federal court.

The best way to find out more about the trademark application process is to visit http://uspto.gov. The Patent and Trademark Office has a wealth of information on its web site about the process, and it offers step-by-step instructions on how to file a trademark application online.

The federal government even operates a help line that you can call to get more information about the filing process. The help line cannot give you legal advice, but it is an extremely helpful, amazing resource. The Trademark Assistance Center's number is 1-800-786-9199.

But there are advantages to hiring a lawyer to help prepare your application. Often, there is a back and forth required with the Patent and Trademark Office in the process, and having a professional working on your behalf can help you obtain the broadest possible rights for your mark.

Picking a Protectable Trademark

Some trademarks are stronger than others. Made-up names (for example, Exxon or Google) or those that have no literal connection to the company (for example, Apple for a computer company) are best to establish strong intellectual property rights. Names that require a slight leap of logic or merely suggest a company's products or services (for example, Titanium for a travel bag company, suggesting strength and durability) are protectable and often strike the right balance between developing strong brands and educating the public about the company.

On the other hand, names that describe what a company does (for example, Online Advertising, Inc., for a company that sells Internet ads) tend not to be initially protectable. Companies often gravitate toward descriptive names because they want the public to immediately understand the company's business. However, choosing a descriptive name can adversely impact a company's long-term bottom line. Here are some reasons:

- It may be impossible to stop a competitor from using the same name.

- A descriptive name (which, by its nature, may be similar to others' names) may require additional marketing costs to differentiate it from a crowded field.

- There may be additional expenses caused by the increased burden of "policing" others who want to use similar names.

As an app maker, you have two important opportunities to brand your app: your app name and your icon. You also have the ability to specify your company name.

First, let's discuss your app name as a brand. The App Store places some unusual business constraints on the app name that you choose. In a non-App Store context, I typically recommend picking a name that does not describe or suggest the function of your product. Descriptive or suggestive trademarks are much more difficult to protect than arbitrary or fanciful ones.

With iOS apps, however, arbitrary marks pose a discovery problem. The App Store will display only the first 17 or so letters of your app's name when listing apps. If you give your app an arbitrary name, casual browsers of the App Store catalog may not find your app or realize that it is something that they need. For this reason, there are business advantages to choosing a less protectable mark; however, you should still seek to make your app name distinctive in some way.

For instance, if you sell a tip calculator and name it Tip Calculator, it is going to be nearly impossible for you to successfully obtain trademark protection for that name. On the other hand, if you name your tip calculator app TipStar and add a distinctive icon featuring a star, you have something that you can argue identifies the app as coming from you, as opposed to simply describing the app's purpose.

In the TipStar example, if another developer published a tip calculator that featured a star-shaped logo or used the word *star*, Ryan Rowe, the developer of TipStar, would have a legitimate claim of infringement. Ryan's TipStar trademark goes beyond simply describing the app and adds something distinctive that exists for the purpose of distinguishing his apps from others. The star name and symbol are unrelated to the purpose of the app, so if Ryan put out an app called WeightStar or ConvertStar, he could build on the goodwill that he created with his initial app.

Your goal should be to create a distinctive name that can identify your app as coming from you, but without completely obscuring the purpose of your app. It is a fine line.

If you choose an app name that suggests the function of your app, you may want to take extra effort to make your icon distinctive. Figure 3–1 shows some examples of distinctive icons, compared with some icons that are less distinctive.

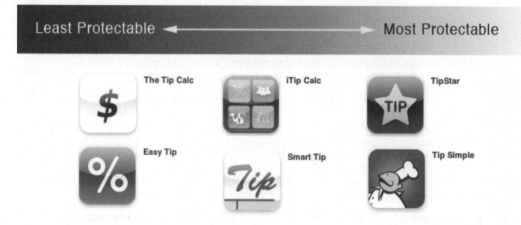

Figure 3–1. *Tip calculator names and icons, from least to most protectable*

Trade Secrets

As a developer, you probably have some secrets worth protecting. Maybe it is the concept for your next game or app, an algorithm that makes your apps more efficient, or the source code behind one of your app's features. Trade secret law is one way you can protect those secrets, and qualifying for the protection is fairly simple.

Trade secret law varies from state to state, but typically provides protection for information that gives the owner of the information an advantage over competitors in the marketplace and that is treated by the owner in a way that can be reasonably expected to prevent the information from being learned by other people, absent some improper action, such as breach of contract or theft. In simpler terms, if you have a secret that gives you a competitive advantage, and you take sufficient steps to keep it a secret, you can sue if it is stolen from you.

How Do You Establish a Trade Secret?

Trade secret protection doesn't require any application or filing with the government. In fact, you don't need to do anything but take reasonable steps to keep the secret confidential. For protecting source code, this might mean keeping the code on a secure server. For protecting your unpublished product ideas, this might mean not talking about your app idea with people who haven't signed a nondisclosure agreement.

The following are some minimum steps to take toward maintaining the confidentiality of information that you want to protect as a trade secret:

- **Education**: Be sure to educate all of your employees and contractors on the importance of maintaining confidentiality of company information. Being able to show that you took efforts to make sure everyone was aware of their responsibilities will help demonstrate that your company acted reasonably.

- **Contractual protection**: Every full-time or part-time employee and all consultants (including founders and officers) should sign an employment agreement that contains provisions protecting confidential information of your company before commencing work and before any company trade secrets are revealed to them. Use nondisclosure agreements to protect confidential information disclosed to any other third parties.

- **Control of tangible materials**: Confidential documents and tangible materials should be marked as "Confidential." Access to these documents and materials should be limited to those employees and contractors who have a need to know such information for the performance of their duties to the company.

- **Control of electronic data and code**: Be sure that source code and other confidential data is stored on secured computers that require a login and password to access.

Nondisclosure Agreements

Nondisclosure agreements (NDAs), also referred to as *confidentiality agreements*, are used to create a confidential relationship that legally binds a party to protect the trade secret information of another party. Although a confidential relationship can be created through an oral agreement or can be implied by the conduct of the parties, I recommend that you always use an NDA when disclosing confidential information. Oral or implied agreements are much more difficult to prove than written agreements.

At the core of most NDAs is the obligation not to use or disclose the other party's confidential information.

If you are in a situation where both you and the other party will be disclosing confidential information to each other, the appropriate agreement would be a *mutual NDA*. Mutual NDAs tend to be drafted in an evenhanded manner, since the rights and obligations apply equally to both parties.

If you are in a situation where you expect to disclose but not receive confidential information, you should consider using a one-way NDA that protects your confidential information but does not create any obligations for your company with respect to information received from the other party. For example, a one-way NDA would be appropriate when you are pitching a product idea to another company or hiring a contractor to perform work for you. In those cases, you might not want to be restricted in how you use information received from the other party, since it will likely apply to the product you are pitching or the work you are hiring the contractor to perform.

NDAs are a critical part of maintaining protection for your trade secrets. Trade secrets are protectable only if they are kept secret, so failure to put a confidentiality agreement in place with a third party before disclosing a trade secret even once can cause a loss of your trade secret rights.

Limitations of Trade Secret Protection

An important limitation to consider is that trade secret protection applies only to nonpublic information, which means there is no protection for information that others can gather by simply inspecting your product. The secret recipe for Coca Cola is a famous trade secret, but its trade secret protection does not stop Coca Cola's competitors from buying a can and trying to reverse-engineer the finished product. This limitation applies equally to the observable elements of your iOS app. Information that your users can access by analyzing your app is not protected under trade secret law because it stopped being secret once you published the app.

To help illustrate this distinction, let's imagine that you created a new search engine that runs on the iPhone. Imagine that this search engine is powered by a top-secret and highly effective algorithm that you invented to determine which search results are most relevant to the user. If it works, this algorithm would probably be your company's most valuable intellectual property asset. The key then would be putting out your app in a way that gives your users the benefit of the algorithm, without exposing exactly how it works.

Now let's assume the Google has learned of your amazing app and wants to incorporate the technology into its search engine. As the developer of this technology, you will clearly want Google to need to license or buy it from you or, better yet, acquire your company to get access to the secret. Before Google can do that, you can assume that it will probably buy a copy of your app and try to figure out how the algorithm works. Assuming you haven't patented your algorithm, if Google's engineers can figure out how your algorithm works by testing and observing your program, Google likely won't need to buy your company to implement something similar.

If you take sufficient efforts to protect the algorithm, and it isn't ascertainable by simply observing your product, you can keep your competitors from using it. If they hack into your computers or bribe one of your employees to disclose the algorithm, you could sue them for trade secret misappropriation.

The fact that trade secret law covers only things that you can keep secret is an important limitation to consider. It means that you will want to look to other forms of intellectual property protection (for example, copyright and/or patent) to protect aspects of your products that are visible to the user.

Patents

If you think of the various forms of intellectual property protection as weapons, patent protection is the doomsday device. Patents are expensive to obtain and expensive to litigate, but they can offer extremely strong protection for inventive ideas and should scare the pants off your competition. Entire business models or core technology can be sunk by a patent on preexisting technology that covers what the company is doing. For this reason, many midsize to large companies amass an arsenal of patents purely for defensive purposes so they will have something to fire back at their competition if they get sued.

Despite their strength, patents tend to be a bad fit for most iOS developers. Costs vary, but typically hiring an attorney to file a patent application and take it through to publication costs more than $10,000. The process often takes two to three years, so your iOS app would need to be a long-term venture for the patent to become relevant.

Games, for instance, have a fairly distinctive sales curve in the App Store. If a game is successful, it will see a spike in sales at or near launch, and then typically sales deteriorate over time. For a patent to be worthwhile, your inventive idea must still be valuable in three years.

Meanwhile, having a patent in process doesn't give you any enforceable rights until the patent issues. Telling your competitors that you are coming for them once you have your patent might keep them from investing too greatly in a competitive app. However, if the competitive app is inexpensive to create (or the competitors already created it), they are likely to continue selling the app until your patent issues. Combine that with the fact that there are iOS developers all over the world. Your patent may not scare a 14-year-old kid in India who is creating a competitive app and doesn't have much to lose by being sued.

All that said, there are cases where patents make a lot of sense for iOS developers. The biggest downside of pursuing patent protection is the cost. If you are working on a particularly big budget or ambitious app, and the $10,000+ it will cost you to pursue a patent is not a huge expense in the scheme of the overall project, obtaining a patent might be a smart move to try to protect your overall investment in the project.

Another time when patent protection makes sense is if your app is a long-term venture. If three years is short in the grand scheme of your product's expected life cycle, the lengthy application process may not be an issue. Seriously think about your ambitions for your app, and decide whether you think people are going to still care in three years.

Is Your Invention Patentable?

Patents protect new and useful processes, machines, articles of manufacture, and compositions of matter, as well as any new and useful improvement to those things. In general terms, among other requirements, to qualify for a patent, your invention must be new and useful, and you must be able to describe it in a way that would allow a person reasonably skilled in the invention's area to make the invention work.

The requirement that the invention be "new" means that you must be the first one to invent it. In the United States, if two people file a patent on the same invention, the patent goes to the first to conceive the invention, not the first to file the patent application. In fact, whether the other inventor files a patent at all, if that inventor conceived of the invention first, your later-filed patent can be invalidated.

Even if no one conceived of the invention before you, the invention itself must be "nonobvious" to a person having ordinary skill in the area of technology related to your invention. This can be a tricky burden, since often the best inventions seem obvious once they have been invented. To this point, the test is whether the invention was nonobvious at the time it was invented. Because this is a difficult thing to determine once the invention is known, often the fact that no one had previously conceived of the invention, despite having access to the same information as the inventor, is used as evidence that the invention was not particularly obvious.

Another requirement for protection is that your invention must be described in your application in a manner that demonstrates that you have "reduced the invention to practice." This means that you have done more than conceive of the invention, but you have also actually determined how to make it work with enough detail that a skilled person in your area of technology could produce it. For example, if I claim to have invented a time machine or a teleportation device, to qualify for a patent, I need to be able to describe how to build the machine or device in a way that actually enables someone to build it.

Assuming your invention qualifies for protection, a US patent gives its owner the right to exclude others from making, using, offering for sale, or "selling" the invention in the United States or "importing" the invention into the United States for a period of 20 years from the date on which the application for the patent was filed in the United States. These rights are particularly powerful compared to copyright and trade secret protection, because your right to prevent other people from making or selling your invention applies whether or not they copied or stole the invention from you. Even if they independently invent the same thing, if you conceived of it first, you may be able to stop them.

Avoiding the On Sale Bar

An invention will not qualify for patent protection unless its patent application is filed less than one year after it is first published, used in public, or on sale in the United States. This means if you demonstrate your invention or app to a potential investor or customer, you write a blog post about it, or your app is submitted to Apple, the clock is running. If you don't file your patent application within one year, you will lose the right to do so. For this reason, if you are considering pursuing patent protection, you should contact a patent attorney fairly early in the process, so that the attorney can help you determine how much time you have to file your application.

How to File for a Patent

Although it is possible to file a patent application on your own, you will almost certainly get a broader and more defensible patent if you work with a patent attorney. Unlike contracts, where a plainly written agreement is actually preferable to a complex one, patent applications have a certain vocabulary that applies specifically to patent applications. Using the wrong phrasing to describe an invention can cause weaknesses in your patent claims.

Patent attorneys and the Patent Office have their own language, and it is worth hiring someone who speaks it to translate your invention into the right terms to maximize the value of your patent. If you do try to draft an application on your own, you might at least hire a patent attorney to look it over before you file it, to see if there are any obvious fixes that the attorney can recommend.

Filing a Provisional Patent Application Yourself

Although the patent process is expensive and generally requires an attorney, there is a preliminary step that you can do yourself for a modest filing fee. This preliminary step is called a *provisional patent application*.

A provisional patent application is basically a description of your invention that you file with the Patent Office to establish an early effective filing date if you decide to file a full patent application on the invention. The provisional patent application just holds your place in line, so that if you file a full application, you can get the benefit of the earlier filing date.

Generally speaking, provisional patent applications are pretty weak. They don't give you any enforceable rights and won't result in a patent unless you later file a full patent application before your time runs out (see the earlier "Avoiding the On Sale Bar" section).

So why bother? A provisional patent application gives you the ability to use the term *patent pending* in connection with your product. The term *patent pending* doesn't mean that you have any legally enforceable rights, but it puts your competitors and potential competitors on notice that you have a patent application in the works. Depending on how expensive it will be for potential competitors to enter your market, making them aware that you are pursuing patent protection may be enough to dissuade them. Many people simply don't know what patent pending means and won't bother to find out.

If you don't file a nonprovisional patent application within the time allotted by the on sale bar, you will lose the ability to claim patent-pending status, but by then, you should know whether your app has a future and decide whether it is worth spending the money to continue pursuing a patent.

You can file provisional patent applications online through the US Patent and Trademark Office web site at https://efs.uspto.gov/efile/portal/efs-unregistered.

The Patent and Trademark Office has some instructions and information regarding provisional patent application on its web site. Additionally, there are some resources available from legal publishers like Nolo Press. For example, *Patent Pending in 24 Hours* by Richard Stim and David Pressman (Nolo, 2009) can walk you through the process.

If you think you are going to follow up with a nonprovisional patent application, you might also want to consult with the attorney who will be filing your full application. Attorneys can file your provisional application for much less than a full application would cost. Also, they might be less restricted when filing the nonprovisional application than they would be if they needed to work from a provisional application that you drafted yourself.

Addressing Intellectual Property in Contractor and Employee Agreements

If you are hiring contractors or employees to help you create your app, it is imperative that you get an agreement in place with them to govern ownership of the intellectual property that they contribute to your app. It is a common misconception that the person hiring a contractor or employee automatically owns the rights to the work he or she creates. In reality, if you hire a contractor to create the code for your app or design your UI, unless you have a written agreement indicating that you own the work product, it is unlikely that you will have all the rights you would like in the work delivered.

Hiring Contractors

Drafting an independent contractor agreement that protects your company involves more than just having the requisite intellectual property assignment provisions. You may want to work with an attorney to get a form in place that will cover your company in the event of a variety of problems that can arise. You may want to include acceptance provisions for deliverables so that you know you will get what you expect. Or you might want to add liquidated damages for late delivery to motivate your contractor to deliver work product in a timely fashion. If your contractors are overseas in countries where intellectual property protection is not particularly strong, you may want to include additional protective provisions around confidentiality. This section, however, is focused on making sure you get the intellectual property rights that you expect from your independent contractor agreement.

In the independent contractor context, the customer does not own the intellectual property rights in the work product created by the contractor, unless there is a written agreement that assigns those rights to the customer. This is contrary to what many people hiring contractors expect.

You may have heard of the "work-for-hire" doctrine. The work-for-hire doctrine does not mean that if you hire someone to do work for you, you own the work product. In fact, if you hire a contractor without a written agreement assigning the intellectual property rights, you will most likely have only a limited license to use the work product. This is problematic for a number of reasons. First, since your license to the work product is not in writing, it can be difficult to determine what is permitted and not permitted. For instance, under this unwritten license, it may be unclear whether you have the right to hire other contractors to modify the work or whether you have the right to sublicense it to other companies.

If you are fortunate enough to have someone try to buy your company or the rights to your app, the lack of written license agreement or assignment of intellectual property could jeopardize the deal. I have seen an initial public offering (IPO) and more than one acquisition almost go south for this reason. In each case, the company that didn't get the agreement in place with its contractor needed to find the contractor and negotiate a deal to buy the missing rights. This negotiation is not an easy one, because the company on the eve of a liquidation event has very little leverage, particularly if the contractor knows of the pending acquisition. Hoping to get an agreement in place retroactively also assumes that you will be able to find the contractor. Years from now, the contractor's company may not exist, or the contractor may have moved to a remote part of the Andes. If you can't find the contractor, no matter how much money you have to try to buy the rights, they won't be available.

If there is one thing that you take away from this chapter, it should be to get an independent contractor agreement in place with anyone who you hire to create anything that will be incorporated into your app. This includes coders, artists, UI designers, and so on—everyone.

I recommend that you work with an attorney to create an independent contractor agreement that is customized for the needs of your company, but for your reference, I have posted an example independent contractor agreement at `http://www.bitwiselegal.com/iPhone`. It should give you an idea of the type of provisions that you, as the hiring company, would want to see in an agreement to hire a contractor.

Hiring Employees

Hiring employees has its own set of complications for your business. From an intellectual property perspective, however, it is simpler than with independent contractors. Unlike with contractors, when you hire employees, you do get some ownership rights in the work product that they create. As with contractors, however, you don't get all the rights that you might expect.

Patent rights in particular are not assigned automatically as part of an employer/employee relationship. Without a written assignment, the employer gets what are referred to as *shop rights*, which means that the employer can use the invention in its business but does not own the underlying intellectual property in the invention.

As when working with independent contractors, you will want to have a written employment agreement assigning intellectual property rights to you as the employer. You should have all employees sign this agreement.

> **CAUTION:** Intellectual property assignments apply to founders, too. Often, when friends come together to form a company, they jointly develop the company's products without signing employment (or contractor) agreements with the company. If there is a falling out and the founders part ways, the company could be left without full rights in its technology. Founders who didn't sign an assignment agreement could later try to sue the company for infringement or use the work that they made to create a competitor to the original company.

Inbound Licensing of Intellectual Property

So, every developer hates to need to re-create something that another coder has already nailed. Sometimes it is more time- and cost-efficient to get code from other people. The third-party code might be better tested and more stable than something you could write from scratch. It might have useful features that you don't have time to build into your own code. The problem is that it isn't yours. Since you didn't build it yourself or hire an employee or contractor to build it for you, you need to obtain the right to use the code from the person or people who made it. This section addresses how to acquire the rights you need to use content and technology that are owned by other people.

Document Your Inbound Licenses

Whenever you use code or other materials that you obtain from a third party, you will want to be sure that you have documented and understand the scope of your license. Sometimes these inbound license agreements will be negotiated and executed between you and the licensor. In other cases, you will have clicked through an agreement with the provider as part of your purchase. In the case of code that you find on the Web, you may be bound by the terms of a license that accompanies the code. If there is no license posted, you might not have the right to use the code at all.

Know What You Are Getting

The main purpose of a license agreement is to grant the licensee the right to use the licensor's code or other content, but licenses also can provide the licensor with certain assurances regarding the quality of the code or content.

If you are negotiating an inbound license, you will want to secure some warranties that the licensor in fact has the right to grant you the license to the code or content. You may also want the licensor to defend you if for some reason your company is sued for infringement caused by the in-licensed materials.

Many click-through or shrink-wrap licenses will not include these types of warranties or indemnification. The result is that you alone may be responsible if something harmful is included in the code provided by a licensor.

Freely available code items, like Joe Hewitt's Three20 framework, are incredible resources. But it is important to understand that code like Three20, licensed under the BSD license, does not come with any warranties. It is effectively "as-is," which means that although it is a great way to save time in your development of apps, you alone will be responsible if that code fails, includes a virus, or infringes. Surprisingly, the same applies to most artwork that you license through stock photography sites, like iStockphoto.com. This is not to say that you shouldn't use Three20 or stock photography, but that you should be aware of the risk that your company bears by doing so.

Avoid Viral Licenses

Some freely available software is licensed under open source licenses that are viral in nature. These open source licenses, like the GNU General Public License (GPL) and Lesser GPL (LGPL), have contributed immensely to the advancement of software, but they carry a fairly strong obligation for anyone who uses the code in their own programs. This obligation is to license the resulting app under a similar open source license. This means that if you accidentally (or intentionally) include some open source code that you found on the Internet in your app, you may be contractually obligating yourself to provide access to your source code and allow other people to redistribute your apps for free. For commercial software, this is a real problem.

The takeaway here is that you should be sure to review the license agreement for any piece of third-party code or content that you incorporate into your app. Everything in your app should be traceable back to its original licensor and linked in your records to a license agreement that you are comfortable provides you with sufficient warranties and does not contain viral provisions that could taint your commercial products.

Don't Use Apple's Trademarks

It is important to know that Apple's developer agreement prohibits the use of Apple's trademarks in your apps. This means that you want to avoid using toolbar icons that look like an iPod, and you don't want to include pictures or images of an iPhone in your app. Also, you shouldn't use the word *iPod*, *iPhone*, or *iPad* in your app or company name.

Using these marks is a violation of your agreement with Apple, and could get your app rejected or possibly stuck in a lengthy and unpredictable approval cycle.

Creating a Custom End User License Agreement

Your end user license agreement (EULA) is the agreement with your users that gives them the right to use your app. In terms of intellectual property, this agreement is where you grant your user a license under your intellectual property rights to use your app.

The Purpose of a EULA

Your EULA is the document that governs your relationship with your users. Among other things, it grants your users the right to use your app and sets out any limitations you want to impose on how it can be used. Like any license agreement, your EULA can grant narrow or broad rights, depending on your goals. Most app developers will want to grant users only a very narrow license that limits the users to only using your app, and not modifying or redistributing it. This model is to some extent baked in to the App Store, since Apple embeds technological restrictions on users' ability to share apps with others.

One of the most important reasons to have a EULA is that it can be used to limit the warranties that users get with your app, and therefore limit your liability to the end user.

Warranty Disclaimers

What should your customer expect when they purchase a copy of your app? The ways these expectations are set from a legal standpoint are with *warranties*.

When you say in your app description that your game has 20 levels or that your Twitter client enables users to post tweets from the app, these are "express warranties" about the app. If a customer buys your app, and it doesn't do the things you said it would do, the user could claim that you breached your warranty.

Most app developers are not looking to disclaim their express warranties, but without the proper warranty disclaimer language in your EULA, you could end up making warranties to the end user that you do not intend. These are implied warranties that can come into existence based on the circumstances of the sale. Examples of implied warranties are the "warranty of merchantability" and "warranty of fitness for a particular purpose." The problem with these warranties is that they are often based on what the customers expect your product to do, rather than the things that you told them it would do.

A detailed description of the various implied warranties and how they come into existence isn't necessary to understand how they fit into your EULA. The point is that with proper disclaimers in your EULA, you can disclaim these implied warranties and limit the users' ability to sue you if your app does not live up to their expectations. As you launch your app on the App Store, you will see how important this is. There are all types of customers in the App Store. Some are mature; some are immature. Some are reasonable; others are crazy. Once you start seeing some of the reviews that people post for apps, it will be clear that often users' expectations for what an app can do are not based in reality.

Limitations of Liability

Another important benefit for developers in an EULA is a provision limiting the developer's liability in connection with the sale of the app. A limitation of liability provision is an agreement between you and your user that sets the maximum liability under your agreement at some amount. Most often, these caps on liability are set at the amount the customer paid for the product. Sometimes they are set even lower than that.

Not all jurisdictions enforce limitations of liability. Often, the judges evaluate whether the limitation of liability provision is fair to the user. Generally, however, courts in the United States will respect people's right to decide for themselves which contracts they want to agree to, and most often limitations of liability are considered enforceable.

A limitation of liability is particularly important if your app, like many iOS apps, sells for only a few dollars. If your customer pays only a dollar for your app, you would not want to be exposed to customers suing you for thousands of dollars if they feel they are harmed by the app. The limitation of liability provision in your EULA can help reduce this risk and can allow you to keep selling your app for a dollar, instead of needing to raise the price to factor in the risk of a customer suing you. The customers get a better price on the app, but agree that if it doesn't work, they won't sue you for more than some fixed amount (most likely the amount they paid for the app).

Apple's EULA

You absolutely should have an EULA that governs your relationship with your users, but you might not need to create a custom agreement for yourself. Apple has a standard EULA that it applies as a default if you don't upload your own.

Apple's default EULA includes some of the basic protections discussed, such as the limited license grant, disclaimer of warranties, and limitation of liability. Apple posts a copy of its App Store Terms and Licensed Application EULA at `http://www.apple.com/legal/itunes/us/terms.html#APPS`.

Apple's current App Store Terms and Licensed Application EULA (dated February 2, 2011) provides most of the basic protection that you would want in such an agreement, and it requires no additional effort to implement. There are some reasons, however, that you might want to create your own agreement.

Reasons to Use Your Own EULA

In my opinion, the biggest weakness in Apple's default EULA is that users are not presented with it for acceptance when they download or install your app. They have agreed to the terms as part of Apple's other click-through agreements. However, one could argue that the agreement would be more likely to be enforceable if users were required to agree to the terms at the time that they decide to purchase your app. This is not to say that the Apple default agreement is not enforceable, only that it gives the users an argument that they otherwise wouldn't have if the EULA were presented to them for agreement at the time of the download.

Another good reason to create your own EULA is if your app or business has specific risks that are not accounted for in Apple's default agreement. For instance, if you are developing a medical app that helps doctors evaluate the needs of their patients, you may want to include some specific disclaimers reminding the doctors that they shouldn't rely solely on your app in providing care. If you are creating an app that involves user-generated content, you may want to include a Digital Millennium Copyright Act Safe Harbor provision that can help protect your company if your users upload infringing content.

Lastly, the privacy provisions in Apple's default EULA may not match how your company uses and/or discloses user information. In fact, the language in Apple's default agreement is fairly vague with respect to how this information can be used by developers. If you plan on collecting any personal information from your users, such as their name and e-mail address, or will be accessing data on their device, such as their music library or address book, you should seriously consider implementing your own

EULA with privacy provisions specific to your business. This is particularly important if you plan to use the information that you receive for any purpose beyond providing the users with the service that they are downloading your app for or if you want to preserve the right to share that information with other companies.

How and When to Pursue Legal Action

So, you have taken the necessary steps to secure yourself some intellectual property rights in your app. Now the competitors have emerged, and you think they may be treading on your rights. What do you do? In the remainder of this chapter, I will cover the prelitigation and litigation options in the context of an app that I believe infringed the trademark of one of my apps.

This story involves one of my early apps called Private-I, which helps iPhone users recover their lost or stolen iPhone. The app features an intentionally intriguing icon with the word *Private* displayed in red letters. The icon is intended to lure someone who finds or steals the user's iPhone into opening the app to find out what the user considers private. When the app is opened, it displays a screen that appears to be loading some private information, when in reality, it is secretly sending the iPhone's owner an e-mail message with a map to the phone's location. I had modest hopes for the app, since it was inherently limited by the fact that the thief needs to open the app for the location tracking to be activated. To my surprise, the app struck a chord with people. It was featured on a number of prominent blogs, like TechCrunch and Engadget.

As with all apps that achieve notable success, similar apps started appearing shortly after my app launched. The total market for the app didn't warrant seeking patent protection for the concept, and I am not sure that the concept would even warrant patent protection, so I accepted that others would be using the idea to make apps. However, one competitor decided to use my exact icon to sell his app, which caused me to consider taking legal action. The following is an explanation of some of the prelitigation and litigation options, and how I evaluated these options in connection with my own copycat situation.

First Steps Toward Dispute Resolution

In my experience, Apple tries to avoid getting involved in disputes between app developers. Nonetheless, before you start considering real litigation, it is worth pursuing a remedy through Apple. Working with Apple costs nothing, and if the company is responsive, it could result in immediate results. Litigation, on the other hand, can be time-consuming and expensive. Trademark-related issues can be submitted to Apple for consideration through the e-mail address appdisputes@apple.com.

In my case, the appdisputes@apple.com e-mail address didn't exist yet, but I sent a request to Apple's copyright officer, as registered with the US Copyright Office. My request was not answered, which led me to the conclusion that Apple lawyers would prefer not to get involved in interdeveloper disputes. Truthfully, I can't blame them. Copyright and trademark disputes can be complicated, and Apple would need to make a determination in each case as to the respective rights of the developers. It's understandable why Apple would prefer to simply wait for the developers to resolve their dispute through litigation or negotiation, and then act in response to a court order or the agreed instructions of the developers.

Nonetheless, e-mailing Apple should be your first step in pursuing an infringer. You should not just assume that Apple is going to resolve the dispute for you.

Prelitigation

If you think a competitor is infringing your intellectual property rights, the first step in the litigation process is to identify the rights it is infringing:

- If the other party has used some of your graphics in its app, you should be focused on your copyright for the graphics.

- If the competitor has given its app a name that is confusingly similar to your app, you should focus on your trademark rights.

- If the competitor has an app that has taken the same concept or idea that you created for your app, if you have filed a patent app (or you still have time to file before the on sale bar restricts your right to do so), you may want to focus on your potential patent rights.

Talking with a lawyer at this stage can help you identify the ways in which your rights are being violated. A lawyer can help you understand if there are any additional steps you need to take to shore up your rights before you start trying to assert them against others. A lawyer can also help you to understand the relative strength or weaknesses of your rights and your likelihood of prevailing in a lawsuit against the competitor.

Going to court is extremely expensive. Fortunately, most disputes are resolved well before you get that far. If you and your lawyer conclude that you have a valid infringement claim against your competitor, your next step will likely be to send the competitor a cease-and-desist letter. The purpose of this letter is to notify the other party that you believe it is infringing your rights and demand that it stops. Depending on the circumstances, your competitor may not realize it is infringing. A cease-and-desist letter serves the dual purpose of notifying the competitor of the alleged infringement to get it to stop and creating documentation to show that it was aware of your rights, should it choose to continue infringing.

So, how did I approach this in the case of Private-I? I evaluated the rights that I believed the copycat infringed. In my case, I believed that the copycat infringed my copyright in the icon because the artwork had been copied, and the trademark was infringed because the use of the same icon on another product was bound to cause confusion with customers. More important, I evaluated the harm that the infringement was causing me and the potential benefit that would come from pursuing a claim. My conclusion was that pursuing the copycat wasn't worth the effort. His duplicate of my app never sold very well and didn't have a large effect on my sales. I was offended that someone would be so underhanded as to copy an entire app and post it on the App Store, but I needed to make a decision as to whether I wanted to spend my time writing letters and interacting with someone who I found distasteful or I would prefer to focus my energy on making apps. I don't regret the decision. Private-I continued to be a strong contender in the Travel category, and the copycat app has almost no exposure on the store.

Litigation

In my case, the copycat app wasn't causing much harm, but if your rights are being infringed and that is causing real harm to your business, litigation is the way to stop the infringement and potentially recover monetary damages from the infringer. Litigation is expensive and time-consuming, but it is an extremely strong weapon.

If the potentially infringing competitor does not stop infringing your rights as a result of your cease-and-desist letter, and your discussions with the representatives have broken down, your next step is to file a claim against the competitor. This is not something that you would want to attempt alone. If you think you have a claim, you should work with an intellectual property litigator to draft and file the complaint.

Summary

Intellectual property law and the general legal issues in running a software business can be difficult to wrap your head around. Fortunately, you don't need to understand everything about intellectual property to be a rights-savvy developer. Even lawyers who work in this space tend to focus on specific portions of the law. My practice, for instance, is focused primarily on helping people draft contracts, while other lawyers are specifically focused on litigation. Others spend their time helping people file patent or trademark applications. Since even lawyers in this field don't know everything about intellectual property, your goal should simply be to get enough exposure to the issues so that you will recognize when it is time to explore more about a particular topic.

Think of these legal issues like the frameworks included in Cocoa. For example, you don't need to know how to use a `UIImagePickerView` until you write an app that requires the use of the camera or photos. But when that time comes, it will be important to know that the class exists and roughly what it can do. Just like learning a programming language, the key to success in expanding your knowledge of business legal issues is being aware of the available resources and how to access them.

Your iOS App Is Your Most Powerful Marketing Tool

Your app icon and screenshots are often the first visual elements users see in the App Store when evaluating your app. A bad first impression can cost you sales and invite negative reviews, so fine-tuning your app's design is a critical component to success. In this chapter, I'll reveal some useful tips for prototyping, creating eye-catching app icons, crafting an intuitive UI, and designing for multiple iOS device targets.

This book is focused on how to improve the marketability of your app. This chapter discusses how interface design comes into play. It spotlights several important factors to consider when designing your UI, and points out a few common pitfalls to avoid.

Getting Your Foot in the Door: First Impressions Are Everything

After performing all of those App Store searches during your pursuit to collect competitive research information (covered in Chapter 2), you undoubtedly noticed that there are a *lot* of low-quality apps clogging the pipeline. You'll see plenty of shoddy apps that were quickly churned out by developers concerned only with exploiting short-term trends.

One of the biggest problems that plagues new iOS developers is app discovery. In a sea of more than 300,000 apps, it's hard for users to successfully wade through the crud to find the true gems. But no matter how much publicity you do to drive traffic and awareness to your app, discovery is only part of the equation.

When people finally do seek out or stumble upon your app's product page in the App Store, you've managed to capture their interest, but only for a moment. You have precious few seconds to convince them to continue exploring your app. This means your app's icon and screenshots need to hook them into wanting to learn more.

In general, most people are both lazy and extremely busy, placing an immense value on their time and a short fuse on their patience. If your app does not captivate them within the first few seconds of viewing your App Store page, they will move on, especially if there are many similar apps to peruse.

The First Visual Cue

Your app icon is the first visual cue your app has to offer. Consumers see your app icon first in the App Store listings. Your icon, combined with your app's name, will be the initial key factor that determines whether a user is interested enough to click through to your app's product page. It also represents your app's brand identity and must be uniquely memorable.

If your icon doesn't look professional, it leaves the distinct impression that your application may not be professionally made. So, with this in mind, an eye-catching, high-quality app icon should be your top design priority. It is your proverbial "foot in the door," granting you a little more of a consumer's time and short attention span.

The Second Visual Cue

When people land on your app's product page in the App Store, your screenshots are the second important visual cue. You cannot rely on people reading your app's entire text description in the App Store. They may read the first couple lines of your app description, but will be immediately drawn to the displayed screenshot.

That first screenshot must be one that best represents the core functionality of your app. Don't waste the opportunity by posting your app's splash or settings screen as that first visual. Although those screens may technically come first in the flow of using your app, they communicate nothing to potential customers.

In those vital few seconds, that first screenshot must convey your app's functionality or defining feature. After one look, consumers should have that "ah-ha" moment, when they immediately understand how your app generally works and/or why they should buy it. At the very least, it should spur them to continue clicking to see more of your screenshots, read more of your app description, and explore your customer reviews and official web site. And if you've done your job right, that winning first impression convinced them to download and evaluate your free lite version (if you offer one).

More Incentive for a Good First Impression

And while I'm on the subject of free lite versions, I'll mention that giving your users the ability to evaluate your app before purchase will help promote the paid version or In-App Purchase items, but it becomes that much more important that your app's UI is designed to impress. If a user downloads your app, tries it briefly, and then decides to delete it, you may never get a second chance to convert that person into a customer.

As noted in Chapter 2, prior to iOS 4, Apple automatically prompted a user to rate the app upon deletion. That flawed approach invited negative reviews. Thankfully, Apple removed that "rate upon deletion" feature in iOS 4. But if users dislike your app enough, they may take the time to visit the App Store and manually post a nasty review. This sure provides extra incentive to make as good of a first impression as possible.

Unfortunately, your app's UI design and functionality are responsible not only for attempting to win a sale for the paid version, but also for avoiding negative reviews (that may be unfairly "judging a book by its cover"). This task may seem overwhelming at first, but after reading this chapter, you'll be armed with some practical design methodology for tackling this problem head-on.

I'll discuss the merits of free lite versions to promote paid apps and In-App Purchase items in Chapters 6 and 8, but first things first. It's time to lay the groundwork for your app's design.

Playing by the Rules in Apple's Sandbox

Violating Apple's *iOS Human Interface Guidelines* (commonly known as the HIG) is one of the most frequent causes for submitted iPhone and iPad apps to be rejected. Although the App Store does contain some exceptions to the rule—approved apps that have broken a few of those UI design rules—it's best to adhere to the guidelines the best you can.

There's no sense playing with fire unless you have a very good reason to do so, and even then, you need to ask yourself whether it's truly worth the risk. Design innovation can give an app that "sexy" visual appeal that helps drive interest and sales, but before you attempt to break too many conventions, keep in mind two very important factors:

- If your design violates too many critical guidelines, Apple won't think twice about rejecting your app, no matter how cool it is. And if you're not in the App Store, your app can't make money.

- Apple's interface guidelines serve the vital purpose of supplying common interface controls and architecture. Familiarity greatly eases the learning curve, which makes the user experience much more intuitive.

In the past, some developers familiar with Apple's infamous rejection letters had lost faith in playing by the rules, especially when the rules often appeared to be a somewhat moving target. For much of 2009, Apple's app review process had been under quite a bit of scrutiny. Developers and the tech media questioned the seemingly inconsistent reasoning behind the rejection of several high-profile app submissions.

Thankfully, Apple resolved the mystery behind its elusive app review criteria by releasing an official set of developer guidelines in September 2010. Written in a very straightforward, informal, and often lighthearted manner, *App Store Review Guidelines* is a welcome and valuable document, shedding light on specific app elements that developers should avoid to help expedite the approval process. The full list can be viewed at http://developer.apple.com/appstore/guidelines.html.

This convenient online resource page provides links to read the *App Store Review Guidelines* and the *iOS Developer Program License Agreement*, as well as the ability to submit an appeal to the App Review Board if you feel your app was unfairly rejected. To access these links, you'll be required to first log in to the iOS Developer Program.

Although many developers have expressed their concern regarding Apple's tight control over the app approval process, this curated, exclusive sales channel is the App Store's greatest strength. By ensuring a certain quality level, the App Store is an attractive mobile marketplace that instills consumer trust, which in turn helps sell more apps—a recipe that has proven wildly successful.

The bottom line is that if you want the opportunity to make money in the hottest, most lucrative mobile platform, you must remember that you're playing in Apple's sandbox. To stay in the game, you need to adhere to the company's rules. You may not like its rules, but that's the real price of admission (beyond your iOS Developer Program fee).

Even with the posted guidelines, it may be impossible to foresee all the potential reasons for rejection (especially if new ones arise), but at least you can do yourself the favor of avoiding the known issues that will earn you a rejection letter. Throughout this book, I'll be spotlighting known rejection causes as they apply to the related design and development topics being discussed, but those select tidbits alone are not enough.

Here are a few important resources that should be required reading for all iOS app developers:

> *iOS Human Interface Guidelines*: This is the bible for iPhone, iPod touch, and iPad app UI design. Obviously, you're encouraged to be creative and inventive, but let the HIG serve as your foundation. This online guide provides a link to download a handy PDF version. You can also access the HIG within Xcode's built-in documentation browser. With so many viewing options, you really have no excuse, so read it, embrace it, live it! Find it at http://developer.apple.com/library/ios/ documentation/UserExperience/Conceptual/MobileHIG/Introduction/ Introduction.html.

> *Official App Store Review Guidelines*: You'll be required to log in to the iOS Developer Program in order to access this direct link. Unlike with the HIG, Apple does not offer a PDF download of the *App Store Review Guidelines*. It's important to note that these guidelines are considered by Apple to be a "living document," which will be updated to reflect new rules and changes as the need arises. This is not to suggest that Apple plans to morph the guidelines to suit its own agenda, but that new app submissions will surely trigger new questions that require new rules and clarification. As the mobile landscape evolves, so, too, will Apple's guidelines. With this in mind, always refer to the latest online version of this document when designing and developing your app. Find it at http://developer.apple.com/ appstore/resources/approval/guidelines.html.

Application Submission Feedback: This blog posts reported reasons for app rejections, as submitted by anonymous developers. This unauthorized site is a great source of information, although Apple's app review team can't be thrilled with its existence. Visit it at `http://appreview.tumblr.com/`.

Designing for Multiple iOS Devices

In Chapter 2, I stressed the importance of embracing multiple iOS device targets when developing your apps. Beyond the technical aspects of supporting the iPhone 4's Retina display and the iPad's larger screen, it's vital that your app's icon and UI elements are designed to best suit the various iOS devices. While your existing 57 × 57 pixel app icon may look great on the home screen of older iPhone and iPod touch models, it will appear quite blurry on the iPhone 4 and iPad.

You don't want your app to simply be compatible with newer versions of iOS. You want your app to look absolutely amazing on the latest iOS devices, enticing potential customers to tap that Buy button in the App Store. One major step to achieving this is including appropriately sized icons and images within your app for all the related iOS targets your app is supporting, but what does that entail?

Preparing UI Art Assets

The large 512 × 512 pixel App Store version of your app icon is one of the only image sizes that's consistently the same across all iOS targets. Everything else requires different sizes, as described in Apple's HIG. The following is a summary of the requirements.

Home screen app icon:

- Older iPhones: 57 × 57 pixels
- iPhone 4 Retina display: 114 × 114 pixels
- iPad: 72 × 72 pixels

Spotlight Search and Settings icon:

- Older iPhones: 29 × 29 pixels
- iPhone 4 Retina display: 58 × 58 pixels
- iPad (Spotlight Search): 50 × 50 pixels
- iPad (Settings): 29 × 29 pixels

Document icon (new to iOS 4):

- Older iPhones: 22 × 29 pixels
- iPhone 4 Retina display: 44 × 58 pixels
- iPad: 64 × 64 pixels and 320 × 320 pixels

Do not design your Document icon to emulate a document with a page curl. iOS automatically adds the document border, drop shadow, and top-right corner page curl. This means that you may need to do a few tests to ensure your icon is positioned properly within the image dimensions, so that it falls within the "safe zone" of the Document icon's dynamically generated border.

Navigation bar and toolbar icons:

- Older iPhones: 20 × 20 pixels

- iPhone 4 Retina display: 40 × 40 pixels

- iPad: 20 × 20 pixels

Those are the approximate icon sizes to fit within bordered buttons. If you opt to use plain-style buttons (no border) in your toolbar, you can experiment with slightly larger sizes.

Tab bar icons:

- Older iPhones: 48 × 32 pixels maximum

- iPhone 4 Retina display: 96 × 64 pixels maximum

- iPad: 48 × 32 pixels maximum

Although these dimensions allow you to have icons that are much wider than their height, if your tab bar includes four or five tabs, I recommend sticking with square icons, or even narrower icons if your tab bar is looking a little cramped.

Default launch image:

- Older iPhones: 320 × 480 pixels

- iPhone 4 Retina display: 640 × 960 pixels

- iPad: 768 × 1004 pixels (portrait); 1024 × 748 pixels (landscape)

Your default launch image for the iPhone should include the status bar area, but oddly enough, the default launch image for the iPad should not include the status bar.

Orientation Considerations on the iPad

With the iPhone's small screen, providing an efficient UI design often requires a dedicated orientation, such as a portrait-only app. That's perfectly acceptable on the iPhone, but the iPad's larger display allows more of your interface elements to be consolidated into a single window, providing enough screen space in both portrait and landscape views. In fact, Apple recommends that iPad apps should support all orientations.

If your iPhone app is locked into a single orientation, you'll want to rethink the design when porting it to the iPad, so that it can accommodate multiple orientations on the larger tablet screen. On the iPad, you should include a default launch image for every orientation that your app supports, since you won't know how the user will be holding the tablet before launching your app.

Double the Fun with Retina Display Screens

Looking at the various icon size differences between the iPhone 4 Retina display and older iPhone models, you'll notice that the Retina display doubles the width and height. This also holds true for all other art assets, such as background images.

So how does your iPhone app differentiate between the two sizes? Apple has made this very easy for developers. If a background image is named *blue-texture.png*, then simply name the double-sized Retina display version *blue-texture@2x.png*. That *@2x* identifier should be placed after the identical file name, but before the *.png* file extension. When run on a Retina display, your compiled app will look for the file with the *@2x* identifier and load that image accordingly. If a Retina display version doesn't exist in your app, the lower-resolution image will be displayed instead.

As I mentioned in Chapter 2, don't just upscale your existing graphics, saving them as larger *@2x* versions. That will only provide blurry imagery on Retina display screens. If you originally created your images in a bitmapped format using Adobe Photoshop or a similar graphics tool, your best bet is to re-create those images specifically for the Retina display sizes, to ensure crisp, high-resolution interface elements. Trust me, perfecting your app's visual appeal is worth all the extra design work involved in supporting Apple's Retina display.

Whenever possible, you should create your icons and UI images in a vector-based format such as Adobe Illustrator, so that you have the flexibility to adapt to any new sizes that Apple requires in the future. That would save you from the hassle of re-creating small bitmap images. I talk more about bitmap and vector-based design in the following section, so keep reading.

Creating an Effective App Icon and Logo

As mentioned earlier, when consumers browse the App Store listings, your app icon is the first visual cue your app has to offer. Your app's icon and name will be the first key factors that determine whether a user is interested enough to click through to your app's product page. Since the icon represents your app's brand identity, its design must be memorable and eye-catching enough to stand apart from the icons of your competition.

At the end of Chapter 2, I recommended reviewing your competition's app icons and starting to think about ideas for your own app icon. For example, if you're building a note-taking app and most of the similar apps currently use a notebook-related app icon, you won't want to emulate that same look. Otherwise, your app may be perceived as an unoriginal "also-ran" app that's simply hopping on the same bandwagon. But your app is going to be different—better. So, let your app icon reflect that with contrasting colors and an original visual theme that set your app apart from similar apps when they are all displayed together in the App Store listings.

Although some app icons utilize photographic imagery, you'll find that most apps have illustration-based icons. Often, a photo includes too much detail, and when shrunk to a tiny 57 × 57 pixel icon, the image looks cluttered and busy. The most successful icons boast a simple, crisp, and clean design that looks vibrant and appealing at any size—big or small. Illustrations tend to work best to meet those design goals.

App Icon Rules and Tools

Many apps use icon imagery that look suspiciously like royalty-free clip art. Using royalty-free stock art can serve as a great foundation for mocking up the initial prototype design of your icon, but you'll want to create your own original artwork for the final icon, especially if you plan to register a trademark for your app logo and icon. You can't trademark someone else's artwork or imagery unless you own all the rights to it.

> **APP REJECTION WARNING:** *Do not use copyrighted or trademarked art or names in your app icon or UI.* This also includes any Apple trademarks. iPhone imagery is strictly hands-off, so don't include it in your icon or interface design. Although a few select apps do display an iPhone in their app icon or UI icons, they are the rare exception. Breaking this rule without receiving prior permission from Apple will quickly earn most new apps a rejection letter. It's also important to note that Apple will also reject your app if it uses unauthorized images of public figures or celebrities. And believe me, Apple is doing you a favor by enforcing this before granting entry into the App Store. The last thing you want is some large Fortune 500 corporation suing you for trademark infringement.

Let me just state for the record that although I know my way around Adobe Photoshop, I'm definitely not an artist. But that's the beauty of designing a simple icon. As long as you know a few layering and filtering tricks, you can create an attractive icon. You don't need to be Michelangelo, but having a good eye for composition—how to structure the layout of an icon—is definitely a valuable trait. But not to worry, even if your graphics skills ended with kindergarten drawings displayed on the refrigerator, the "Tips for the Artistically Challenged" section later in this chapter provides helpful advice and links to online resources.

If you're not a talented artist, it's definitely worth finding room in your budget to hire a professional designer. Your app icon will greatly benefit from the skilled eye of an experienced graphics guru. Again, your app icon is a very important visual component of your overall app marketing strategy. If you're truly serious about succeeding in the App Store, hiring a professional designer to develop your icon, as well as your logo and even some of your UI elements, is a smart investment.

But what if you are a struggling independent developer, working with a small, shoestring budget? Let's see what you can do on your own to produce a worthy, high-quality icon.

Most professional design work is done in either Adobe Illustrator or Photoshop (http://www.adobe.com/):

- Adobe Illustrator is a vector-based drawing program, which means it creates illustrations that can be set to any size without losing any pixel quality. It's perfect for designing software icons and logos that may need to be available in many different sizes for anything ranging from a small desktop icon to a large trade-show poster.

- Adobe Photoshop is a bitmap-based graphics program that also includes many vector-based tools.

I tend to be partial to Photoshop, but most designers would probably recommend Illustrator for this specific task. And since Apple keeps introducing new iOS devices and screen resolutions, creating a vector-based icon design gives you the flexibility to handle larger sizes in the future without sacrificing image quality.

If Illustrator or Photoshop is too expensive for your budget, cheaper graphics tools are available. Just search your favorite online software directories for comparable alternatives. But if you plan on creating your own graphics for all your software products, web site, and marketing materials, I highly recommend investing in Adobe's applications. If you buy the Creative Suite, you'll get all of Adobe's best design apps bundled together for a discounted package price.

When submitting your app to the App Store, you'll need to provide Apple with a large 512×512 pixel icon. So if you're creating your icon in Photoshop, make sure your master design is at least that big. Since you'll probably want to use your icon in marketing materials as well, you should strongly consider creating your master icon at an even bigger size. Keep in mind that print advertising (magazine ads, trade-show posters, and so on) should be at least 300 dots per inch (dpi), so if your biggest icon is only 512×512 pixels, your icon is only 1.7 inches big when used in 300-dpi print materials.

If you create your master icon at a large size of several inches, you'll always be sure to have the right size for any occasion. You can always resize the icon smaller with great results, but you can't increase the size of an existing bitmap-based icon without it looking terribly pixelized. If you're creating a vector-based icon in Illustrator, resizing up or down is not an issue.

Don't make the mistake of previewing your app icon on only an iPhone 4 or the very latest iPod touch models. Almost everything looks nice on a crisp, high-resolution Retina display. Also make sure your design looks good at the smallest home screen app icon size, which is 57×57 pixels. The trick is for your icon to look professional and sophisticated, while remaining simplistic enough to display well in almost any size. This is no easy feat, especially for a nondesigner, but we'll take a stab at it by using a few clever little graphics tricks.

APP REJECTION WARNING: *Your app icon and App Store icon must match!* Don't try to work around icon legibility issues by crafting a complex, detailed 512 × 512 icon and then a vastly simplified version for the 57 × 57 app icon. The icons don't need to be precisely identical, so you can do minor touch-ups to the small icon if the resize muddied a few elements. But when placed next to each other, both icons should look like the same design. If there's a major difference between the two, your app risks being rejected by Apple's app review team.

Enough talk about rules and tools. Let's dive into some design work!

Designing a Custom App Icon

Remember the fictional app example from Chapter 2—the parked-car locator called Breadcrumbs? As an example, we'll now design an original app icon for it.

Since the fictitious Breadcrumbs app will help locate your parked car, you obviously know that including a car in the icon would be beneficial. But you don't want to look like any other competing app icons, so you'll draw your car from scratch using very simple shapes. You'll also incorporate a trail of dots (to emulate breadcrumbs) leading up to the car to help visually communicate the logic behind the app name. In this example, we'll take an illustration-based approach.

First, let's start with a rough sketch of the icon by drawing the objects in outline form (see the left icon in Figure 4–1). I recommend using a graphics program that supports layers (as Photoshop and Illustrator do), so that you can place each separate object in its own layer. For example, the car windshield is the top layer, with the car bumper layer beneath. Under that are the car frame layer and the car tire layer. Another separate layer holds the breadcrumb dots. The bottom layer is the background.

Figure 4–1. *After designing an initial outline (left icon), you can experiment with contrasting colors (middle icon), and then add a professional polish with easy-to-use effects and filters (right icon).*

Why go to all the trouble of maintaining so many layers? By keeping the objects separated, it allows you to easily move around individual layers or groups of layers until you have a composition that looks balanced and complete. Separate layers also allow you to modify the outline stroke and filter effects of a selected object without affecting the other objects.

Keep the basic icon outline very simple. Its raw, unfinished appearance will tempt you to add detailed lines and textures, but resist the urge. Too many fine lines will not translate well when the image is resized into a small 57 × 57 icon, so it's best not to enhance the design in that way.

Once you have a layout you like, you can start experimenting with color (see the middle icon in Figure 4–1). Leaving the outline stroke black, I filled the car frame object with red, the bumper with light gray, and the windshield with light blue. I also added a blue gradient for the sky and a light-tan gradient for the ground. Notice that the gradient fades lighter toward the middle horizon. This helps give the background a little more dimension, with the illusion of sunlight shining from the horizon line. Since this book is printed in grayscale, you won't be able to see the nice contrast of the red car against the blue sky, but try to visualize it in your mind.

Although this color version is an improvement from the previous black-and-white outline, it still looks very childish, like it was drawn by an amateur illustrator. Remember that I'm a programmer, not an artist.

Now for the fun part! With just a few tricks using the built-in tools and effects included in both Photoshop and Illustrator, you can transform that amateurish icon into a polished work of art (see the right icon in Figure 4–1).

NOTE: If you have trouble locating the various tools, effects, and filters described in the icon-creation steps, consult the Photoshop or Illustrator documentation for details.

The current black outlines give the icon a cartoonish, comic-book look, so the first thing you need to do is change the color of the stroke outlines for all the objects. Select the layer that contains the car frame object, and change its stroke outline to a dark red to nicely complement the car's bright red color. Make the headlight's and bumper's stroke outline dark gray. Then decrease the opacity of the white dots' stroke outline to 60 percent, allowing the stroke to take on the subtle shades of blue and tan from the background behind the dots. By just changing the stroke outline colors, you've already made a huge improvement.

Next, use the built-in Bevel and Emboss layer style on the car bumper object and the white dots to give them a three-dimensional feel. Adjust the Highlight and Shadow modes until you get the look you want. Since you want to create the illusion that there's one central light source, make sure all your Bevel and Emboss modified objects use the same Shading Angle value for consistency. You can then add the Drop Shadow layer style to the car's grill and drop its opacity to 60 percent.

Using the Gradient tool, continue shading and highlighting strategic areas of the car to enhance the three-dimensional effect. In Photoshop, when the Gradient tool is chosen, you can modify its settings to customize how the gradient will draw itself. For example, with the car's headlight object selected, I changed the Gradient tool's mode to Radial so that the white to yellow gradient would make the headlight's surface appear rounded. Changing the Gradient tool's mode to Linear and selecting the car frame object, I added a light red to dark red vertical gradient, which provided shading near the bottom of the car frame. A small, lighter gradient was added to the car's hood as a highlight.

With the car windshield object selected, I added a horizontal Linear gradient of white to light blue. But the windshield still did not look like glass. So, I added an artificial "glint" of light near the top of the windshield. To do this, create a new layer above the existing car windshield layer. Draw an arced, white sliver on this new layer, and then change its opacity to 60 percent. Ah, much better. Now it looks more like glass.

Now here's the hard part: creating the angled sunbeams in the sky. These sunbeams give the icon that extra "pop," so it's worth the additional effort. First, darken the existing blue background, making it a darker blue vertical gradient (with the lighter color ending at the middle horizon line). Then create a new layer above the background (but below the car object layers). Draw a white rectangle that fills the entire sky area, and then change its opacity to 30 percent. This will make the sky look washed out, until you start cutting out angled slices that allow the darker sky underneath to shine through. The cut-out angled slices are actually the spaces between the sunbeams, so space them evenly, with all of them angled toward the same central point on the horizon. In this case, the central reference point I used is directly behind the car's headlight.

The last task is to create a shadow below the car. This is as easy as creating a new layer below the existing car object layers and then drawing a fairly flat, horizontal oval that is slightly wider than the car. Fill the oval with black, change its opacity to 50 percent, and then apply the built-in Blur filter until it looks like an authentic shadow.

And that's it! By using Photoshop and/or Illustrator's built-in shapes, stroke outlines, Gradient tool, layer styles, and Blur filter, you were able to transform a basic design idea into a professional-looking app icon. I hope you'll be able to put these simple little tricks to good use when designing your own app icons.

The true test now is in resizing the finished icon to the required sizes. If the design still looks good in both 512 × 512 pixel and 57 × 57 pixel icon sizes, then you accomplished your mission. Don't worry about the rounded edges and glossy beveled look that iOS app icons typically have. The iOS system and the App Store automatically add those elements to the icon for you.

Although you can't do anything about the dynamically added rounded edges, you do have the ability to disable the beveled gloss effect from your app icon if desired. The Breadcrumbs app icon would probably look better without it, but let's test it by previewing the app icon in Xcode's iOS Simulator (see Figure 4–2).

Figure 4–2. *You have the option to disable the default beveled gloss effect if your app icon looks better without it. Previewing the example Breadcrumbs app icon with the glossy effect (left) and without (right).*

As you can see in Figure 4–2, the default beveled gloss effect interferes with the underlying icon design, so let's disable it. After you've added your 57 × 57 pixel icon and 114 × 114 pixel icon (Retina display)—such as *Icon.png* and *Icon@2x.png*, respectively—to the Resources folder of your iPhone app project in Xcode, you'll need to open your project's plist file. Xcode displays the contents of your plist file as a nicely formatted list (see Figure 4–3).

Key	Value
▼ Information Property List	(13 items)
Localization native development region	English
Bundle display name	${PRODUCT_NAME}
Executable file	${EXECUTABLE_NAME}
Icon file	Icon.png
Bundle identifier	com.yourcompany.${PRODUCT_NAME:rfc1034identifier}
InfoDictionary version	6.0
Bundle name	${PRODUCT_NAME}
Bundle OS Type code	APPL
Bundle creator OS Type code	????
Bundle version	1.0
Application requires iPhone environment	☑
Main nib file base name	MainWindow
Icon already includes gloss and bevel effects	☑

Figure 4–3. *Adding a new plist property, "Icon already includes gloss and bevel effects," and setting it to True will disable the default beveled gloss effect from your iPhone app icon in Xcode.*

First, you'll want to add your *Icon.png* file name to the Icon property. Then click the gray plus (+) symbol button on the bottom-right side of the list to add a new entry to the plist file. In the new blank row, click the tiny arrows in the left Key column to display a contextual menu of additional properties, and select "Icon already includes gloss and bevel effects" from that menu. It may not seem like the intuitive choice, but setting its value to True will disable the default beveled gloss effect from your app icon. Save the plist file, and run your Xcode project in the iOS Simulator to preview your app icon.

When displaying your app icon on an iOS device's home screen or the 512 × 512 pixel icon in the App Store, Apple checks your app's plist file first, so your preferred setting is honored with both icon sizes.

If you prefer to preview the various app icon sizes with rounded corners during the design process, you may want to check out these helpful Photoshop and Illustrator files donated to the community by generous developers:

- Cocoia Blog's iPhone/iPhone 4/iPad App Icon PSD Template (http://blog.cocoia.com/2010/iphone-4-icon-psd-file/)

- Nick Farina's iOS Icon Template for Perfectionists (http://nfarina.com/post/1185879730/ios-icon-template-for-perfectionists)

- Neven Mrgan's iOS App Icon PSD Template (http://mrgan.tumblr.com/post/708404794/ios-app-icon-sizes)

- Jon Hick's iOS Icon Template for Illustrator CS5 (http://hicksdesign.co.uk/journal/ios-icon-template-for-illustrator-cs5)

Don't Forget About a Logo

After sweating over your icon design, keep those creative juices flowing and tackle a logo for the app. This is another visual element that would benefit from the wizardry of a professional designer, so if you hired a designer to create your app icon, you should have that same expert create a logo to match. But don't worry if a constrained budget forces you to continue carrying the graphics burden on your own. A logo does not need to be complicated. In fact, like your icon, the more simplistic your logo is, the more flexibility you have to use it in various small sizes while still maintaining readability.

Just as with your master icon, you'll want to create a master logo that's at least several inches long with a 300-dpi resolution so that it will look good in any and all print-related marketing materials you may create in the future. For best results, you may want to choose the vector-based Illustrator program for creating your logo, especially if your icon was constructed in Illustrator. Take advantage of the design work you've already done, and incorporate the existing icon into the logo design. Not only does this save you a lot of design time, but it also helps reinforce the branding you already established with the app icon.

Since I'm not a trained artist, I opted to follow my own advice and keep things simple with the Breadcrumbs logo example. Sometimes crafting an appealing, simple logo is just a matter of finding an interesting font. I opted to use a rounded, condensed serif font for the name *Breadcrumbs*. After trying several different fonts, a font with rounded edges seemed to perfectly complement the rounded lines within the app icon. To add a little flavor to the font, I gave it a thick black stroke outline with a white fill color, and then employed a Drop Shadow layer style.

CAUTION: If you do use a third-party font, it's important that you purchase the proper font licensing to use it in commercial projects. Some fonts can be quite expensive, so if money is an issue, I recommend using royalty-free fonts when possible. See the "Tips for the Artistically Challenged" section later in this chapter for some helpful font library resources.

With only the icon and adjoining app name, the logo still felt too basic. To really drive home the breadcrumbs metaphor, I extended the trail of white dots to flow from the icon to a "Parked Car Locator" caption beneath the app name (see Figure 4–4). Wow, such a simple element, and yet it really pulled the entire logo together to form an original and cohesive design.

Figure 4–4. *This fictional Breadcrumbs logo is a simple extension of its app icon design.*

Creating an app icon for inclusion in your Xcode project seems like a no-brainer at this early stage in the game, but why design a logo now, when the app hasn't even been developed? Obviously, you'll want to have your logo ready to use on your app's official web site, as well as available for any prerelease publicity efforts you do. But the biggest reason to design your logo now is for trademark registration (as explained by Michael Schneider in Chapter 3). The trademark application and approval process can take several months, so if you plan on registering a trademark for your app logo, it's best to start this ball rolling as soon as possible. If all goes well, you'll ideally have the trademark officially registered before your app is available in the App Store.

Maintaining a Consistent Brand Identity

To reinforce your brand identity, you'll want to use the same app icon and logo across all your marketing efforts. If you use too many visual variations for promoting the same iOS app, you're likely to cause confusion among consumers.

By consistently using the same icon and logo, your app's brand will start to become recognizable to people. This familiarity will help consumers easily recall your app name when searching the App Store and recommending your app to friends and family. Having a recognized brand also helps you promote new iOS apps to those users who are familiar with the visual branding of your previous app.

For example, to reinforce the logo branding of Touchgrind, a popular skateboarding game, Illusion Labs included the same logo and color palette within various screens of the app, as well as in the app's YouTube video trailer and official web site (see Figure 4–5). Notice that even though the Touchgrind logo is a very simple design, its consistent use is nonetheless quite effective (good news for all you nonartists out there).

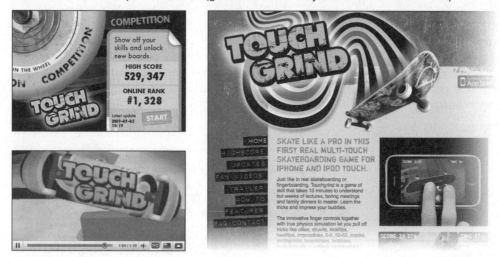

Figure 4–5. *Illusion Labs uses the same Touchgrind logo within the app itself (top left), its Touchgrind YouTube video trailer (bottom left), and its Touchgrind.com web site (right) for consistent branding.*

If you're porting an existing app to the iPhone or iPad from another platform, such as Mac OS X or Windows, take advantage of the brand equity you've already established by using a similar icon and logo for the iOS version. This is a great way to attract new customers who are already familiar with your app from another platform.

For example, when Cultured Code created an iPhone version of its award-winning Mac application, Things, it used the same branding but modified the icon slightly. The icon is still instantly recognizable as Things and cements the fact that the iPhone app is directly related to its Mac cousin. But the minor design tweak to the iPhone version's icon plays an important role. Not only does the change help the image display better as a small iOS icon with rounded edges, but it also helps position the iPhone app as a stand-alone version (see Figure 4–6).

Figure 4–6. *The Things Mac icon (left) and the Things iPhone icon (right)*

The Things iPhone icon is another great example of an image that is both simple and sophisticated at the same time. Although there are dozens of competing to-do lists and task management apps in the App Store with similar check mark–themed icons, the Things iPhone app stands out from the pack because of its photorealistic icon. The icon gets its high-quality feel from the little design nuances, such as the high-contrast colors, the inner drop shadow on the white square, and the subtle gloss effect on the surrounding blue box. In my opinion, the Things icons for both Mac and iOS are perfect models of effective app icon design, where less is more—delivering sheer simplicity with visual impact.

As you discovered while experimenting with Photoshop effects and filters while designing the Breadcrumbs icon example, sometimes the only things separating an amateur drawing from a professional-looking design are a few minor graphical touches.

Interface Design: Think Like a User, Not a Developer

Because I stressed its importance earlier in this chapter, you've taken the time to read Apple's IOS HIG, right? No? Then go ahead. I'll wait….

You're back already? Great! Now that you understand Apple's suggested boundaries and recommended design practices for iOS UIs, your first step in the development process is to put that knowledge to good use. No, I'm not talking about writing code just yet. Think about your app's core functionality and the key features it will include. How do you package that feature set into a compact, user-friendly interface for a small mobile device? Answering that question should be your first development task. You may already be an experienced iOS programmer, well versed in Objective-C and Cocoa Touch (and if you're not, plenty of great iPhone and iPad development books are available from Apress), but many developers have trouble translating their app concept into an efficient UI that's intuitive and easy to use.

When showcasing your app in the App Store, users want to see its interface. It's the front end that they will be interacting with on a daily basis when using your app, so they'll be checking to see whether it satisfies their specific needs and is easy to learn. Since they may have many alternatives to choose from, your app needs to be more visually appealing than your competitors. It's not just about being the app with the most features. Offering the features that consumers want may initially grab their attention, but the app with the best overall user experience will win their hard-earned money.

Take off your "developer hat" for a moment to think about your own purchasing habits. When you compare several similar apps to evaluate which one to buy, it's your visual senses that first kick into gear. You're looking at an app's screenshots in the App Store, and maybe even watching a video demo trailer on the developer's web site or playing with a free lite version. Obviously, customer ratings and reviews play a huge part in your decision, but let's say two similar apps offer the same features and have received roughly the same glowing reviews. When compared side by side, if one app offers a very plain, boring UI and the other offers a slick, attractive UI, a consumer is going to gravitate toward the app that's more visually enticing.

This type of thinking does not apply only to games, which require unique interfaces and original game play. Even if you're developing a utility or productivity app that performs mundane tasks, that doesn't mean that it can't be exciting and fun to use. Your customers will thank you for it.

The Immense Value of Prototyping

Prototyping can reveal awkward workflows and unintuitive architecture in your app. An interface concept can play like a good idea in your head, but once you map it out on paper and scrutinize a semi-working prototype, you may change your mind. In fact, sometimes a prototype can lead you to new ideas that end up enhancing the marketability of your app. At the very least, prototyping will expose actions that are overly complicated, leading you to find new solutions to streamline the user interaction—something that's crucial to the success of a mobile app.

Prototyping can also save you countless hours of development time and prevent you from writing unusable code. "How is that possible?" you ask. "Wouldn't it be faster to just jump into Xcode right now and start hammering out a quick-and-dirty demo?"

If you're developing an app for a client or your boss, he may want to see your ideas before signing off on the project. The key word here is *see*. More often than not, many business executives—especially those with no creative background—have trouble visualizing an interface. No matter how well you communicate your idea in a meeting, they just can't picture it in their head. Putting together wireframes or screenshot mock-ups of your interface concept is an easy, time-saving method to quickly show your client or boss what you're proposing. This way, if he comes back to you with a lot of changes or (gasp!) a major shift in direction, you won't have wasted a lot of precious time in Xcode and Interface Builder.

If you're outsourcing your app development, then prototyping can also be extremely valuable in properly communicating your UI concept to third-party programmers, especially if there's a substantial language barrier. When they're charging you by the hour, the less time you need to spend explaining your ideas and goals, the less money the outsourced development will cost you. A picture is worth a thousand words.

Even if you're an independent developer working solo on an app, the most important benefit of prototyping is the amount of valuable time and potential headaches it can save you later during the beta testing stage. You don't want to spend months slaving over an app, only to receive overwhelming feedback from your testers that the UI is impossible to grasp, making it difficult for them to figure out how to use the app or access certain features. Those are issues best solved before you get too deep into the development process.

Drawing Your Ideas on Paper

Don't overlook the value of sketches on graph paper! Getting your ideas down on paper is a quick way to map out the basic look and feel of your app. Designing a game that requires a completely custom interface? Drawing your concept on paper may be your only rapid option, since it would be impossible to do with only the standard controls available in Interface Builder. Sketch it first by hand to work out the design kinks, and then construct the final custom artwork in Illustrator or Photoshop.

Tired of drawing the same buttons and other standard interface elements over and over again? Thanks to several prominent designers and developers, predrawn iPhone and iPad sketch templates are available online (see Figure 4–7):

- Erik Loehfelm's iPhone UX Sketch Templates (http://erikloehfelm.blogspot.com/2009/05/iphone-ux-sketch-templates.html) are offered in multiple formats such as PDF, Photoshop, EPS, PNG, and OmiGraffle.

- Full of Design's iPhone App Wireframe Templates (http://www.fullofdesign.com/posts/iphone-app-wireframe-template) are available in PDF format.

- Kapsoft's iPhone and iPad Stencils (http://www.mobilestencil.com/) are durable IMA acrylic stencils. You can also get downloadable sketchbook pages in PDF format.

- UI Stencils' iPhone and iPad Stencil Kits (http://www.uistencils.com/) are stainless steel stencils.

Figure 4–7. *iPhone-related sketching templates and stencil kits are available from third-party designers.*

Although all the downloadable templates are truly well done, I couldn't find a comprehensive solution that matched my personal design needs, so I opted to publish my own unique, grid-based templates in *The Developer Sketchbook for iPhone Apps* and *The Developer Sketchbook for iPad Apps* (Electric Butterfly, http://www.developersketchbook.com/). These books include hundreds of pages of portrait and landscape UI templates, app navigation flowcharts, and app icon design templates. Also available are Dean Kaplan's *iPhone Application Sketch Book* (Apress, 2009) and *iPad Application Sketch Book* (Apress, 2010). If you're looking for an iOS app design notebook to take with you when you're away from the office or simply a central place to keep all your app ideas organized, these printed solutions are worthy additions to your development arsenal.

Beautiful Mock-Ups in Illustrator and Photoshop

If drawing on paper is not your thing, and you're more comfortable working in Adobe's Photoshop, Illustrator, or even Fireworks, other resourceful designers have graciously donated comprehensive sets of interface elements to the iOS developer community. These are conveniently stored in layered files, making the creation of pixel-perfect mock-ups extremely easy (see Figure 4–8).

- Mercury Intermedia's iPhone UI Vector Elements, for Illustrator
  (http://www.mercuryintermedia.com/blog/index.php/2009/03/iphone
  -ui-vector-elements)

- Iconshock's iPad Vector GUI Elements, for Illustrator
  (http://iconlibrary.iconshock.com/icons/ipad-vector-gui-
  elements-tabs-buttons-menus-icons/)

- Teehan+Lax's iPhone GUI and iPad GUI, for Photoshop
  (http://www.teehanlax.com/blog/)

- ThreeTwentyFourEighty's iPhone Interface PSD, for Photoshop
  (http://www.320480.com/)

- Smashing Magazine's iPhone PSD Vector Kit, for Photoshop
  (http://www.smashingmagazine.com/2008/11/26/iphone-psd-vector-
  kit/)

- iPhone GUI as Adobe Fireworks Rich Symbols
  (http://code.google.com/p/iphone-gui-fireworks-symbols/)

- Metaspark.com's iPhone Mockup Toolkit for Fireworks
  (http://blog.metaspark.com/2009/02/fireworks-toolkit-for-
  creating-iphone-ui-mockups/)

Figure 4–8. *Just a small sample of the many iOS elements available in layered Photoshop files and vector-based Illustrator files from third-party designers*

Other Software Tools for Designing Mock-Ups

If you don't own a license for Photoshop or Illustrator, or you're looking for a more budget-conscious prototyping option, here are some other tools for designing mock-ups:

OmniGraffle (http://www.omnigroup.com/applications/omnigraffle/): This is an inexpensive solution for Mac users. Although originally developed as a diagramming tool, OmniGraffle has become a popular choice for constructing wireframes and interface design mock-ups.

Graffletopia (http://www.graffletopia.com/): The third-party web site Graffletopia offers an extensive free library of user-contributed OmniGraffle stencils. Several iPhone-related stencils are available for download, which I've listed here for your convenience:

- Ultimate iPhone Stencil by Patrick Crowley

- Mobile iPhone by Yahoo! (part of the Yahoo! Design Stencil Kit)

- iPhone 3G Stencil by Theresa Neil

- iPad and iPhone Design by da5id

Keynotopia (http://keynotopia.com/): If you prefer using presentation software for client meetings, you may want to check out the various Keynote templates for prototyping iPhone and iPad apps available at Keynotopia.

*Balsamiq Mockups (*http://www.balsamiq.com/products/mockups/*)*: One of my personal favorites, Balsamiq Mockups is a robust, cross-platform Adobe AIR application that features a vast toolkit of "hand-drawn" UI elements for both desktop apps and iOS apps. This unique approach produces mock-ups that are very clean and professional, while still looking as though they were drawn on paper.

Designing Apps with Mobile Apps

What about those frequent occasions when inspiration hits while you're away from your desk? A few innovative iPhone and iPad apps provide powerful wireframing and prototyping features from the convenience and comfort of wherever you are.

If you're interested in exporting Xcode projects of your mock-ups, you'll definitely want to check out Dapp and Interface. If you're already a fan of OmniGraffle on the Mac, OmniGraffle for iPad may be an obvious solution for you (although it's worth noting that some of the third-party templates available at Graffletopia.com may not be supported on the current iPad version of OmniGraffle). Loyal users of Balsamiq Mockups will value the Balsamiq export feature in Endloop Systems' excellent iMockups.

The following are some of the available mobile mock-up tools:

- OmniGraffle for iPad
  (http://www.omnigroup.com/products/omnigraffle-ipad/)

- iMockups for iPad (http://www.endloop.ca/imockups/)

- Dapp (http://dapp.kerofrog.com.au/)

- Interface for iPhone and iPad (http://lesscode.co.nz/interface)

- App Layout for iPad (http://macspots.com/app-layout/)

- SketchyPad for iPad (http://sketchyapp.com/)

- Stencils App Modeler (http://www.stencilsapp.com/)

- AppMockUp (http://www.redbotsoftware.com/Apps/AppMockup.html)

Paper Prototyping

Whether you've designed your initial mock-ups via desktop graphics software or hand-drawn sketches, many developers have found it beneficial to create printed paper prototypes of their UIs. With scissors, glue, and even a little tape, you can emulate a very rough look and feel of the app's navigational flow. You may decide to get fancy with moving pieces of paper that slide within iPhone and iPad frames, or stick to a more conventional storyboard approach that spans several pages (like directors do before shooting movie scenes). Either way, this is a convenient method for performing very basic usability testing, working out any major flaws before crafting a more refined prototype in Xcode and Interface Builder.

Of course, if you're simply designing an app for yourself as a solo developer, then this step may seem a little excessive, especially if you're skilled enough to cobble together fast prototypes in Interface Builder. But if you're working with a client who is infamous for requesting countless UI changes, then creating functional paper prototypes may allow you to quickly refine the design and get your client's approval without wasting any actual programming time.

Testing User Interactions to Your Prototype

After you've created and tweaked your design, and you're finally happy with the way your interface looks, it's time to fire up Xcode and Interface Builder. Creating a new Xcode project, you could immediately go to work re-creating your UI design with real UIKit components or your own custom controls in Interface Builder, but before you put too much effort into writing a lot of code, you may want to first test the usability of your new UI design.

You can quickly create a semifunctional prototype of your app by coding only the bare minimum of UI elements needed to emulate the intended flow of actions. Although you may assume this would include writing at least basic code for most of the controls in your app, there's actually a lot you can "fake" to avoid that and save time. This is especially handy if you just want to quickly test a UI concept in the iOS Simulator or compile and distribute a quick prototype to others to receive feedback. This step can be immensely valuable in finding questionable areas of your app's navigational flow that could benefit from streamlining or simplifying actions. And when allowing a select group to test such an early prototype, you gain important insights about which interface elements are not intuitive to other people, allowing you to make important changes to your design before investing months pursuing a wrong direction.

For example, if your app is managed by a navigation controller or tab bar controller, then add that controller to your window in Interface Builder. In Xcode, write only the controller code necessary to enable moving from one screen to the next. Don't worry about re-creating the individual UI controls in every screen. If you've already created mock-ups of your app's various screens in Photoshop, Illustrator, or some other graphics editor, then simply crop and save those screens as PNG files. Import those PNG files into your Xcode project. By adding new subviews with UIImages to display each PNG file, the temporary UIImages can serve as dummy placeholders for those screens in Interface Builder (see Figure 4–9).

Figure 4–9. *Create quick prototypes by adding a minimum amount of navigation code needed to move from one screen to the next. Each screen subview can be faked by displaying Photoshop PNG files of your interface mock-ups in UIImages.*

As shown in Figure 4–9, a navigation controller is wired up with enough code to move between your app's various screens. On the selected subview in the example, an image is added and set to display the PNG mock-up of the default background with a fake text field. To enhance the prototype with additional functionality, you can add a few lines of code so that a mouse click on that image triggers the display of a new subview layer that shows a PNG mock-up of a fake iOS keyboard. Based on your own needs, you can decide how much extra interactivity you want to add to your prototypes.

After testing the prototype, receiving valuable feedback, and making any improvements to your app design, you can strip out the small amount of temporary code and related UIImage elements. Now you're ready to build the real subviews and controls on top of your existing controller code to start fleshing out the interface and feature set of your newly optimized app architecture.

As an alternative, if you've already created PNG or JPEG mock-ups of your various app screens using Photoshop or a similar graphics tool, and you're interested in previewing them on an actual iOS device, then the following solutions are worth exploring:

- Briefs (http://github.com/capttaco/Briefs)
- LiveView for iPhone and iPad (http://www.zambetti.com/projects/liveview/)
- Mockabilly (http://www.mockabilly.com/)
- Review (http://www.getreviewapp.com/)

LiveView, Mockabilly, and the highly recommended (and open source) Briefs also allow you to assign interactions to specific regions of each screen (such as buttons and table view rows) for testing on-device usability.

Pushing the Envelope with a Custom Interface

Creating a custom UI for a nongame app can be very rewarding. Why should games have all the fun? There's no reason utility and productivity apps can't be just as visually appealing. Unique and exciting UIs can get people talking, which results in free publicity for your app. Mac OS X users saw this strategy work wonders for Delicious Monster with the cutting-edge UI of its successful Delicious Library software application.

If you have your heart set on creating a custom interface, here's one important rule to remember: don't overthink the design. Being innovative is good, as long as it does not make your UI less intuitive to use. In such a small screen for mobile usage, less is more. Take special care that your custom design does not add extra complexity to your interface.

Convertbot by Tapbots breaks convention with a totally unique interface design (see Figure 4–10). The app provides unit conversion for hundreds of formats, such as currency, speed, temperature, length, mass, time, and so on—a very utilitarian service that could have easily been presented in a basic screen layout using standard UIKit controls. Instead, the developers opted to produce a clever and innovative design, turning the typically mundane task of unit conversion into a fun user experience. The beautiful interface of Convertbot has earned Tapbots a lot of free buzz in the iPhone community, with countless reviewers and users praising the thoughtful and creative design behind its UI.

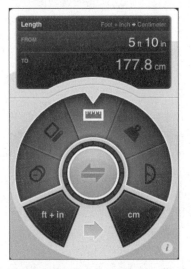

Figure 4–10. *The Convertbot UI effectively balances beauty and simplicity to provide a satisfying and intuitive user experience.*

What makes the Convertbot design so effective and easy to use is that behind the meticulously crafted UI is an extremely simple concept: a single large dial. So, even though the interface is unlike any of the usual UIKit elements, everyone knows how to use a dial (especially classic iPod users).

Another good example of an app that delivers a beautiful custom interface while remaining very easy to use is BRID's Awesome Note. Although there are already dozens of note-taking apps in the App Store, most of them use standard table views to organize and list groups of notes. Instead of a simple table view row for each notes category, Awesome Note sets itself apart from its competitors by wrapping the same functionality into a graphical, cascading tab folder theme (see Figure 4–11). Because we're all familiar with using folders in the physical world (and also on our desktop computers), the elements in this design remain instantly recognizable. The custom UI of Awesome Note succeeds in offering a unique user experience with no additional learning curve.

Figure 4–11. *The stunning UI of Awesome Note remains easy to use by integrating familiar tab folders and sticky note elements.*

As long as you avoid known issues that can get your app rejected by Apple, and remember to think like a user to maintain a UI that's intuitive and easy to use, pushing the envelope on interface design can offer an attractive user experience with the potential to garner increased publicity and sales.

The Comfortable Familiarity of UIKit

Before choosing to design a custom interface instead of using the standard UIKit controls provided by Apple, make sure you have very valid reasons to do so. As previously mentioned, the custom controls in BRID's Awesome Note app help reinforce its unique tab folder theme while staying true to the familiar functionality of similar UIKit components. In that particular situation, BRID's design intentions appear well served and justified, but don't reinvent the wheel just for the sake of being clever.

If you're building a complex, feature-rich app that's intended to store a lot of data, you may want to think twice about introducing a custom UI with new visual metaphors. If your app's interface appears to be too cluttered and complicated, you run the risk of overwhelming users. Your custom design elements may seem intuitive to you because you created them, but to newcomers, your unique visuals may feel foreign and confusing. Anything that causes frustration can lead to negative customer ratings and reviews, which obviously won't help your app sales.

With thousands of apps already using Apple's standard UIKit framework, users already know how to operate those standard components. By relying on UIKit, your app minimizes the learning curve for new customers. This allows people to focus on your app's core functionality without getting bogged down in figuring out how to use your interface.

Cultured Code takes advantage of UIKit components with its iPhone version of Things, which specializes in making task management as easy as possible. The main Things iPhone screen consists of standard UIKit components, such as a navigation controller and grouped table views (see Figure 4–12). To brand this basic UI with its own unique visual identity, Cultured Code integrated beautiful custom icons that match the ones used in its Mac OS X version of Things.

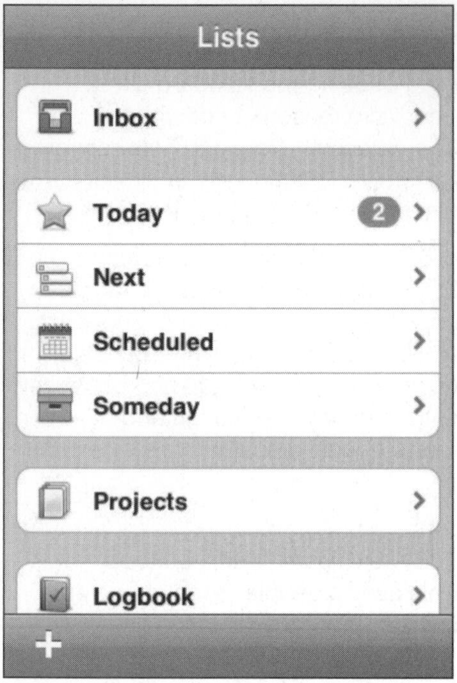

Figure 4–12. *The Things iPhone app utilizes a combination of standard UIKit components with custom icons to create a very clean and straightforward working environment.*

By keeping the interface extremely simple, Things provides a very clean and uncluttered working environment, enabling users to focus on creating and organizing their tasks. No matter how many tasks are added, the simplicity of the design gives the content room to breathe on the screen. For a productivity app like Things, sheer simplicity can prove to be the most alluring trait. With an interface that never appears cramped in such a small mobile screen size, even long lists of tasks fail to overwhelm users—an impressive feat that underscores the power of UIKit.

Apple has put a lot of thought into its native interface elements to ensure they visually communicate their function using a highly compact, streamlined approach. If you can't create something better than what's already included in UIKit, then don't.

In the case of Things, one look at the first screenshot in the App Store, and you automatically understand how it works. There's no learning curve. You just "get it" at first glance. That screenshot alone is a powerful marketing tool, making Things extremely attractive to people looking for an easy-to-use task management app.

Extensibility is an important factor to keep in mind when designing your interface. If there are four distinct sections in your app, a tab bar controller may seem like the best UI choice for easily accessing each of the sections. But before you decide to go that route, think about the features you have planned for future updates. If you plan on later integrating additional sections, a tab bar controller is probably not the best choice, since it can comfortably display only four or five tabs in portrait mode. To give your app room to grow in the future, you may want to consider using a table view to list those sections. A grouped table view, like the one used in Things for iPhone (Figure 4–12), can be scrolled, so it can accommodate an endless number of new additions while still remaining easy to use.

Extensibility is a consideration for every aspect of your UI design, since you don't want to be forced to radically change the interface in version 2.0 or 3.0 because you ran out of room. Requiring your customers to learn how to use a new UI after they've grown accustomed to using your original UI will only agitate them. It may even cost you a few customers who decide to switch to a competitor's app out of frustration.

If you're interested in using UIKit elements in your app but worry about your interface looking too much like other similar apps, you can do several things to make your UIKit-driven interface unique. Let's look at a few options.

Icons and Images

As you saw with Things, the icons and imagery you use within your app's interface can make a huge difference in giving your app a unique visual identity. Try not to use stock clip art for your icons, which will only cheapen the look of your UI. You want all of your icons to be consistent in design and not a motley collection of stock clip art from different styles. You also do not want any of your users to recognize any of your icons as clip art they've seen in other places, since that automatically lowers the perceived quality of your app.

If you don't have the design chops to create your own artwork, as I've said before, I highly recommend hiring a professional graphic designer. If you've already had someone create your app icon and logo, see whether that person is also able to design your UI icons and imagery for a consistent overall theme.

Designing single-color white icons for use in buttons and tabs in toolbars and tab bars is a lot harder than most people assume. With no additional colors, you must design white icons that distinctly communicate an action or topic by its unique symbolism. Not to sound like a broken record, but this is yet another occasion when simplicity works best to ensure that the user can easily understand the meaning behind each and every icon. Showing a rough prototype to a select group can help pinpoint icons that people are having trouble identifying, so that you can modify their design accordingly long before you start beta testing a finished app.

When designing for multiple iOS device targets, you may find that resizing your Retina display toolbar and tab bar icons for older iPhones and the iPad provides less than stellar results. Shrinking a little white icon to an even smaller size can sometimes make certain elements of the icon appear blurry. Frequently, I find that to perfect an icon for each target size, I end up either doing some touch-up work to the icon after resizing it or simply re-creating it from scratch for that smaller size. Yes, that's a lot of extra work, but in the long run, it's worth the additional time spent on beautifying my app for every iOS device it supports.

APP REJECTION WARNING: *Use system-provided icons only in the way that users expect them to work.* Apple has generously included several icons in the iOS SDK that developers can use in their own apps, such as Add, Compose, Reply, Action, Search, and many more. This can save you from needing to create custom icons for common tasks that are already covered by Apple's system icons. Just keep in mind that Apple provides these icons to represent consistent behavior across all apps that use them. When employing these system icons in your own app, be sure you're using them in their intended manner, or else your App Store submission may be quickly rejected. For example, don't use the Reply icon for a back button, and don't use the Bookmarks icon to open an e-book.

Toolbar Colors

You can modify the color of navigation controllers and toolbars. Don't feel obligated to use the black or default color choices.

Browsing the App Store, you'll see a lot of apps using distinct toolbar colors, such as dark blue, brown, green, and red (see the Nike+ GPS app's red toolbar in Figure 4–13). Just make sure to choose a high-contrast color so that embedded text labels and buttons are easy to read.

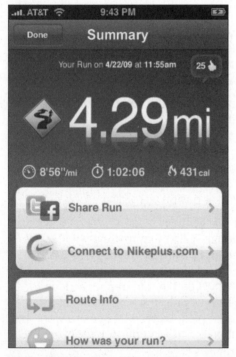

Figure 4–13. *The Nike+ GPS app utilizes red toolbars and red background image textures to reinforce its brand colors and give the interface a unique and attractive visual theme.*

Set the color of the navigation and toolbar components by first opening your *.xib* file in Interface Builder and selecting the navigation bar or toolbar with its attributes visible in the inspector palette. Then under Attributes, keep the Style set to Default and change the Tint to your desired color, using the included Color Picker button.

Background Colors and Images

If you use a custom color for your navigation bar and/or toolbar, you'll also want to modify the background of your views from the default blue/gray to a new color or image of your choice.

The Nike+ GPS app (see Figure 4–13) is a nice example of the use of the background. It employs a subtle red cross-hatch texture image as the background of the view below the red-tinted toolbar. Using a dark red to lighter red gradient from top to bottom, the background adds a subtle three-dimensional depth to the interface as it flows behind the large white text and the grouped table view rows.

Designing for Accessibility

Another important visual design factor to consider is Apple's accessibility feature, White on Black. This enables any iPhone 3GS, iPhone 4, iPod touch (Retina display), and iPad user to change the display to white text on a black background in any application. When turned on, this high-contrast feature inverts the screen's colors, making the text easier to read for some vision-impaired folks. As a developer, you should test your app's interface design in White on Black mode to ensure that it remains readable and its usability does not suffer from the inverted colors. It does not appear that the iPhone Simulator supports the White on Black mode, so for now, you'll need to test your app on an actual iOS device. In the Settings panel, choose General, then select Accessibility, and finally tap the White on Black switch to ON.

Another important subject that's often overlooked by software developers is color blindness. Although complete color blindness is a rare condition, quite a large percentage of the world population suffers from some form of color-deficient vision. This means their eyes still see full color but are unable to differentiate between some key colors like red and green. Although very few females exhibit color problems, would you believe that a whopping 8 percent of males demonstrate some sort of color deficiency? To put that into perspective, roughly 1 in 12 males of European descent have color-deficient vision. Considering that many iOS developers create games and other apps specifically geared toward guys, being aware of color-deficiency issues when you're designing your interface is crucial in making your app accessible to the broadest audience possible.

Here are a couple of helpful resources for checking accessibility:

> *Vischeck* (`http://www.vischeck.com/`): This web site should be a required stop for all software developers. It provides helpful online tools for revealing color problems in your applications. Upload screenshots of your interface into the online Vischeck simulator to see how your UI design will look through color-deficient eyes. Upload

screenshots to the online Daltonize tool to color-correct your interface for the three most common color deficiencies. The site also offers downloads of the Vischeck simulator as a free Photoshop plug-in for testing your interface screenshots directly within Photoshop.

Sim Daltonism, for Mac OS X (http://michelf.com/projects/sim-daltonism/): This time-saving desktop application by Michel Fortin is a simple floating palette that allows you to test your iPhone app's interface in real time. Run your Xcode project in the iPhone Simulator while running the Sim Daltonism floating palette along one side. Select a color-deficiency type from the palette's menu, and then move your mouse pointer over the iPhone Simulator to see how your app's UI looks through color-deficient eyes in the palette window. (If you find Sim Daltonism useful, you're encouraged to support its continued development by making an online donation at Michel's web site.)

Tips for the Artistically Challenged

The do-it-yourself route is not for everyone, especially when designing something as important as custom artwork for your iOS app icon, logo, and UI. Remember that Photoshop, Illustrator, and other graphics programs are merely tools. Those tools are only as useful as your ability to wield them. To put the tools to good use, you must have the creativity and patience to translate the ideas from your head into actual pixels on the screen. Need some help? Here, I'll recommend a few time-saving solutions and resources that might give you just the boost you need.

Finding Graphics and Icons

Looking for premade icons for your app's toolbars and tab bars? Lucky for you, there are numerous third-party icon collections designed specifically for use in iOS apps. These icon sets are royalty-free and inexpensive (or free)—perfect for budget-conscious, commercial app projects. Graphics are available as bitmap images, vector-based images, or both formats, so you're sure to find some great icons to help enhance your app's UI. Here are some resources:

- Glyphish Icons (http://glyphish.com/)

- Pictos Interface Icons (http://pictos.drewwilson.com/)

- Default Icon Repository (http://www.defaulticon.com/)

- eddit's iPhone UI Icon Set (http://eddit.com/shop/)

- PixelPressIcon's Whitespace Icon Collection (http://www.pixelpressicons.com/?page_id=118)

- The Working Group's iPhone Toolbar Icons (http://blog.twg.ca/2009/09/free-iphone-toolbar-icons/)

- App-bits Tab Bar Icons (http://www.app-bits.com/free-icons.html)

- Tabs Interface Icons for iOS (http://www.tabsicons.com/)

- Dezinerfolio's Vector Icons
  (http://www.dezinerfolio.com/freebie/30-free-vector-icons)

As far as full-color icons are concerned (for use in your table views and other related UI elements), dozens of web sites offer icon design tutorials, free stock icons, commercial icon sets, and custom icon design services.

If you do find some free stock icons that you would like to use in your app, be sure to check the licensing terms to ensure that the icons are royalty-free and can be used in commercial software. Some free icons require giving credit to the designer in your app or documentation.

Also, as previously mentioned, if you do decide to use stock icons in your iOS app, consider modifying them so that you app retains a unique feel (provided you still adhere to the related license terms). You don't want to cheapen the perception of the quality of your app by using the same stock icons that people have already seen countless times in other software and web sites. Here are a select handful of online resources:

- The Iconfactory (http://iconfactory.com/)

- Stockicons (http://stockicons.com/)

- IconDock (http://icondock.com/)

- Icon Archive (http://www.iconarchive.com/)

- FreeIconsWeb (http://www.freeiconsweb.com/)

- IconsPedia (http://www.iconspedia.com/)

- Iconshock (http://www.iconshock.com/)

- Iconfinder (http://www.iconfinder.net/)

- iStockphoto (http://www.istockphoto.com/)

NOTE: Although most people know iStockphoto as a destination for purchasing inexpensive stock photography, it also has an extensive library of beautiful vector-based background imagery and icons.

Choosing Fonts

For most iPhone and iPad apps, using the native iOS system fonts will be sufficient, so font licensing will not be a concern. If you're developing a game, kids' app, or entertainment app that uses a special font in its interface graphics, you'll want to make sure the unique font you've chosen has affordable licensing terms. Royalty-free fonts are obviously the most cost-effective, as long as they allow use in commercial projects.

Pay close attention to the licensing agreement of each custom font you're interested in using. At first glance, many font libraries appear to be free or royalty-free, but often the fine print specifies personal use only, with separate licenses (and higher price tags) available for commercial purposes, such as web sites, software, and so on. Do your homework before you purchase specialty fonts for use in your iOS apps.

Here are a few font directories to explore:

- dafont.com (http://www.dafont.com/)

- MyFonts (http://www.myfonts.com/)

- Search Free Fonts (http://www.searchfreefonts.com/)

- Discover Fonts (http://www.discoverfonts.com/)

- Fonts.com (http://www.fonts.com/)

- FontSpace (http://www.fontspace.com/)

- UrbanFonts (http://www.urbanfonts.com/)

- 1001 Free Fonts (http://www.1001freefonts.com/)

Adding Audio and Music

If you're building a game or entertainment app, audio and music are often big factors in the enjoyment of it. If you're not a sound designer or have very little experience composing and editing audio, you may want to hire someone to do the music and sound effects cues. If you can't afford to hire a digital musician or sound designer, you may want to consider licensing stock sound libraries. As with fonts, make sure any stock audio or music you purchase is royalty-free and licensed for commercial use.

Here are some audio and music directories:

- Sound Effects Library (http://www.sound-effects-library.com/)

- SoundMATTER (http://soundmatter.thegamecreators.com/)

- StockFuel (http://stockfuel.com/stock_audio.html)

- AudioJungle (http://audiojungle.net/)

- IndieSFX (http://www.indiesfx.co.uk/)

- NEO Sounds (http://www.neosounds.com/)

- The Music Bakery (http://www.musicbakery.com/)

- Sounddogs.com (http://www.sounddogs.com/)

- Soundrangers (http://www.soundrangers.com/)

- iStockphoto Audio Tracks (http://www.istockphoto.com/audio)

Using Professional Design Services

If creating artwork or custom audio proves difficult for you—like pulling teeth—then instead of allowing the experience to become overly frustrating and unrewarding, you may want to consider hiring a professional designer. Don't succumb to any egotistical notions that you must create and control every aspect of the design and development process if your app stands to suffer from your own creative limitations. The success of your app is far too important.

Knowing your own limitations as a developer will give you the freedom to bring on outside help so that you can build the best-quality app possible. Even when delegating the work to professional designers, you're still in charge of the project.

If money is an issue, then be creative. Do you have any talents that a professional designer may need? Perhaps the designer needs some web site or software programming assistance? If so, then there's an opportunity to barter services.

Another option is to offer a small percentage of your app sales in exchange for the designer's ongoing graphics support. In essence, the designer is becoming a partner, sharing in the risk. If the app fails to reach an audience, then no one involved makes any money. Some designers, depending on their availability, may not be open to such a gamble. Even if you have a great concept, they may prefer to get paid up front. But if a profit-sharing option is your best option, it can't hurt to offer it.

There are far too many professional design services and freelance artists to list within these pages. Here are a just few notable resources worth considering:

- They Make Apps (http://theymakeapps.com/)
- Get Apps Done (http://www.getappsdone.com/)
- 99designs (http://99designs.com/)
- oDesk (http://www.odesk.com/)
- Elance (http://www.elance.com/)
- Guru.com (http://www.guru.com/)

When exploring outsourcing marketplaces, online search engines, or even your local yellow pages, never settle for the first listing you find. Ask for recommendations from your peers, either directly or via developer mailing lists and online forums. You want to find out from other developers which companies and consultants are trusted and respected for their design work on icons, logos, music, sound effects, and other outsourced creative elements. Even when you find a designer you like, ask to see her portfolio to make sure her design style and skills are capable of bringing your specific vision to life.

Communication is key when working with designers. Although they may be extremely good at their craft, they can't read minds. The more information you give them about your creative needs, the better equipped they will be to deliver exactly what you want.

Creative Boost

Wow, that was a lot of information packed into a single chapter! Are you now fueled with new ideas and enough inspiration to kick-start your own app interface design work? Good! Turning your iOS app into a powerful marketing tool does not end here. In the next chapter, you'll explore the benefits of integra.

Chapter 5

Social Inception: Promoting Your Apps Within Apps

Building upon Chapter 4's quest to transform your app into its own marketing powerhouse, this chapter will take you one step further. You'll learn how to integrate convenient sharing and social media elements such as In-App Email, Twitter, and Facebook. You'll also explore tactics for gracefully encouraging App Store user reviews within your app, and improving app discovery with in-app cross-promotion and third-party social gaming platforms. The sample code in this chapter demonstrates how to implement these various ingredients for effective results.

Encouraging User Reviews Within Your App

You've put a lot of work into perfecting your app's user experience in the hopes that your efforts result in sales and positive customer ratings.

As I've noted in earlier chapters, prior to iOS 4, when a user deleted an app from the home screen, Apple automatically prompted the user to first rate the app. Although that was a convenient way to solicit customer feedback, it was certainly not the most opportune time to ask for an opinion. If the user had chosen to delete your app, then he probably didn't like it or had not found it useful. In either situation, if he did opt to post a rating, odds were it would be a negative one.

Thankfully, Apple removed that rate-upon-deletion feature in iOS 4. But even with that welcome fix, unhappy users are typically much more motivated than satisfied users to visit the App Store on their own and manually post a review. They have a bone to pick and want everyone to know about it. Let's consider how to encourage ratings from users who are happy with your app.

Seeking Feedback at Runtime

We're all painfully aware that customer ratings and reviews in the App Store can greatly affect the sales of an app. So, how does a developer combat the uneven emphasis on negative feedback? Obviously, the first answer is to make a well-thought, polished app. But what can you do beyond that?

Why not prompt your satisfied users for positive feedback within the app? It's as easy as having your app display its own UIAlertView, asking users who like the app to please rate it. You can do this with only a handful of code lines.

First, fire up Xcode and create a new iPhone project, using the View-based Application template as the foundation. (You can just as easily create this as an iPad project if that's the device you prefer to target.) Let's name the project **AskForRating**. In this example, you'll simply be adding a button to the AskForRating project's main screen. In your own apps, you may want to give the user the option to rate your app at any time by including a button on your Settings or Info screen.

Next, you'll need to add a reference to the UIAlertViewDelegate in the @interface call of your *AskForRatingViewController.h* header file. You'll also want to add an IBAction method for the button you'll be creating in Interface Builder later. Your *AskForRatingViewController.h* file should now consist of the following code:

```
#import <UIKit/UIKit.h>

@interface AskForRatingViewController : UIViewController <UIAlertViewDelegate> {

}

- (IBAction)buttonPressed:(id)sender;

@end
```

After saving that file, open the *AskForRatingViewController.m* implementation file, and add the following code:

```
- (IBAction)buttonPressed:(id)sender {
    UIAlertView *buttonAlert = [[UIAlertView alloc] initWithTitle:@"Help Spread the
Word" message:@"If you like this app, please rate it in the App Store. Thanks!"
delegate:self cancelButtonTitle:@"Maybe Later" otherButtonTitles:@"Rate It Now", nil];
    [buttonAlert show];
    [buttonAlert release];
}

- (void)alertView:(UIAlertView *)alertView clickedButtonAtIndex:(NSInteger)buttonIndex {
    if (buttonIndex == 1) {
        NSURL *url = [NSURL URLWithString:@"YOUR APP STORE URL"];
        [[UIApplication sharedApplication] openURL:url];
    }
}
```

The (IBAction)buttonPressed method receives the tapped button action and proceeds to display the UIAlertView, asking the user to rate the app. The alertView code is called when the user chooses either the Maybe Later or Rate It Now button in the UIAlertView dialog box. If the Rate It Now button is selected, your App Store URL is launched, sending the user directly to your app's page in the App Store.

Don't forget to replace the placeholder string "YOUR APP STORE URL" with your unique App Store URL.

> **TIP:** To grab the correct App Store URL, simply locate your app in the desktop Mac version of iTunes, select **Copy Link** from either the pop-up menu next to the Buy button or the contextual menu that appears when you Ctrl-click your app icon, and then paste it into the URL string in your code.

Save the file in Xcode, and move on to the last task: creating your button. Double-click the *AskForRatingViewController.xib* file to open it in Interface Builder. Add a Round Rect Button to your view. Rename the button's title to **Rate This App**. If desired, you could create your own custom button instead. Then wire the button's Touch Up Inside connector to the File Owner's buttonPressed connector. Save and close the XIB file.

If you run your Xcode project in the iOS Simulator, you'll see that pressing the Rate This App button successfully prompts you to rate the app with a UIAlertView dialog box (see Figure 5–1). However, if you click the Rate It Now button, the App Store URL won't load within the iOS Simulator, so you'll need to test your app on an actual iPhone, iPad, or iPod touch to ensure it properly fetches your app's page in the on-device App Store.

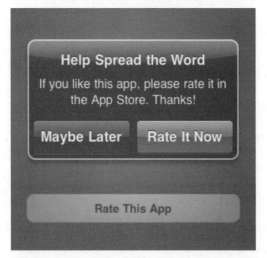

Figure 5–1. *Encourage users to rate your app with a built-in custom prompt.*

Take note of the wording used in our example's UIAlertView. By using the title "Help Spread the Word" as the call to action, you're inviting fans to help evangelize your app. And with the message "If you like this app, please rate it in the App Store," you're specifically addressing your satisfied users. Of course, that won't stop haters from using this feature, but the wording does set a positive tone. Even the cancel button is labeled Maybe Later, letting users know that their feedback is always welcome at any time.

When to Ask for Ratings

Although our previous example provides a nice solution, it's still a passive one, relying on the users to tap the Rate This App button to initiate the action. If you place the button on your Settings or Info screen, users may stumble upon it only while looking for help with your app. And if they're searching for help, they may be frustrated—not a good time to hit them up for a review.

You want to ask users to rate your app when they're in the best possible mood, such as moments when they are enjoying your app. You may want to consider taking a more proactive stance, initiating the display of your UIAlertView at strategic times such as the following:

- After several days of usage, if users have not deleted your app yet, they must have found some positive value in it. Include code to check the NSUserDefaults, determining how many days the app has been installed upon app launch. Depending on how often your app is likely to get used (daily or weekly), pick an appropriate time to pop up the rating request dialog box—maybe after 5 to 15 days of being installed.

- If your app is a game, display the rating request dialog box when they're feeling good, like after finishing a difficult level or achieving a high score.

- If it's a productivity app, you may want to display the rating request dialog box when users have a positive sense of accomplishment— after writing a document, editing a photo, checking off a list of tasks, and so on.

Lima Sky's popular Doodle Jump uses a fun pop-up banner image on the game's main menu screen to solicit positive App Store ratings (see Figure 5–2). Notice the implied request for a good rating by showing five stars in the banner. You can see that the caption "Love Doodle Jump?" specifically addresses the game's happy customers. These are subtle yet effective strategies to inspire users to help out.

Figure 5–2. *Lima Sky customized the app rating request in Doodle Jump to match the fun style of the game.*

With any of these approaches, take care not to be overly aggressive. If you annoy users by constantly asking them for a rating, this ploy will backfire on you. The users you annoy will be driven to post negative ratings, complaining about how much they hate being pestered for their feedback. For best results, ask only once or in a very few select places. If customers choose Maybe Later, they can always rate your app when it's convenient for them by accessing the Rate This App button on your Settings or Info screen.

If you're interested in prompting users after a specific number of days and/or app launches, but would rather not spend time implementing that extra bit of code and making it multitasking-aware, check out Arash Payan's open source Appirater class, at http://github.com/arashpayan/appirater/. (And if you find the free Appirater code helpful, then return the favor by downloading his iPhone app, Jabeh.)

Tell a Friend with In-App Email and Social Networking

Similar to the concept of a Rate This App button, you can also include a Tell A Friend button in your app, enabling your customers to recommend your app to their friends and family. This is good old-fashioned grassroots marketing. By supplying your users with convenient options to talk about your app, you've taken a proactive step in the hopes of increasing your app's exposure and sales through the proven power of word of mouth. Nothing helps sell a product more effectively than recommendations from trusted peers.

What options would you want to offer? You can send e-mail directly from within your app using the iOS SDK's In-App Email functionality, so that's an easy yet powerful feature to include. And with Twitter and Facebook being such popular social networking sites, you may want to consider adding support for those platforms as well.

Using Third-Party Web Services

If you do decide to connect with a third-party web service, you'll want to first read the API license agreement to confirm that it allows you to access the API in a commercial software application for mobile devices. And even if it does allow commercial use, take into consideration that the company's terms may change in the future, or it may cease to operate, forcing you to remove that feature. If your app lists supported web services as buttons on a UIActionSheet, that gives you the flexibility to easily remove one of the buttons if needed in a future app update.

Even beyond licensing terms, a third-party web service might make an API change that could break your app, causing you to scramble to submit a new fixed update to the App Store. Remember Twitpocalypse—the Twitter API change that briefly disabled many of the iPhone Twitter client apps back in June 2009? Unlike the instant availability of posting new software downloads on your web site, you may need to wait days for your updated version to make its way through the App Store review process before customers can get their hands on it.

Relying on a third-party web service also makes you vulnerable to any API outages or glitches that may surface due to server maintenance, bugs, or too much traffic. You'll want to defensively code your app to gracefully handle situations when a supported service is temporarily unavailable. If your app's social networking feature is not functioning properly and the app fails to notify the users that the third-party service is down, they will automatically assume the culprit is your app, not Twitter or Facebook.

Web services offer amazing content that is perfect for mobile app consumption, but definitely keep these potential issues in mind when deciding how much of your app's functionality will depend on a third-party web service.

Connecting Users with In-App Sharing

Without any further ado, let's try our hand at a little code, shall we? Create a new project in Xcode, but this time choose the Window-based Application template with Universal selected in its Product pull-down menu, and name it TellAFriend. This way, you can use the same shared code for both iPhone and iPad, yet you'll see how the interface appears slightly different on the two devices.

Before you start working on TellAFriend's primary functionality, you'll want to first set the stage with some basic UI elements. Since many apps use the standard action button to present these kinds of sharing features, let's build a navigation controller with an action button. This requires a few extra steps, so you can either follow along or download the completed project from the book's companion code examples at http://iPhoneBusinessBook.com/ or http://www.apress.com/.

With the *Shared* folder selected in the Xcode project, choose **File ➤ New File…**, and then add a new UIViewController subclass with an XIB file and *.h* file. Name the new class **RootViewController**, and set it aside for now. We'll come back to it in a few minutes.

Open the *AppDelegate_iPhone.h* file and add two new lines of code (shown in bold):

```
#import <UIKit/UIKit.h>

@interface AppDelegate_iPhone : NSObject <UIApplicationDelegate> {
    UIWindow *window;
    UINavigationController *navigationController;
}

@property (nonatomic, retain) IBOutlet UIWindow *window;
@property (nonatomic, retain) IBOutlet UINavigationController *navigationController;

@end
```

You'll also need to add those bold code lines to the same places in your *AppDelegate_iPad.h* file. This code is for the navigation controller that we'll be adding to the UI soon.

Next, open the *AppDelegate_iPhone.m* file and modify its contents with a few new code lines (shown in bold):

```
#import "AppDelegate_iPhone.h"
#import "RootViewController.h"

@implementation AppDelegate_iPhone

@synthesize window;
@synthesize navigationController;

#pragma mark -
#pragma mark Application lifecycle

- (BOOL)application:(UIApplication *)application
didFinishLaunchingWithOptions:(NSDictionary *)launchOptions {

    [self.window addSubview:navigationController.view];

    [self.window makeKeyAndVisible];

    return YES;
}
- (void)dealloc {
    [navigationController release];
    [window release];
```

```
        [super dealloc];
}

// There are several other default application methods also included in this
// file, which we'll omit from this code listing to conserve page space, but
// DO NOT remove them from the actual file.

@end
```

As with the header files, you'll also need to add those bold code lines to the same places in your *AppDelegate_iPad.m* file. This new code essentially adds the navigation controller's view to the window and displays it.

Now with all the code groundwork out of the way, open *MainWindow_iPhone.xib* in Interface Builder and add a UINavigationController. Wire the app delegate's referencing outlet navigationController to the UINavigationController. Then with the UINavigationController's view selected in the attributes inspector panel, assign the view's NIB name to RootViewController with the Resize View From NIB option checked (see Figure 5–3). And, in the identity inspector panel, set the class to RootViewController. Save that file. Then perform the same steps with the *MainWindow_iPad.xib* file.

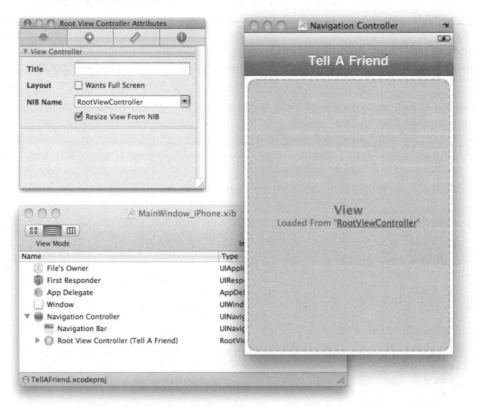

Figure 5–3. *Setting up the navigation controller for the iPhone UI in Interface Builder. The same steps will also need to be performed for the iPad UI in this universal app example.*

You'll want the app to include a Tell A Friend button that displays a UIActionSheet with various buttons for e-mail, Twitter, and Facebook. Why use a UIActionSheet? It allows you to add the Tell A Friend feature with a single button, so as not to be intrusive in your existing interface design. It also consolidates all of the supported social networking services into a single list, making it easy to add or remove options as needed. Want to add support for another social networking platform? Just add another button to your UIActionSheet, without disturbing your app's main UI design.

Open the *RootViewController.h* header file, and modify the code to read as follows:

```
#import <UIKit/UIKit.h>

@interface RootViewController : UIViewController <UIActionSheetDelegate> {

}

- (IBAction)showShareOptions:(id)sender;

@end
```

Notice the added delegate reference to the UIActionSheetDelegate and the IBAction method for the button you'll be creating in Interface Builder. Save that file, and now open the *RootViewController.m* implementation file. Change the code to read as follows:

```
#import "RootViewController.h"

@implementation RootViewController

- (void)viewDidLoad {
    [super viewDidLoad];

    // Add action button to the navigation bar.
    UIBarButtonItem *actionButton = [[UIBarButtonItem alloc]
initWithBarButtonSystemItem:UIBarButtonSystemItemAction target:self
action:@selector(showShareOptions:)];
    self.navigationItem.rightBarButtonItem = actionButton;
    [actionButton release];
}

- (IBAction)showShareOptions:(id)sender {
    // Action button was tapped, so display Action Sheet.
    UIActionSheet *actionSheet = [[UIActionSheet alloc] initWithTitle:@"Like This App?
Tell A Friend!" delegate:self cancelButtonTitle:@"Maybe Later"
destructiveButtonTitle:nil otherButtonTitles:@"Send Email", @"Post on Twitter", @"Share
on Facebook", nil];
    [actionSheet showInView:self.view];
    [actionSheet release];

}

- (void)actionSheet:(UIActionSheet *)actionSheet
didDismissWithButtonIndex:(NSInteger)buttonIndex {
    if (buttonIndex != [actionSheet cancelButtonIndex]) {
        if (buttonIndex == 0) {
            // Add Email code here.
        }
```

```
            if (buttonIndex == 1) {
                // Add Twitter code here.
            }
            if (buttonIndex == 2) {
                // Add Facebook code here.
            }
        }
    }

    - (void)didReceiveMemoryWarning {
        [super didReceiveMemoryWarning];
    }

    - (void)viewDidUnload {
        [super viewDidUnload];
    }

    - (void)dealloc {
        [super dealloc];
    }

    @end
```

In viewDidLoad, an action button is being dynamically added as the right button in the navigation bar. Since RootViewController is the view assigned to the navigation controller in both the iPhone and iPad interfaces, this new action button will display itself on both the iPhone and iPad versions of the app.

If the user taps the action button, the showShareOptions method is called. This is where you display the UIActionSheet with the title "Like This App? Tell A Friend!" Buttons for e-mail, Twitter, and Facebook have been added (see Figure 5–4). As a UIActionSheetDelegate, the RootViewController is notified when a user chooses an option from the action sheet. The user's selection is captured in the action sheet's didDismissWithButtonIndex event.

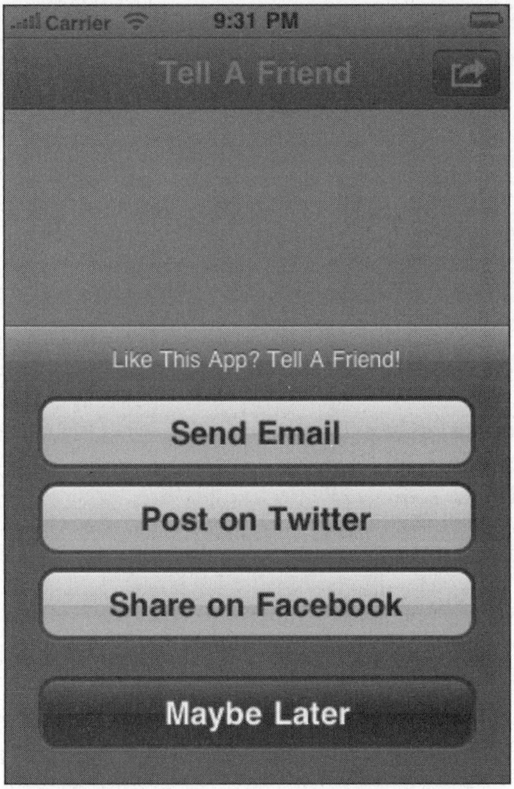

Figure 5–4. *The Tell A Friend example app in action on the iPhone*

When running the app on the iPad, you'll notice that the `UIAlertSheet` is displayed as an iPad-centric popover (see Figure 5–5). The Maybe Later (cancel) button is discarded by the system, since popovers are dismissed by tapping anywhere outside the popover window.

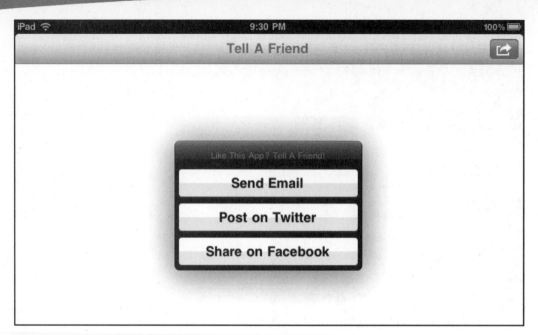

Figure 5–5. *The same Tell A Friend example app running on the iPad*

Tapping on the Send Email, Post on Twitter, or Share on Facebook button does nothing but dismiss the `UIAlertSheet`, but that's because you haven't added the functionality yet. On to the next steps…

Adding E-mail Support

With the basic foundation of the Tell A Friend app finished, now you need to add functionality to the Send Email button. The iOS SDK includes framework support for an In-App Email feature, which allows users to compose and send an e-mail message directly within your own app! Apple has made In-App Email relatively easy for developers to employ, so adding this functionality requires much less effort than you might expect.

Before you write any code, the required MessageUI framework must be added to the Xcode project. To add it, Ctrl-click the project's *Frameworks* folder, and from the contextual menu that appears, select **Add ➤ Existing Frameworks…** (see Figure 5–6). Select MessageUI.framework from the list that appears.

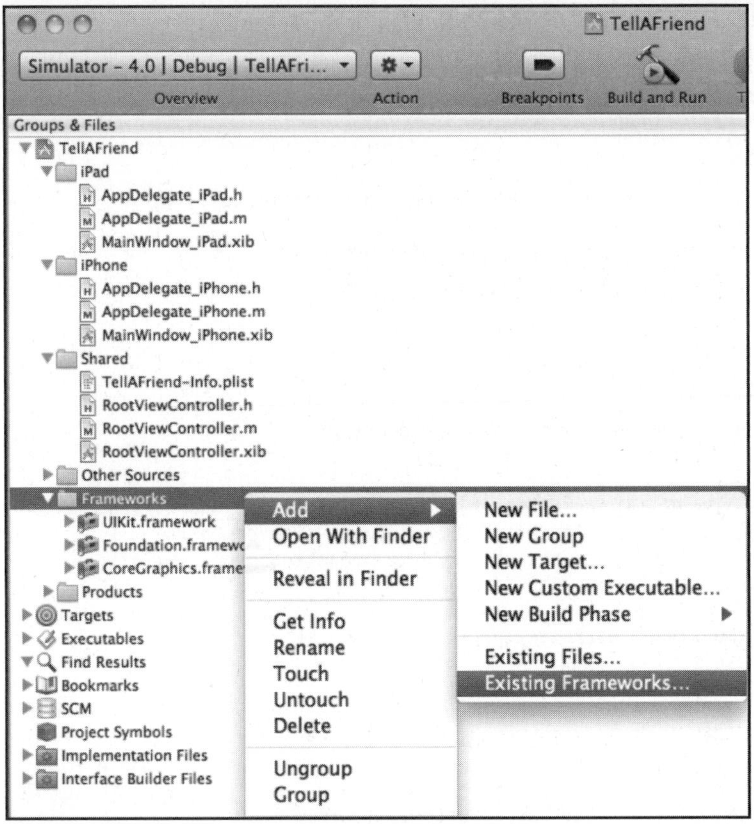

Figure 5–6. *To add a new framework, choose Existing Frameworks from the contextual menu's Add submenu, and then select the MessageUI.framework from the list that appears.*

Once the MessageUI framework is included in your project, you can dig into some programming. Open the *RootViewController.h* header file, and modify the code as follows:

```
#import <UIKit/UIKit.h>
#import <MessageUI/MessageUI.h>
#import <MessageUI/MFMailComposeViewController.h>

@interface RootViewController : UIViewController <UIActionSheetDelegate,
MFMailComposeViewControllerDelegate> {

}

- (IBAction)showShareOptions:(id)sender;
- (void)showMailComposer;

@end
```

As you can see from the new code elements highlighted in bold, the MessageUI framework classes have been imported, a new mail delegate was added to the @interface, and a showMailComposer function is referenced. Save this file.

Now open the *RootViewController.m* implementation file, and without changing the existing code, add the following two methods:

```
// Displays an email composition interface inside the app
// and populates all the Mail fields.
- (void)showMailComposer {

    Class mailClass = (NSClassFromString(@"MFMailComposeViewController"));
    if (mailClass != nil) {
        // Test to ensure that device is configured for sending emails.
        if ([mailClass canSendMail]) {

            MFMailComposeViewController *picker = [[MFMailComposeViewController alloc] init];
            picker.mailComposeDelegate = self;

            [picker setSubject:@"Check out this cool new app!"];

            // Fill out the email body text
            NSString *emailBody = @"Check out this cool new app for iPhone, iPad, and iPod touch - now available in the App Store!\n\nBreadcrumbs - Parked Car Locator\n\nWatch a video and learn more at:\nhttp://www.breadcrumbsapp.com/";
            [picker setMessageBody:emailBody isHTML:NO];

            [self presentModalViewController:picker animated:YES];
            [picker release];

        } else {
            // Device is not configured for sending emails, so notify user.
            UIAlertView *alertView = [[UIAlertView alloc] initWithTitle:@"Unable to Email" message:@"This device is not yet configured for sending emails." delegate:self cancelButtonTitle:@"Okay, I'll Try Later" otherButtonTitles:nil];
            [alertView show];
            [alertView release];
        }
    }
}

// Dismisses the Mail composer when the user taps Cancel or Send.
- (void)mailComposeController:(MFMailComposeViewController*)controller didFinishWithResult:(MFMailComposeResult)result error:(NSError*)error
{
    NSString *resultTitle = nil;
    NSString *resultMsg = nil;

    switch (result)
    {
        case MFMailComposeResultCancelled:
            resultTitle = @"Email Cancelled";
            resultMsg = @"You elected to cancel the email";
            break;
        case MFMailComposeResultSaved:
            resultTitle = @"Email Saved";
            resultMsg = @"You saved the email as a draft";
            break;
        case MFMailComposeResultSent:
            resultTitle = @"Email Sent";
```

```
                    resultMsg = @"Your email was successfully delivered";
                    break;
              case MFMailComposeResultFailed:
                    resultTitle = @"Email Failed";
                    resultMsg = @"Sorry, the Mail Composer failed. Please try again.";
                    break;
              default:
                    resultTitle = @"Email Not Sent";
                    resultMsg = @"Sorry, an error occurred. Your email could not be sent.";
                    break;
        }

        // Notifies user of any Mail Composer errors received with an Alert View dialog.
        UIAlertView *mailAlertView = [[UIAlertView alloc] initWithTitle:resultTitle
message:resultMsg delegate:self cancelButtonTitle:@"Okay" otherButtonTitles:nil];
        [mailAlertView show];
        [mailAlertView release];
        [resultTitle release];
        [resultMsg release];
        [self dismissModalViewControllerAnimated:YES];
}
```

Let's step through the new code so you can see exactly what's happening. The showMailComposer function does all the heavy lifting of crafting an e-mail message and then displaying it in a new embedded MFMailComposeViewController. For this example, the message tells a friend to check out the fictional Breadcrumbs app in the App Store. It even includes a link to the official web site. Supplying all of this for the user makes sharing extremely convenient and simple. All the user needs to do is type a friend's e-mail address in the To field and tap the Send button (see Figure 5–7).

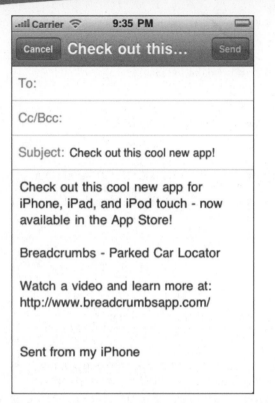

Figure 5–7. *When users tap the Send Email button, the Mail Composer is displayed within the app.*

Working our way down, below the showMailComposer method is the mailComposeController event, which is called when the user presses the MFMailComposeViewController's Cancel or Send button. This is the place to add code that notifies the users of the status of their e-mail action. As you can see from the listed code, you can test the received results for the status of the e-mail, and then report to the user that the e-mail was successfully delivered or that the process failed for some reason.

> **TIP:** It's always a good idea to provide users with frequent status updates, especially when sending data via an online connection. If a user clicks the Send button and the MFMailComposeViewController is dismissed without any further communication, the user is left waiting, wondering whether the e-mail was delivered. In the example mailComposerController event, if the received result signals a successful delivery, then the user is notified via a UIAlertView. The user is also notified if the e-mail could not be sent. In your never-ending quest to avoid negative customer ratings in the App Store, communicating the current status of e-mail actions will help prevent users from getting frustrated.

The very last piece of the puzzle is to have the Send Email button call the showMailComposer method when tapped. This is easily accomplished by adding a single line to the action sheet's didDismissWithButtonIndex event (see the code highlighted in bold):

```
- (void)actionSheet:(UIActionSheet *)actionSheet
didDismissWithButtonIndex:(NSInteger)buttonIndex {
    if (buttonIndex != [actionSheet cancelButtonIndex]) {
        if (buttonIndex == 0) {
            // In-App Email, requires iOS 3.0 or higher
            [self showMailComposer];
        }
        if (buttonIndex == 1) {
            // Add Twitter code here.
        }
        if (buttonIndex == 2) {
            // Add Facebook code here.
        }
    }
}
```

When running the TellAFriend project in the iOS Simulator, the app will report that your e-mail was successfully delivered, but it does not actually send your message. For best results, test your In-App Email code on an actual iOS device with at least one e-mail account already set up in the Mail app.

And that's all there is to it! Adding In-App Email support to your app actually requires very few lines of code compared to how much functionality you get in return.

Integrating Twitter and Facebook

Beyond sending e-mail, you may want to also give users the ability to post messages to their Twitter and Facebook accounts. And although it's nice when users blatantly promote your app, another, more subtle way to increase awareness for your app is to deeply integrate social networking with other core features in your app. For example, if you're building a game, enabling users to share their high scores via Twitter and Facebook will not only breed synergy among players, but may also attract new customers who want to get in on the action. Lima Sky's Doodle Jump includes a seamless user option for sharing high scores via Twitter and Facebook (see Figure 5–8).

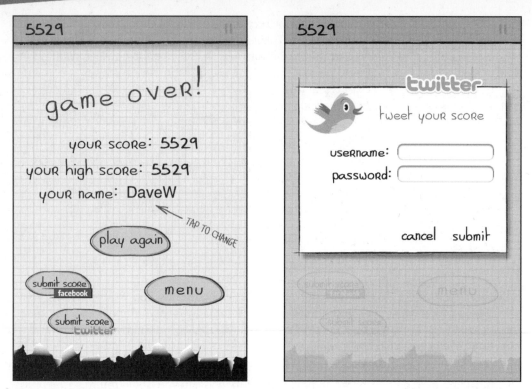

Figure 5–8. *After finishing a game in Lima Sky's Doodle Jump, users are prompted to share their high scores on Twitter and Facebook.*

What gets posted is the following message: "I just got up to 5,529 in #DoodleJump!!! Beat that! http://bit.ly/DoodleJump-App."

Besides flaunting your high score, it throws down a challenge to anyone who thinks they can beat it with a convenient link to Doodle Jump in the App Store. That's a great way to get your customers to help promote and sell additional copies of your game while they're busy sharing high scores with their friends!

A more comprehensive extension of community building is to integrate one of the many social gaming platforms currently available for iOS games, as discussed later in this chapter. For now, let's look at Twitter and Facebook.

Accessing Twitter's API

Instead of trying to write your own custom library of classes for communicating with the Twitter API, save yourself valuable time by using existing contributions from the developer community. Many iOS Twitter clients rely on the popular open source solution, MGTwitterEngine, created by prominent developer Matt "Legend" Gemmell. Originally developed for Mac OS X software applications, Matt's Twitter code has since been updated for use in iOS app projects. It's available for download from http://mattgemmell.com/source.

MGTwitterEngine is an Objective-C class library that encompasses the Twitter API and returns data as native Cocoa objects, making it extremely easy to use. And you'll be happy to know that Matt's license terms are very generous, allowing developers to use MGTwitterEngine royalty-free in commercial products. All he requires is that you credit him as the author of the MGTwitterEngine code included in your app. (Of course, if you find his code helpful, it would be a nice gesture to send him a PayPal donation. Open source developers put a lot of hard work into their contributed code, so they always appreciate knowing when people find their efforts useful.)

The Twitter API performs authentication via OAuth, which enables Twitter to know the source of a posted tweet. If you want the source attribution of tweets to say "from [*My App Name*]," you'll need to register your application with Twitter. Registered apps are given a unique API key and secret token for properly identifying themselves when posting to Twitter.

Register your app with Twitter at `http://dev.twitter.com/apps/new`.

Using the Facebook SDK for iOS

Facebook allows iOS developers to access their platform using their open source Objective-C software development kit (SDK), available from `http://github.com/facebook/facebook-ios-sdk`. Having access to your list of friends and their profile information, as well as connecting with them in real time, brings the full power of the Facebook platform into your iOS app.

It may seem like overkill to integrate such an extensive framework into your Xcode project just so your users can post status updates to their Facebook page. But if you're developing an iOS game or any kind of peer-to-peer community app, you may soon find yourself using additional Facebook features in other parts of your project.

Before you can use the Facebook SDK in your iOS app, you'll need an API key and secret token in order to authenticate your Facebook requests. This requires you to have an active Facebook account of your own. Once logged into your account, visit the Facebook Developer Create Application page at `http://www.facebook.com/developers/createapp.php` and register your app.

When setting up a new Facebook application, be sure to give it the same name as the iOS app you're building, since that application name will be listed as the source when users post status updates from your iOS app. For the same reason that you should register your app with Twitter, this is a subtle yet effective way to get your app's name displayed on users' Facebook pages—great exposure for your app.

Once your new Facebook application is created on the Facebook Developer site, the application's profile will list your unique API key and secret token. Save those two text strings in a safe place, because you'll need them when customizing the Facebook code in your own iOS app.

APP REJECTION WARNING: Your app must notify users when an online connection attempt fails. If your app relies on connecting with a third-party web service, you must include appropriate error-handling code so that in the case of a failed connection or data request, your app handles the failure gracefully and notifies the users of the current status. If a bad data request freezes your app or leaves the user waiting without any indication of what's happening, the App Store review team will most likely reject your submission. If you provide a demo account for use during the review process, make sure that demo account works! Or provide two demo accounts, just in case one fails during the review. It's also a good practice to always notify users if and when your app requires an online connection, especially since iPad and iPod touch devices may not always be logged in to a Wi-Fi network.

Now you're ready to integrate social networking into your own iOS apps! Following the documentation and sample code included with MGTwitterEngine and the Facebook iOS SDK, see whether you can add support for posting to Twitter and Facebook in the existing Tell A Friend example project. I bet you'll have it up and running in no time!

Using ShareKit

If you feel that diving into MGTwitterEngine and the Facebook iOS SDK is too daunting or time-consuming, then you're in luck. Respected developer Nate Weiner has produced a turnkey, open source class library called ShareKit that supports a long list of services such as e-mail, Twitter, Facebook, Delicious, Google Reader, Tumblr, Pinboard, Instapaper, and Read It Later. Beyond sharing URLs, ShareKit also supports sharing images, text, and files. Because it's open source, the UI is customizable, and anyone can add services to ShareKit at anytime. Download ShareKit from http://www.getsharekit.com/.

Since you already have the Tell A Friend example created, let's step through the process of adding ShareKit to your project (or you can open the completed Tell A Friend with ShareKit project from the book's companion code examples). You'll need to set the project's base SDK to iOS 4 or higher. Since this is a universal app, iPads running iOS 3.2 can still be supported by setting the project's iOS deployment target to iOS 3.2.

After downloading ShareKit, open the ShareKit example project in Xcode and drag its *ShareKit* folder (located within the *Classes* group) into your open Xcode project. When prompted, make sure "Copy items into destination group's folder (if needed)" is checked. ShareKit requires a few additional Apple frameworks as well. You should already have the MessageUI framework included from the previous In-App Email example. Using the same method, add the SystemConfiguration and Security frameworks. When completed, your project's Groups & Files list should look like the one shown in Figure 5–9.

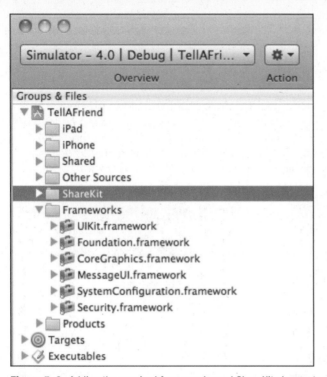

Figure 5–9. *Adding the required frameworks and ShareKit classes to your project*

In the previous sections, I mentioned the need to register your app with both Twitter and Facebook in order to acquire API keys and secret tokens. Using the ready-made ShareKit does not excuse you from those two tasks. You'll need to store those unique API keys in ShareKit's *SHKConfig.h* file. Nate has included extensive instructions in that file as code comments, making this step as easy to follow as possible.

Last, but certainly not least, is calling ShareKit from the project's action button. To accomplish this, open the *RootViewController.m* file and add the following line at the top to import ShareKit's header file:

```
#import "SHK.h"
```

Next, rip out the existing code in the showShareOptions method, replacing it with the following new code (shown in bold). This assigns the text and URL to be posted, and launches ShareKit's custom action sheet.

```
- (IBAction)showShareOptions:(id)sender {
    // Action button was tapped, so launch ShareKit.

    // Create the item to share (in this example, a url)
    NSURL *url = [NSURL URLWithString:@"http://breadcrumbsapp.com/"];
    SHKItem *item = [SHKItem URL:url title:@"Check out Breadcrumbs, the new parked car
locator app for iPhone and iPad!"];

    // Get the ShareKit action sheet
```

```
SHKActionSheet *actionSheet = [SHKActionSheet actionSheetForItem:item];

    // Display the action sheet
    [actionSheet showFromToolbar:self.navigationController.toolbar];
}
```

Since ShareKit is now doing all the work, you no longer need any of the previously added code for handling UIActionSheet and In-App Email. All of that unused code can now be safely removed from the RootViewController class. When running the Tell A Friend app, instead of the original UIActionSheet implementation, you should now see ShareKit's custom action sheet (see Figure 5–10).

Figure 5–10. *With the Tell A Friend app now configured to use ShareKit, you should be able to post data to Facebook and several other social networking services.*

TIP: There may be a newer, updated version of ShareKit available by the time you read this book. Since ShareKit is continually being enhanced with new features and services, I strongly recommend that you download the very latest version of ShareKit from its official web site (http://www.getsharekit.com/) and use that in the apps you plan on submitting to the App Store. And while you're at it, drop Nate Weiner an e-mail, thanking him for his wonderful open source contribution and letting him know which of your apps feature ShareKit.

Strength in Numbers: Building Synergy with In-App Cross-Promotion

A major factor that has contributed to the success of Optime Software's apps is its heavy use of in-app cross-promotion. Upon launching one of Optime's free ad-supported apps, a splash screen briefly appears. While the user is waiting for the app to load, the splash screen not only promotes the premium version of the free app they're using, but also lists several of Optime's other free apps (see Figure 5–11). Each app listed is a live link. Tapping the app name will take you to its respective page in the App Store so that you can learn more about the app and download it.

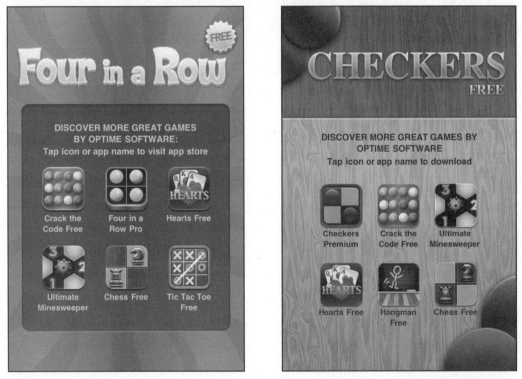

Figure 5–11. *The splash screens in Optime Software's free apps effectively cross-promote its other apps.*

While Optime Software has seen sales increase four to five times from cross-promoting its apps across in-app advertising networks (which will be explored in Chapter 7), doing its own in-app cross-promotion has also proven to be a valuable method for boosting awareness of all of its free apps to existing users. The more downloads it receives, the more the company eventually earns from ad revenue and premium app sales.

"Splash-screen cross-promotion has been a very effective tool for us," says Optime Software's founder and CEO, Jon Schlegel. "We track the click-through rates from our splash-screen advertising, but not the conversion rates. We've seen click-through rates as high as 10 percent for some of our splash-screen ads. Click-through rates for the splash-screen ads tend to decline over time though, as regular users become acclimated to the ads and start to ignore them. We're looking into ways to make the splash-screen advertising more dynamic in order to increase its effectiveness."

APP REJECTION WARNING: Even though Apple's iOS HIG says that it frowns upon splash screens, they seem to be prevalent in countless applications in the App Store. But upon submitting your app via iTunes Connect, if it gets rejected because of a splash screen, then you'll know you went too far with the concept. If you do utilize a splash screen in your app, then before submitting it, make sure it doesn't linger on the screen for too many seconds and doesn't go over the top with a blatant hard sell. Since splash screens fall into that mysterious gray area of the approval process, take great care that when designing your splash screen as a cross-promotional tool, it remains visually effective without calling too much attention to itself.

Circumventing the splash-screen approach, many game publishers include a More Games button on their app's main screen. In some apps, selecting More Games launches the publisher's web site in Mobile Safari. That takes users away from the game they were playing, which is never optimal.

Setting Up Shop

In a move to keep users engaged within the app, NimbleBit opted to embed its own custom "app store" into its games. Tapping the More Games button in its apps displays the NimbleStore screen, which cross-promotes all of its available apps (see Figure 5–12). Rather than automatically redirecting the user to the respective page in the App Store, tapping an app icon in the NimbleStore screen displays an embedded, custom screen for the app. This allows NimbleBit to tailor its own enhanced sales pitch, along with providing a link to its App Store page.

Figure 5–12. *Tapping the More Games button in one of NimbleBit's games displays its embedded NimbleStore, which cross-promotes its catalog of apps with video trailers and more.*

The beauty of the embedded NimbleStore is that it is a remote mini-site displayed in a UIWebView. Not only does this allow NimbleBit to modify the NimbleStore pages at http://m.nimblebit.com/ without requiring updates to the iPhone and iPad games themselves, but it also lets the company use Google Analytics to track which store pages are being accessed by users. According to NimbleBit's statistics, approximately 85 percent of the people who visit the NimbleStore within their apps go on to further explore one of the specific game pages. In only the first nine months, the NimbleStore received a little more than 1.6 million page views and has been responsible for 13,170 game sales!

Having the NimbleStore remotely hosted enables NimbleBit to dynamically alter pricing based on regions and limited-time sale offers. Apple tends to reject apps that display app pricing, so I'm not sure how NimbleBit escaped that particular restriction (unless having the pages hosted remotely makes the difference). So, just to play it safe, you probably should not list prices in your own in-app cross-promotion efforts.

When users choose to buy an app from the NimbleStore, tapping the App Store button sends the user to the iTunes App Store to make the purchase. As any smart iOS developers should set up, all redirects to the App Store are iTunes affiliate links, so any time a user purchases one of the games listed in the NimbleStore, NimbleBit makes an affiliate commission. The iTunes Affiliate Program also enables NimbleBit to track the commissions earned, which reports the total number of games being purchased from NimbleStore leads.

The "Apps We Love" games listed in the NimbleStore (such as Harbor Master) are not NimbleBit games. Although those specific purchases won't net NimbleBit an App Store royalty, they will earn the company affiliate commissions. So, if you don't have enough apps to fill your own embedded mini-store, you can always list some of your favorite apps from other publishers. You'll be supporting your fellow developers, as well as making a little money yourself from the referrals. You'll learn more about the iTunes Affiliate Program in Chapter 6.

If you have only a few apps and would rather limit your cross-promotion efforts to your lite version's Info screen where you're currently up-selling the paid version, just be careful not to dilute your marketing message too much. If encouraging users to upgrade to the paid version is your priority, make sure that any mention of your other apps on that same screen does not upstage the sales pitch for the paid version.

United We Prosper

If you like the idea of integrating your own mini-store within your app to cross-promote your other app offerings, but you don't have enough apps to fill it, consider partnering with a select few of your developer peers. With several developers integrating a shared "community" store in all their apps, you'll benefit from having a populated storefront. You'll also get the increased synergy of cross-promoting your apps not only within your own apps, but also across all the other apps in this community network. It's a win-win situation for all the developers involved.

This strategy is exactly what a few independent iOS game developers set out to achieve when they banded together to form App Treasures. The developers originally involved in App Treasures were The Blimp Pilots (Koi Pond), Imangi Studios (Harbor Master), Snappy Touch (Flower Garden), Streaming Colour Studios (LandFormer), and Veiled Games (Up There). They positioned the App Treasures label as a seal of quality that consumers can trust. If players like one of the games, they'll most likely enjoy other games in the App Treasures family.

Accessible from the More Games button within all the participating games, App Treasures is an embedded view that spotlights apps from those developers. As seen in Harbor Master HD for the iPad (see Figure 5–13), the App Treasures button is listed alongside the Imangi Studios' promoted apps on the More Games screen.

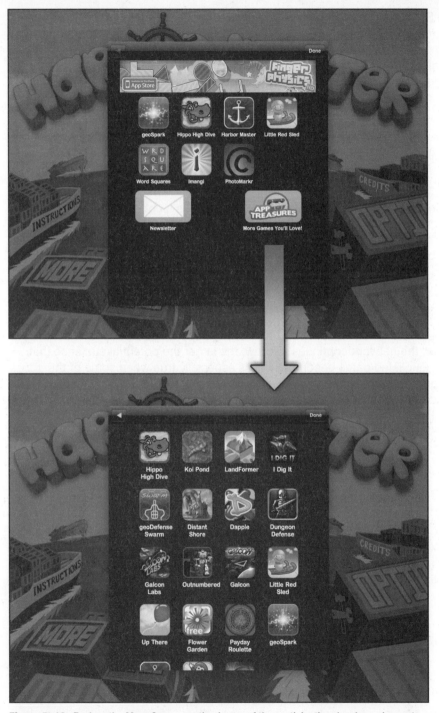

Figure 5–13. *Explore the More Games section in any of the participating developers' apps to access the cross-promotional App Treasures screen.*

With the App Store's games category so often dominated by the big game publishers such as Electronic Arts and Gameloft, the feeling was that it was more difficult for smaller, independent developers to gain the same level of visibility. Keith Shepherd, CEO of Imangi Studios, said that App Treasures "is our way of combining resources to become a bigger player, while retaining our independence and without any of the drawbacks and strings attached that come from working with a publisher."

What makes this kind of shared, cross-promotional network especially valuable is that when one partner's app becomes successful, the other partners benefit from the heightened exposure. When Harbor Master skyrocketed into the App Store's Top 25, the embedded App Treasures screen was receiving as many as 10,000 views a day, which resulted in a sales surge for the other App Treasures games listed there.

If cross-promoting your games across a network of apps is a concept that appeals to you, but you don't really know other developers or don't have the time to build your own in-app mini-store, third-party solutions are available. One such alternative is PlayHaven, a free mobile promotion service that provides a ready-made, embedded app catalog that looks and functions similar to the custom ones used by NimbleBit and App Treasures. You can sign up for

PlayHaven at http://www.playhaven.com/.

The advantage of using PlayHaven is that as more and more app developers join this free service and the network continues to grow, the larger the potential audience that may discover your listed game becomes. This is especially true when some of the participating games become best sellers, such as The Playforge's Zombie Farm. These hits greatly increase the number of consumers tapping that More Games button, browsing the PlayHaven network, and checking out some of the lesser-known games (see Figure 5–14).

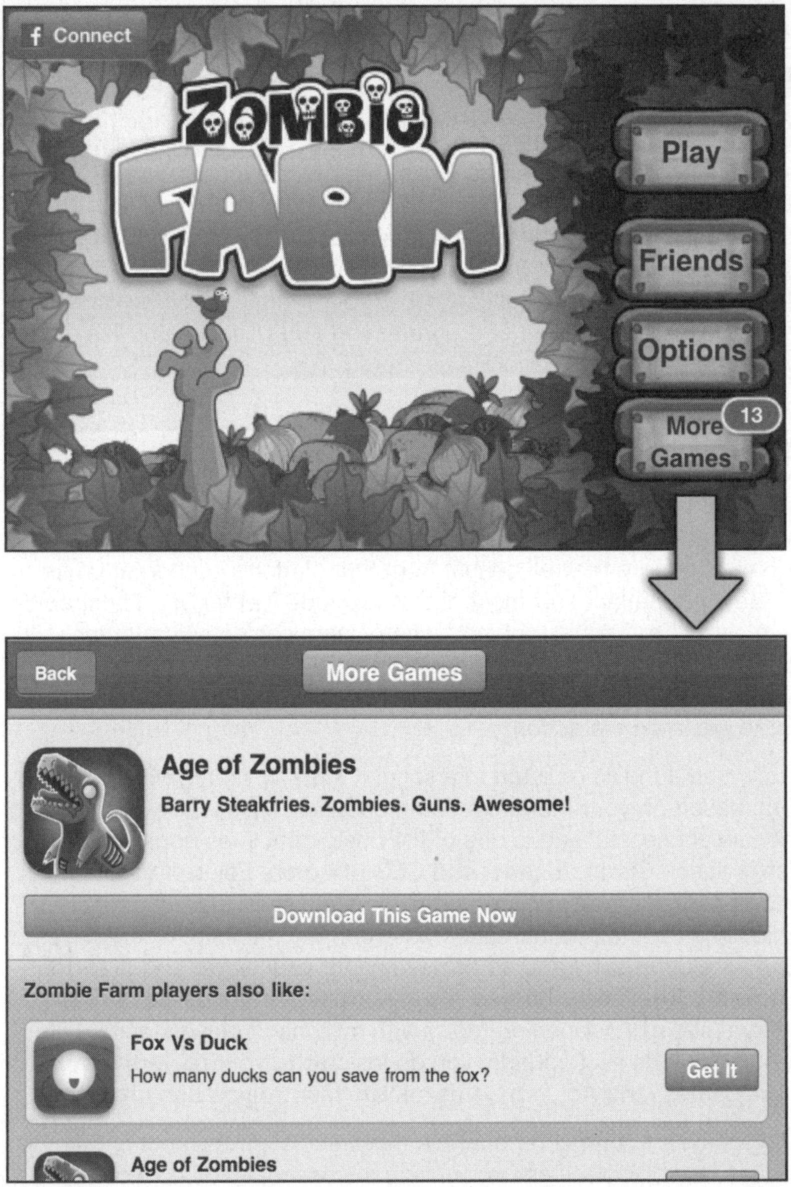

Figure 5–14. PlayHaven offers a free in-app cross-promotion service that provides exposure for your games across its entire network of participating apps.

For game developers, another great solution for in-app cross-promotion and increasing app discovery is by integrating one of the many third-party social gaming platforms such as OpenFeint and Apple's Game Center into your game. Keep reading…

Get Your Users Talking with Third-Party Social Gaming Platforms

If you're a game developer, you're most likely familiar with the social gaming platforms available for iOS, such as OpenFeint, Scoreloop, Plus+, and Apple's own Game Center. The obvious benefit to using one of these platforms is that they provide ready-to-use hosted services—such as high-score leaderboards, multiplayer connectivity, and social challenges—which alleviates the need for you to code this complex functionality yourself. By integrating a third-party social platform into your iPhone and iPad games, you're potentially saving hundreds of hours of programming time. This seems like a no-brainer, especially since most of these platforms are free to use.

Enthusiasm Is Contagious

What some developers don't realize is that many of the social gaming platforms also provide powerful environments for increased app discovery. The more games that use the same social platform, the more they all benefit from that platform's inherent cross-promotional synergy. Beyond the fact that most of them include Twitter and Facebook support, some of them also offer "virtual lobbies," where users can see what other people are playing and which games are connected with that platform. The sheer influence of what's currently popular in these arenas helps drive new app sales, because interested users want to get in on the action.

"If a friend tells you to watch a movie or listen to a song, it's pretty likely you're going to buy that movie or song based on your friend's recommendation. This is why Facebook's App Platform has been so successful and is one of the basic principles upon which OpenFeint is built," says Jason Citron, founder and CEO of Aurora Feint. "OpenFeint provides Xbox Live–style hosted game services such as multiplayer, leaderboards, challenges, chat, achievements, etc., that create cross-promotion events when players interact with them. So, for example, by adding achievements and leaderboards to your game with OpenFeint, you will sell more games. It's important to mention that this isn't some dry sales pitch—we see this happening today with millions of players across hundreds of games. As ridiculous as it sounds, you do less work, your players have more fun, you sell more games, and Apple pays us affiliate fees so you don't have to."

In fact, app discovery is such a strong component in these social environments that the companies that run these free platforms are monetizing their services by collecting iTunes affiliate fees. Aurora Feint's OpenFeint and ngmoco's Plus+ feature prominent in-app game catalogs, promoting all of the participating games on their respective networks (see Figure 5–15). OpenFeint is even experimenting with additional promotional opportunities for developers, such as its Free Game of the Day feature.

Figure 5–15. *Beyond their many social features, Aurora Feint's OpenFeint (left) and ngmoco's Plus+ (right) provide appealing cross-promotion opportunities for game developers, which enable users to see what other people are playing and even purchase the listed games to join in the fun.*

Choosing a Social Gaming Platform

So, which social gaming platform is right for your game? When choosing a platform, there are two major factors to consider:

- The platform that is being adopted by more of the high-profile best sellers will attract a larger audience. More players congregating in one online community equal more exposure for your app.

- Although app discovery is definitely a vital component, your number-one priority should be to choose the platform that works best for your app's specific game play. It needs to make your game more fun, not more complicated or frustrating. If your players are having a great time, that enthusiasm will show in the online social community, which will in turn drive additional sales.

With the advent of Apple's Game Center built into iOS 4.1 (and higher), many of these third-party social gaming platforms have quickly adapted with new functionality that sets them above and beyond the current basic feature set of Game Center. In fact, some of them, like OpenFeint, have embraced Game Center by offering deep compatibility.

OpenFeint's strategy is that by enabling developers to mix and match the best features from both OpenFeint and Game Center, the end result is a win-win for both OpenFeint and its massive user base of existing game players.

Since Game Center is baked right into iOS, and Apple is heavily promoting apps in the App Store that support Game Center with special logo badges and featured selections, adding support for Game Center into your game should be a no-brainer. But Game Center is the newest kid on the block. It has fewer features than some of its rivals and has not yet accumulated the large user base of existing networks like the popular OpenFeint. Many developers are integrating support for *both* Game Center and OpenFeint so that their app can provide a more comprehensive set of social gaming features and is accessible to the biggest possible audience of gamers.

If you're an iOS game developer, I highly recommend exploring all of the social gaming platform web sites and easy-to-use SDKs to find the one that best fits your specific development and marketing needs. Get started with the following list:

- Apple's Game Center for Developers (https://developer.apple.com/devcenter/ios/gamecenter/)
- OpenFeint (http://openfeint.com/)
- Scoreloop (http://scoreloop.com/)
- AGON Online (http://developer.agon-online.com/)
- ngmoco's Plus+ (http://plusplus.com/)
- Chillingo's Crystal SDK (http://www.crystalsdk.com/)

Earning Your Stripes

This and the previous chapter covered a vast number of topics, and you even played around with some code (yeah, I thought you would appreciate that). I told you we would be talking about more than just research and marketing concepts.

You've definitely earned yourself a pat on the back and a well-deserved break after all you've tackled so far. So, go put up your feet and enjoy a few levels of your favorite iOS game.

When you're ready for more, just turn the page to dive into the next chapter.

Chapter 6

Money for Nothing: When It Pays to Be Free

Unlike the traditional desktop software world, the App Store currently does not allow time-limited or feature-crippled trial versions. To work around this restriction, many developers offer an In-App Purchase–supported "freemium" model or a free "lite" version of their apps, hoping users will buy in-app content or the separate paid edition to gain access to premium features. In this chapter, you'll learn when and how to harness the power of *free* for effective results, plus how to tap into the additional revenue opportunities of affiliate programs.

Generating Revenue from Free Apps

In Chapter 4, you explored the value of designing an eye-catching app icon and elegant UI to help make your app more visually attractive in the App Store. But once you have people's attention, will your screenshots be enough to convince them to purchase your app? Don't think that just because your app is priced at only 99 cents everyone will automatically buy it. Most of the apps in the Top 25 go for 99 cents, so why should consumers pick your app over the thousands of others with the same price? Unfortunately, the current App Store ecosystem has a very skewed outlook on pricing, with everyone racing to the bottom with lowered prices to gain traction in the Top 100.

So, what's a developer to do? Don't forget the big lesson from the previous chapters: your app is its own powerful marketing tool. Let's take that concept to the next level by giving consumers something for free.

Free? Yes, you read that correctly. Don't worry. The objective here is still to make money. Free is a very powerful motivator to get people to download your product. Who doesn't love to get free stuff? I know I do, and according to the App Store statistics, I'm not alone. Although free apps account for only 25 percent of the App Store's catalog, they represent a whopping 95 percent of the total downloads!

Free Strategies

You can take advantage of this demand for free apps by employing one or more of the following strategies:

- Offer a free lite version of your app to help drive sales for the paid version, or use a freemium model with premium features available through In-App Purchase.

- Give away your app for free to get as many people using it as possible. After you've cultivated a large loyal customer base that depends on your app, use that basic free version to up-sell a separate premium version or In-App Purchase items that offer additional "must-have" features.

- Make your app free, supported by in-app advertising. Implementing mobile ads in your app is discussed in Chapter 7.

Which of those scenarios will work for your particular situation greatly hinges on what kind of app you're developing. For example, in-app advertising may not be an appropriate solution for an educational app for kids. Parents may not condone apps that advertise to their young children. Also, the majority of users may be running the app safely offline on an iPod touch, unreachable by ad network servers.

And don't forget about affiliate programs. If your app currently links to an external web site that offers an affiliate program, you should be benefiting from the traffic you're sending your affiliates' way. Do you have a music app that includes links to buy selected songs in the iTunes Store? Does your app include web links to books on Amazon.com or products listed on eBay? If your app takes advantage of affiliate links, you can earn commissions on all sales you drive to those web sites.

Try Before You Buy

As an iOS developer, you're undoubtedly no stranger to the concept of free lite apps. Like me, your iPhone or iPad home screen is probably littered with several "pages" of lite apps downloaded from the App Store. And after evaluating them, you've probably bought the paid versions of at least a few of them. Without the ability to try the lite version first, would you have purchased the paid version? Maybe not. So, it's easy to see the enormous value that free lite versions can have in boosting paid app sales.

Developers of desktop software have known this important fact for decades. Making trial demo versions available for free download is one of the primary marketing tools for selling commercial software. The trial versions of most modern Mac and Windows applications offer built-in purchase mechanisms. These enable users to easily buy a license online and receive a serial number that unlocks the demo app, instantaneously transforming the trial version into the full-featured application.

Try before you buy. It sounds like a no-brainer for the App Store, right? Unfortunately, Apple does not currently allow iOS app developers to offer free trial demos with crippled features that can be unlocked by purchasing the app. This limitation forced developers to work around the issue by producing two separate versions of their app: a free lite version and a paid version that offers additional features not found in the lite version. For the first year of the App Store, this was the closest anyone got to the "try-before-you-buy" concept.

When Apple announced the inclusion of the new In-App Purchase feature in the iPhone SDK 3.0 back in 2009, developers were hopeful that it would finally solve this problem, but that was not quite the case. Even though In-App Purchase does enable users to purchase App Store items within an iOS application, Apple is very particular about how In-App Purchase is utilized. Free apps are allowed to offer In-App Purchases, but this built-in e-commerce API cannot be used to unlock previously crippled features, because apps are still prohibited from presenting features as disabled. If the free app includes a feature—such as a button in the toolbar—then it must be a functional feature. The current implementation of In-App Purchase enables developers to provide *additional* features that are not currently included in the app, such as subscription services, new content, and add-on game levels.

Choosing a Path: Lite vs. In-App Purchase

With the advent of In-App Purchase, many developers were quick to predict that it would render lite versions obsolete. However, with the complexities of implementing In-App Purchase combined with how apps are positioned in the App Store charts, a free lite version is still a very valid and effective business model. Again, which approach is best for you depends on the kind of app you're developing.

The most obvious reason many developers still opt to produce both a free lite version and a separate paid version is that it is much easier to implement than In-App Purchase. If you've ever taken the time to glance through Apple's Store Kit documentation, you'll have noticed that In-App Purchase requires quite a bit of additional programming and back-end infrastructure. For newcomers to the iOS developer platform, the Store Kit API may seem a little overwhelming. And it's easy enough to compile two versions of your app within Xcode: one as a lite version and the other as a more robust paid version.

If your app's functionality can be divided neatly into a free feature set and additional premium features made available for a small upgrade fee, then In-App Purchase may be the better model to suit your needs. For example, if your free app is a first-person shooter that includes five levels of game play, additional levels and weapons could be offered as In-App Purchase items.

ngmoco found success with this model in its popular Eliminate Pro app. This app is offered for free, and additional game play, weapons, and armor can be bought via In-App Purchase. In fact, ngmoco's foray into In-App Purchase has proven so effective that it switched over to a freemium business model with all subsequent app releases, such as Touch Pets, We Rule, and We Farm.

NOTE: You can't replace the existing app binary with a new binary via In-App Purchase, so for most games, this requires including the extra game levels and content within the free app in a hidden or locked capacity. When the customer purchases that item, your app unlocks that new weapon or game level.

But In-App Purchase may not be suitable for every type of application. Some single-function utility apps are structured in such a way that attempting to target specific features to be offered via In-App Purchase can be problematic.

In the case of most games, In-App Purchase seems to be a good fit, but keep in mind that unlocking additional content via In-App Purchase requires your application to be that much bigger (to store that hidden content). And when dealing with the download bandwidth limitations on mobile devices, the file size of your free app can make a huge difference in its effectiveness as a promotional sales tool.

Many phone carriers, such as AT&T, limit file downloads through their mobile networks to only 20MB. So, if users want to download your 35MB free game onto their iPhone, they will need to wait until they are logged in to a local Wi-Fi network. That defeats potential impulse buys and spur-of-the-moment downloads. By the time they are within range of a Wi-Fi network, they may have already forgotten about your app.

With a lite version, only the content that it is offered for free is included, which in turn compiles to a much smaller file size than the larger, full-featured paid version. If the free lite app binary weighs in at under 20MB, it will be accessible to a much broader audience of potential customers, since they will have the ability to download it onto their iPhones through their carrier's mobile network if Wi-Fi isn't available.

With all that said, a major drawback to the free lite model is that purchasing the paid version is a separate app download, so transferring any existing user data from the lite version to the paid version is quite a logistical headache for developers. In-App Purchase unlocks the new features or content directly within the app, so there's no need to transfer existing user data.

Another important consideration is that paid apps are required to provide free updates to existing customers. The App Store does not currently support a mechanism for charging for updates. So, even if your lite version successfully persuades a user to buy your paid app, that single purchase price is the only time the customer will invest in the app. That means you need to continually attract new customers to support the ongoing development costs of releasing updates. If your app is priced at only 99 cents and doesn't consistently sell large quantities, that's a tough model to follow to properly sustain and grow your business.

With In-App Purchase, if you're always giving customers the option to buy additional features and add-on content, then you're giving them a way to continue purchasing items at their convenience and comfort level. They can spend as little or as much as they want, which is great for your bottom line. Flexibility wins hearts! A large portion of your revenue will come from a small percentage of loyal customers buying multiple In-

App Purchase items. An effective, long-term business model is one that never limits the amount of money a customer can spend.

Even though freemium apps include In-App Purchase items, they are free to download, which means your app is eligible to appear only in the App Store's Top Free Apps chart. On the other hand, releasing a free lite version and a paid version gives your product a chance to potentially place on both the Top Free Apps and Top Paid Apps in the App Store.

While it's certainly true that appearance in the App Store charts leads to increased app discovery and sales, it's no longer as critically important to the survival of your business as it once used to be. Snappy Touch's Noel Llopis saw an exponential increase in revenue after he integrated In-App Purchase in his acclaimed app, Flower Garden.

"The common sense approach to make money on the App Store used to be to do anything to get on the Top charts. In-App Purchases changed all of that," said Noel in a recent blog post on his `GamesFromWithin.com` site. "Good In-App Purchases can make your app profitable without being anywhere on the charts, and are the best hope for the independent developer."

I do believe In-App Purchase is a very powerful avenue for mobile sales and will soon become the most popular method for monetizing app development on the iOS platform. If this model fits nicely with your application's feature set and architecture, then stay tuned! Chapter 8 provides detailed coverage on when and how to implement In-App Purchase.

The Lite Approach: Tastes Great, Less Filling

Later chapters of this book are dedicated to producing profitable free apps supported by in-app advertising and In-App Purchase. Here, we'll cover the case where your product idea is best served as a paid application, and explore how to use a free lite version to promote your paid app. But before diving into effective marketing strategies, let's go over some guidelines for developing lite apps.

Playing It Safe: Lite Version Restrictions

To avoid rejection from the App Store, make sure your lite version adheres to the following guidelines. Although these rules may not be written in stone, this checklist appears to have worked for countless lite versions currently available in the App Store.

- **The lite version must be a fully functional app.** Your free lite version can contain fewer features than the paid version as long as this limited feature set allows the user to enjoy the lite version as a complete, stand-alone experience. The core functionality of the app should be accessible in both versions. For example, if your app's primary functionality is writing documents, then both the lite and paid versions should include the ability to create, edit, and save documents. To entice users to purchase the paid version, you can make additional enhancements exclusive to the paid version, such as file-synchronizing services, extra style formatting options, and so on. You may even limit the number of documents a user can store in the lite version (lite: ten files; paid: unlimited), as long as the core functionality remains intact.

- **The lite version cannot contain crippled features.** A free lite version may not contain disabled features that, when accessed, inform users that the selected functionality is available only in the paid version. For example, if your app is a game and the ability to save high scores is limited to the paid version, do not include a reference to high scores in your lite version's interface. Don't include a High Scores button in the lite version that, when selected, notifies the user that high scores is a full-version, paid-only feature with a blatant Buy Now button. In the eyes of Apple, that's considered a *crippled feature*. If your lite version includes a High Scores button, it must provide that functionality.

- **The lite version cannot remind users to buy the paid version.** Although you can definitely include a Buy Full Version button in your lite version's main Info screen, you cannot prompt the user to upgrade via a `UIAlertView` or a custom pop-up view while they are using your app. This constant "nag" window may be acceptable for desktop shareware, but it will quickly earn you a rejection letter from Apple's app review team.

- **The lite version cannot time out or disable features.** In the world of desktop software, a common approach to expedite the full-version purchase is to create a time-limited demo version that disables either certain features or the entire app after being installed for a set number of days. This is a big no-no in the App Store. iOS apps are not allowed to ever expire or time out in any way.

- **The lite version cannot be referenced as a demo.** Since all iOS apps are required to be fully functional, you'll have trouble getting approved in the App Store if you use words like *demo* or *trial* in your app name, or anywhere in your UI. Your app can include the word *lite* or *free* to denote a lite version.

Can a Free Lite Version Really Boost Paid App Sales?

If done right, your lite version can be a finely tuned sales machine, turning thousands (or maybe millions) of users into paying customers. So, how many free lite downloads does it actually take to see a spike in paid app sales?

On average, most iOS developers report conversion rates between 0.5 percent and 3 percent. This means that for every 100 downloads of their free lite version, they're selling approximately one to three paid versions. If you're selling your paid version for 99 cents, and your lite version is getting only 100 downloads per day, your app sales may bring in only a few dollars each day. That's not going to generate enough revenue to financially support yourself or your development costs.

This is where success really becomes a numbers game. Volume is king. You'll need to heavily promote your lite version to increase the number of downloads it receives. The more lite downloads you have, the more your paid app sales will rise.

Ethan Nicholas, the developer behind the best-selling iShoot app, reported conversion rates as high as 8 percent. The popularity of Ethan's iShoot Lite helped propel iShoot to the number-one spot in the App Store's Top Paid Apps chart. Although 8 percent may not seem like a lot, the numbers quickly add up if your lite version becomes popular. The free iShoot Lite received millions of downloads, and with iShoot priced at $2.99 at the time (January 2009), that small conversion rate reportedly earned Ethan more than $700,000 in just the first few weeks of release. Just keep in mind that was back when the App Store had less than 100,000 apps. Now Apple's mobile marketplace is packed with more than 300,000 titles, so most apps and games will never see conversion rates that high.

Specialized niche apps often see higher conversion rates than mainstream apps, since interested users are looking for specific features that only a handful of apps offer. A popular niche app may not rank high enough to be listed in the Top 100, but it could potentially benefit from conversion rates of 10 to 20 percent. Why such a big difference?

Popular mainstream apps that hover in the Top 100 have much more visibility, drawing the attention of a broader, general audience who may download many free lite versions out of sheer curiosity. Special niche apps are usually found by consumers with a genuine interest or need for that specific functionality, so the odds they will purchase the full version are much better. This is why many niche apps are priced higher than games and novelty apps. What they lack in sales volume, they try to make up for with a higher profit margin per unit sold.

Regardless of the actual conversion rate, it's important to have your lite version available at the same time you release your paid app. This allows you to capitalize on the buzz and visibility surrounding the initial launch. One of the biggest success stories of 2010 was not a best seller right out of the gate. Rovio's Angry Birds had lukewarm sales when it was first released as a paid app in December 2009. It wasn't until the free lite version was made available a few months later that sales started to skyrocket (see Figure 6–1). As more and more people were trying the free lite version, the word-of-mouth spread quickly, and Angry Birds was eventually showcased as a featured game in the App

Store. The groundswell of attention, combined with its addictive, fun game play, propelled Angry Birds to the phenomenon it is today, with more than 40 million downloads of the free lite and paid versions for the iPhone and iPad.

Figure 6–1. *Rovio's sales for Angry Birds didn't skyrocket to the top of the paid charts until the free lite version was released, followed by Apple showcasing it as a featured game in the App Store.*

Very few developers will experience the same level of success as Ethan Nicholas or Rovio, especially with the staggering number of apps now competing for attention in the App Store. But if you develop a solid lite version strategy, there is still potential to make quite a bit of money. A lot of factors go into building an effective lite version. Here's where attention to detail can really pay off.

They Won't Buy the Cow If the Milk Is Free

Most developers immediately understand the marketing value of offering a free lite version, but since Apple requires lite apps to be fully functional, a major concern is giving too much away. If your lite version includes enough functionality to satisfy people's needs, why would anyone buy the paid version?

The answer lies in all of the market analysis and competitive research discussed in Chapter 2. If you know the audience your app is targeting, who your competition is and what features those apps offer, and which key features are important to users, then planning your lite version strategy will be that much easier.

The trick is to understand which features to include in the lite version without cannibalizing your paid app sales. If your competitors offer specific features in their lite versions, you'll want to take a similar approach, especially if users are expecting those features. But if your app has some cool new feature that no one else offers—that innovative X factor that sets your app apart from the competition—then you'll want to figure out a way to allow users to test-drive that feature in your lite version, while providing a more comprehensive version of it in your paid app.

You want to whet their appetite without giving away the whole meal.

Lite Versions of Productivity and Utility Apps

For productivity, utility, and nongame apps, choosing lite version features can be challenging, which is why many of them do not offer free lite versions. Instead, they rely on reviews, external publicity, video trailers, and screenshots to help sell the app. How do you limit the lite version functionality enough to encourage paid app sales and yet still get approved into the App Store?

If you're building an app that creates documents or notes, you'll need your lite version to be fully functional, allowing users to create, edit, and save those files. Since users will want the ability to import/export their documents via e-mail or synchronize files with a remote server (such as Google Docs or Dropbox), then obviously those are features your app will need to remain competitive in the App Store, but they could be offered as premium features available only in the paid version.

If your app enables users to create to-do tasks or lists of some kind, one effective approach is to limit the number of items that can be created within the lite version. To properly set user expectations, your lite version should openly communicate the current limitations, encouraging users to upgrade to the paid version for the full, unlimited experience.

Marco Arment adopted this strategy for Instapaper Free, the lite version of his acclaimed Instapaper app, which is a useful tool for saving web pages for reading later. Instapaper Free limits storage to ten web page articles—enough to convince people of the benefits and convenience of this service. Once they're hooked and require more space, they will be more inclined to upgrade to the paid version, which offers unlimited storage, iPad compatibility, and a bevy of additional features (see Figure 6–2).

Figure 6–2. *Marco Arment's Instapaper Free is limited to saving ten web page articles for later reading, encouraging users to upgrade to the paid version for unlimited article storage, iPad compatibility, and additional features.*

Lite Versions of Games

For games, devising a free lite approach is usually a much simpler task. Game developers typically include the first few levels in the lite version. If users want more, they need to purchase the paid version, where they are rewarded with dozens of additional levels, enhancements, and special features.

Depending on your app's game play, limiting the lite version to only a handful of introductory levels may not be enough to adequately showcase the game's true value. Matt Rix ran into this issue when he developed the lite version for his best-selling game, Trainyard.

"The paid game has around 150 puzzles, and at first, I thought about including only the first few puzzles in the lite version, hoping users would see the potential and want to buy the full game," said Matt. "The problem is that during the first 10 or 15 puzzles, players are just starting to get a feel for the mechanics. The 'ah ha!' moments don't come until 40 or 50 puzzles into the game, when you get a sense of just how cool the puzzles can be. That left me in a bit of a tricky spot. I could give away the first 50 puzzles in the lite version, but then if users decided to buy the paid game, there was no smooth upgrade path. They'd have to solve those 50 puzzles again in the full game. I considered adding a cheat to the full game that skipped the first 50 puzzles, but that still didn't seem like the best solution."

Instead, Matt came up with a clever alternative. He created 60 brand-new puzzles for the lite version. Opting not to use the word *lite* or *free*, he named this edition Trainyard Express and refers to it as a "prequel" to the full paid version of Trainyard (see Figure 6–3).

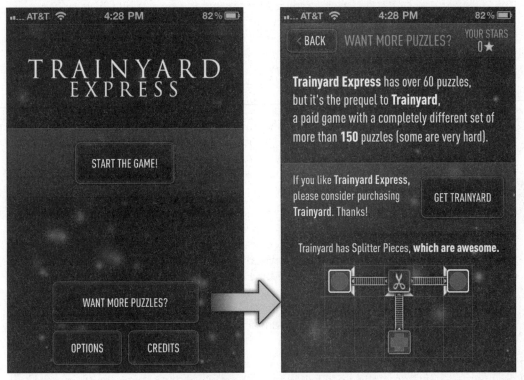

Figure 6–3. *Matt Rix's free Trainyard Express offers 60 unique puzzles to avoid overlapping the 150 puzzles in the paid Trainyard game. This strategy increases the perceived value of both versions.*

Matt admits that this unconventional path required a lot of extra development work, but there was quite a bit of strategic thinking behind the effort. He added, "I really want people to fall in love with the mechanic, and I think this might just be the best way to do it. I also increased the difficulty curve quite a bit, so that the sixtieth puzzle in the free Express is as hard as the hundredth puzzle in the full game."

In positioning Trainyard Express as its own stand-alone precursor to the full paid game, fans of Trainyard will want to download both versions in order to play all 210 puzzles. This incidentally helps boost the game in both the paid and free charts, for greater visibility in the App Store.

When to Release the Lite Version

Giving away so much free content may seem like a risky gamble, but depending on your particular app's functionality or game play, it can be winning move that earns you a faithful following of loyal customers.

The initial concern that a lite version may potentially impede paid app sales is a scary prospect for any new app business. Due to this fear, many independent developers shy away from lite versions. Some developers wait until app sales drop off, thinking that introducing a free lite version at the tail end of an app's life span will help resuscitate sales. Although that may drum up a little extra business, they are really not maximizing the true potential of the lite version as a promotional tool. The timing is all wrong.

Developers who have taken this delayed approach do see an increase in paid app sales when introducing a free lite version at such a late stage, but by then, all of the free publicity generated from the initial launch has long since faded, so the new sales bump is often not enough to push the paid version back into the App Store's Top 200. If only those developers had made a free lite version available when their app's release was benefiting from the initial wave of publicity!

If you plan on releasing a free lite version, you should make it available from the very beginning when you first launch your paid version. This way, your free lite version can take advantage of all the publicity and word-of-mouth generated during the app's initial release. The more traffic you drive to downloading the free lite version, the more conversions you'll have for the paid app. Many developers who advertise their apps online link the ads to their free lite versions to encourage click-throughs. This makes their advertising campaigns much more effective, since people love free. Then let your lite version work its magic, giving users a small taste of what they will get if they buy the paid version.

If you worry that the exclusive features in your paid version are not enticing enough to get users to switch from the free lite version, then you need to rethink the division of features between the two versions to make the upgrade more appealing, or you may want to consider adding in-app advertising to your free lite version. Offering a paid version without any advertisements can be a powerful lure, and it also provides a way to monetize your free lite version with ad revenue. Chapter 7 provides details about in-app advertising.

Of course, not all applications lend themselves well to the concept of a free lite version. But if you can figure out a way to make it work in your favor to generate app sales, then it's a gamble that will pay off in the long run.

Perfecting Your In-App Sales Pitch

To design a more effective lite version, you need to think of it as a virtual sales assistant. You can't personally be there to walk each user through the benefits of your app, so you need your lite version to do the talking for you. This means you need to carefully craft the sales pitch within your lite version to properly communicate your message. You already know what the guidelines are for lite versions, so for the moment, take off your developer hat. It's time to think like your users, putting yourself in their shoes.

Placing the Buy Button

Many lite versions promote the paid version on their splash screen, which is displayed for the first few seconds when the app is launched. Although this is a great way to take advantage of your users' undivided attention as they briefly wait for the app to load, it should not be the only place that the "buy" button is located.

After users finish a session with your app, if they are interested in learning more about the paid version, they will look on your app's main screen, Info screen, and/or Settings screen (depending on which of those screens you've included in your app). This may sound like common sense to you, but I'm always surprised to find lite versions that don't make that buy button easily accessible within the app or, worse yet, don't even include it at all!

If people can't find the buy button, they can't purchase your app. Don't rely on them remembering to manually visit the App Store on their own. Odds are, they might forget, and you've just lost those potential customers.

When it comes to selling anything, especially software, make the act of buying your product as easy and painless as humanly possible. And unlike most online e-commerce systems that overly complicate the process with too many steps, Apple has designed the iTunes App Store to be the simplest, most convenient way to buy software, so you really have no excuse. If someone loves your free lite version and is interested in upgrading to the paid version, that next step should be only a finger tap away.

So, now that you've integrated a buy button into your lite version's main screen or Info screen, what should it say? That may sound like a stupid question, but the answer is really much more subtle and complicated than you might think.

Words like *buy* and *purchase* communicate one thing to iPhone, iPad, and iPod touch users: tapping that button will take them to the App Store. Yes, your refined sales pitch is already there in the App Store—complete with a detailed description and screenshots—making this very convenient from a development standpoint. As you learned in Chapter 5, launching your iTunes store URL within your app can be done in only a few lines of code. ZeptoLab's popular Cut the Rope Lite uses a similar tactic, with a Full Version button placed above the familiar Available on the App Store badge. This shows up on the game's main menu screen and is also displayed when the user reaches the end of the free levels (see Figure 6–4). Tapping on those buttons will take you directly to the Cut the Rope paid game's page in the App Store. You'll also find the same App Store buttons in Rovio's Angry Birds.

Figure 6–4. *In ZeptoLab's Cut the Rope Lite, the Full Version button and Available on the App Store badge link directly to the Cut the Rope paid game's page in the App Store.*

Although some apps have found success with this simple approach, it is not necessarily the most effective, especially for an unknown, new product. As much as we would all like to believe that our apps are just as addictive as Cut the Rope and Angry Birds, those two phenomenal best sellers are the exceptions to the rule. Odds are good that we mere mortals will need to be a little more aggressive with our in-app marketing strategies.

Adding Upgrade Info to the Lite Version

Jumping to the App Store from that buy button takes users out of your app, someplace they may not want to be at that very moment, especially if they mistakenly think it will automatically initiate a purchase. As developers, we understand that's not possible without the users first entering their iTunes password in the App Store, but some consumers may not be tech-savvy enough to recognize that. Why would they want to buy the app without first knowing which additional features they would gain? They wouldn't, so they might ignore the button. And if that happens, your free lite version just failed its one and only mission.

Any known reason that might make a user hesitate about tapping that buy button should be eliminated whenever possible. If there's anything you can do to remove that hesitation or fear, then it's worth the extra development time to implement it.

So, how do you solve the problem at hand? Instead of instantly redirecting users away from your app to the App Store, why not include your sales pitch directly inside your app? Once you've sold them on upgrading to the full version, you can safely close the deal with a buy button linked to the App Store.

One of my favorite examples is Digital Chocolate's 3D Rollercoaster Rush Free. On the app's main screen, the What's Full Version? button leads to a screen that tells you exactly what you'll get if you select it. You're expecting detailed information about the features included in the paid version, and that's precisely what you receive (see Figure 6–5). The promotional screen that appears is very well designed to match the game's visual theme. The screenshots and key selling points are crafted for maximum impact. All this is communicated without forcing the user to leave the app, giving people the choice to either buy the paid app or tap the Back button to return to the game. I was convinced to tap the Get the Full Version button, and I'm a very jaded iPhone user who rarely plays games, so the sales pitch is definitely effective.

Figure 6–5. *3D Rollercoaster Rush Free is a great example of the up-sell done right.*

On the iPad's larger display, you have more screen real estate, so it's easier to insert upgrade information for the paid version in a popover window (UIPopover) or a centered modal view (UIModalPresentationFormSheet) without dominating the entire screen. In Illusion Labs' Labyrinth 2 HD Lite, the menu of free mazes includes a small banner ad for the paid version. Tap the banner, and a popover window appears with a scrollable description of premium features, screenshots, and an App Store buy button (see Figure 6–6).

Figure 6–6. *Illusion Labs' Labyrinth 2 HD Lite presents the paid version up-sell in a popover window on the iPad.*

The beauty of a UIPopover is that the UIView it displays can be easily reused and shown again in another UIPopover elsewhere in the app. Beyond the mazes that Illusion Labs provides, the company also hosts a free online community where customers can upload and share their own contributed maze creations. From within the free Labyrinth 2 HD Lite app, users can browse the list of third-party mazes, but they will quickly notice that the paid version is required in order to download and play those community mazes. That's a great motivator to upgrade to the full game. In the lite version, the download button is conveniently replaced with a Full Version Info button. When tapped, that button displays the same paid version information in a UIPopover as previously seen in other sections of the app (see Figure 6–7). The popover window provides the upgrade information when needed, without being intrusive to the rest of the interface.

Figure 6–7. *Requiring Labyrinth 2 HD Lite users to buy the paid version in order to download the thousands of free, third-party mazes contributed by the Labyrinth community is a great incentive to upgrade.*

APP REJECTION WARNING: You should not display the app's price within your application. When promoting the full version within your free lite version, don't list the price. Apple has localized App Stores in many countries around the world, supporting many different currencies, so it frowns upon hard-coded prices displayed in your app. Apple's app review team does not always flag this as a cause for rejection, but it happens enough that you'll want to avoid doing it. Beyond the risk of rejection, it's important not to list the price in your app so that you have the flexibility to change the App Store price at any time for special sale offers without needing to submit an update.

Including Analytics

It's important to include analytics in your lite version so that you can track how many people are tapping that buy button. Those analytics reports combined with your iTunes Connect statistics will help you to determine the effectiveness of your lite version as a promotional tool. You'll know how many people are downloading your lite app, how often they use it, how many users tap the buy button, and how many sales your paid version is pulling in. With all that data at your fingertips, if the conversion rate of lite-to-paid sales is much lower than expected, you can experiment with the wording and button placements in subsequent updates in an effort to improve results.

Of course, knowing how customers use your paid app can be just as valuable, so if you do add analytics to your development strategy, make sure to wire it into all your apps—both lite and paid—for the most comprehensive picture of how they are performing. Apple recently changed its rules on what information third-party analytics are allowed to collect. To learn the facts on in-app analytics, check out Chapter 7.

> **TIP:** If you're an iOS developer, you should join the iTunes Affiliate Program. Any links you have pointing to the App Store should be affiliate links. There's no reason not to earn some affiliate commissions for all the traffic you're sending Apple's way. This means all the buy buttons in your lite version, cross-promotions, web site, and so on should be coded with iTunes affiliate links. We'll be exploring the lucrative world of affiliate programs later in this chapter.

Bulletproofing Your Lite Version

As developers, we work hard to create high-quality products, so no one purposely releases buggy software. Showstopper bugs happen to the best of us, but if there was ever a time to ramp up your testing and quality control efforts, it's with your free lite version.

Since users will be evaluating your lite app to determine whether the paid version is worth their hard-earned money, they will be test-driving it with a very critical eye. Since it's free, the app will attract a much broader audience, with many people merely kicking the tires out of curiosity. Without any emotional investment in the app, people are often quick to make snap judgments. As evidenced by the lower ratings of most lite versions compared to their paid-app counterparts, people have no problem giving an app a dismal one-star rating for the most minor of reasons. Even though the lite version was free, reviews often can be harsh if the experience left users frustrated.

Ensure that your lite version includes ample built-in instructions to help alleviate any potential confusion that might arise if someone can't figure out how to use the app. Many lite versions ask users upon launch if they would like to watch or read a brief tutorial before exploring the app. Although this does require a little extra development effort, it is a very proactive approach that may help avoid many of those unwarranted one-star reviews. If you feel your app would benefit from offering in-app tutorials, see Chapter 9 for details on this topic.

Migrating Data from the Lite Version to the Paid Version

If users purchase your app, they should not be penalized by losing the data they had in the free lite version. If that happens, prepare to receive a slew of negative customer reviews in the App Store.

For most games, there's nothing to lose, since high-score leaderboards are usually stored on a remote server. But what if it's a productivity app that saves information in a plist file or database records?

Unlike the more flexible environment of desktop operating systems, iOS restricts each app to its own data "sandbox" for storing files. App A is not allowed to access the saved files from app B, and vice versa. This protects each installed app from malicious behavior, but makes it incredibly difficult to share data between apps.

Starting with iOS 3.2, Apple introduced a new built-in file-handling mechanism called Document Support, which allows developers to register their app with the iOS system to create and/or open specific file types. This is wonderful for apps that require their own unique file type (such as a word processor) or offer support for popular file types (such as PDF, image, and video formats). This enables a file in one app to be opened in or copied to another app that is registered to also support that same file type. If you need to transfer some information from a plist file or a few database records from your lite version to the paid app, this Document Support feature is overkill, adding a lot of programming overhead that's unnecessary in the particular situation.

iOS 3.2 also added a desktop synchronization feature, which enables an app to display its file directory in a special file sharing list within the desktop iTunes when your iOS device is synchronized with your computer. Technically, if your apps supported this feature, your users could copy the stored data file from your lite version onto their desktop, and then drag it back into iTunes onto the *File Sharing* directory of your paid app. But that's asking your customers to do a *lot* of extra work for something they shouldn't need to deal with in the first place. If you value your customers and want them to have a satisfying user experience, you'll avoid this solution.

Obviously, this is where In-App Purchase would make your life much easier, side-stepping the hassles of passing data from a lite version to a separate paid app. But don't despair—there are other ways to accomplish this task.

Syncing with the Cloud

Some developers have solved the problem of migrating data by implementing a synchronizing service that enables customers to sync their app data to a remote server. Popular apps like Flixoft's Grocery Gadget encourage users to sign up for a free group account so that data from the lite version can be easily transferred to the paid version.

If your app stores large amounts of complex data, or if you simply want to give customers a way to access their data from alternative locations and devices (such as their iPad or desktop computer's web browser), then maintaining a synchronizing service might be your best bet. If this sounds like an appealing solution for your app needs, here are a few affordable cloud services worth checking out:

- Dropbox for Developers (http://www.dropbox.com/developers)
- Google App Engine (http://code.google.com/appengine/)
- Amazon S3 (http://aws.amazon.com/s3/)
- Rackspace Cloud (http://www.rackspacecloud.com/)

If you don't want the hassle of developing and maintaining a server-side web application to handle the synchronizing of data between your native app and the cloud, you may want to first look at Dropbox's SDK for iOS. Dropbox has become a very popular choice for mobile developers who need to synchronize data across multiple devices. But if you need to transfer only a very small amount of data from one app to another, there is yet another option.

Transferring Data via URL

Some developers have found success transferring data across a unique URL command. For example, if an iOS app makes an open URL request for an HTTP web site address, Mobile Safari automatically launches and processes the request, since it is the default app registered to handle HTTP. In a nutshell, the app just sent data to Mobile Safari. You can put this same concept to work for your own apps by setting up a unique URL protocol handler.

For your URL protocol to work, it needs to use a prefix that is not already being used by any other application. Since you have no idea what unique protocols other iOS apps might be using for this same purpose, you should come up with your own prefix that is obscure enough to prevent conflicts with those other apps.

For the purposes of this exercise, let's create a unique protocol for our fictional parked-car locator app, Breadcrumbs. We want users of the lite version to be able to transfer their saved parking locations to the paid version. Since the amount of data is very small (just a few GPS coordinates) and does not contain any confidential information, transferring the data via an open URL command would work quite well.

For our URL prefix, we'll use bcrumbs. If your app has an original name (which it should), then that name (or a variation of it) might lend itself nicely as a unique prefix. First, the bcrumbs URL protocol needs to be registered with the iOS system as being assigned to the full version of Breadcrumbs. This is done by adding a new URL type to the paid app's *Info.plist* file in Xcode (see Figure 6–8).

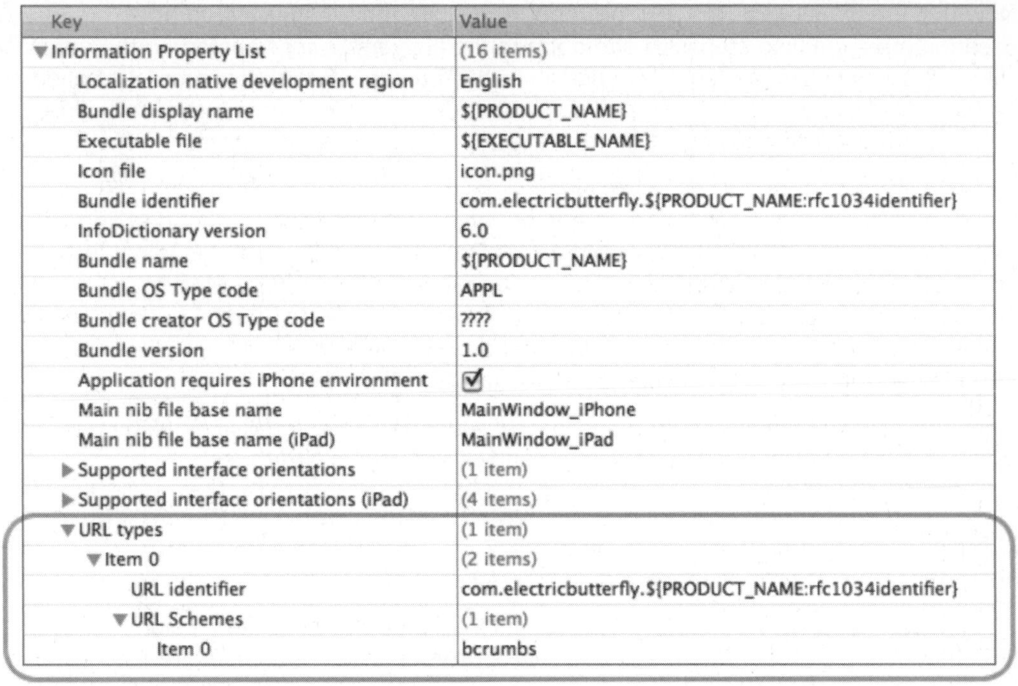

Key	Value
▼ Information Property List	(16 items)
Localization native development region	English
Bundle display name	${PRODUCT_NAME}
Executable file	${EXECUTABLE_NAME}
Icon file	icon.png
Bundle identifier	com.electricbutterfly.${PRODUCT_NAME:rfc1034identifier}
InfoDictionary version	6.0
Bundle name	${PRODUCT_NAME}
Bundle OS Type code	APPL
Bundle creator OS Type code	????
Bundle version	1.0
Application requires iPhone environment	☑
Main nib file base name	MainWindow_iPhone
Main nib file base name (iPad)	MainWindow_iPad
▶ Supported interface orientations	(1 item)
▶ Supported interface orientations (iPad)	(4 items)
▼ URL types	(1 item)
▼ Item 0	(2 items)
URL identifier	com.electricbutterfly.${PRODUCT_NAME:rfc1034identifier}
▼ URL Schemes	(1 item)
Item 0	bcrumbs

Figure 6–8. *Open your full version's Info.plist file within Xcode's plist editor to add a new URL type.*

To add a new entry to the *Info.plist* file, select the last row in the plist editor, and then click the gray plus symbol (+) button on the right side. In the new blank row, choose **URL Types** from the contextual menu list that appears in the left Key column.

With the new URL type now added to your *Info.plist*, open its disclosure triangle to configure its nested properties. Under its Item 0 key, you'll need to add the unique com.company.Application property of this paid app to the URL identifier field. For the fictional Breadcrumbs app, that would most likely be com.electricbutterfly.Breadcrumbs.

Next, click the plus button again to add another nested key directly below URL identifier, and choose **URL Schemes** from the new key's contextual menu. The URL scheme is where you define your unique URL protocol handler, so in the case of the Breadcrumbs example, it's bcrumbs.

> **NOTE:** If you have a single Xcode project set up with two compile targets—one target build for your lite version and one target build for your paid version—you'll need to create a separate plist file for each target. Only the plist file of your app's full version can contain the unique URL protocol handler definition. If your lite version's plist file references this same URL type, then your lite version will end up receiving its own URL requests, which will cause a conflict. When your lite version sends the unique URL request, you want only your paid version to respond to it.

Now that the unique `bcrumbs` URL protocol is assigned to the full version of Breadcrumbs, the next step is to add code to the lite version for transferring the data via URL. Let's say you've added a new button to the lite app's Settings screen. It's called Transfer My Data to Full Version, and it has already been wired up in Interface Builder. Let's also assume that the event handler already includes code for obtaining the data from the lite app's sandbox (such as content from an XML file or a plain-text file).

You can't send raw data via a URL query, so it first must be Base64-encoded and/or URL-encoded. The iOS SDK does not include Base64 encoding and decoding, but several third-party Objective-C libraries, such as Google Toolbox for Mac (http://code.google.com/p/google-toolbox-for-mac/), provide Base64 support for iOS. If only URL-encoding is sufficient for your needs, you can easily call the native iOS NSString method `stringByAddingPercentEscapesUsingEncoding`.

Once the data is Base64-encoded and/or URL-encoded and stored in an `NSString`— let's call it `encodedData`—it can be sent as part of the unique URL query:

```
NSString *urlQuery = [NSString stringWithFormat:@"bcrumbs://localhost/importData?%@",
encodedData];
NSURL *url = [NSURL URLWithString:urlQuery];
[[UIApplication sharedApplication] openURL:url];
```

When a user taps the Transfer My Data to Full Version button, the lite version makes that URL request. iOS recognizes the `bcrumbs` URL protocol handler as being registered to the full version of Breadcrumbs, so that unique URL is passed to the paid app. The full version of Breadcrumbs launches to receive and parse that URL command.

For that last part to succeed, the paid app must include the `application:handleOpenURL` handler in the application delegate's implementation. For example, my *BreadcrumbsAppDelegate.m* file includes the following code:

```
- (BOOL)application:(UIApplication *)application handleOpenURL:(NSURL *)url {
    if([@"/importData" isEqual:[url path]]) {
        NSString *urlData = [url query];

        // First, you should ask users if they want existing
        // data replaced by the new imported Lite data.

        // Then depending on how the string was initially encoded, you'll
        // need to either decode the Base64 via a third-party library
        // -OR- decode the URL-encoding by calling the NSString
        // method stringByReplacingPercentEscapesUsingEncoding.

        // Lastly, you'll want to parse and save the data
        // to this full version's own app sandbox.

        return YES;
    }
    return NO;
}
```

And that's all there is to it! Just keep in mind that transferring data via URL is practical only for small amounts of data such as XML files or text files that are less than a few hundred kilobytes. You'll also want to defend your paid app against hackers who figure out your unique URL protocol by coding your `application:handleOpenURL` handler to accept only the specific data you want and to ignore invalid URL strings.

Securing Market Share: Give It Away Now and Up-Sell Later

Is the success of your iOS app dependent on being adopted by as many people as possible, such as a social networking app that requires multiple participants in order for it to be useful? If so, you may want to consider giving away the app for free. The only way to get millions of people to adopt your service on such a grand, global scale is to make it freely available to everyone. Think Facebook, Foursquare, and Twitter.

The goal is to get everyone and anyone to use your app frequently enough that it eventually becomes an indispensable part of their daily lives. The fewer barriers to entry, the easier this task is to accomplish. Beyond being free, for best results, your app should also be void of any potential deterrents such as advertising.

After your app has cultivated a large loyal following, you can introduce a premium version of the app that offers additional features for a price. An alternative option is to offer premium features as In-App Purchase items (as discussed in Chapter 8). The basic version will always be available for free, which is what the majority of users will choose.

So, how do you make any money if most people use only the free basic version? This is yet another example of how volume will ultimately dictate your success. If you've created an innovative user experience and you've done your job right as a marketer, then your free app has penetrated the mainstream as a "must-have" app and is currently used by millions. For example, let's say the free basic version is frequently used by 10 million people. If only 8 percent of that user base decide to upgrade to the $1.99 premium version, after subtracting Apple's 30 percent App Store fee, you would net more than $1.1 million in revenue. For a more conservative estimate, even if only 5 percent upgrade to the premium version, that would still produce $700,000 in revenue.

Again, volume is the name of the game for this strategy to work. Most apps will not be appropriate for this kind of business model. But if your app relies on peer-to-peer interaction between users, this approach might just be your ticket to capturing the lion's share of the market for that particular niche. If your app is the market leader, you'll fare much better at successfully up-selling more users to the premium version.

In Chapter 2, I mentioned the cool Bump app by Bump Technologies, Inc., which enables users to instantly send contact information to each other by bumping their hands together. But for it to work, the two people must both have Bump installed on their iPhones or Android phones. The more people who have Bump, the more useful it becomes. The hope is that it will eventually be ubiquitous enough among mobile phones that it becomes the standard method for users to swap virtual business cards and other data. And the plan seems to be working. As it stands now, the app has become quite popular among iPhone users and has even been featured in one of Apple's iPhone commercials.

Will Bump always be free? To continue the adoption momentum, that's the goal for the foreseeable future. Instead of taking a traditional path with a premium edition, Bump Technologies, Inc. is hoping to successfully monetize its business by licensing its core bump technology to other large-scale, commercial developers who would benefit from this functionality. The Bump API is free to use within your app as long as it doesn't overload the Bump servers or generate incremental revenue with each bump. If your app makes money from bumps or requires significant bandwidth from the Bump servers, you can purchase the appropriate licensing tier.

By offering this API with easy-to-use SDKs for iOS and Android, Bump is not only solidifying its position in the mobile world as the de facto platform for peer-to-peer data sharing, but it's also building a long-term infrastructure for monetizing its core strength. And with the Bump API already adopted in dozens of mobile apps by independent developers, as well as by high-profile clients like PayPal and ABC Family, it would appear Bump's strategy is definitely paying off.

The newspaper industry is another good example of a business that's attempting to grow a loyal mobile audience by offering a free service. With print newspaper ad sales and circulation continuing to fall at a rapid pace, struggling newspapers are looking to transition to a digital platform with a sustainable revenue model. Competing with so much free online content, paid newspaper apps have failed to work in the past, especially since re-creating the newspaper experience on a small mobile phone screen had proven challenging. But with the immense popularity of the iPad and the fact that a tablet encourages similar layback viewing behavior as newspaper reading, there's finally a viable mobile platform for this medium.

Major newspapers such as the *New York Times* and the *Washington Post* have begun experimenting with new dedicated iPad apps that offer their entire daily newspapers free for a limited time. With the iPad's larger screen, these apps are able to present a satisfying digital reading experience that's comparable to print, while taking advantage of modern touchscreen technology. They provide 100 percent free content for several months, and hope that consumers will grow to depend on receiving the "paper" this way. Then it will be an easy decision to switch to an in-app purchase subscription when the free service ends (see Figure 6–9).

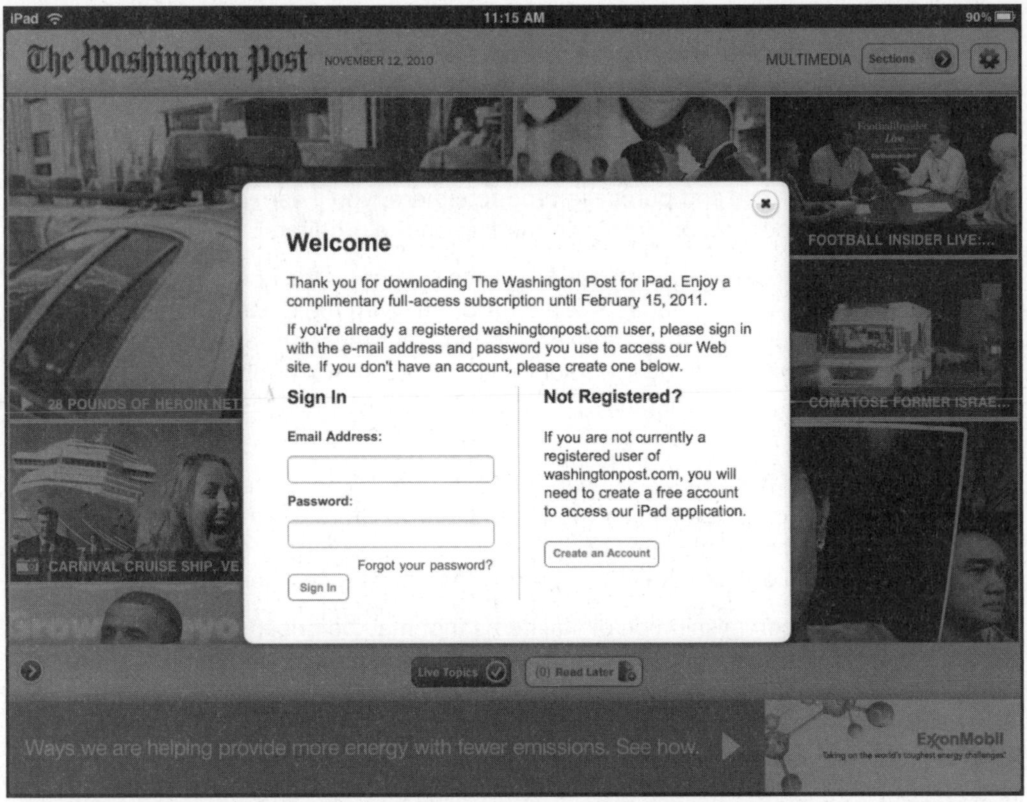

Figure 6–9. *The Washington Post is one of several newspapers hoping that its free iPad app will eventually turn loyal readers into paid subscribers by offering 100 percent free content for a limited time.*

If you need to earn revenue sooner rather than later to finance your development efforts, these free strategies may not be the right path for you. But if your development is currently supported by existing cash flow from investors, sponsors, or other sources, and you can afford to wait several months for your app to gain traction in the mobile marketplace, free can be an effective business model with the right implementation.

Mining Additional Revenue with Affiliate Programs

Earlier in this chapter, I mentioned the use of iTunes affiliate links when sending users to the iTunes Store. Here, we'll take a closer look at how affiliate programs can generate income for you.

How Affiliate Programs Work

The way affiliate programs work is quite simple. Participating companies want to encourage software and web site owners to send traffic to their retail sites. As an incentive to do so, a small commission fee is earned for sales that are generated. This is tracked by using special URLs that include unique affiliate IDs. The commissions earned by an affiliate are based on a percentage of the sales that were derived by customers who came from that affiliate's links.

Most bloggers and web site owners are very familiar with Amazon.com Associates, one of the oldest and most popular affiliate programs online. If your site visitors follow your affiliate link to Amazon.com and purchase products there, you'll earn a commission on that sale (typically 4 percent or higher, depending on the products).

Although there are thousands of affiliate programs out there, the one you should be most interested in is Apple's iTunes Affiliate Program. With the iTunes Store and the App Store built into every iPhone, iPad, and iPod touch, it's easy for apps to link to the store pages of music, movies, TV shows, audiobooks, and even other applications. Free lite apps do it all the time, redirecting users to the full paid version in the App Store, in the hopes they will buy it.

So, there's no lack of links here. Thousands of iOS apps and their related web sites are chock-full of links back to the iTunes Store and the App Store. What I find odd is that a large percentage of those links are not affiliate links. I'm constantly surprised by just how many developers still do not take advantage of this free revenue-generating opportunity.

Earning a 5 percent commission on digital items that may be priced at only 99 cents does not sound like a windfall of money, but just like low-priced app sales, this business model is all about volume. If you're sending app users or site visitors to the iTunes Store, and Apple is making money from your links, why shouldn't you be compensated for the sales you're generating for Apple? It's hard enough to make money in the App Store if you're not in the Top 200, so why would you ignore an easy option to earn some extra cash? As a software business owner, you should be looking for any and all possible revenue streams that your iOS app and web site can deliver for you (legitimately, of course). And in this case, all it requires you to do is sign up for the free affiliate program and modify your existing URLs.

Not yet convinced that it's worth the effort? Here's a little tidbit that might pique your interest.

Pandora is one of the most beloved Internet radio services available online, and its Pandora iOS app is a perennial favorite, forever hovering in the App Store's Free Music Apps Top 10. Listeners who like the currently playing song can easily purchase that track by tapping the Buy from iTunes button (see Figure 6–10). The button uses an affiliate link to send the user to the related song page in iTunes. If the track is purchased by that user, Pandora earns a commission fee.

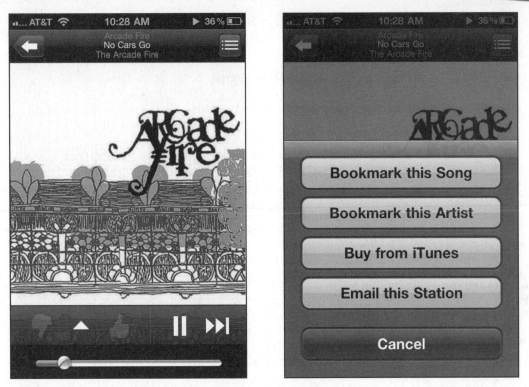

Figure 6–10. *The Pandora Internet radio app includes affiliate links to the iPhone's embedded iTunes Store, enabling listeners to easily buy the currently playing song.*

Pandora's Chief Technology Officer, Tom Conrad, revealed that between Pandora's web site and iOS app, Pandora listeners are buying approximately 1 million songs a month through their affiliate links! And of those song sales, Pandora's iOS app is responsible for a whopping 20 percent of that.

It's not difficult to see how a large customer base can generate substantial traffic to the iTunes Store, turning those affiliate links into a major revenue stream. The commissions earned from iTunes affiliate links are one of the primary sources of income for many of the social gaming platforms, such as OpenFeint (discussed in Chapter 5), which is why they are able to provide those feature-rich gaming services for free to iOS developers.

The great thing about the iTunes Affiliate Program is that when users follow your affiliate link to the iTunes Store, you'll earn a 5 percent commission on everything they buy within a 24-hour session or until they click another affiliate link. Pandora has seen many of its listeners not only buy the song from the affiliate link they followed, but also go on to purchase a few other songs as well, which just adds more commissions to Pandora's earnings.

Granted, your iPhone or iPad app may not have as many users as Pandora (not many apps can match that level of popularity), so let's examine a more realistic scenario. Let's say your app drives about 50,000 people to the iTunes Store every month. Even if only half of them end up buying one or two 99-cent digital items, at a 5 percent affiliate commission, you would be earning $1,250 to $2,500 per month. That's a lot of money for doing nothing but a one-time URL change to your embedded iTunes Store links.

Joining the iTunes Affiliate Program

To sign up for the iTunes Affiliate Program, head over to

`http://www.apple.com/itunes/affiliates/`.

There are different affiliate networks for specific regions. Currently, your options are LinkShare (United States), TradeDoubler (Europe), LinkShare Japan (Japan), and dgm (Australia and New Zealand). Do not sign up for the affiliate network that represents your own location, but rather choose the one that best suits your app's target audience.

Here, we'll step through the process using the primary US-based affiliate network, LinkShare. Clicking the LinkShare link will take you to LinkShare's sign-up form. If you already have a LinkShare account, simply log in at `http://www.linkshare.com/`.

Once you've completed the sign-up process and logged in to your LinkShare account, there's still one more step. LinkShare is the affiliate network for hundreds of retailers, so within your LinkShare account, you're required to apply for the individual affiliate programs you're interested in joining. Perform a search of LinkShare's advertiser network for the keyword *iTunes*, and the iTunes Affiliate Program will be displayed in the listed results (see Figure 6–11). Click the Apply button, and agree to Apple's terms and conditions.

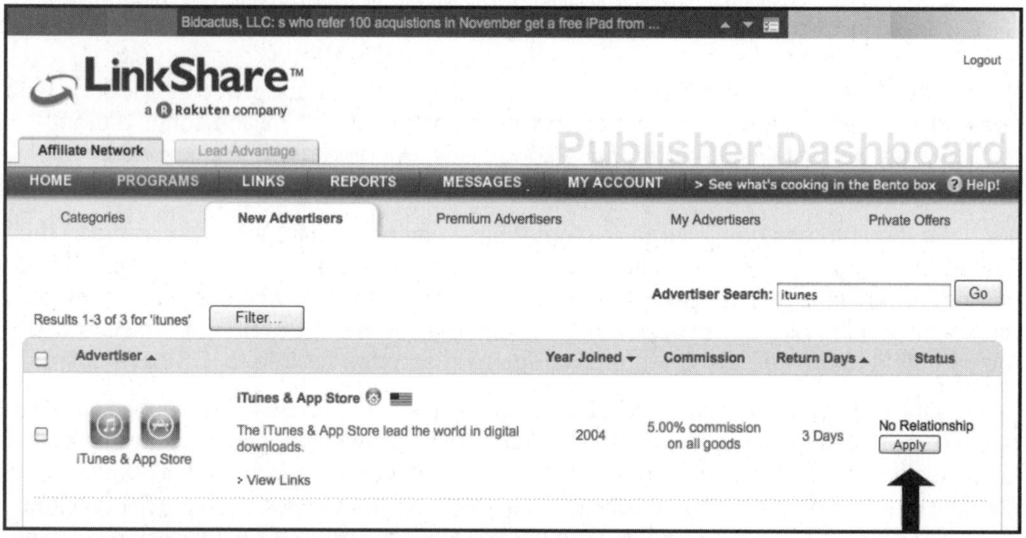

Figure 6–11. *After signing up for LinkShare, you'll need to apply for the iTunes Affiliate Program within your LinkShare account. Search for iTunes, and then click the Apply button.*

Since Apple manually approves all of its affiliates, you'll need to wait until you receive approval confirmation (via e-mail) before you can create any affiliate links.

Once approved by Apple as an official iTunes affiliate, log back into your LinkShare account, and navigate your way over to the iTunes Affiliate Program page (listed in the My Advertisers section). You should now see a blue iTunes Create Links banner with a row of buttons underneath (see Figure 6–12).

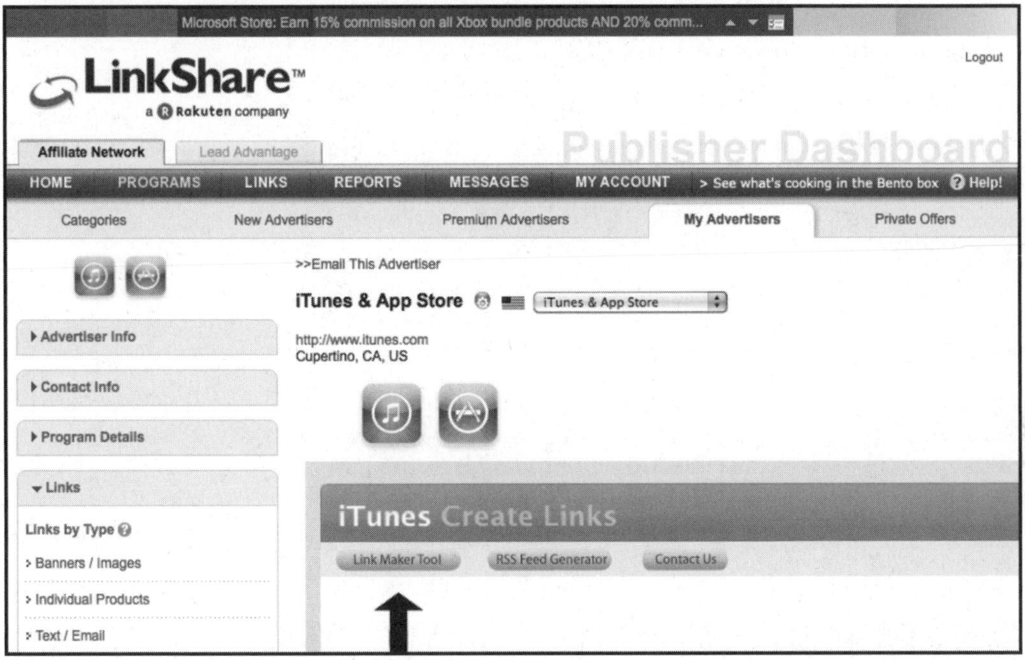

Figure 6–12. *To generate affiliate links for items in the iTunes Store, you'll need to use Apple's special Link Maker Tool.*

To generate iTunes affiliate links for use in your iOS apps and web site, click the Link Maker Tool button. (Do not use LinkShare's link-builder features.) Apple's Link Maker Tool is very easy to use. You can easily search for a specific product, and then copy the custom affiliate link that the online tool provides.

It's really that simple. Use those special links (which include your affiliate ID) in your apps and web site to start earning some extra money for all that traffic you're sending to the iTunes Store.

Shifting Gears

Paid apps are not the only avenue to make money in the mobile universe. Do you want to really leverage the power of free to generate more revenue? Promotional lite versions and the other business models discussed in this chapter are only the tip of the iceberg. The next two chapters will explore in-app advertising and In-App Purchase.

Monetizing Free Apps with iAd and Other In-App Advertising Opportunities

Mobile advertising is widely perceived as the next great marketing frontier, with advertisers racing to target that growing audience. In this chapter, the world of in-app advertising is thoroughly examined, educating you on the mobile ad networks available for iOS apps and the value of tracking usage through in-app analytics. Alternative advertising models, such as sponsorships and product placement deals, are also explored.

When to Use In-App Advertising

At one time or another, we've all downloaded free apps that display some kind of in-app advertising, and many of us have even tapped the ads. Based on current trends, the research experts at Gartner anticipate mobile ad spending to surpass $13 billion by 2013. Even Apple has jumped into this lucrative market with the introduction of its iAd platform for serving ads in iOS apps. But the big question is this: can app developers make any money from it?

In-app advertising can be an effective way to monetize your free app without relying on paid content sales, but it may not be a viable business model for all apps. You need to take an in-depth look at what kind of app you're building, as well as how people will be consuming your app.

Knowing Your Audience

If you're developing a free app that would appeal to a broad mainstream market and experience frequent usage, you might be able to earn quite a bit of revenue from in-app advertising. The key is *volume*.

The more people who use your app, the more ad impressions and click-throughs that will accrue. And if your app is "sticky" enough to retain the user's attention for a long span of time, it will be able to display many more banner ads, which will net you more ad-sharing revenue.

If your free app has limited appeal to a niche market, then it may not generate enough advertising revenue to support your business. On the other hand, catering to a niche market may earn you higher rates from premium ad networks whose brand advertisers are eager to target that audience. Even though this kind of niche app will ultimately attract fewer users than a mass-market app, it may be able to make up the difference in revenue by earning more money per ad.

Here are some factors to consider:

- **Apps that use the Internet**: If your app requires an Internet connection, such as to access GPS information, web services, or an online social network, adding in-app advertising will not be an imposition for your users, since they will already be online when running your app. This is important to keep in mind, because even though an iPhone typically has a constant connection (via Wi-Fi or cellular carrier), iPod touch and iPad users may not have a Wi-Fi connection at all times. If the majority of your customers tend to use your app offline, then your in-app advertising will not make you any money. If your app cannot communicate with the ad network servers, it can't serve up ads.

- **Apps for a younger audience**: If your app is a game or educational app aimed at a younger demographic, in-app advertising may not be appropriate. For one, parents may not appreciate apps that directly advertise to their kids. And advertising to young children may be illegal in some regions, so it's important to do your legal homework.

- **Entertainment apps and casual games**: Many entertainment apps, especially casual games and board games, can fare quite well with in-app advertising, especially the ones that require an Internet connection for logging in to an online leaderboard or game network. If the UI design is done right, banner ads inserted at the very top or bottom of the screen should be unobtrusive to the game play. An example is Angry Birds Free, which earns revenue from in-app advertising. The development company, Rovio, prevents the actual game play from being obscured by creatively sliding the ad banners in and out of view at the top of the screen (see Figure 7–1).

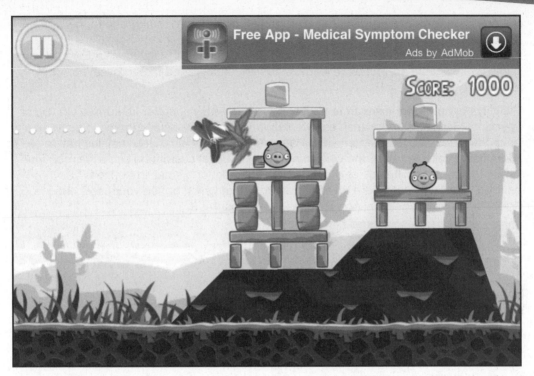

Figure 7–1. *Angry Birds Free slides ad banners in and out of view at the top of the screen to prevent obscuring actual game play.*

- **Immersive games**: In-app advertising can be very difficult to successfully integrate into full-screen, immersive 3D games. Often, the only option in those cases is to display advertisements in between game levels. This is usually not ideal, since that would drastically reduce the number of ad impressions your app could generate, especially if game levels take a long time for users to complete.

If you do decide to monetize your free iOS application with in-app advertising, be sure to do it from the very beginning, with your initial 1.0 release. If your app has always included advertising, users will simply accept it as the price for a free download. If your app has already gained a loyal following of users who have enjoyed several versions of your app ad-free, then the sudden introduction of in-app advertising in a later update is bound to upset many of your fans. As always, you want to avoid receiving negative customer reviews in the App Store, so carefully plan your free app strategy up-front.

In-App Advertising As a Sales Tool

If you're not sold on relying entirely on advertising revenue and decide to release a free lite version to promote your paid app, consider using in-app advertising in only your lite version. Depending on the kind of app you're developing, it can be an effective way to not only monetize that free app, but also help motivate users to upgrade to the paid app if they want an ad-free version. That's the business model behind Angry Birds Free (see Figure 7–1), which offers a dozen free game levels with in-app advertising. For additional game levels and an ad-free experience, users are encouraged to purchase the Angry Birds paid app.

Even if you don't offer a separate paid app, some users will prefer an ad-free version of your app. Many free apps, such as Tweakersoft's AroundMe (see Figure 7–2), offer a paid option to remove ads via In-App Purchase. This way, your app remains free to download, available to anyone who wants to try it. Loyal customers can either continue to use the app free with ads or opt to remove the ads for a small in-app fee. This enables your app to generate revenue, regardless of which option your users choose. For in-depth coverage of In-App Purchase, see Chapter 8.

Figure 7–2. *Tweakersoft's free app, AroundMe, offers an ad-free option with an In-App Purchase to remove ads.*

Selecting a Mobile Ad Network

Apple made quite a media splash with its iAd launch in 2010. News of participating apps earning impressive profits from ad impressions and click-throughs has attracted hordes of iOS developers to the iAd Network. For app interfaces that are designed to accommodate banner ads, iAd is an enticing choice. And Apple has been working hard to ramp up the iAd Network's ad inventory and increase availability beyond the United States to improve its reach and value to developers. But iAd is certainly not the only game in town, and it may not be the most ideal ad solution for your specific app needs.

Investigating the Choices

It's important to thoroughly investigate all the iOS-compatible ad networks to find the ones that offer the solutions you need. Although there are dozens of mobile advertising platforms available, I'll limit the focus here to only the major players that offer an in-app advertising SDK for iOS developers.

Here are some ad network sites worth exploring:

- iAd (http://developer.apple.com/iad/)

- AdMob by Google (http://www.admob.com/)

- Greystripe (http://www.greystripe.com/)

- Millennial Media (http://developer.millennialmedia.com/)

- InMobi (http://www.inmobi.com/)

- iVdopia (http://www.ivdopia.com/)

- Jumptap (http://www.jumptap.com/)

- Medialets (http://www.medialets.com/)

- MobFox (http://www.mobfox.com/)

- Mojiva (http://www.mojiva.com/)

- Rhythm NewMedia (http://www.rhythmnewmedia.com/)

- Say Media (http://saymedia.com/)

- Smaato (http://www.smaato.com/)

- YuMe (http://www.yume.com/)

At the end of the day, the most important factors in a successful ad-supported app are ensuring a 100 percent fill rate (with an ad always available to display) and earning the best rates for your app's ad space. Accomplishing these goals may require supporting more than one ad network in your app. Many developers take advantage of ad mediation layers and ad exchange platforms, such as offered by the following services:

- AdWhirl (http://www.adwhirl.com/)

- Burstly (http://www.burstly.com/)

- Mobclix (http://www.mobclix.com/)

Which Ad Network Is Right for You?

Beyond the lure of easy-to-use SDKs that can be integrated into your app within five to ten minutes, all of these ad networks are also free and offer similar features, so which one should you choose? It really comes down to the actual needs of your app. You should make your decision based on the following criteria:

- Supported ad sizes and formats
- Reporting and analytics
- Global availability and targeting
- Earnings and fill rates

Let's take a closer look at how these factors can greatly impact your app's success with in-app advertising.

Supported Ad Sizes and Formats

First and foremost, the mobile ad network you choose must support ad sizes that will fit nicely within your iOS app's UI and screen dimensions. For example, some ad networks offer only fixed portrait and landscape banner ad sizes for the iPhone and iPod touch, which would prove problematic for the larger screen of an iPad app.

And what if banner ads aren't suitable for your app's specific interface needs? Some ad networks specialize in full-screen, rich media ads or video-based ads, which may be a better fit for games and custom UIs where traditional banner ads would be impractical.

If cross-promotion is a valuable feature for your free ad-supported app to utilize, then pay special attention to the ad networks that allow you to assign some of your ad inventory with custom "house ads." You can use these to promote your other apps and/or In-App Purchase offerings from within your free app, as well as possibly trade ads with other third-party apps as part of an exchange network. While you won't be earning any ad revenue from those kinds of cross-promotional ads, they can help drive a lot of traffic and sales to your other paid apps and content, if your free app enjoys a large user base.

Reporting and Analytics

In order to properly evaluate the effectiveness of your in-app advertising business model, you must have the ability to measure the frequency and performance of ads displayed within your app. All of the ad networks offer web-based reporting on the ads run within your app, but some are more comprehensive than others. You should try to check out an example of a report before making your decision.

But earned ad revenue is not the only set of statistics worth tracking. Most (if not all) of the mobile ad networks also offer an integrated analytics package as part of their SDKs.

This can be significant in tracking app usage and figuring out which sections of your app receive the most traffic. This knowledge will help you to fine-tune in-app ad placement to improve ad revenue, as well as enhance the app's overall performance and design to better match how people are using it. In 2010, Apple changed its policy on analytics, allowing only third-party analytics when used to track and improve in-app advertising efforts. I discuss in-app analytics in greater detail later in this chapter.

Global Availability and Targeting

One ad network alone may not cater to every App Store region where your app is sold, so consider how to provide in-app ads to all of your users, regardless of their location. This may require a combination of ad networks or that you take advantage of a service that supports multiple ad networks and mediation layers.

When Apple's iAd Network first launched, it was initially limited to the North American continent. In the months that followed, Apple began slowly rolling out iAd in other regions, such as Europe and Japan. By the time you read this, iAd may be well established in enough regions to make it a viable in-app advertising solution for globally available apps.

But if you're worried about some regions or countries going unserved, you may want to support more than one ad network in your app. Many developers program their apps to serve up iAds for US users, MobFox or InMobi for European users, and AdMob for the rest of the world. This is where location awareness and in-app analytics can help determine which ad networks to call on for each individual user.

Another vital component to your success is ad targeting. Make sure the ad network you choose is capable of matching the right ads to your app's unique audience. For example, if your app caters to mostly males (such as Maxim HD for iPad), then ads for women's fashion and makeup would most likely be the wrong fit for that demographic. Unrelated ads that do not capture the attention of your users will not get tapped. The fewer click-throughs, the less ad revenue you earn.

Earnings and Fill Rates

Ad-sharing revenue is based on the effective cost per thousand (eCPM). Apple's iAd Network currently holds the highest eCPM rate in the mobile advertising space due to its big-name brand advertisers.

As a new venture, during the first six months of operation, iAd had a small ad inventory. So even though ad rates were high, there weren't enough ads to fill the pipeline of participating apps in the network. As a result, critics complained of iAd's low fill rates. Although Apple has worked hard to pump up its ad inventory since then by adding more brand advertisers and launching the iAd for Developers program, it's never a bad idea to support multiple ad networks to ensure a 100 percent fill rate in your app.

Due to iAd's high eCPM rates, many developers assign iAd as the first ad network to send a request for an ad. If there isn't an iAd available, then the app automatically requests an ad from a second ad network, such as Google's popular AdMob.

One of the primary advantages of using an ad mediation layer service, like AdWhirl or Burstly, is that it ensures the best fill rate and a good eCPM average. Not only do AdWhirl and Burstly support a long list of leading ad networks, but they also support iAd. Mobclix is another appealing platform that supports several major ad networks.

Differentiate which ad networks pay out only for actual click-throughs on ads versus the ones that also pay out for ad impressions (views). Some ad networks claim high eCPM rates without mentioning that those attractive rates are often only a small fraction of their ad inventory, and available only to select apps that reach a specific demographic.

Again, be sure to do your homework before choosing an ad network. Just keep in mind that if your app does not have a large user base or capture a coveted demographic, then your app may not be able to command the high eCPM rates.

Building a Business with Ad-Supported Apps

Can iOS developers make a living solely based on revenue earned from in-app advertising? When trying to decide whether you should release your product as either a paid app or a free ad-supported app, it's important to do the math. A paid app sale would earn you at least 70 cents (based on a 99-cent price). If it was an ad-supported free app, would it generate enough ad impressions and click-throughs to net you more than 70 cents per user? With a heavily used app, you could confidently answer "yes" to that question, but with very few users, the answer may be a surprising "no."

If you're averaging an eCPM that hovers around $1, then to make more than $1,000, your in-app advertising will need to receive at least 1,000,000 ad impressions. With more than 160 million iOS devices out there, it shouldn't be too hard for your free app to drum up 1 million ad impressions, right?

Just because your app is free does not guarantee an avalanche of downloads. There are simply too many apps in the App Store vying for people's attention. Only a small percentage of those apps enjoy a healthy customer base of hundreds of thousands of users, with some of the top apps benefiting from millions of users. But that's not the norm. More than half of the free apps in the App Store have been downloaded by only a few thousand people. If your app falls into that latter category, you would net only a handful of dollars each day in ad revenue—definitely not enough to sustain a full-time salary for yourself.

While that may sound rather bleak, keep in mind that your app doesn't need to be a Top 10 best-selling phenomenon in order to make money from in-app advertising. There are quite a few free, ad-supported apps that pull in consistent revenue due to the thoughtful, strategic planning and marketing creativity of the developers who created them.

Balancing UI Design Aesthetics with Ads

You'll need to consider how the display of ads will affect your UI. Whether you have a single version that has an option to remove the ads or you offer dual apps consisting of a free version with ads and a paid version without them, your UI design will need to accommodate your selected approach.

Designing Free Apps with Removable Ads

Hog Bay Software's Jesse Grosjean made his first foray into the world of mobile advertising with the release of his free writing app, PlainText for both iPhone and iPad. His previous iOS products, the popular TaskPaper and WriteRoom, were released as paid apps. But with the cloud-based Dropbox file-synchronizing option in PlainText, the user needs an online connection. This presented a unique opportunity for Jesse to experiment with in-app advertising.

The goal of PlainText is to provide a minimal, distraction-free UI for writers, so it was important to Jesse not to clutter the screen with ugly banner ads. Most iAd banners are nicely designed, so instead of juggling multiple ad networks to leverage the best eCPM and fill rates, he felt it was more important to preserve the integrity of the app's UI design and support only iAd. When an iAd is available, the entire PlainText UI shifts up, making room for an iAd at the bottom. If there's no iAd to display, the PlainText UI reverts back to its normal state, hiding the ad banner frame (see Figure 7–3).

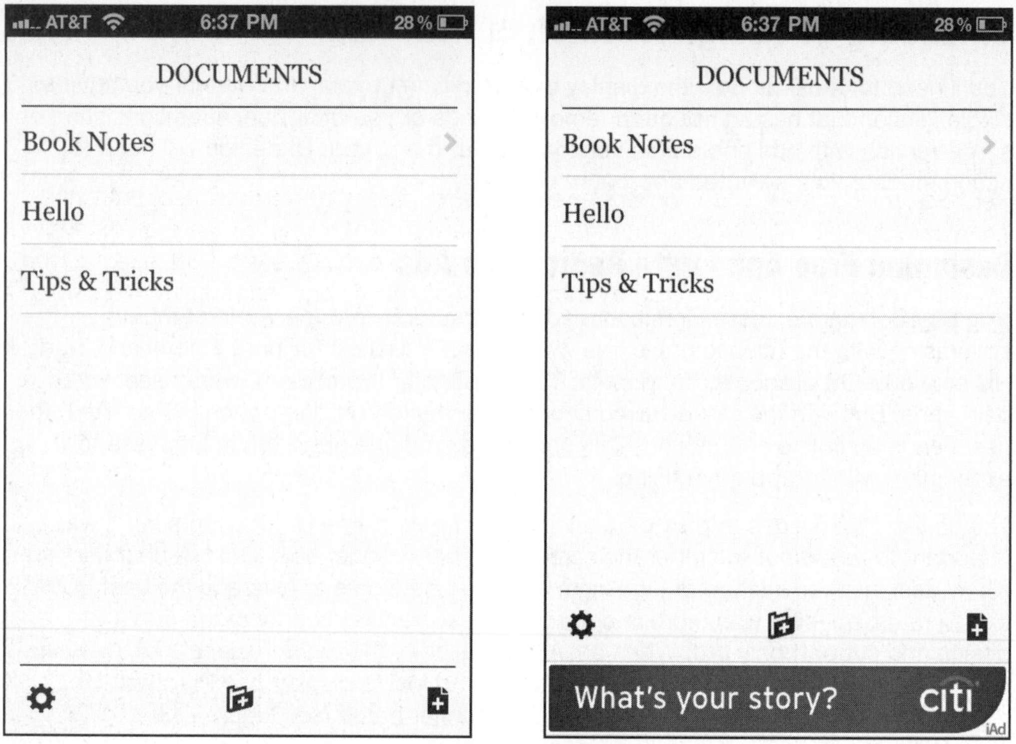

Figure 7–3. *PlainText by Hog Bay Software dynamically adjusts the height of the app's UI based on whether an iAd is available for display at the bottom of the screen.*

Jesse admitted that his decision to use iAd exclusively doesn't allow him to truly optimize his in-app advertising efforts, especially since iAd requires iOS 4, so users running PlainText on iOS 3 are not seeing any ads. Regardless of that limitation, he has been pleased with the results. The free app also offers an In-App Purchase option to remove the ads.

"Compared to my paid apps, PlainText has had many more downloads, but with less profit," Jesse revealed. "In a little over two months, PlainText has had about 225,000 downloads and has made a little over $3,000 via In-App Purchases and about $7,000 via iAd."

Even though the number of people who chose to buy the "Remove Ads" In-App Purchase item represents only roughly 1 percent of total PlainText users, it is still a significant portion of the revenue that the app earns. This hybrid model of a free, ad-supported app with an In-App Purchase component for removing ads and/or selling additional features can be a very powerful combination.

Designing Two Versions: With and Without Ads

Instead of offering an In-App Purchase option to remove ads, some developers simply release two versions of the app: a free, ad-supported app and a paid, ad-free app. This is the strategy employed by Optime Software, a business built from the ground up on mobile ad revenue. The company launched with only free app releases—Checkers Free, Dots Free, Chess Free, Tic Tac Toe Free, Four in a Row Free, and other classic games. And many of their free apps continuously rank high in the App Store charts.

In response to user requests, Optime Software started offering ad-free, premium versions of its games. CEO Jon Schlegel explained, "Many users outside of the United States don't have all-you-can-eat data plans and were concerned about the cost they were incurring due to ad downloads. The response we have received from users to the premium versions has been very favorable. Most users will buy the premium version of a game if they use it regularly."

Unlike the resizing UI of PlainText to dynamically show or hide the ad banner frame, Optime Software specifically designs its free app interfaces with banner ads in mind. The ad-free, premium versions are able to span the entire screen, spacing out the various game elements and giving the overall UI design a little more breathing room (see Figure 7–4).

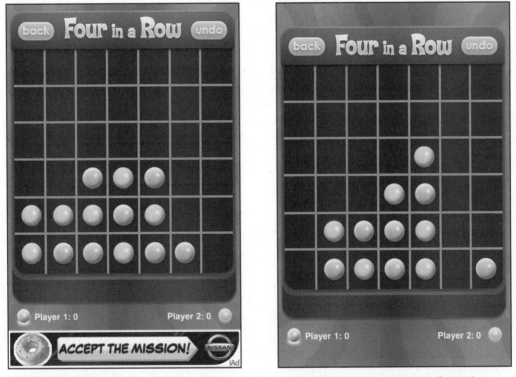

Figure 7–4. Optime Software modifies the placement of various UI elements in its games depending on the version. A free app requires adequate space at the bottom of the screen for an ad banner (left), whereas a premium paid version does not (right).

The obvious disadvantage to this approach is the development maintenance of two separate versions. Optime Software was utilizing this strategy long before the introduction of In-App Purchase, but the stellar benefit here is the presence of two apps in the App Store, instead of only one. The increased visibility of having apps on both the free and paid App Store charts can help promote both versions. Jon admitted, "We earn significantly more from our ad-supported free apps than from our premium applications, but the free apps also help drive visibility and create uplift for our premium apps. Many of our premium applications have made it onto the Top 100 lists for their categories entirely based on up-sell conversions from the free version of the app."

Finding the Best Mix of Ad Networks

Mark Johnson of Focused Apps has quite a bit of experience working with in-app advertising in many of his free apps, which include Focus for Facebook, Hit Tennis 2, and Santa's Lil' Zombies. He was kind enough to share some valuable insights he has learned from all the experiments he has conducted to find the best mix of eCPM and fill rates.

"Making money with third-party ads is hard. For us, it's a smaller part of our revenue. To make free+ads work, you need volume and a sticky app," Mark stated. "In other words, you need lots of downloads, an app that people use often, and that they keep on their phone and return to over a long period of time (as opposed to just deleting it after a week of play)."

Focus for Facebook displays ads from iAd, AdMob, and other leading ad networks. The ad banner frame appears at the bottom of the screen, with the table view scrolling behind it (see Figure 7–5). The placement enables the ad to remain highly visible at all times without interfering with the reading of a user's Facebook newsfeed.

Figure 7–5. *The free Focus for Facebook app is supported by in-app advertising, displaying ads from iAd (left), AdMob (right), and other ad networks.*

"In one of our apps, we use Burstly as an ad network integrator so that if iAd doesn't have an ad for us, Burstly will put in an ad from one of the other ad networks," Mark said. "The different ad networks vary in fill, eCPM, quality of ads, and all those factors vary from country to country. Around half of our ad inventory is shown in the US, the other half in other countries. We've been trying different ad networks in order to see what fill rates and eCPMs we can get in different countries. No one ad network performs the best in every country. Naturally eCPMs are higher in richer countries, but the ad network's sales presence in each country affects the volume and value that they can sell there, and of course, English text ads won't be as good as ads in the local language. iAd pays well in the US at the moment, and it's growing. I recommend that developers first look at iAd, supplemented by AdMob and your own house ads (AdMob has a good built-in solution for house ads). Also consider using AdWhirl or Burstly."

Harnessing the Power of House Ads

As I mentioned earlier in this chapter, house ads are custom ads you create for display in your app's ad banner frame. If you're willing to forego some of the third-party ads to show your house ads, they can be a great way to promote other revenue-generating services and products, such as your paid apps. Mark Johnson had a lot to say on the subject:

"Naturally free apps get a lot more downloads, and that's a huge benefit. We use the ad space in the free app for a lot more than just showing third-party ads. We show house ads to do things like up-sell the paid app version; up-sell in-app-purchases; promote our other apps; ask users for feedback to help us plan the next version of the app; get people to join our mailing list; get people to tweet out an ad for us. I'd say the biggest advantage of making free apps isn't the ad revenue, but getting in front of a lot of people, and then using house ads creatively to aid other lines of business. This works really well. Something like 95 percent of our mailing list sign-ups come from a 'join our mailing list to unlock a free level' house ad, compared to only 5 percent from our 'contact us' screen."

Displaying house ads in free apps to cross-promote other paid apps and In-App Purchase offerings is a strategy that has also benefited Backflip Studios. Many of its apps, such as the ultra-popular Paper Toss (see Figure 7–6), are perennial favorites, ranking quite high in the App Store charts. With more than 47 million iOS app downloads, Backflip Studios makes $500,000 per month with in-app advertising in several free apps. And that's with only 60 percent of the ad impressions dedicated to third-party ads, such as AdMob. The remaining 40 percent of the ad impressions are house ads assigned by Backflip Studios to promote all of its other apps, both free and paid.

Figure 7–6. *Paper Toss HD Free for iPad utilizes the dedicated ad space to display not only third-party ads, but also house ads promoting other apps by Backflip Studios.*

The average free app usage declines rapidly in the first few weeks after download, with less than 5 percent of users returning to the app after 30 days. For in-app advertising to be a lucrative revenue source, your app needs to serve up as many advertisements as possible, which requires continued usage by a large number of users.

If your app is supported entirely by in-app advertising, it's crucial that you have marketing and development strategies in place that not only drive new users to your app, but also extend your app's life span beyond that initial 30-day average. So, even when offering free apps, developers cannot rest on their laurels, waiting for the ad revenue to roll in. You should expect to work just as hard promoting and continuously updating a free, ad-supported app as you would for a paid app to ensure that your in-app advertising solution pays off.

But if your free app becomes a runaway hit, rising into the App Store's Top 100, it's possible to make a lot of money from in-app advertising. And if you have several top-ranking free apps generating ad revenue at the same time, you could have a very profitable business on your hands.

Implementing Apple's iAd in Your iOS Apps

After reading about the success other developers have had with in-app advertising, you're probably anxious to try your own hand at it. Due to page constraints, it wouldn't be practical for this book to include implementation instructions for every third-party mobile ad network out there, so for our examples, we'll stick with iAd. Once you have a good handle on how to use Apple's iAd framework in your iOS apps, learning other third-party SDKs like AdMob on your own will prove very easy.

We'll start with the basics of working with the iAd Network, and then take an extensive walk-through of designing and programming your app to support iAd. So roll up your sleeves and let's get started.

> **NOTE:** If you're interested in learning more about iAd, check out these official Apple Developer links (your iOS Developer Program login may be required): iAd Development (`http://developer.apple.com/iad/`) and App Store Resource Center for iAd (`http://developer.apple.com/appstore/resources/iad/`).

Joining the iAd Network

Before you can start working with iAd, even when testing in Xcode's iOS Simulator, you're required to first join the iAd Network. This is done in iTunes Connect, so log in— `http://itunesconnect.apple.com/`—and then navigate to the Contracts, Tax, and Banking section to apply for the iAd Network (see Figure 7–7).

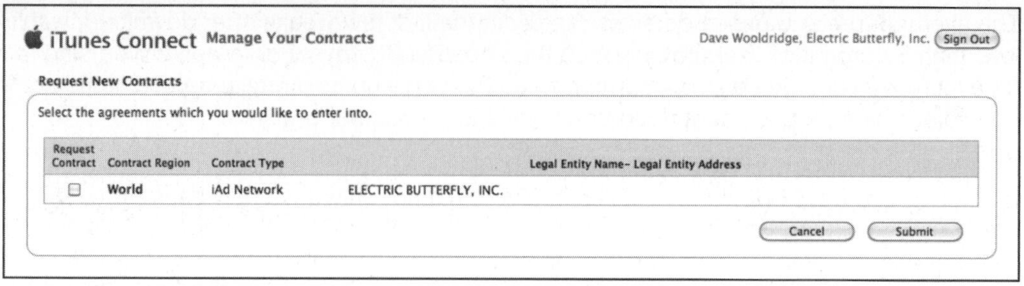

Figure 7–7. *You must first join the iAd Network within iTunes Connect before you can begin working with the iAd framework in your apps.*

Once your iAd Network contract request has been approved by Apple, you'll be able to successfully develop and test your apps with the iAd framework.

It's important to note that the only ad you'll see when running your app in the iOS Simulator and on your test devices is the default iAd test advertisement. Tapping the test iAd banner will display only the test ad view. Your app won't display real live iAd banners until you submit the app in iTunes Connect with iAd enabled for that app in iTunes Connect.

Designing Your App for Displaying iAd Banners

There are two types of iAd advertisements. One is the typical iAd Banner View, which can be seen in many ad-supported iOS apps (see Figures 7–3 and 7–4, for example). The other is a full-screen, immersive ad called an iAd Interstitial View, which was introduced in iOS 4.3. For the sake of simplicity, we'll focus on only the more popular iAd Banner View type within these pages. If you're interested in learning more about implementing the iAd Interstitial View, check out the documentation online at Apple's iOS Dev Center.

If you've already seen iAds in iOS apps, you're familiar with the general concept of how they operate. An iAd banner is placed strategically in an app's UI, and when tapped, the user does not leave the app. Instead, a full screen advertisement is shown as a modal view within the app. Closing the modal advertisement view brings the user back to the app.

As you might expect, the iAd banner sizes are very similar to other mobile ad sizes:

- iPhone portrait iAd banner: 320 points wide × 50 points tall

- iPhone landscape iAd banner: 480 points wide × 32 points tall

- iPad portrait iAd banner: 768 points wide × 66 points tall

- iPad landscape iAd banner: 1024 points × 66 points tall

The goal is to insert the ad banner into your app's UI without it being too intrusive to the user experience. But at the same time, you want the ad to be placed where it will be easily seen by users to gain impressions and click-throughs.

If you plan on placing the iAd banner frame at the top of the screen, Apple recommends positioning it above your top navigation bar or toolbar. If you plan on displaying the iAd banner frame near the bottom of the screen, Apple also recommends adding it above toolbars or tab bars, but that doesn't necessarily work in all cases. For example, if an iPad app uses a split view controller with toolbars along the bottom, a landscape ad banner can't be placed above those toolbars, since there are essentially two different views (the master pane and the details pane are side by side in landscape mode). In that scenario, you need to place the ad banner below the toolbars.

What may come as a surprise to many developers is that an iAd Banner View must be added as a subview to a UIView. If you know your app is always going to display ads at a specific fixed position on the screen, why not just add an iAd Banner View to an existing UIView in Interface Builder? If your app supports multiple ad networks, you'll always have an ad available to show, so why not? There are actually three very important reasons to ensure your ad view can be dynamically removed from the UI while the app is running, as demonstrated in Hog Bay Software's PlainText (see Figure 7–3):

- If the user's device loses cellular or Wi-Fi connectivity, you do not want your app to display an empty ad banner frame. Having a large, blank rectangle consume valuable screen real estate within your UI is ugly and very unprofessional.

- Apple's app review team will reject any apps that display a blank ad space when either an iAd banner is not available or the iAd Network's server cannot be reached. Apple's iAd framework makes this easy to detect in code by sending your app a message via the iAd banner delegate when an ad cannot be retrieved.

- If you plan on offering an In-App Purchase option to remove ads for those loyal users who would prefer an ad-free experience, you won't want an unused, empty ad banner frame to remain on the screen after purchase, cluttering the app's UI for no reason.

For those of you who plan to have an iAd appear above a UITableView or a game-based canvas in a specific UIView, making the iAd banner visible on the screen via code is fairly trivial. But for those developers who need to resize multiple controls to make room for the iAd banner frame, this will undoubtedly require some retooling of the design of your UI components and parent controllers.

Don't automatically give in to the easy path by compromising your app's design to accommodate an iAd banner. Take the time to figure out how to integrate the iAd banner without sacrificing the integrity of your app's UI. If you have not built your app yet, then this is simply a matter of planning your UI with ad banners in mind. But for existing apps, this may require rebuilding many of your views to include new parent UIViews, such as an underlying view that holds the nested subviews of the iAd banner frame and the top view containing your app's UI components (see Figure 7–8).

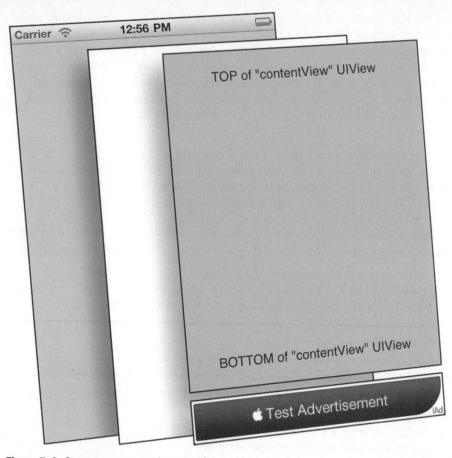

Figure 7–8. *Some apps may require reworking the hierarchy of views to accommodate an iAd banner frame, which must be a subview of a UIView.*

In Figure 7–8, the top `UIView` (assigned in code as `contentView`) acts as a parent view container for your app's UI controls. If you need this parent view to resize itself to make room for an iAd banner at the bottom of the screen, you will want to set the autosizing masks of the nested UI controls, so that they also resize or move accordingly. As shown in Figure 7–8, the `UILabel` with the text "BOTTOM of 'contentView' UIView" has its autosizing mask set to move up relative to the resizing of its parent `UIView`'s height.

The very bottom layer in Figure 7–8 represents the app's main window with an embedded view controller. The white middle layer is the main `UIView` called by the view controller. This `UIView` is assigned the outlet `view` by default. The `contentView`-named `UIView` and the iAd banner frame are both subviews of the parent `UIView` (known as `view`).

If any of this is a little confusing to you, don't worry. It will make perfect sense when we step through the process of integrating iAd into an Xcode example project in the following section. You'll understand the reasoning behind the hierarchy of `UIView`s when you see it in action.

As far as appearances are concerned, you don't want the iAd to instantly pop into view with everything shifted. That can be jarring for the user. It's much more elegant to gracefully transition the iAd onto the screen, sliding it in and out of view using UIView animation. You'll see how to use UIView animation with an iAd banner frame when we build the Figure 7–8 example as a universal app for both iPhone and iPad. Keep reading...

Programming Your App to Support Ads

Let's tackle some code! First, it's important to understand exactly what we need this example project to do before diving into Xcode. Here's an outline of the basic functionality:

- Check the device's Internet connectivity. If there's no connection, then do nothing, leaving the app's UI in its normal, full-screen state.

- If the device does have Internet access, then request an iAd banner from the iAd Network.

- If the iAd Network sends a message that the iAd banner request was successful, then prepare the iAd banner frame, and the ad banner is ready to display.

- If the iAd Network replies that an iAd banner is not available, then prepare an alternate ad banner to show. In this example, we'll show a built-in house ad, but you could just as easily modify the example code to support a second ad network instead (such as AdMob).

- When an ad banner is ready for display—either an iAd or the house ad—use UIView animation to slide the advertisement up into view at the bottom of the screen and adjust the positioning of affected UI elements to make room for the ad banner frame.

- If the app was previously showing an ad banner, and either the device loses Internet connectivity or there's no new ad banner to display, then use the same UIView animation technique to slide the ad frame out of view, reverting the app's UI to its normal, full-screen state.

If you just want to display an iAd banner above your existing UI, you may find this extensive tutorial to be a bit overkill for your needs. For simple iAd code examples, check out Apple's sample project, iAdSuite, available online at the iOS Dev Center: http://developer.apple.com/library/ios/#samplecode/iAdSuite/.

But for those of you interested in the features I've outlined, the advanced example project we're about to build might just be the solution you're seeking. This tutorial contains a lot of code (compared to other examples in the book), so to avoid all of that manual typing, I highly recommend downloading the book's companion code examples (from http://www.iPhoneBusinessBook.com/ or http://www.apress.com/), and then opening the included InAppAdv project in Xcode. Even if you want to work through the steps yourself, copying and pasting some of the code from the InAppAdv example project could save you some valuable time.

Creating a New Xcode Project

iAd has been available for iPhone and iPod touch since iOS 4.0, but iAd wasn't supported on the iPad until iOS 4.2. To accommodate all readers, we'll build a universal app example, showing how to implement iAd code for both iPhone and iPad targets.

Launch Xcode and create a new iOS project, choosing the Window-based Application template. When selecting that project template, make sure its **Product** drop-down menu is set to **Universal**, but leave the Use Core Data for storage box unchecked. Name the new project InAppAdv.

Adding the iAd Framework to the Project

Apple's iAd framework is required in order to successfully run and compile your app with iAd-related code. To add this framework to your project, Ctrl-click the project's *Frameworks* folder, and from the contextual menu that appears, select **Add ➤ Existing Frameworks…** (see Figure 7–9). Then select iAd.framework from the list that appears.

Figure 7–9. *Add the required iAd.framework to your Xcode project.*

To remain focused on the task at hand, the example project requires iOS 4.2. If your app needs to support older iOS versions, you can weak-link the iAd framework in your project. To do so, select the project's app name in the Targets group, click the Get Info button, and within the General tab that appears, choose Weak as the linking method for iAd.framework (see Figure 7–10).

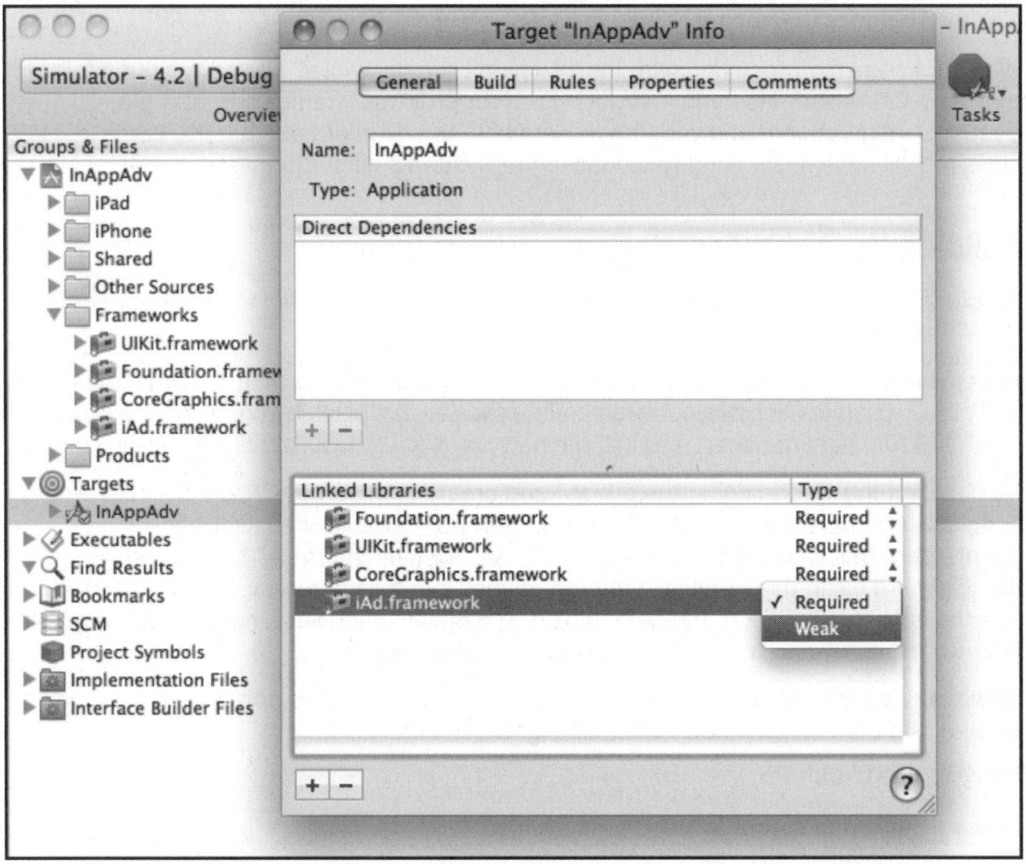

Figure 7–10. *Weak-linking the iAd.framework for backward-compatibility with pre-iOS 4 devices*

You'll probably also need to use conditional coding within your app, so that on iOS 4 devices, an iAd banner ad is displayed, but on older iOS versions, a house ad or another third-party ad banner is shown instead. For more information about implementing backward-compatibility, check out the iOS Dev Center.

Adding Apple's Reachability Class to the Project

When the app is running, you'll want the code to check for Internet connectivity. Without access to the Internet, there's no sense requesting an ad banner. Instead of spending hours crafting your own custom network-detection code, Apple recommends using its own Reachability class, which can be downloaded from the iOS Dev Center as part of the Reachability sample project, at http://developer.apple.com/library/ ios/#samplecode/Reachability/.

Once you've downloaded the Reachability project, open it in Xcode. Drag and drop the *Reachability.h* and *Reachability.m* class files from the Reachability project into the *Shared* folder of your InAppAdv Xcode project window (selecting the option to copy the files rather than move them).

We'll add code for interacting with the Reachability class later. For now, simply follow the same framework-insertion instructions as for previous examples to add the SystemConfiguration framework to your project. As you might expect, the Reachability class requires the networking functions in the SystemConfiguration framework.

Building the App's Foundation

Before programming the core functionality of our project, we need to construct some initial files and write some basic code.

With the *iPhone* folder selected in the Groups & Files column, create a new file based on a UIViewController subclass. Assign an interface to this class by checking the box "With XIB for user interface," and call the new class MainViewController_iPhone.

Next, select the *iPad* folder in the project and create another new UIViewController subclass, appropriately named MainViewController_iPad. As with its iPhone counterpart, make sure the check box "With XIB for user interface" is selected. Even though we're using this class for the iPad, please leave Targeted for iPad unchecked, so that the autosizing mask of the default UIView remains unlocked. This will come into play later when we need to modify the UIView autosizing mask.

Now that we have the necessary new classes created, open the *AppDelegate_iPhone.h* file and add the following new code, highlighted in bold:

```
#import <UIKit/UIKit.h>

@class MainViewController_iPhone;

@interface AppDelegate_iPhone : NSObject <UIApplicationDelegate> {
    UIWindow *window;
    MainViewController_iPhone *viewController;
}

@property (nonatomic, retain) IBOutlet UIWindow *window;
@property (nonatomic, retain) IBOutlet MainViewController_iPhone *viewController;

@end
```

As you can see, the bold lines of code assign a new viewController property and IBOutlet to the MainViewController_iPhone class.

Also add the same code to *AppDelegate_iPad.h*, taking care to replace all MainViewController_iPhone references with MainViewController_iPad.

After saving those header files, open the *AppDelegate_iPhone.m* implementation file and add the new code, shown in bold:

```
#import "AppDelegate_iPhone.h"
#import "MainViewController_iPhone.h"

@implementation AppDelegate_iPhone

@synthesize window;
@synthesize viewController;

#pragma mark -
#pragma mark Application lifecycle

- (BOOL)application:(UIApplication *)application
didFinishLaunchingWithOptions:(NSDictionary *)launchOptions {

    // Override point for customization after application launch.

    [window addSubview:viewController.view];
    [self.window makeKeyAndVisible];

    return YES;
}

- (void)applicationWillResignActive:(UIApplication *)application {
}

- (void)applicationDidEnterBackground:(UIApplication *)application {
}

- (void)applicationWillEnterForeground:(UIApplication *)application {
}

- (void)applicationDidBecomeActive:(UIApplication *)application {
}

- (void)applicationWillTerminate:(UIApplication *)application {
}

#pragma mark -
#pragma mark Memory management

- (void)applicationDidReceiveMemoryWarning:(UIApplication *)application {
}

- (void)dealloc {
    [viewController release];
    [window release];
    [super dealloc];
}

@end
```

This new code adds viewController as a subview to the app's main window.

Also insert the same new code in *AppDelegate_iPad.m*, taking care to #import *MainViewController_iPad.h* instead of *MainViewController_iPhone.h*.

With the proper code in place, it's time to do a little UI work. Follow these steps:

1. Open *MainWindow_iPhone.xib* in Interface Builder.

2. Drag a UIViewController from the Library palette to the browser window and wire its referencing outlet viewController to the app delegate module.

3. With the UIViewController selected in the browser window, assign its NIB to *MainViewController_iPhone.xib* in the inspector palette's Attributes tab, with Resize View from NIB checked (see Figure 7–11).

4. In the inspector palette's Identity tab, change its class to MainViewController_iPhone.

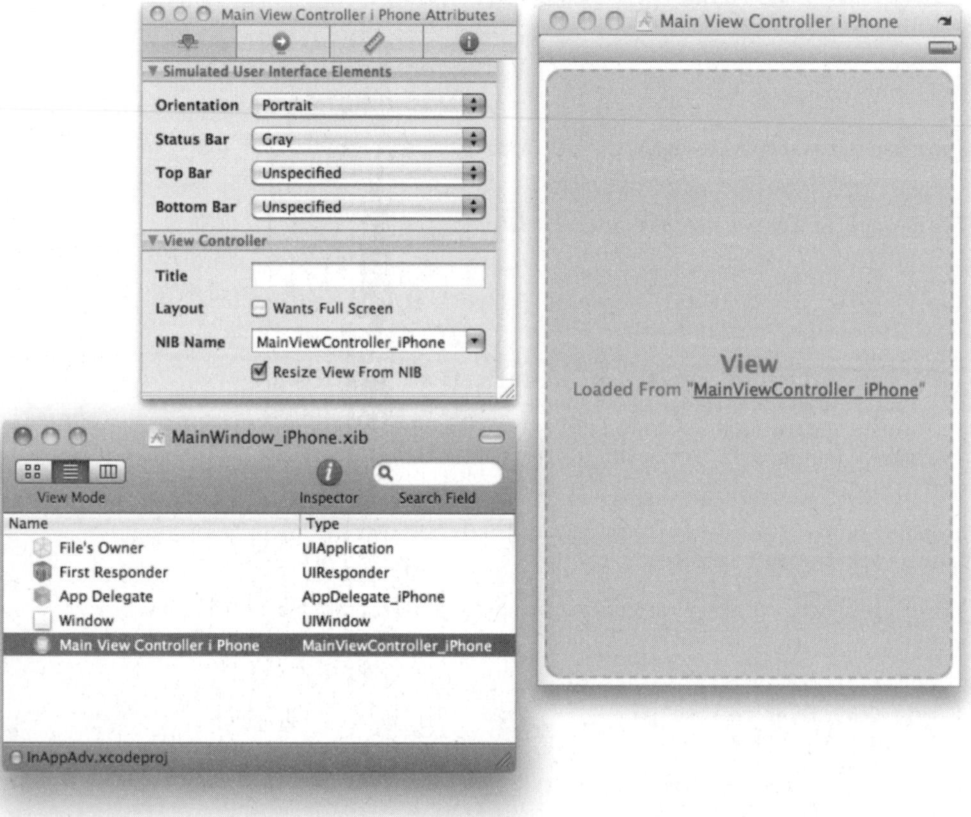

Figure 7–11. *Configuring MainWindow_iPhone.xib with a new UIViewController that loads MainViewController_iPhone*

You'll need to perform the same steps in Interface Builder with *MainWindow_iPad.xib*, except that the UIViewController's NIB should be assigned to *MainViewController_iPad.xib* and its class changed to MainViewController_iPad.

Checking the iOS Device's Network Connection

Remember adding Apple's Reachability class to the project? Now you get to write code that taps into the power of that handy network-detection class. Open the *MainViewController_iPhone.h* file in Xcode and add the following bold code:

```
#import <UIKit/UIKit.h>

@class Reachability;

@interface MainViewController_iPhone : UIViewController {

    UIView *contentView;
    Reachability* netReachable;
    BOOL isNetAvailable;
}

@property (nonatomic, retain) IBOutlet UIView *contentView;

- (void)reachabilityChanged:(NSNotification*)note;

@end
```

Essentially, this code sets up some Reachability-related properties and a method, as well as a new UIView property and IBOutlet reference called contentView. You'll need to also add the same new code lines to *MainViewController_iPad.h*.

Moving on to the *MainViewController_iPhone.m* implementation file, add the following new code, highlighted in bold:

```
#import "MainViewController_iPhone.h"
#import "Reachability.h"

@implementation MainViewController_iPhone

@synthesize contentView;

// Uncommented viewDidLoad and added Reachability code.
- (void)viewDidLoad {
    [super viewDidLoad];

    // Check the current device's Internet connection
    // using Apple's Reachability classes. When the status
    // changes, a notification is posted, calling the
    // reachabilityChanged method.
    [[NSNotificationCenter defaultCenter] addObserver: self selector:
@selector(reachabilityChanged:) name: kReachabilityChangedNotification object: nil];
    netReachable = [[Reachability reachabilityWithHostName: @"www.apple.com"] retain];
    [netReachable startNotifier];
}
```

```
// Uncommented and return YES.
- (BOOL)shouldAutorotateToInterfaceOrientation:
               (UIInterfaceOrientation)interfaceOrientation {
    // Return YES to support both Portrait and Landscape orientations.
    return YES;
}

//Called by Reachability whenever status changes.
- (void) reachabilityChanged: (NSNotification* )note {

    NetworkStatus netStatus = [netReachable currentReachabilityStatus];
    switch (netStatus)
    {
        case NotReachable:
        {
            isNetAvailable = NO;
            break;
        }
        case ReachableViaWiFi:
        {
            isNetAvailable = YES;
            break;
        }
        case ReachableViaWWAN:
        {
            isNetAvailable = YES;
            break;
        }
    }
}

- (void)didReceiveMemoryWarning {
    [super didReceiveMemoryWarning];
}

- (void)viewDidUnload {
    self.contentView = nil;
    [super viewDidUnload];
}

- (void)dealloc {
    [contentView release];
    [[NSNotificationCenter defaultCenter] removeObserver:self];
    [super dealloc];
}

@end
```

The newly added code sets up access to the Reachability functionality and the NSNotificationCenter, so that this class can check the current status of the device's network connection, and is always notified if that status changes. This determines if your app has Internet access, which is vital information to know before attempting to communicate with ad network's servers. If viable network connectivity is detected, then the Boolean `isNetAvailable` is set to YES.

As with the previous steps in this tutorial, you'll need to add the same bold code lines to *MainViewController_iPad.m* as well.

Building the App's Interface and UIView Hierarchy

You probably noticed the new `UIView` property called `contentView` in the `MainViewController_iPhone` and `MainViewController_iPad` classes. Now that the `IBOutlet` code is in place, let's complete the configuration of that `UIView` in Interface Builder, along with some other UI elements for this example.

1. Open *MainViewController_iPhone.xib* in Interface Builder.

2. In the browser window, you should already see a `UIView` listed, wired to the default `view` referencing outlet. Drag a new `UIView` from the Library palette to the browser window, carefully positioning it as a nested `UIView` within that existing `UIView`. Wire the outlet of `contentView` from the File's Owner module to that new, nested `UIView`. The nested `UIView` (named `contentView`) and the iAd banner frame will both be subviews of the main parent `UIView` (named `view`).

3. With that nested `UIView` selected, navigate to the View Size tab of the inspector palette and modify the autosizing mask to automatically expand full screen (see Figure 7–12). The parent `UIView` should also have the same autosizing mask settings (if it doesn't already by default).

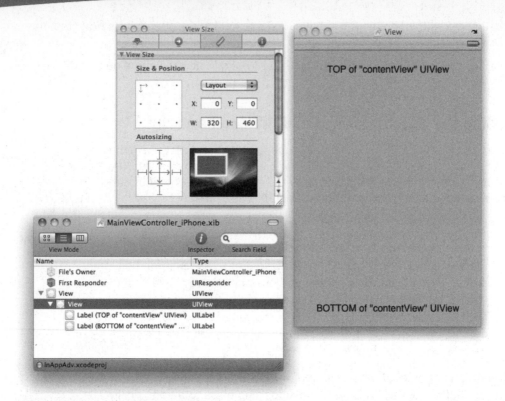

Figure 7–12. *Within MainViewController_iPhone.xib, construct the nested UIView hierarchy, UI elements, and autosizing masks.*

NOTE: Even though the Library palette does offer an iAd BannerView component, do *not* add it to the view within Interface Builder. For this example, it's crucial that the iAd banner frame is only added programmatically, so that the iAd can dynamically slide in and out of the screen based on availability and other factors at runtime. You'll see how to write that iAd code soon.

4. With the nested UIView (named contentView) selected, change its Color Tint in the inspector palette's Attributes tab to 75 percent grayscale, so that we can easily differentiate this UIView from its white parent UIView when displayed on the screen. This gray UIView is where you will place all of the UI elements for this screen. Think of it as a container for your app interface, with its height resized when needed to make room for the ad banner frame at the bottom of the screen.

5. To keep things simple for demonstration purposes, add two UILabels from the Library palette to that nested UIView.

6. Move one `UILabel` to the top of the view with label text that reads **TOP of "contentView" UIView**. Set the autosizing mask for that `UILabel` to always stay rooted at the top of the screen.

7. Move the second `UILabel` to the bottom of the view and give it the label text **BOTTOM of "contentView" UIView**. Set the autosizing mask of this second `UILabel` to always stay rooted at the bottom of the screen.

> **NOTE:** If you're not quite sure how to configure the brackets on the autosizing mask, check out the book's downloadable `InAppAdv` project to see an example of how they are set.

Remember to also make all of these same additions and modifications to *MainViewController_iPad.xib*.

Why the `UILabels`? They serve as visible markers, indicating where the top and bottom of the gray `contentView`-assigned `UIView` is located when resizing it via code to make room for the ad banner frame. This will be obvious when you run the app in the iOS Simulator or on a test device and see it in action. But we're not ready to do that quite yet.

The last step is the most important piece of the project: writing the code that manages the entire in-app advertising process from ad banner request to display on the screen.

> **NOTE:** You may find that several UI components, such as a `UINavigationController`, cannot be added to a `UIView` in Interface Builder. For those scenarios, the solution is to create those UI components programmatically in Xcode, adding them to the `UIView` as a subview via code.

Copying Your House Ad Image Files to the Project

In the event that there isn't an iAd available to display, you'll want to show an alternate ad banner instead. For this example, let's show a house ad. Before you start writing code for handling iAd and your alternate ad banner, you'll need to create the actual image files for your house ad and add them as resources to the Xcode project.

To support all of the device orientations and display resolutions for both iPhone and iPad, you'll need to create your house ad in six different sizes with the exact file names and PNG format listed here, so that they work with the example code:

- *adbannerportrait-iphone.png* (320 pixels × 50 pixels)
- *adbannerportrait-iphone@2x.png* (Retina: 640 pixels × 100 pixels)
- *adbannerlandscape-iphone.png* (480 pixels × 32 pixels)
- *adbannerlandscape-iphone@2x.png* (Retina: 960 pixels × 64 pixels)
- *adbannerportrait-ipad.png* (768 pixels × 66 pixels)
- *adbannerlandscape-ipad.png* (1024 pixels × 66 pixels)

For consistency, the house ad uses the same banner sizes as supported by iAd. The iAd Network dynamically serves up high-resolution iAd banners for Retina display devices, so to maintain the same resolution quality, you should also create Retina display banner sizes for your house ad.

If you don't want to spend time designing your own house ad just to complete this tutorial, then as a placeholder, copy the six house ad PNG image files from the book's downloadable InAppAdv project to your Xcode project's *Shared* folder.

Crafting the In-App Advertising Code

For this last step, you'll finally add the code for managing the iAd banner frame and the alternate house ad, along with the dynamic resizing of the app's UI to accommodate the ad banner. This part requires the addition of a *lot* of new code. To avoid all of that manual typing, I'll once again recommend downloading the book's companion code examples, so that you can copy and paste the relevant code from the included InAppAdv project into your Xcode project.

Open *MainViewController_iPhone.h* and add the following new code lines (shown in bold):

```
#import <UIKit/UIKit.h>
#import <iAd/iAd.h>

@class Reachability;

@interface MainViewController_iPhone : UIViewController <ADBannerViewDelegate> {

    UIView *contentView;
    ADBannerView *adBannerView;
    UIButton *altAdBannerButton;
    Reachability* netReachable;
    BOOL isNetAvailable;
}

@property (nonatomic, retain) IBOutlet UIView *contentView;
@property (nonatomic, retain) IBOutlet ADBannerView *adBannerView;
@property (nonatomic, retain) IBOutlet UIButton *altAdBannerButton;

- (void)reachabilityChanged:(NSNotification*)note;
- (void)prepareAdBannerView;
- (void)prepareAltAdBanner;
- (void)adjustAdBannerPosition:(BOOL)animated;
- (void)tappedAltAdBanner;

@end
```

In a nutshell, this new code imports the *iAd.h* header file and initializes several new ad-related properties and methods for dealing with iAd and the alternate house ad.

Notice that the iAd banner type being used is the ADBannerView. In order to receive messages from the iAd Network, this class is assigned as an ADBannerViewDelegate. To ensure the house ad is tappable, like a real banner ad, it will be created as an image-based UIButton via code. I'll explain how the preparation and display of the iAd and alternate house ad are programmed when we add those respective methods to the *MainViewController.m* file.

Of course, you'll also need to add the identical bold code to *MainViewController_iPad.h*:

```objc
#import <UIKit/UIKit.h>
#import <iAd/iAd.h>

@class Reachability;

@interface MainViewController_iPad : UIViewController <ADBannerViewDelegate> {

    UIView *contentView;
    ADBannerView *adBannerView;
    UIButton *altAdBannerButton;
    Reachability* netReachable;
    BOOL isNetAvailable;
}

@property (nonatomic, retain) IBOutlet UIView *contentView;
@property (nonatomic, retain) IBOutlet ADBannerView *adBannerView;
@property (nonatomic, retain) IBOutlet UIButton *altAdBannerButton;

- (void)reachabilityChanged:(NSNotification*)note;
- (void)prepareAdBannerView;
- (void)prepareAltAdBanner;
- (void)adjustAdBannerPosition:(BOOL)animated;
- (void)tappedAltAdBanner;

@end
```

Now we tackle the biggest chunk of code yet, which adds the bulk of the app's in-app advertising functionality. Open the *MainViewController_iPhone.m* implementation file and insert the following new code, highlighted in bold:

```objc
#import "MainViewController_iPhone.h"
#import "Reachability.h"

@implementation MainViewController_iPhone

@synthesize contentView;
@synthesize adBannerView;
@synthesize altAdBannerButton;

- (void)viewDidLoad {
    [super viewDidLoad];

    // Check the current device's Internet connection
    // using Apple's Reachability classes. When the status
    // changes, a notification is posted, calling the
    // reachabilityChanged method.
    [[NSNotificationCenter defaultCenter] addObserver: self selector:
@selector(reachabilityChanged:) name: kReachabilityChangedNotification object: nil];
    netReachable = [[Reachability reachabilityWithHostName: @"www.apple.com"] retain];
    [netReachable startNotifier];
```

```objc
    // Configure and request an iAd banner.
    [self prepareAdBannerView];

    // Configure an alternate ad banner in the event
    // that an iAd banner is not available.
    [self prepareAltAdBanner];

    // Adjust the app UI to display the ad banner
    // view at the bottom of the screen.
    [self adjustAdBannerPosition:NO];
}

-(void)viewWillAppear:(BOOL)animated
{
    [super viewWillAppear:animated];
    [self adjustAdBannerPosition:NO];
}


- (void)willRotateToInterfaceOrientation:(UIInterfaceOrientation)toInterfaceOrientation
duration:(NSTimeInterval)duration {

    [self adjustAdBannerPosition:YES];
}

- (BOOL)shouldAutorotateToInterfaceOrientation:
                (UIInterfaceOrientation)interfaceOrientation {
    // Return YES to support both Portrait and Landscape orientations.
    return YES;
}

//Called by Reachability whenever status changes.
- (void) reachabilityChanged: (NSNotification* )note {

    NetworkStatus netStatus = [netReachable currentReachabilityStatus];
    switch (netStatus)
    {
        case NotReachable:
        {
            isNetAvailable = NO;
            break;
        }
        case ReachableViaWiFi:
        {
            isNetAvailable = YES;
            break;
        }
        case ReachableViaWWAN:
        {
            isNetAvailable = YES;
            break;
        }
    }
}

- (void)prepareAdBannerView {
```

```objc
    // This method creates and configures the iAd banner view offscreen.

    // Calculate the size of the banner view based on the device's current orientation.
    NSString *adBannerSize = UIInterfaceOrientationIsPortrait([UIDevice
currentDevice].orientation) ? ADBannerContentSizeIdentifierPortrait :
ADBannerContentSizeIdentifierLandscape;

    // Initially, this iAd banner view will be placed offscreen.
    // Once an ad is ready to be shown, then the ad banner view will be displayed.
    CGRect adFrame;
    adFrame.size = [ADBannerView sizeFromBannerContentSizeIdentifier:adBannerSize];
    adFrame.origin = CGPointMake(0.0, CGRectGetMaxY(self.view.bounds));

    // Create the iAd banner.
    ADBannerView *adBanner = [[ADBannerView alloc] initWithFrame:adFrame];

    // Set iAd banner's delegate to self, so that iAd notifications can be received.
    adBanner.delegate = self;

    // Inform the iAd network of the ad sizes the app supports
    // (in this case, both portrait and landscape).
    adBanner.requiredContentSizeIdentifiers = [NSSet
setWithObjects:ADBannerContentSizeIdentifierPortrait,
ADBannerContentSizeIdentifierLandscape, nil];

    // Add the iAd banner view to the parent view.
    // It is now requesting an ad from the iAd Network.
    [self.view addSubview:adBanner];
    self.adBannerView = adBanner;
    [adBanner release];
    [adBannerSize release];
}

- (void)prepareAltAdBanner {
    // This method creates and configures a custom house ad banner offscreen
    // in the event that an iAd banner is not available. But the code below could
    // be easily replaced to show an ad from another ad network like AdMob.

    // Create the alternate ad banner based on the device's current orientation.
    UIImage *altAdImg = [[[UIImage alloc] init] autorelease];
    NSString *adBannerImage = [[NSString alloc] init];
    if (UIInterfaceOrientationIsLandscape([UIDevice currentDevice].orientation)) {
        adBannerImage = @"adbannerlandscape-iphone.png";
    } else {
        adBannerImage = @"adbannerportrait-iphone.png";
    }
    altAdImg = [UIImage imageNamed:adBannerImage];

    UIButton *altButton = [[UIButton buttonWithType:UIButtonTypeCustom] autorelease];
    [altButton setBackgroundImage:altAdImg forState:UIControlStateNormal];
    [altButton addTarget:self action:@selector(tappedAltAdBanner)
forControlEvents:UIControlEventTouchUpInside];
    self.altAdBannerButton = altButton;
```

```
        // Initially, this ad banner will be placed offscreen.
        // Once the ad is ready to be shown, then the ad banner will be displayed.
        CGRect adFrame = CGRectMake(0.0, CGRectGetMaxY(self.view.bounds),
    altAdImg.size.width, altAdImg.size.height);
        self.altAdBannerButton.frame = adFrame;

        // Add the alternate ad banner to the parent view.
        [self.view addSubview:self.altAdBannerButton];
        [adBannerImage release];
    }

    - (void)tappedAltAdBanner {
        // The user has tapped the alternate ad banner, so perform an action.
        // For this simple example, the alternate ad banner links to a URL.
        NSURL *url = [NSURL URLWithString:@"http://www.iPhoneBusinessBook.com/"];
        [[UIApplication sharedApplication] openURL:url];
    }

    - (void)adjustAdBannerPosition:(BOOL)animated {
        // Set up some initial properties for calculating positions and animation.
        CGFloat animationDuration = animated ? 0.3 : 0.0;
        CGRect viewFrame = self.view.bounds;
        CGFloat iAdPosition = self.view.frame.size.height;
        CGFloat iAdHeight = 0.0;
        CGFloat altAdPosition = self.view.frame.size.height;
        CGFloat altAdWidth = 0.0;
        CGFloat altAdHeight = 0.0;
        UIImage *altAdImage = [[[UIImage alloc] init] autorelease];

        if (UIInterfaceOrientationIsLandscape([UIDevice currentDevice].orientation)) {
            // Landscape iPhone Height: 320 - 20 pixel status bar = 300.
            adBannerView.currentContentSizeIdentifier =
    ADBannerContentSizeIdentifierLandscape;
            iAdPosition = 300.0;
            // Landscape iAd Banner Size: 480 width, 32 height.
            iAdHeight = adBannerView.frame.size.height;
            altAdImage = [UIImage imageNamed:@"adbannerlandscape-iphone.png"];
            altAdPosition = 300.0;
        } else {
            // Portrait iPhone Height: 480 - 20 pixel status bar = 460.
            adBannerView.currentContentSizeIdentifier =
    ADBannerContentSizeIdentifierPortrait;
            iAdPosition = 460.0;
            // Portrait iAd Banner Size: 320 width, 50 height.
            iAdHeight = adBannerView.frame.size.height;
            altAdImage = [UIImage imageNamed:@"adbannerportrait-iphone.png"];
            altAdPosition = 460.0;
        }
        [altAdBannerButton setBackgroundImage:altAdImage forState:UIControlStateNormal];
        altAdWidth = altAdImage.size.width;
        altAdHeight = altAdImage.size.height;

        // Check status of Internet connection to decide whether or not to show an ad.
        if (isNetAvailable) {
```

```objectivec
        // YES, Internet connection is available, so show ad banner.

        if (adBannerView.bannerLoaded) {
            // An iAd was successfully loaded into the ad banner,
            // so slide it into view. Also resize contentView height
            // to make room for the ad banner at the bottom.

            // Adjust height for contentView above iAd banner.
            viewFrame.size.height -= iAdHeight;

            // Since alternate ad banner is not being used,
            // adjust its position offscreen.
            altAdPosition += altAdHeight;

            // Now adjust onscreen position for iAd banner.
            iAdPosition -= iAdHeight;

        } else {
            // iAd not available or an error occurred,
            // so show alternate ad banner instead.
            // For this example, a custom house ad is shown,
            // but the code below could be easily replaced to
            // show an ad from another ad network like AdMob.

            // Adjust height for contentView above alternative ad banner.
            viewFrame.size.height -= altAdHeight;

            // Since iAd is not being used, adjust iAd position offscreen.
            iAdPosition += iAdHeight;

            // Now adjust onscreen position for alternate ad banner.
            altAdPosition -= altAdHeight;
        }

    } else {
        // NO, Internet connection is NOT available, so hide ad banner.

        // Move both banner views offscreen.
        iAdPosition += iAdHeight;
        altAdPosition += altAdHeight;
    }

    // Slide the requested ad banner into view,
    // and move the other ad banner view offscreen.
    [UIView animateWithDuration:animationDuration animations:^{
        contentView.frame = viewFrame;
        [contentView layoutIfNeeded];
        adBannerView.frame = CGRectMake(0.0, iAdPosition, adBannerView.frame.size.width,
adBannerView.frame.size.height);
        altAdBannerButton.frame = CGRectMake(0.0, altAdPosition, altAdWidth,
altAdHeight);
    }];
}
```

```objc
// As an ADBannerViewDelegate, this class will receive messages from the
// iAd framework, notifying your app if an iAd banner was loaded or not.
#pragma mark ADBannerViewDelegate methods

- (void)bannerViewDidLoadAd:(ADBannerView *)banner {

    [self adjustAdBannerPosition:YES];
}

- (void)bannerView:(ADBannerView *)banner didFailToReceiveAdWithError:(NSError *)error {

    [self adjustAdBannerPosition:YES];
}

- (BOOL)bannerViewActionShouldBegin:(ADBannerView *)banner
willLeaveApplication:(BOOL)willLeave {
    return YES;
}

- (void)bannerViewActionDidFinish:(ADBannerView *)banner {
}
// End of the ADBannerViewDelegate methods

- (void)didReceiveMemoryWarning {
    [super didReceiveMemoryWarning];
}

- (void)viewDidUnload {
    self.contentView = nil;
    adBannerView.delegate = nil;
    self.adBannerView = nil;
    [super viewDidUnload];
}

- (void)dealloc {
    [contentView release];
    adBannerView.delegate = nil;
    [adBannerView release];
    [altAdBannerButton release];
    [[NSNotificationCenter defaultCenter] removeObserver:self];
    [super dealloc];
}
```

@end

I sprinkled helpful comments through that code, so after a quick read through of *MainViewController_iPhone.m*, you might already have a good understanding of the concepts at work here. But for the sake of being thorough, let's step through it and look at how each piece operates.

Beyond synthesizing and releasing the ad-related properties in the appropriate sections, you'll notice that the viewDidLoad event calls prepareAdBannerView, prepareAltAdBanner, and adjustAdBannerPosition, so let's start with those methods.

The `prepareAdBannerView` method creates a new instance of `ADBannerView`, sets its ad frame size based on the device's current orientation, and then sends an iAd request to the iAd Network. Initially, this iAd banner frame is placed off the screen. When an iAd banner has been successfully received from the iAd Network, only then will the iAd banner frame be displayed on the screen. Moving the iAd into view is done in the `adjustAdBannerPosition` method.

So how does your app know when an iAd banner is available to display? As an `ADBannerViewDelegate`, this class receives messages from the iAd Network after the `prepareAdBannerView` method sends the request. When an iAd Network reply is received, the `bannerView:didFailToReceiveAdWithError:` event fires. If an iAd banner cannot be loaded, then the Boolean `ADBannerView.bannerLoaded` is set to NO. If an iAd is successfully loaded, then that Boolean is set to YES. When the received iAd is finished loading into the `ADBannerView` frame, the `bannerViewDidLoadAd` event is fired. When either the `bannerView:didFailToReceiveAdWithError:` or bannerViewDidLoadAd events fire, the `adjustAdBannerPosition` method should be called, regardless of whether there is an iAd to display.

Just in case the iAd Network is unable to provide an iAd, this example project includes a backup plan to show a house ad instead. The `prepareAltAdBanner` method creates a new instance of an image-based `UIButton` to show the alternate house ad in the event that iAd is unavailable. This `UIButton` is configured and placed off-screen until it is needed. Of course, if you would rather use a third-party ad banner as a fallback option instead of a house ad, you could easily customize this method with your own code that requests and configures an advertisement from another ad network, like AdMob or InMobi.

The `adjustAdBannerPosition` method does all the heavy lifting of moving the appropriate ad banner onto the screen and resizing the existing UI elements to accommodate the ad banner frame. It is also responsible for removing the ad banner and reverting the app's UI to its normal, full-screen state if network connectivity is lost. This transition of sliding the ad banner in and out of view is achieved using `UIView` animation (see Figure 7–13).

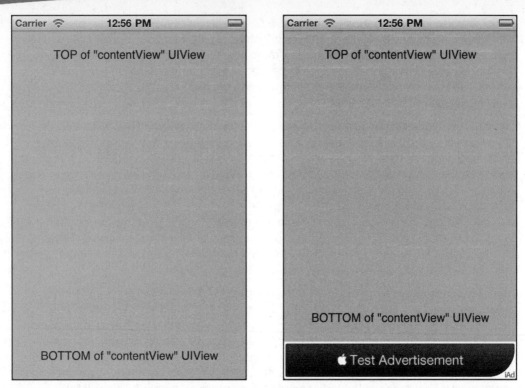

Figure 7–13. *Using UIView animation, the adjustAdBannerPosition method is responsible for sliding the ad banner in and out of view and adjusting the rest of the app's UI as needed.*

The `adjustAdBannerPosition` method configures and juggles the placement of the iAd banner frame and the house ad `UIButton`. If an iAd is available, then the iAd banner frame is assigned a pixel position on the screen, and the house ad is given an off-screen position. And if there's no iAd to display, the opposite occurs, with the house ad receiving on-screen placement, and the iAd banner frame being relegated to off-screen coordinates (see Figure 7–14). If the device loses network connectivity, then both the iAd banner frame and the house ad `UIButton` are given off-screen pixel positions.

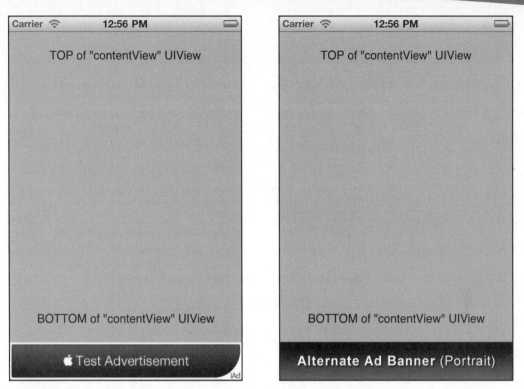

Figure 7–14. *If an iAd is available, then it is displayed on the screen. In the absence of an iAd banner, the alternate house ad is shown instead.*

To ensure that the displayed ad banner and the affected UI elements are properly positioned (with the correct ad size) when the device's orientation is changed, you need to also add the native Cocoa Touch events viewWillAppear and willRotateToInterfaceOrientation to the *MainViewController_iPhone.m* code. When either of those events fire, the adjustAdBannerPosition method should always be called.

If an iAd banner is tapped, the iAd modal view advertisement is displayed, taking over the screen (with the host app idling in the background until the iAd is dismissed). But when the alternate house ad is displayed, what happens when a user taps that banner? As a UIButton, its action selector is set to call the tappedAltAdBanner method. Right now, the example code within that method launches http://www.iPhoneBusinessBook.com/ in Mobile Safari, but you could easily replace that code with a custom action of your choice.

To complete this project, don't forget to add the new code from *MainViewController_iPhone.m* to its iPad companion, *MainViewController_iPad.m*. All of the new code should be identical, with the exception of the prepareAltAdBanner and adjustAdBannerPosition methods, which both contain iPad-specific code, as follows:

```
- (void)prepareAltAdBanner {
    // This method creates and configures a custom house ad banner offscreen
    // in the event that an iAd banner is not available. But the code below could
```

```
    // be easily replaced to show an ad from another ad network like AdMob.

    // Create the alternate ad banner based on the device's current orientation.
    UIImage *altAdImg = [[[UIImage alloc] init] autorelease];
    NSString *adBannerImage = [[NSString alloc] init];
    if (UIInterfaceOrientationIsLandscape([UIDevice currentDevice].orientation)) {
        adBannerImage = @"adbannerlandscape-ipad.png";
    } else {
        adBannerImage = @"adbannerportrait-ipad.png";
    }
    altAdImg = [UIImage imageNamed:adBannerImage];

    UIButton *altButton = [[UIButton buttonWithType:UIButtonTypeCustom] autorelease];
    [altButton setBackgroundImage:altAdImg forState:UIControlStateNormal];
    [altButton addTarget:self action:@selector(tappedAltAdBanner)
forControlEvents:UIControlEventTouchUpInside];
    self.altAdBannerButton = altButton;

    // Initially, this ad banner will be placed offscreen.
    // Once the ad is ready to be shown, then the ad banner will be displayed.
    CGRect adFrame = CGRectMake(0.0, CGRectGetMaxY(self.view.bounds),
altAdImg.size.width, altAdImg.size.height);
    self.altAdBannerButton.frame = adFrame;

    // Add the alternate ad banner to the parent view.
    [self.view addSubview:self.altAdBannerButton];
    [adBannerImage release];
}

- (void)adjustAdBannerPosition:(BOOL)animated {
    // Set up some initial properties for calculating positions and animation.
    CGFloat animationDuration = animated ? 0.3 : 0.0;
    CGRect viewFrame = self.view.bounds;
    CGFloat iAdPosition = self.view.frame.size.height;
    CGFloat iAdHeight = 0.0;
    CGFloat altAdPosition = self.view.frame.size.height;
    CGFloat altAdWidth = 0.0;
    CGFloat altAdHeight = 0.0;
    UIImage *altAdImage = [[[UIImage alloc] init] autorelease];

    if (UIInterfaceOrientationIsLandscape([UIDevice currentDevice].orientation)) {
        // Landscape iPad Height: 768 - 20 pixel status bar = 748.
        adBannerView.currentContentSizeIdentifier =
ADBannerContentSizeIdentifierLandscape;
        iAdPosition = 748.0;
        // Landscape iAd Banner Size: 1024 width, 66 height.
        iAdHeight = adBannerView.frame.size.height;
        altAdImage = [UIImage imageNamed:@"adbannerlandscape-ipad.png"];
        altAdPosition = 748.0;
    } else {
        // Portrait iPad Height: 1024 - 20 pixel status bar = 1004.
        adBannerView.currentContentSizeIdentifier =
ADBannerContentSizeIdentifierPortrait;
        iAdPosition = 1004.0;
        // Portrait iAd Banner Size: 768 width, 66 height.
        iAdHeight = adBannerView.frame.size.height;
        altAdImage = [UIImage imageNamed:@"adbannerportrait-ipad.png"];
```

```
        altAdPosition = 1004.0;
    }
    [altAdBannerButton setBackgroundImage:altAdImage forState:UIControlStateNormal];
    altAdWidth = altAdImage.size.width;
    altAdHeight = altAdImage.size.height;

    // Check status of Internet connection to decide whether or not to show an ad.
    if (isNetAvailable) {
        // YES, Internet connection is available, so show ad banner.

        if (adBannerView.bannerLoaded) {
            // An iAd was successfully loaded into the ad banner,
            // so slide it into view. Also resize contentView height
            // to make room for the ad banner at the bottom.

            // Adjust height for contentView above iAd banner.
            viewFrame.size.height -= iAdHeight;

            // Since alternate ad banner is not being used,
            // adjust its position offscreen.
            altAdPosition += altAdHeight;

            // Now adjust onscreen position for iAd banner.
            iAdPosition -= iAdHeight;

        } else {
            // iAd not available or an error occurred,
            // so show alternate ad banner instead.
            // For this example, a custom house ad is shown,
            // but the code below could be easily replaced to
            // show an ad from another ad network like AdMob.

            // Adjust height for contentView above alternative ad banner.
            viewFrame.size.height -= altAdHeight;

            // Since iAd is not being used, adjust iAd position offscreen.
            iAdPosition += iAdHeight;

            // Now adjust onscreen position for alternate ad banner.
            altAdPosition -= altAdHeight;
        }

    } else {
        // NO, Internet connection is NOT available, so hide ad banner.

        // Move both banner views offscreen.
        iAdPosition += iAdHeight;
        altAdPosition += altAdHeight;
    }

    // Slide the requested ad banner into view,
    // and move the other ad banner view offscreen.
    [UIView animateWithDuration:animationDuration animations:^{
        contentView.frame = viewFrame;
        [contentView layoutIfNeeded];
        adBannerView.frame = CGRectMake(0.0, iAdPosition, adBannerView.frame.size.width,
adBannerView.frame.size.height);
```

```
        altAdBannerButton.frame = CGRectMake(0.0, altAdPosition, altAdWidth,
altAdHeight);
    }];
}
```

The difference here is that these two methods have been customized with iPad-specific ad banner sizes and screen coordinates to fit the larger dimensions of the tablet's display (see Figure 7–15).

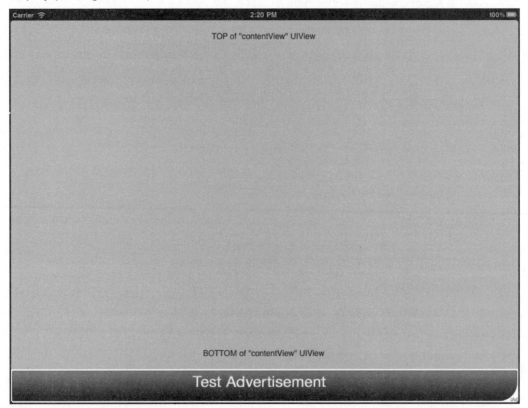

Figure 7–15. *The iPad target requires modified prepareAltAdBanner and adjustAdBannerPosition methods to accommodate iPad-specific ad sizes and placement.*

NOTE: Experienced iOS developers may find the similarities between the iPhone and iPad code fairly repetitive. I'll be the first to admit that much of the code could be refactored for sharing between the two targets to reduce the redundancy. But there really is a method to my madness. The book's readers are a very diverse bunch, ranging from entry-level beginners to advanced programmers. By leaving all of the related code in one place for each target, this approach makes it much easier for readers to follow the code and quickly learn how the project works, regardless of skill level.

If you run into any snags incorporating this example code into your own app projects, or if you need to build a more advanced solution, check out Apple's extensive iAd documentation available online at the iOS Dev Center:

- *iAd Programming Guide*
  (http://developer.apple.com/library/ios/#documentation/UserExpe
  rience/Conceptual/iAd_Guide/)

- *iAd Framework Reference*
  (http://developer.apple.com/library/ios/#documentation/UserExpe
  rience/Reference/iAd_ReferenceCollection/)

Enabling Live Ads in Your App

Before submitting your app to the App Store, Optime Software's Jon Schlegel offers some sound advice: "Don't forget to disable the 'test ad' mode before you go live in the App Store. I know several developers who have forgotten to do that and have lost quite a bit of money as a result [from displaying test ads that don't earn revenue]. We trigger a compiler warning in all of our apps when the 'test ad' mode is enabled to make sure that we don't go live with the test ads."

If you're using third-party ad networks such as AdMob, be sure to check their respective SDK documentation for instructions on how to disable the test ad mode (if applicable) before publishing your app in the App Store.

For iAd, activating live ad banners within your app requires a few steps in iTunes Connect. You'll need to first upload your app to iTunes Connect, and then within the Manage Your Applications section of the online portal, enable iAd for that application listing. Once your app is available in the App Store, you'll be able to monitor and track your iAd performance and revenue via the iAd Network module in iTunes Connect.

Knowledge Is Power: Tracking App Usage Through Analytics

Any successful web developer understands the immense value of tracking web site traffic statistics with tools like Google Analytics. Mobile applications are no different. Knowing as much as possible about your users' demographics and their usage patterns will help you to make better development and marketing decisions. How much time do they spend using your app? Which features are popular, and which ones are rarely accessed? Having this kind of knowledge at your fingertips will empower you with the ability to improve your app's user experience and sales potential.

In 2010, Apple revised its policy on in-app analytics, prohibiting apps from collecting and sending device-related data to a third party (such as an analytics service). Apple still allows in-app analytics, but only if the transmitted data is directly relevant to in-app advertising or the use of the app. Because of this major policy change, it appears the only analytics services that remain compliant are the ones integrated with some kind of in-app advertising solution.

Here are a few analytics services to consider:

- Flurry (http://www.flurry.com/)

- Mobclix (http://www.mobclix.com/)

- Medialets Analytics (http://www.medialets.com/)

Mobclix and Medialets both offer mobile advertising solutions, so if you currently use one of those companies for in-app advertising, you also benefit from the comprehensive app analytics features that are integrated into their respective SDKs. Flurry provides an innovative AppCircle advertising option for app recommendations and cross-promotions as part of its popular analytics SDK to comply with Apple's terms.

Even though in-app analytics services collect anonymous, aggregated data, consumers are becoming more and more protective of their privacy. If you do plan on integrating analytics into your app, I recommend that you let users know up-front what kind of information you're collecting, and give them a convenient in-app method to opt out. The popular ad-supported, free app, AroundMe, provides this courtesy (see Figure 7–16).

Figure 7–16. *AroundMe notifies users of analytics data that the free, ad-supported app collects and provides a convenient, in-app method to opt out.*

Even with Apple's restrictions, acceptable in-app analytics are still being approved in the App Store, so don't let this shift in policy deter you from exploring how analytics can improve your own development efforts. Thousands of apps in the App Store still actively employ in-app analytics.

Take the time to plan an effective analytics strategy that not only provides you with valuable app usage data, but also gives you the peace of mind that your app complies with Apple's terms and satisfies consumer privacy needs.

Contemplating Sponsorships and Product Placement Deals

Similar to in-app advertising, sponsorships and product placement offer an innovative way to monetize a free lite version, but they're typically more tightly integrated within the app than traditional advertising. This provides a much more elegant solution for users, while enabling the sponsor to directly connect with a very targeted audience. Since the sponsor would be eager to promote its affiliation with the app, the added marketing support can help reinvigorate interest in an existing app, bringing a flood of new users that you can later up-sell additional paid content and other apps.

Firemint's Real Racing is one of the most popular racing games in the App Store. Possibly for fear of cannibalizing sales of the paid version, the developers initially opted not to release a free lite app. But that soon changed. By partnering with Volkswagen, Firemint was able to offer a free Real Racing GTI version in the App Store. Real Racing GTI features the same game engine as the original Real Racing app, but all the race cars are the new 2010 Volkswagen GTI models. Even the sponsor stickers and track billboards are Volkswagen ads (see Figure 7–17). The game also includes a virtual showroom, providing a closer look at the GTI.

Figure 7–17. *Firemint's free Real Racing GTI game features 2010 Volkswagen GTI race cars and sponsored billboards on the racetrack.*

With this sponsored product placement deal, Volkswagen can promote its 2010 GTI to this highly targeted audience, and Firemint now has a way to monetize the free lite version. With the free Real Racing GTI game available to a greater number of users, it also presents Firemint with a much bigger audience to up-sell the additional features in the paid version of Real Racing and its sequel, Real Racing 2.

Even the app icon for Real Racing was customized to better promote the sponsored version. Not only does the altered app icon help differentiate the free version from the original paid game, but it's also an important visual element within the App Store that helps reinforce the sponsor's brand (see Figure 7–18).

Figure 7–18. *The custom app icon (right) helps differentiate the free version from the original paid game (left) and serves as an important visual element within the App Store that reinforces the sponsor's brand.*

As evident by the success of Real Racing GTI, partnering with a sponsor can breathe new life into an existing app, extending its reach to a much larger audience with a free version. In fact, this approach proved so popular that Firemint expanded the concept in the paid sequel. Real Racing 2 features 30 officially licensed cars that you can race in the game, including BMW, Chevrolet, Ford, Jaguar, Lotus, and several other brands.

Obviously, these kinds of sponsorship deals are not appropriate for all apps. For example, if your iOS app is a mobile guide to the latest movies and local theaters, then recruiting Warner Bros. as the exclusive sponsor would present a conflict of interest when listing new movies from other studios such as Universal and Paramount. And if your app's subject matter is too broad or your app does not currently reach enough people, you may have trouble finding an interested sponsor. Companies are in the business of selling more products, so a sponsorship proposal would be appealing only if your app can deliver a large audience in a very targeted market.

The Tipping Point

Whew! This was a long chapter, jam-packed with a *lot* of information to digest. But with the insatiable consumer demand for free apps, learning how to monetize your development efforts with mobile advertising is time well spent. Ready for more?

Where once traditional app sales and in-app advertising were the dominant business models for iOS developers, In-App Purchase is fast becoming one of the top-grossing revenue streams in the App Store, especially for free apps and games. Chapter 8 shows you why and explains how to tap into the power of In-App Purchase.

Exploring the Freemium Model with In-App Purchase

In-App Purchase was one of the more exciting and highly anticipated features introduced in iPhone SDK 3.0. The option to integrate e-commerce within both free and paid iOS apps opened up a new frontier for developers to create additional revenue opportunities beyond just traditional app sales. In-App Purchase enables you to sell subscriptions, services, virtual goods, and add-on content, such as premium features or additional game levels—all within your app.

With average app prices being so low and coming with free updates, it's important for you to embrace new business models to better monetize continued development costs. It's time to get creative! In this chapter, we'll explore how to take advantage of the power of In-App Purchase to help sustain your business for the long run.

Loyalty Pays: Existing Users Make the Best Customers

In the world of desktop software, customers who are happy using your application are more likely to purchase subsequent upgrades, especially if they use your product frequently. Their motivation to stay up-to-date with the latest version is usually driven by either satisfaction with the user experience or dependence on the unique features your software provides (or both, if you're lucky).

This is why Mac and Windows software developers spend so much time strengthening the relationship with their customers. Sure, finding new customers is crucial, but selling upgrades to existing customers is what supports continued development on a particular application. Developers can afford to offer products at low introductory rates (or even free) to entice new customers, knowing they will be able to sell additional upgrades to those users in the future. And beyond that, loyal customers who are already sold on the product quality are typically more inclined to buy other applications from you than new users who are unfamiliar with your offerings.

Up-selling new products and upgrades is the lifeblood of the desktop software industry. Developers are already translating this model to mobile platforms on a smaller scale. Microtransactions are the key to the mobile economy. But the App Store has its own unique buying culture combined with strict app guidelines, both of which introduce a new set of challenges that iOS developers must overcome to sustain a long-term business.

Supporting the Long Tail: Monetizing Continued Development

The App Store is no stranger to "the long tail," a concept described by acclaimed author Chris Anderson. New products experience an initial sales spike, and then, after they've plateaued or reached saturation, their sales gradually drop off. This eventual downward slide of sales, or the *long tail* (as it looks on a graph), is where app developers start to scramble to figure out ways to increase sales or find alternative methods to monetize app development.

Because of how the App Store was initially set up, once a user purchased an app, any updates were required to be free. Unlike traditional desktop software, there was no way to charge existing iOS app customers for an upgraded version. This was a great value for users, especially if the app cost only 99 cents. But it was financially difficult for developers, who were expected to frequently update their apps without a way to fund those development efforts.

Some game developers worked around this limitation by releasing new versions as completely separate apps. As a follow-up to its successful Real Racing game, Firemint spent a lot of time and money developing version 2. Rather than releasing it as a free update, Firemint made the wise decision to launch Real Racing 2 as a separate stand-alone app, enabling the company to charge a fee for this worthy sequel.

For games, the separate app strategy is much easier for consumers to accept, since that has been the standard practice for years on other gaming platforms, such as Xbox and PlayStation. For other types of applications, such as productivity apps, existing customers are used to either receiving free updates or discounted upgrade pricing on Mac and Windows software, so they often expect a similar path to be offered for mobile apps, too. With no App Store option for paid upgrades, iOS developers are limited to two buying mechanisms to pay for new features or additional content: traditional app sales and In-App Purchase.

In the case of Bolt Creative's wildly popular Pocket God game, a big factor in its early success was the near weekly free updates of new game play the company delivered to customers. Each new episode included a massive amount of fresh content, which not only helped attract new customers, but also sustained user engagement with every updated adventure. At only 99 cents (which includes all released episodes), it remains one of the best values in the App Store.

But frequent updates packed full of new content and hours of game play can become quite costly to produce. With so many new games flooding the App Store, unless your game is a perennial best seller like Angry Birds or Pocket God, it would be difficult to deliver enough of a sales spike with each new update to financially support the same, consistent level of accelerated development indefinitely.

Even though Pocket God continues to sell very well, in order to better support the product's ongoing development costs, Bolt Creative began offering In-App Purchases of skin packs and other add-on items. With Pocket God's customers accustomed to receiving so much new content for free, Bolt Creative's Dave Castlenuovo admitted that the primary challenge in introducing In-App Purchase items was in properly communicating that the addition of microtransactions was not an act of greed, but merely the means to help subsidize the continued free updates of new episodes.

The Challenge of Changing User Perception

Since the App Store infrastructure has bred a shopping culture where iOS users expect to receive a lifetime of free updates for the apps they've purchased, shifting their mind-set to accept in-app microtransactions has taken a little longer than most developers anticipated. Streaming Colour Studios quickly discovered this with the launch of its first freemium game, LandFormer.

Released in June 2010, LandFormer received stellar reviews from the media, praising it for being an innovative and addicting puzzler. I'm not a big gamer myself, but it's easily one of my favorite iOS apps. It's a great example of a well-executed freemium strategy.

Streaming Colour Studios' founder, Owen Goss, remarked, "My other games [Dapple and Monkeys in Space] are both paid games, and Dapple has a separate lite version for people to 'try before they buy.' The thing I don't like about the lite model is that it requires players to download two separate apps if they then want to buy the game. It always felt kludgy to me."

Ultimately, Owen decided to release LandFormer as a free app that includes 12 levels. More than 70 additional levels are available via In-App Purchase (see Figure 8–1). To help build a community around the game, LandFormer also enables users to create and share their own levels.

Figure 8–1. *Streaming Colour Studios' LandFormer is a great example of a freemium app that enables users to play the first 12 levels for free, then buy additional levels and themes from the game's virtual shop via In-App Purchase.*

"This is a really exciting monetization path for several reasons," said Owen. "The in-game store allows me to continue releasing new level packs and themes without having to update the app binary itself. As a free game, it gets maximum visibility in the App Store with a lot more downloads. But with banner ads and In-App Purchase, I still have a way to earn some money. And the ads are disabled if the player buys any content from the in-game shop."

"However, it's not all rainbows and unicorns," added Owen. "One thing I was not at all prepared for was a backlash from users over the pricing model. I thought that players would be happy that they were given an opportunity to try the game before spending any money on it. Instead, the reaction from some players was, 'hey, a free game!' but then they're angry when they discover they can't play all the levels for free. My app description clearly states that you only get the beginner levels for free and have to buy the others. The app page in the App Store also lists the top In-App Purchase items. But what I learned is that no one reads that stuff."

In-App Purchase was launched back in mid-2009, but consumers were slow to acclimate to the concept of paying for new content within apps that they had already purchased or downloaded for free. Even a year later, new games like LandFormer and other freemium titles were still experiencing resistance from a percentage of users. But with the proliferation of so many exciting freemium apps in the second half of 2010, the tide was gradually turning, with a majority of iPhone, iPad, and iPod touch users finally embracing microtransactions with open arms.

Where once traditional app sales and in-app advertising were the dominant business models for iOS developers, In-App Purchase has become one of the biggest revenue streams in the App Store. In January 2011, the App Store-monitoring firm Distimo reported that almost 50 percent of the revenue from the top-grossing iPhone apps was now coming from In-App Purchase items!

Much of this evolution can be attributed to popular games such as FarmVille, We Rule Quests, Zombie Farm, and Pocket Frogs. These freemium apps are based on using virtual currency to further your progress in the game. Users quickly learn that in order to grow their farms, build their empires, or nurse their pets, they need to use game points to purchase crops, tools, food, and other required items in the virtual market (see Figure 8–2). These repeated trips to the in-game market conditions users to shop within the app. So, making the jump to purchasing other market items, like Mojo or magic potions, with real money becomes a small extra step (see Figure 8–3).

It's important that consumers never feel misled about what they're selecting. For example, We Rule Quests is careful to clearly display the currency type for every item in its virtual market, so that users can see if an item can be bought with digital points or with real money via In-App Purchase. As shown in Figure 8–3, in order to acquire Mojo, a real price is displayed, requiring an In-App Purchase transaction. Also, In-App Purchase items are categorized as "We Rule Store" products to visually set them apart from other virtual market items.

Figure 8–2. *ngmoco's We Rule Quests for iPad is a kingdom-building game that uses earned points to buy various items in the virtual market.*

Figure 8–3. *We Rule Quests informs users when virtual items like Mojo cost real money, requiring an In-App Purchase transaction (iPad version shown here).*

Even though microtransactions are now widely accepted by the App Store user community, developers may periodically encounter backlash from some customers who resent the à la carte pricing structure of In-App Purchase. Just remember they represent only a small percentage of your overall customer base. Typically, these are the same vocal minority of users who complain about needing to pay more than 99 cents for a full-featured game that would cost 50 times as much on Xbox or PlayStation. While it's important to keep as many customers satisfied as possible, these individuals are usually only happy with free. And unless you're independently wealthy, your business can't afford to give away *everything* for free.

A key factor to succeeding with In-App Purchase is offering exciting add-on items that users are eager to buy. If your app can effectively communicate the distinct difference between free updates to the core functionality versus the additional content available as In-App Purchase items, you may have a profitable business model that can sustain continued development.

With this in mind, it's never too early to look at ways your app could benefit from In-App Purchase. Loyalty pays! In the long run, even if your app eventually attracts fewer and fewer new customers, your satisfied users could continue to support you through In-App Purchases!

When and How to Use In-App Purchase

So, you're ready to tackle In-App Purchase in your application, but what can it be used for? Unlocking additional game content and new levels are obvious choices, but what if you're not developing a game? The best way to approach this is to take a good look at your app's current functionality and future road map of features to see whether In-App Purchase can help extend its product life span and sales potential.

In-App Purchase is a great way to generate additional revenue streams and support continued development, but it isn't suitable for every application. Don't try to force this functionality into your app if you don't have a good reason to do so. It should not be treated as a solution in search of a need. You certainly won't want to wear out your goodwill with loyal customers by "nickel and diming" them to death for core features they expected to get as part of the original purchase price.

Understanding the Fundamentals

In-App Purchases are categorized into four distinct product types: Non-consumable, Consumable, Auto-renewable Subscriptions, and Subscriptions. It's essential that you understand the differences between these product types because your choice affects how purchased items are handled within your app. Additionally, there are a few rules that you need to follow.

In-App Purchase Types

Here's a quick rundown of the four types of In-App Purchase product types:

- **Non-consumables**: Items that are purchased only once and should always remain available within the app on all devices associated with the customer's iTunes account. Typically Non-consumables are additional functionality or add-on content. So if it's a new game level that was purchased within a game on Johnny's iPhone, not only should that new level be persistent every time Johnny runs the game on his iPhone, but it should also be made available within the same game installed on Johnny's iPod touch. The Store Kit framework provides support for querying the App Store for purchased items so that your app can be programmed to restore those items on a specific device, even if it was initially purchased and installed on another device owned by the same customer. I'll talk more about this when we walk through an Xcode project example later in this chapter.

- **Consumables**: Items that can be used up or depleted and then purchased again multiple times. A good example of a Consumable item is weapon ammunition in a game. Once the customer depletes the stock of ammunition that was purchased, it cannot be retrieved again. To continue using that weapon, the customer needs to buy another round of ammunition. Because of the disposable quality of this type, Consumable items are not required to be available across all of a customer's related devices. If you plan to offer this type of In-App Purchase item, you should always state in very clear language within your app that once it's used up, it's gone, but a new one can be purchased.

- **Auto-renewable Subscriptions**: Items much like Non-consumables, except that they are assigned a limited duration. If the customer bought a 30-day subscription to a service within your app, when that term expires, the App Store automatically renews the subscription, billing the customer's iTunes account. Like Non-consumables, Auto-renewable Subscriptions must always be made available within the same app on all devices associated with the customer's iTunes account. So if Johnny has your app installed on both his iPhone and iPod touch, the subscription he purchased should be persistent within the app on both devices. The customer has the option to cancel future renewals, which deactivates the subscription after the current paid subscription period expires.

- **Subscriptions**: An older mechanism that predates the Auto-renewable Subscriptions product type. A limitation of this older Subscriptions type is that it does not currently support a duration term—there is no automatic renewal billing (although Subscriptions may be purchased multiple times. like Consumables). It's up to your app to self-monitor customer subscription expiration dates and renewal notifications. Due to this limitation, Apple recommends using Auto-renewable Subscriptions instead.

Cool, right? Did that give you any ideas for use within your own app?

Additional functionality is usually categorized as a Non-consumable. Add-on content— depending on whether it's a disposable item (ammunition, seeds, magic potions, and so on) or a permanent addition (such as new game levels)—may be a Consumable or a Non-consumable, respectively.

If you plan on unlocking services within your app—such as premium access to a web service, newspaper and magazine content, or a notification service—those are typically categorized as Auto-renewable Subscriptions. Alternatively, a service could be offered as a Non-consumable one-time In-App Purchase. But before going that route, make sure such a model would provide enough revenue to financially support the ongoing upkeep of that service.

In-App Purchase Guidelines

Before you start planning your next major masterpiece with In-App Purchase, you need to know about a few strict rules that you must follow:

- In-App Purchase items must be digital elements that can be delivered within your app. You cannot use In-App Purchase to sell physical products and services outside your app. For example, you can't use it to sell a printed book, but you can definitely sell an e-book, as long as it can be delivered within your app immediately after purchase confirmation.

- In-App Purchase items are not allowed to contain prohibited content, such as pornography or hate speech.

- In-App Purchase items cannot represent virtual currency, unless it's directly related to in-app game play, as seen in apps like Zombie Farm and We Rule Quests. If Apple feels your In-App Purchase items are not properly represented, confusing users as to which goods or services they are buying, your app may get rejected.

■ The Store Kit framework cannot be used to create trialware. As I mentioned in Chapter 6, In-App Purchase is not intended for unlocking previously crippled features, since Apple still prohibits iOS apps from presenting features as disabled. The current implementation of In-App Purchase enables developers to provide *additional* features that are not currently included in the app.

■ Most important, you cannot facilitate a complete payment transaction inside your app without using In-App Purchase. Implementing your own homemade version of In-App Purchase within your app is guaranteed to earn you a rejection notice from Apple's app review team.

The Power of Simplicity

The best part about In-App Purchase is that beyond the handful of guidelines, it does not impose any kind of predefined business model. The Store Kit framework that powers In-App Purchase is nothing more than a secure payment-collection gateway. It does not include a prefabricated storefront like the App Store, which gives you the ultimate creative flexibility to integrate In-App Purchase in any manner that best suits your app's current UI.

In-App Purchase's flexibility is especially helpful if your app offers only one In-App Purchase item. Displaying an entire store window to list only a single item is not an effective use of screen space. With only one or two In-App Purchase items, you can easily implement those buy buttons seamlessly into your existing UI. This may sound like it leaves a lot for you to program yourself, but truthfully, In-App Purchase requires a lot less code than you might think. We'll walk through the steps of adding In-App Purchase to an Xcode project later in this chapter.

Since all In-App Purchase transactions are done through the App Store, they retain the same business terms as those that apply to purchasing standard apps within the store. You, the developer, receive 70 percent of the In-App Purchase price, and Apple keeps 30 percent as a service fee. Although some developers may cringe at giving up 30 percent of In-App Purchases, you need to remember that not only does this cover credit-card fees, fraud protection, and refund-related chargeback fees, but it also provides an elegant microtransaction model in the secure, trusted environment of the App Store.

There's no need to maintain your own customer account management and e-commerce system. The Store Kit framework makes the transaction process seamless for your customers, enabling them to use their existing iTunes login account for a quick and painless purchase experience.

Every item that you want to sell via In-App Purchase needs to be configured in iTunes Connect as its own In-App Purchase product, similar to how standard iOS apps are submitted. Each In-App Purchase item is assigned to its related parent app so that the iTunes App Store knows the relationship between the products. Just like a regular app, each In-App Purchase item needs to be approved by Apple's app review team before it can be made available within your app. This entire setup process is described in detail later in this chapter.

Selling More Content

So, what does a typical In-App Purchase look like to the consumer? One of my favorite apps, Comics by ComiXology, serves as a great example. Comics is a free digital comics reader with an innovative viewing engine for easily reading comics on an iPhone or iPad screen. The app includes access to dozens of free digital comics from popular publishers, such as DC, Marvel, and Image Comics.

Most of the free comics are the first issues of popular series, providing a great entry point for new readers. Comics not only gives customers a lot of immediate value, but the free comics also get people hooked on various series. When they want more, In-App Purchase comes into play.

Within Comics is an easy-to-use store catalog of available comics, ranging from free to $1.99 each. All of the pay comics are configured in iTunes Connect as individual In-App Purchase items. If you decide to purchase a specific comic book issue, the App Store displays a default dialog box asking you to confirm your purchase request for this item (see Figure 8–4).

If you tap the dialog box's Buy button, you're asked to enter your iTunes login, just as with any other purchase through the iTunes Store. Once the login is confirmed, the secure transaction is completed using your existing iTunes account's billing information, and your purchased item immediately begins to download into the Comics app (see Figure 8–5). And that's it! No tedious order forms to contend with. It's a drop-dead simple purchase process, requiring only a few finger taps.

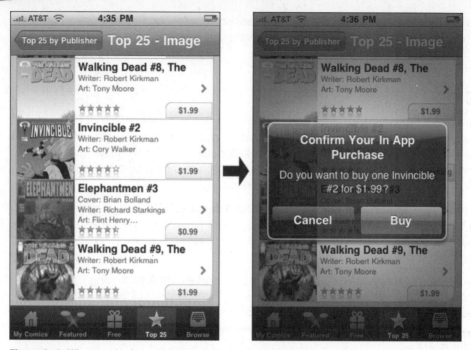

Figure 8–4. *When purchasing a digital comic book within the Comics app (left), the App Store displays a default dialog box requesting confirmation of your In-App Purchase request for this item (right).*

Figure 8–5. *After confirming your purchase and your iTunes login (left), the transaction is completed, and your purchased digital comic immediately begins to download into the Comics app (right).*

You probably noticed that the Comics catalog list looks similar to the App Store. But you can design your in-app storefront to emulate your own custom UI design. As you've seen in previous examples such as LandFormer and We Rule Quests, the Store Kit framework gives you complete flexibility to customize how those items are displayed within your app.

Most people assume that games and entertainment titles will be the dominant champions of In-App Purchase, since selling digital comics, e-books, new game levels, and other virtual-world components seems like such a natural fit for microtransactions. But the truth is that with a little creativity, In-App Purchase can be an effective revenue vehicle for almost any category genre—travel, lifestyle, productivity, and others. A case in point is *Men's Health Magazine*.

The *Men's Health Magazine's* fitness app, Men's Health Workouts, includes an extensive collection of workouts and exercises for an initial price of $1.99. But it also provides additional workout packs that can be purchased in-app (see Figure 8–6). There's a smart play here in that one free add-on workout is uploaded each month (accessible within the app), which not only encourages continued user engagement, but also helps promote the other add-ons available for sale. On top of that, the In-App Purchase items offered in Men's Health Workouts are presented in the same design theme as the rest of the app's custom interface, providing a seamless user experience.

Figure 8–6. *Not just for games! Apps like Men's Health Workouts prove that In-App Purchase can be just as powerful in other category genres. And the Store Kit framework gives you complete flexibility to customize how those items are displayed.*

Offering Services and Subscriptions

We've looked at several examples of downloadable content, but what about services and subscriptions? Simplenote is a great example of both, using an in-app subscription model for its annual Premium service. Beyond the basic note synchronization that's included free in Simplenote, the Premium service offers additional synchronizing features and enhanced support, and hides the in-app ads (see Figure 8–7).

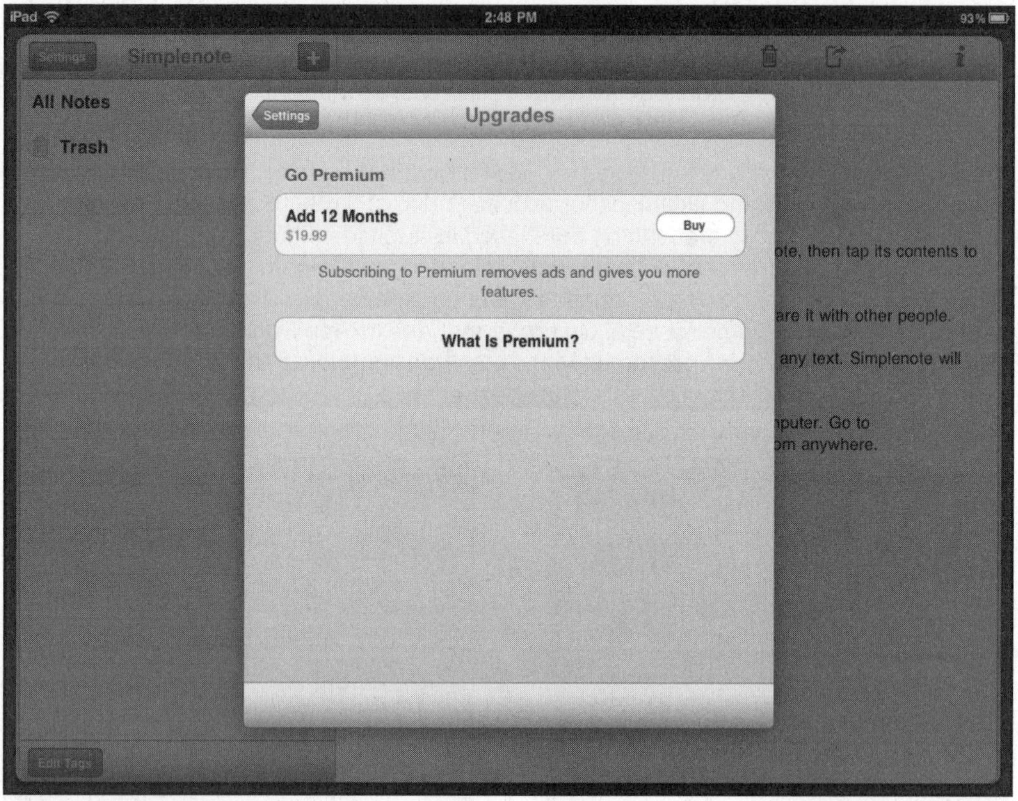

Figure 8–7. *The free note-syncing app, Simplenote (iPad version shown here), uses In-App Purchase to sell a subscription, encouraging users to upgrade to its annual Premium service.*

The one quibble I have with the otherwise excellent Simplenote is that the Upgrades screen (see Figure 8–7) does not include details on the specific benefits provided by the Premium service. For more information, you're forced to tap the What's in Premium? button, which jumps from the app to the Mobile Safari browser, loading a page on the Simplenote web site. Granted, Simplenote's note-synchronizing service is also available as a web-based application, as well as through numerous third-party apps, so directing all inquiries to a central Premium web page enables the developers to manage only one source of information for all the related apps. But how many Simplenote users actually take the time to tap that button?

Convenience is a big factor in impulse buys. Simplenote does well with its Premium service, but just think how many more subscription plans might be sold if the details of the Premium features were actually promoted right there on the Upgrades screen within the app.

Presentation Is the Key to Success

How do you get users to buy your In-App Purchase products? The same way you got them to buy your app in the first place: by offering an appealing package that they will want. Beyond creating great add-on content, you must communicate to your potential customers why they need to buy it.

Remember the promotional full version screens from the free lite app examples in Chapter 6? Since In-App Purchase items are essentially their own products, you'll want to devise a similar in-app sales pitch for them as well. Your visual presentation of these items is just as important as the presentation for promoting the parent app itself. Don't rely on only a single sentence or caption with a buy button. Users want to know exactly what they will receive by buying that In-App Purchase item. But that doesn't mean you should write long, verbose descriptions. Mobile users want quick answers, so brevity can be very effective, as long as the details provided are compelling.

Ramp Champ by The Iconfactory and DS Media Labs accomplishes this task quite nicely with a very straightforward approach that consumes very little screen real estate. Ramp Champ is a fun skee-ball-style game with several built-in themed ramps. Additional ramp packs are offered in the app's Add-ons section. Each add-on pack is listed in a very compact manner, allowing users to quickly scroll through the list of available items. The concise bullet points describe exactly what a buyer gets in each pack, along with visually enticing images from the included ramps (see Figure 8–8).

When crafting In-App Purchase item descriptions, you need to be very clear about what people will receive. Ambiguous descriptions often result in frustrated users. They may post negative customer reviews for your app, complaining that the purchased add-on item was not what they had expected. Communication is vital in preventing confusion.

Customers like knowing up front how much an item costs before tapping the buy button, so you should include pricing within your in-app storefront whenever possible. You can dynamically list the prices of available In-App Purchase items within your app, which is especially helpful when localizing your app across several regions. In fact, since the App Store localizes prices for different country currencies, Apple strongly discourages the inclusion of static prices.

Figure 8–8. *Ramp Champ notifies users when new add-on ramp packs are available (left). The concise bullet points and screenshots effectively describe exactly what a buyer would get in each add-on ramp pack (right).*

If you frequently release new In-App Purchase items for a game (such as additional levels), don't rely on your customers to check your game's virtual shop on a regular basis. When new add-on content becomes available for purchase, let your users know by displaying a `UIAlertView` or a custom notification upon launch, such as the one displayed by Ramp Champ in Figure 8–8.

Finding the Sweet Spot

Although your app's core functionality will be the primary attraction that brings in new customers, your In-App Purchase strategy will succeed only if you're offering enticing add-on content at a reasonable price that makes sense to consumers. Even though App Store shoppers are accustomed to getting full-featured games and apps for as low as 99 cents (or even free), it's perfectly all right if your In-App Purchase items are priced higher than the related parent app, as long as the inherent value is apparent to your customers.

Including the Right Mix of Ingredients

For a paid app, it's important to know which features your customers consider to be the app's primary draw. Those are the features that should be included in your app's price. Additional features that enhance the core offering are the ones better suited as potential In-App Purchase items. You don't want to charge an in-app fee for a feature that users believe should be part of the original app price—some core functionality that they thought they were getting right out of the box.

Networks In Motion ran into this problem when it first released its GPS navigation app, Gokivo, in 2009. At only 99 cents, it included a lot of features, such as Yahoo! Local Search, maps, traffic, and favorites. But to unlock the turn-by-turn, full GPS navigation service, an additional $9.99 monthly subscription fee via In-App Purchase was required. Consumers perceived the turn-by-turn GPS feature as core functionality that should be included with the app. Although the other features were nice, the turn-by-turn navigation service was the primary reason they bought the app in the first place. Upon discovering they needed to shell out another $9.99 a month to get the feature they assumed they had already purchased (regardless of the fact that the app was only 99 cents), many users felt duped.

Networks in Motion went to great lengths to explicitly clarify its pricing structure in the App Store description, but somehow the message was not getting through to some of its customers. Many people were not taking the time to thoroughly read the description before purchasing the app.

The company's eventual solution to the issue was to raise the price of the app to $9.99 and include a 30-day subscription to its turn-by-turn navigation service. This way, customers were able to access the core feature they wanted immediately after purchasing the app. After 30 days, they could renew their subscription for another month via In-App Purchase.

Even though we're talking about the same amount of money in both scenarios, the perception is vastly different. It comes down to the principle of the purchase and satisfying user expectations.

Heading into 2011, Networks in Motion revamped its business model even further. To remain competitive in the saturated navigation market, Gokivo GPS Navigator was made available as a free iPhone app, and it still includes a 30-day subscription to the turn-by-turn navigation service. As a free download, this gets the app into many more hands and gives users a chance to try out the app and become reliant on the service. The options are to renew the subscription via In-App Purchase for only $4.99 a month or $39.99 a year.

Allowing Users to Spend As Much Money As They Want

Snappy Touch's Noel Llopis is no stranger to In-App Purchase. His popular universal app, Flower Garden, lets users grow and nurture digital flowers and send virtual bouquets to friends. This app was a perfect fit for offering consumable add-ons such as extra fertilizer and seed packs (see Figure 8–9). With the in-app Flower Shop included in both the paid and free versions, it's no surprise that most of Flower Garden's revenue comes from In-App Purchases. In fact, paid app sales make up only 17 percent of Flower Garden's revenue; the rest is driven by In-App Purchase sales.

Figure 8–9. *Snappy Touch's Flower Garden offers multiple fertilizer bundles in its in-app Flower Shop, giving users a choice as to how much money they wish to spend.*

Upon seeing how games like FarmVille and We Rule Quests were finding success in selling tiered bundles of consumable items, Noel began wondering if he was underestimating what players were willing to spend by offering only one 99-cent fertilizer option in Flower Garden. He was surprised to find the App Store's top-selling In-App Purchases for many of these popular games were never 99-cent ones. People were spending $4.99 and up for weapons, ammunition, bottles of Mojo, magic potions, farm coins, and other virtual currencies. Some of the top-ranking In-App Purchase items were priced as high as $29.99, $49.99, and even $99.99.

"I decided to run a little experiment by adding two more fertilizer options to Flower Garden: 80 doses of fertilizer for $2.99 and 200 doses of fertilizer for $5.99," said Noel. "Each bundle gives you a slightly better deal on fertilizer. That was still nothing compared to the price tags I was seeing in those other games, but I didn't want to alienate users by slapping on some ridiculously high bundle prices."

The result? Based on the number of sales, the most popular In-App Purchase item was still the 99-cent fertilizer option, but a lot of customers *did* take advantage of the other two fertilizer bundles as well.

Even if you don't sell as many of the higher-priced items, they can still represent a large percentage of your overall revenue. Noel's bundle experiment was a success. In-App Purchases of fertilizer alone now account for a staggering 45 percent of Flower Garden's total revenue.

After adding multiple fertilizer bundles to the growing collection of seed pack offerings, Noel discovered that the top Flower Garden users were spending more than $100 in the game.

If the In-App Purchase items provide ample value for the money and a user continues to enjoy the game, there's no limit to the amount of money that customer may spend.

Noel points to two very good reasons why bundles are great for consumable In-App Purchases: choice and commitment. He explains, "Having different levels of bundles give players more choice on how they want to purchase something. And whenever a user buys a larger bundle, they became more committed to your game. They will continue to keep playing to get their money's worth from that purchase. Even if they had the intention of coming back to your game without the purchase, having spent that money is a nice reminder to do so. And having people come back to your game is what this is all about. They will explore more of the game, get more hooked, make more In-App Purchases, and show it to more of their friends."

Delivering and Managing In-App Purchases

In-app purchased content can be built into your application and then unlocked after purchase, or it can be downloaded from a remote server. Which method you choose will depend on what kind of content you're delivering and the extensibility your app requires.

Unlocking Built-in Content

Unlocking built-in content is by far the easiest route, requiring far fewer steps that can all be completed from within your app. There's no need to maintain a server, and you don't need to worry about security issues when communicating between your app and server. Just a few interactions with the App Store, and then purchased content is unlocked from within your app (see Figure 8–10).

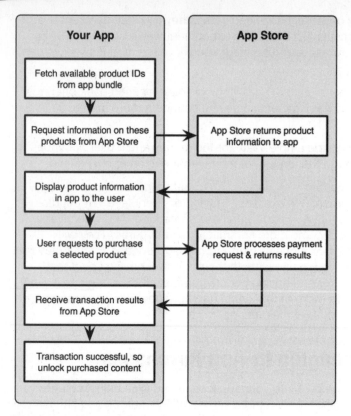

Figure 8–10. *The built-in In-App Purchase delivery model*

If you're new to iOS development, the process illustrated in Figure 8–10 may appear quite daunting, but it's actually not that complicated. True, there are several steps involved in configuring your app to use In-App Purchase, but not to worry. Later in this chapter, I'll walk you through the entire setup process and the creation of a basic Xcode project, so that you can see exactly how all of these pieces fit together.

Using this built-in model requires all your related In-App Purchase content to already be embedded in the app, hidden away from users. When a customer purchases a particular item, your app simply unlocks access to it. This works great for providing integrated content such as new levels in a game or additional features in a productivity app, or for activating subscription-based functionality.

Store Kit does not support any way to "patch" your app binary with a downloaded update from a remote server. If your app requires the purchased content to be integrated within the app bundle, you should include it in your application before submitting it to the App Store. Then after a customer purchase, your app can simply unlock this content.

The easiest way for your app to record and remember unlocked content is to store the information in your app's preferences, which are backed up when users sync their devices with their computer via iTunes. Having the app's preferences backed up will help prevent purchases from being lost, even if the app is deleted on a user's device. Your app needs to remember which items have already been purchased, so that the next time the user runs your app, the purchased content is still readily accessible.

The one major drawback to using this built-in unlocking model is that if you decide to make additional In-App Purchase items available in the future, you'll need to submit a new, updated application binary that includes the new content to the App Store.

Downloading Content from Your Server

If you're constantly adding new In-App Purchase items for your application, using the server download approach is the recommended route. This requires quite a few more steps and saddles you with a lot of server management responsibilities, but it provides the most flexibility and future growth possibilities for your app (see Figure 8–11).

The Comics app by ComiXology (showcased earlier in this chapter) is a perfect example of this model. The app fetches the latest list of product IDs for available digital comics from the server. When a user purchases a specific digital comic book, the app downloads the file from the server. The app can open and view any selected digital comic file from the user's downloaded collection of purchased issues.

This approach enables new digital comics to be made available every week as In-App Purchase items, without requiring any updates to the actual Comics application. New In-App Purchase items are submitted for review through iTunes Connect. When they are approved, ComiXology simply adds their product IDs to the database on its server. Then the next time the Comics app checks for new items, it retrieves the latest list of new digital comics from the server.

You cannot patch your app binary with a downloaded app update from a remote server. If your app requires the purchased content to be integrated within the app bundle, then delivering purchased content from your server is not the appropriate path. You'll need to use the built-in model of embedding the content in your application before submitting it to the App Store. Then after a customer purchase, your app can simply unlock this content.

And what if you plan on delivering the same content to more than just iOS users? The server-based model is recommended if you allow customers to access their purchased content on multiple platforms, such as via the iPhone, an Android phone, a web browser, and so on. This way, all of the content and customer records can be easily managed in one central location (such as a database on your server), with all supported devices connecting to it.

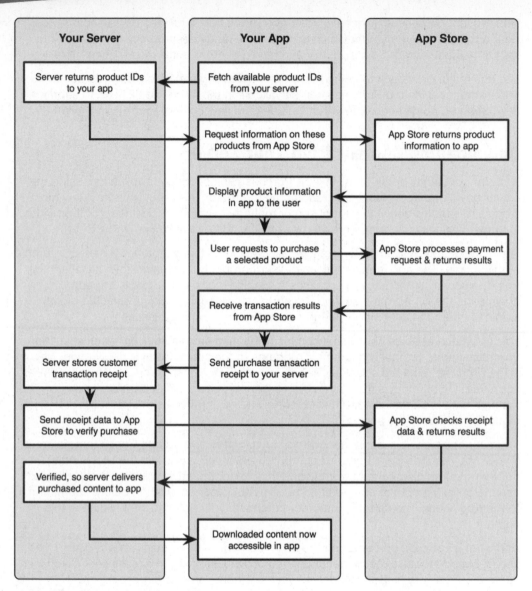

Figure 8–11. *The server-based In-App Purchase delivery model*

Another benefit of downloading content from a server is that it gives you the flexibility to also offer free items along with your In-App Purchase products. If a customer selects a free item, your app can simply bypass the In-App Purchase process and download the item directly from your server. If your users know that free content is often made available in your app's virtual store, that will motivate them to browse your add-on offerings more frequently, and may increase the sales of In-App Purchase items.

The big drawback to the server-based model is that Store Kit does not provide any kind of infrastructure for communicating with your server. It's up to you to develop and implement your own custom server-side applications for interacting with your iOS app.

The Store Kit does offer a method for your server to verify a received transaction receipt. This added verification layer is a recommended security mechanism to help prevent piracy of your server-based downloads. When your iOS app notifies your server that a purchase was successfully completed, it should send a transaction receipt to the server. As I'll discuss in greater detail later in this chapter, when an In-App Purchase transaction is finished, the App Store returns a transaction receipt to your iOS app. By sending this transaction receipt to your server, you've now given your server the data needed to communicate with the App Store via JavaScript Object Notation (JSON) to verify the purchase. This prevents hackers from tricking your server into granting free downloads of content that were never legitimately purchased.

If you're not an experienced web developer, the prospect of creating custom web applications and server-side infrastructure for communicating with your iOS app can seem overwhelming, to say the least. This server-based model also puts the burden of reliable scalability and security on your shoulders. If your app enjoys a large customer base, testing your server to withstand a lot of traffic and potential security threats is essential. Server-related problems affect not only the perceived performance quality of your iOS app, but also your business reputation (and liability).

> **NOTE:** If you're interested in the server-based model, Apple provides a comprehensive tutorial on verifying In-App Purchase transactions via JSON. Read the "Verifying Store Receipts" section of the official *In-App Purchase Programming Guide*, located online at the following URL: `http://developer.apple.com/library/ios/#documentation/NetworkingInternet /Conceptual/StoreKitGuide/`.

Finding Help in the Cloud

Many of us are software programmers, feeling most comfortable when coding Objective-C in Xcode. If just the idea of spending countless hours learning, developing, and maintaining web applications and expensive server systems makes you break out in a sweat, then rest easy. If you need to employ a server-based download model for your In-App Purchases, several third-party services offer comprehensive In-App Purchase support:

- Urban Airship (`http://urbanairship.com/`)
- Push.IO (`http://push.io/`)
- Burstly (`http://www.burstly.com/`)
- iLime:Purchase (`http://www.ilime.com/in-app-purchase/`)
- dodaii (`http://dodaii.com/en/`)

These third-party services take care of the related server management hassles, such as scalability, security, performance monitoring, App Store receipt verification, content delivery, and app integration. Urban Airship even supplies you with a convenient, ready-to-use storefront UI and the ability to deliver free downloads within your app (both not currently offered through Apple's Store Kit framework).

Unless you have some compelling reason to host, troubleshoot, and manage custom web applications and the server yourself, letting the experts handle this back-end architecture will save you time and money (and help alleviate those stress-induced headaches). This allows you to stay focused on what you love doing most: creating apps.

Configuring In-App Purchase in iTunes Connect

Later in this chapter, we'll program an In-App Purchase example in Xcode. For that, you need to create an iTunes Test User account and your In-App Purchase items. You create both online in iTunes Connect. As previously mentioned, In-App Purchase items are added to iTunes Connect as individual products, so they need to be created before you can test purchasing them.

Setting Up an iTunes Test User Account

Why do you need a Test User account? You'll want to test your application's In-App Purchase functionality extensively before submitting it to the App Store. Using a Test User account will enable you to perform test purchases without actually getting billed for them. Whew! That's definitely good news. Now you can do all the In-App Purchase testing you want without worrying about draining your pocketbook in the process.

Log into iTunes Connect at `https://itunesconnect.apple.com/`. On the main iTunes Connect page, click the Manage Users link, and then select the user type Test User (see Figure 8–12). On the Manage Test Users page, click the Add New User button.

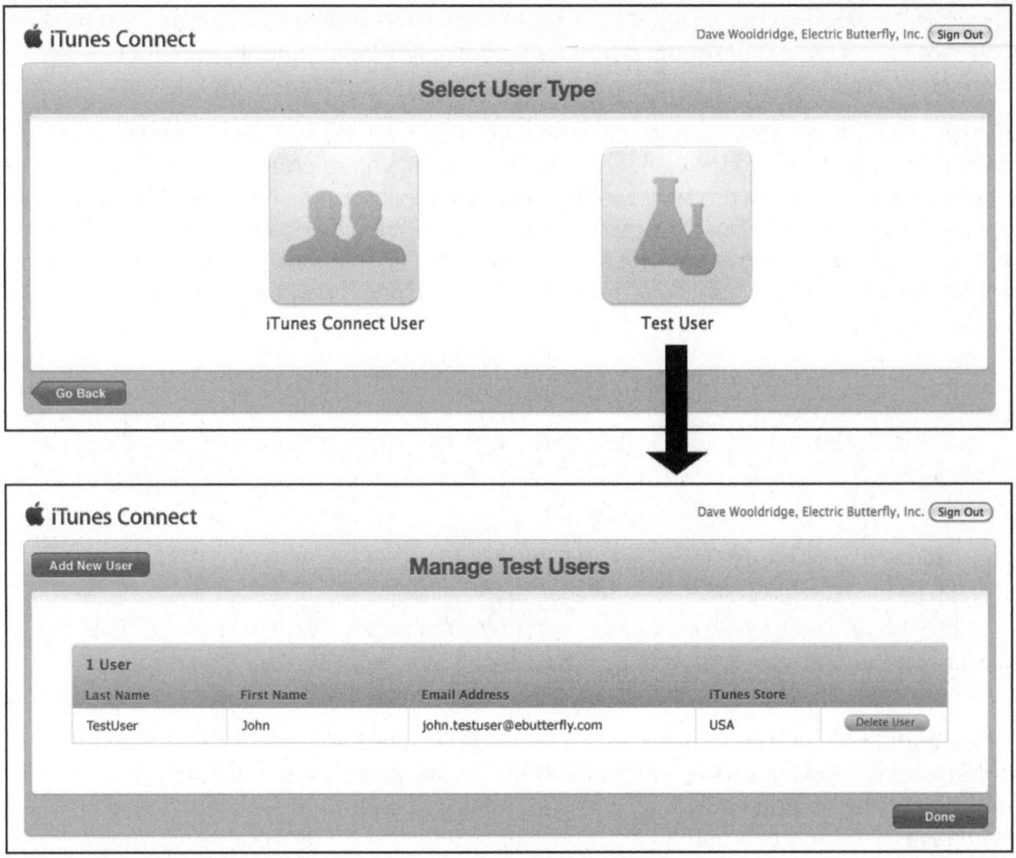

Figure 8–12. *Adding a new Test User account within the Manage Users section of iTunes Connect*

When completing the required form fields, be sure to use an e-mail address that is valid but is *not* associated with any existing iTunes accounts. This is very important. Using an e-mail address that is already assigned to an iTunes Connect or iTunes Store account will invalidate your Test User account. Plus, you don't want your test purchases to accidentally be charged to an existing credit card–enabled iTunes account.

After creating the new Test User account, you can view or delete it from within the Manage Users section of iTunes Connect. There does not appear to be a way to edit an existing user account, so if you want to modify the e-mail address or password, you'll need to delete that Test User account and then create a new one to replace it.

Creating In-App Purchase Items

Now that you have a Test User account in place, the next step is to add your In-App Purchase item to iTunes Connect as its own individual product.

You can create an In-App Purchase item within either your app listing in the Manage Your Applications section or the Manage Your In-App Purchases section of iTunes

Connect. If Manage Your In-App Purchases is not listed in your iTunes Connect, then you probably have not yet submitted your Paid Applications Contract to iTunes Connect, which is required in order to create an In-App Purchase item.

iTunes Connect will allow you to add a new In-App Purchase item only if you already have an app listed in iTunes Connect. This way, when you're creating the In-App Purchase item, you can properly assign the listed application as its parent app. But what if this is your first app? Don't worry. Testing In-App Purchase does not require your app to already be in the App Store. But in order to create and test In-App Purchase items, you must first add your app's information to iTunes Connect and assign the app a unique bundle ID.

> **NOTE:** A bundle ID is based on an app ID you've already created in the iOS Provisioning Portal. In order for In-App Purchase to work within your app (even during testing), you must use an app-specific app ID that is enabled for In-App Purchase. Do not use general-purpose wildcard app IDs (that include asterisks) like the one found in the default Team Provisioning Profile. You'll also need to generate a provisioning profile based on that app ID and the iOS device you'll be using to test your Xcode project's In-App Purchases. If you're unfamiliar with the process of creating app IDs and provisioning profiles in the online iOS Provisioning Portal, read the extensive tutorial in Chapter 9.

When adding a new app to the Manage Your Applications section of iTunes Connect, do *not* upload an app binary yet. Without an app binary, your iOS app will not be prematurely submitted for review, but you'll still be able to set up related In-App Purchase items and test purchases. Your app listing in Manage Your Applications should display a status of Prepare for Upload (see Figure 8–13). For details on how to add a new app listing in iTunes Connect, see the comprehensive instructions provided in Chapter 11.

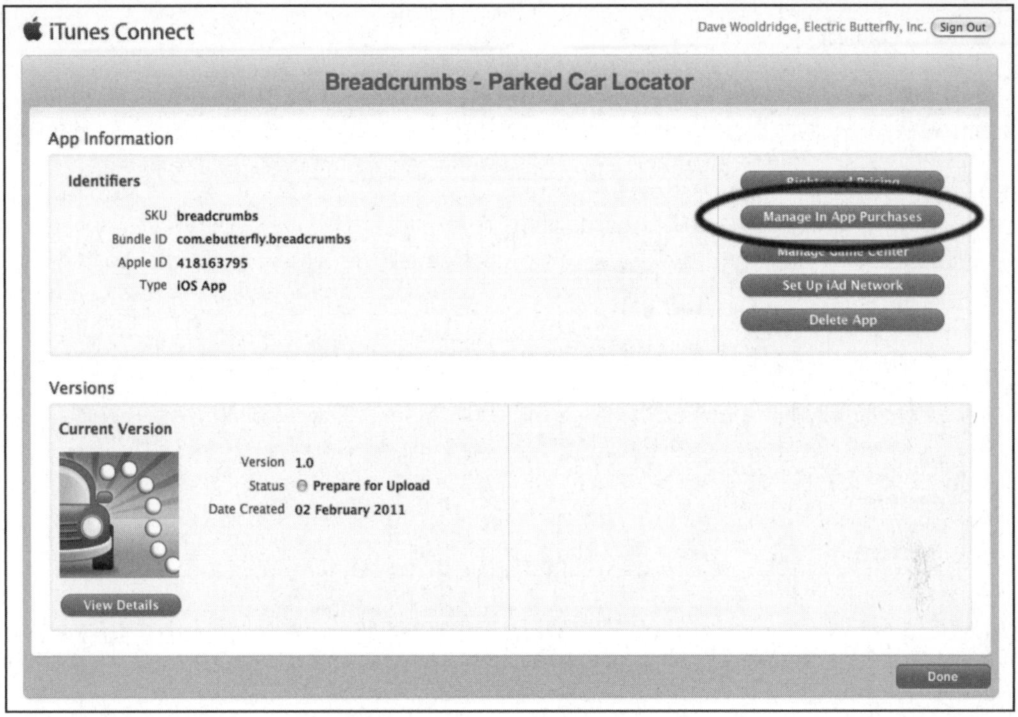

Figure 8–13. *Select your app from within the Manage Your Applications section of iTunes Connect, and then click the Manage In-App Purchases button to create a new In-App Purchase item.*

Within your app's main page, click the Manage In App Purchases button (see Figure 8–13), and then click the Create New button to add a new In-App Purchase item for that app. Complete the web form that appears (see Figure 8–14). You're required to fill out all of the fields, with the exception of the For Review screenshot of the purchase in action. That screenshot is only for the app review team, so you can wait to upload it when you're ready to submit it (after you've finished testing).

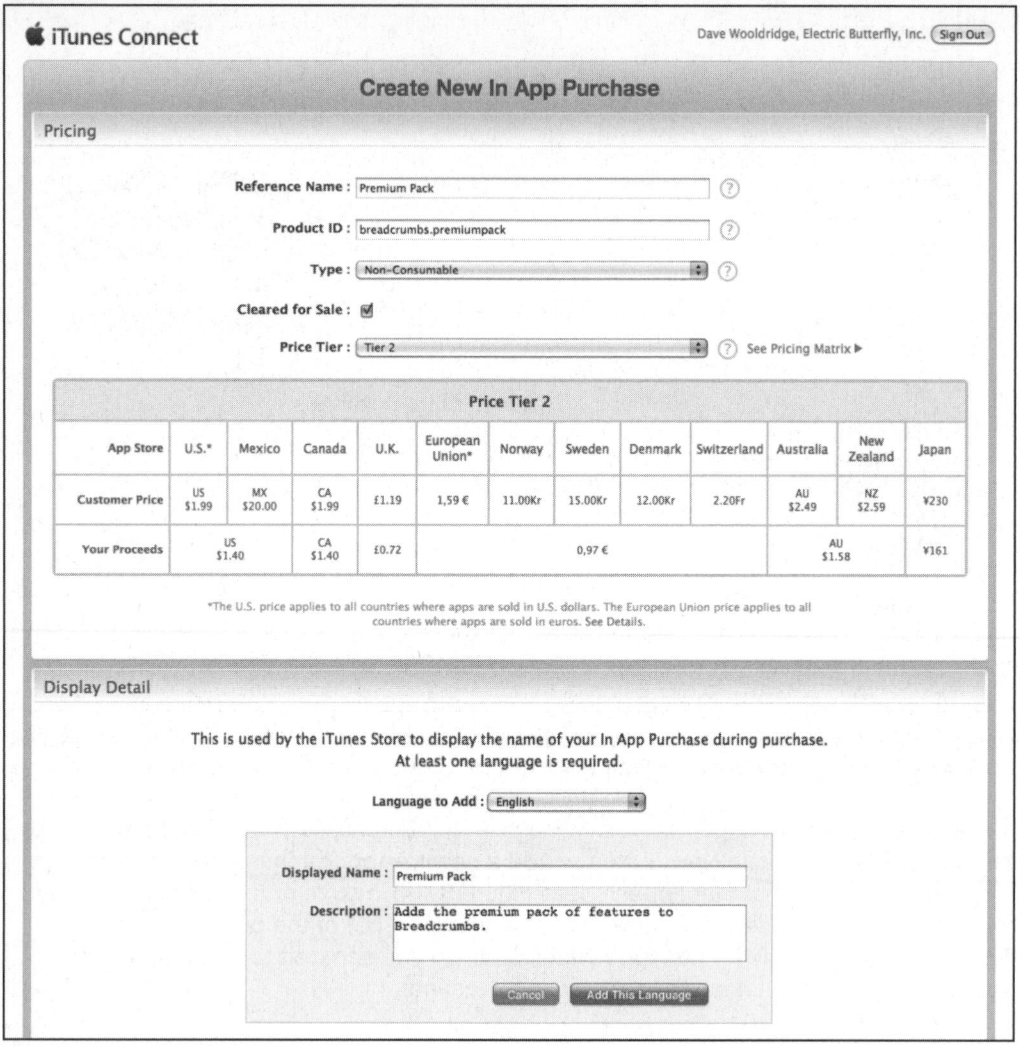

Figure 8–14. *Create a new In-App Purchase item for your app in iTunes Connect.*

Let's walk through the form in Figure 8–14:

- **Reference Name**: This field represents the name of your In-App
  Purchase item in iTunes Connect, but it may not necessarily be the
  name that is displayed in the App Store (if a customer's device has a
  different language setting than your iTunes Connect default language).
  See the Language field description for your item's actual display
  name.

- **Product ID**: Every product in iTunes Connect requires a unique ID, and In-App Purchase items are no exception. Any UTF-8 string can be used to identify this product, but it's recommended to use a common ID system across all of your products. Many iOS developers use *com.company.appname* as the naming scheme for all application SKU numbers, and related In-App Purchase product IDs could use an extension of that, such as *com.company.appname.productid*. Since our fictional Breadcrumbs app in the example screenshots uses breadcrumbs as its SKU, the In-App Purchase product ID for the Premium Pack could be breadcrumbs.premiumpack to visually reference its relationship to the parent app. This simple system gives you an easy and consistent naming scheme across all your own products, as well as unique IDs that no one else would be using. This is a significant factor, since iTunes Connect does not allow any two products to have the same ID.

- **Type**: This is the most important field to understand before submitting this form, especially since it cannot be edited after you've saved your new In-App Purchase item in iTunes Connect. Type defines what kind of In-App Purchase item you're creating. As discussed earlier in the chapter, currently, there are four types: Non-consumables, Consumables, Auto-renewable Subscriptions, and Subscriptions. If Auto-renewable Subscriptions is selected, you'll also be required to define a duration for your subscription (such as monthly or annually), so that the App Store will know when to bill customers for renewals.

- **Cleared for Sale**: If this check box is left unchecked, your In-App Purchase item will not be available for listing within your app. But even if you select this box, that doesn't mean your In-App Purchase item can be publicly purchased. As individual products, all In-App Purchase items need to be reviewed and approved by Apple before they are made available in the App Store. But for testing purposes (as well as when you're ready to go live), you definitely want this box to be selected.

- **Price Tier**: This drop-down menu provides a list of available pricing tiers for assigning a specific price to your In-App Purchase item. You can modify the price of In-App Purchase items to hold a special promotional sale, but they can never be offered for free—not even for a limited time. In-App Purchase, items must be priced, with 99 cents as the minimum. To offer free downloadable content within your app, you'll need to implement your own system for retrieving those items from your server, outside the App Store.

- **Language to Add**: This is where you choose the languages you want to support. For each language selected, you fill in the localized Displayed Name field and the Description field for your In-App Purchase item. Type carefully, since the In-App Purchase item name and description you submit here are what Apple displays to customers within the App Store and your application. Your In-App Purchase item must support at least one language. If you have only one language listed, make sure it is the same as the language set for the related parent app.

- **Screenshot**: This is for review purposes only and will never be displayed in the App Store. When first creating a new In-App Purchase item, you'll leave this field empty. After you've extensively tested In-App Purchase within your app, you'll need to take a screenshot of that purchase process in action. Upload that image to this Screenshot section. This image will aid Apple during the review process of your In-App Purchase item, so upload a screenshot only *after* the item has successfully passed your own testing and is ready for submission.

Managing Your In-App Purchase Items

After saving your new In-App Purchase item within iTunes Connect, you can make changes to it later by accessing it via your app listing's Manage Your In-App Purchases section (see Figure 8–15). Until you submit the item to Apple for review, its status will be Pending Developer Approval, and you can freely edit or delete it.

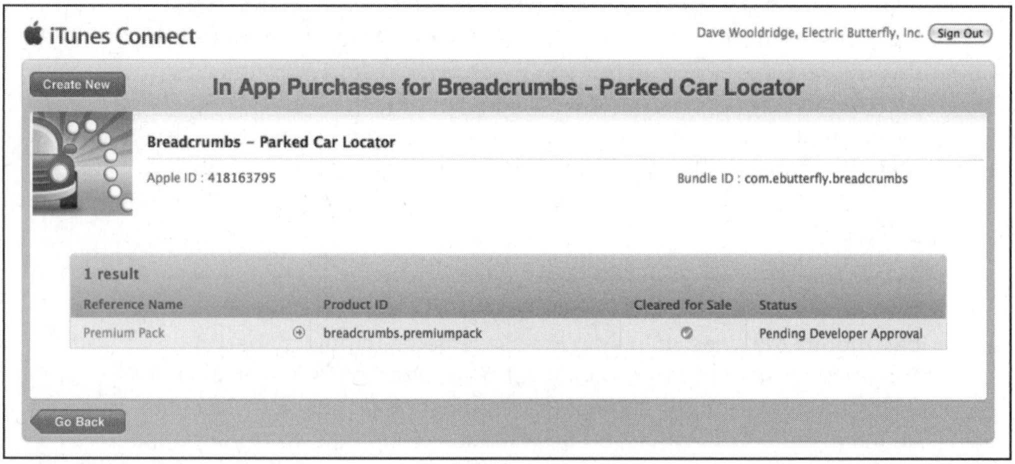

Figure 8–15. *After your In-App Purchase item is created, it is listed in your app's Manage Your In-App Purchases section of iTunes Connect.*

After you've completed your testing and uploaded a screenshot of an In-App Purchase in action, click the Approve button to submit your In-App Purchase item for review. You'll be prompted to choose one of two options:

- **Submit Now**: If your existing iOS app is already supporting In-App Purchase and you're merely adding yet another In-App Purchase item to an existing list of offerings, you can select Submit Now to send it directly to the review queue.

- **Submit with Binary**: If your In-App Purchase item requires a new or updated version of your application, you'll want to select Submit with Binary to ensure that both products are reviewed together and go live in the App Store at the same time.

When the In-App Purchase item's status is Waiting for Review or In Review, you will not be able to make any further changes while it's being reviewed.

After your In-App Purchase item has been rejected or approved by Apple, any additional modifications you make will require it to be reviewed again. If it gets rejected, then Apple requires you to re-create it as a new In-App Purchase item before resubmitting it for review.

You can create up to 3,000 In-App Purchase items per parent application. If you delete an In-App Purchase item from iTunes Connect, that unique product ID can never be used again for another item. Even if you're replacing the deleted item with a similar In-App Purchase item, you'll be required to use a different product ID for it.

Preparing Your Test Device

Unfortunately, the iOS Simulator does not support In-App Purchase. To properly test an In-App Purchase transaction, you'll need to run through it on an iOS device using your new Test User account.

To avoid account issues, you must log out of any existing iTunes accounts on your test device. To do this, simply launch the device's Settings app and tap on Store. On the Store screen, tap the Sign Out button to log out of the iTunes Store (see Figure 8–16). I cannot stress enough how important this step is. Clearing out existing accounts from the device's Store settings will prevent a nontest account from accidentally being used during your In-App Purchase test transactions. Just leave the Store setting empty. Do *not* log in here with your Test User account. Doing so may invalidate it as a test account.

In the Restrictions section of your test device's General Settings, make sure the In-App Purchases feature is switched on under Allowed Content (see Figure 8–16).

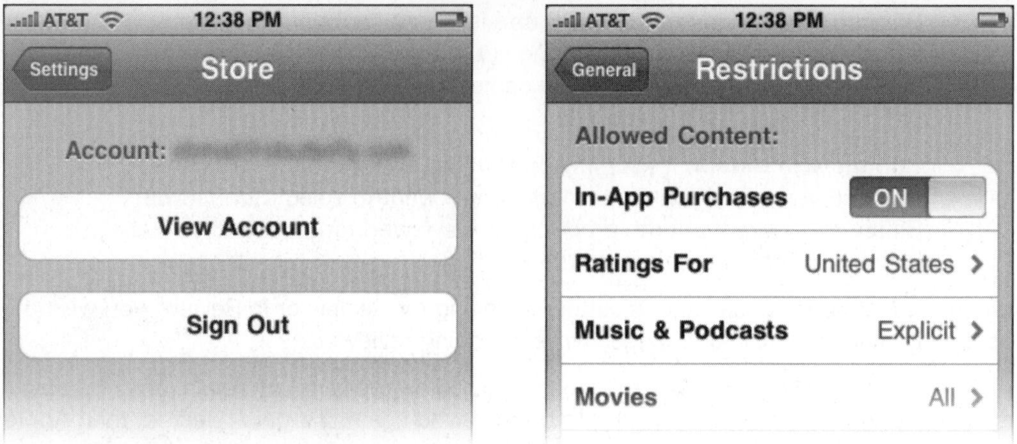

Figure 8–16. *You must sign out of your iTunes account on your test device before testing In-App Purchase (left). You'll also need In-App Purchases turned on in your test device's Allowed Content settings (right).*

Now that your device is ready, simply connect it to your development computer. To compile and test your project on your device, make sure you select Device as the Active SDK in Xcode's drop-down menu. As I mentioned earlier, you'll also want to ensure that you've properly installed the correct provisioning profile in Xcode Organizer—the one that's assigned to this device and the related app ID.

When running an Xcode debug build of your application on your test device, the Store Kit framework communicates with a special "sandbox" test environment instead of the live App Store. If an In-App Purchase request is made, the Store Kit will prompt you to confirm the purchase. Then Store Kit will display an iTunes sign-in screen. Select Existing Account, and log in with your Test User account. In this special test environment, successfully completing a transaction will return an order receipt, but no money is transferred, and no invoice is generated.

Never use your Test User account in a live production environment. Your test account should be used only when debugging your app in Xcode. Doing otherwise will invalidate your account credentials. The *only* way to ensure that you're running the app in Apple's sandbox test environment is to launch it from Xcode onto your test device. If you launch the app from your device's home screen, Store Kit will connect to the live App Store and invalidate your Test User account.

Tapping into the Store Kit Framework

Time to start programming! Fire up Xcode and create a new iOS project, selecting the View-based Application template for iPhone. You could just as easily apply the example code to an iPad or universal app, but to remain focused on the task at hand, let's keep things simple. Name the example project InAppPurchase. If you would rather save time and just follow along, you can download and open the completed InAppPurchase project from the book's companion code examples at `http://iPhoneBusinessBook.com/` or `http://www.apress.com/`.

> **NOTE:** The example project we're about to build should not be viewed as a functional app on its own. For it to work, you'll need to plug in your own In-App Purchase item product IDs and other related data in various places in the code. In outlining the steps needed to complete an example purchase, I'll explain where to insert your custom In-App Purchase information.

Configuring the Project for In-App Purchase

Before we write any code, the required Store Kit framework must be added to the Xcode project. This is done in the same way you've seen in previous examples in the book. Ctrl-click the project's *Frameworks* folder, select **Add** ➤ **Existing Frameworks…**, and choose StoreKit.framework from the list that appears.

Since In-App Purchase is not supported in the iOS Simulator, select Device in the top-left Overview drop-down menu in Xcode's main project window to reflect your connected test device.

Next, open the *InAppPurchase-Info.plist* file and change the bundle identifier to the one that's now assigned to this app in iTunes Connect. As an example, the bundle ID for our fictional Breadcrumbs app is com.ebutterfly.breadcrumbs (as shown in Figure 8–13).

The last configuration task is to specify the Xcode project's provisioning profile, so that the appropriate provisioning profile is used when Xcode runs the app on the connected test device. To accomplish this, select the project name at the top of the Groups & Files pane, and then click the Info toolbar button. In the window that appears, select the Build tab and scroll down to the Code Signing section. Under Code Signing Identity's Any iOS, choose the provisioning profile that's assigned to your app's bundle ID (as previously discussed in the "Creating In-App Purchase Items" section).

If you don't see that provisioning profile listed, you'll need to generate it in Apple's online iOS Provisioning Portal, download it to your computer, and install it in Xcode Organizer while your test device is connected. If you've never created provisioning profiles before, read the tutorial in Chapter 9, so that you can complete this step before moving forward.

Setting Up the Basics

First, you'll need to add a new class to the project, so select the *Classes* folder in the Groups & Files column, and then choose **File** ➤ **New File…**. Next, in the New File dialog box that appears, select the Objective-C Class template from the Cocoa Touch Class category, and configure the Subclass drop-down menu to make it a subclass of `NSObject`. Click the Next button, and have Xcode create both the .*h* and .*m* files, naming them both *InAppPurchaseObserver*. We'll add some code to this class a little later in the process, and I'll explain its purpose then.

For now, let's move on to the InAppPurchaseViewController class. You'll want to design your own storefront UI, especially if you're offering several In-App Purchase products within your app. However, for this basic example, you'll use a simple UIButton for a single In-App Purchase item.

Open the *InAppPurchaseViewController.h* header file, and modify the code as follows:

```
#import <UIKit/UIKit.h>
#import <StoreKit/StoreKit.h>
#import "InAppPurchaseObserver.h"

@interface InAppPurchaseViewController : UIViewController <SKProductsRequestDelegate> {
    InAppPurchaseObserver *inappObserver;
    UIButton *inappButton;
}

@property (nonatomic, retain) InAppPurchaseObserver *inappObserver;
@property (nonatomic, retain) IBOutlet UIButton *inappButton;
-(IBAction)buyInApp:(id)sender;

@end
```

The code highlighted in bold represent new additions. The Store Kit framework has been imported, and a new UIButton and buyInApp method are referenced. This enables you to modify the button's properties via code, and it will call the buyInApp function when the button is tapped.

You'll also notice the assignment of the SKProductsRequestDelegate. This allows the InAppPurchaseViewController to receive responses from the Store Kit framework, which will come into play later when you start adding Store Kit code to the project.

The new InAppPurchaseObserver class has also been imported and can be referenced via the inappObserver property. This will enable the InAppPurchaseViewController to send Store Kit transaction responses to the InAppPurchaseObserver class. We'll talk about that more later in this chapter. For now, save your changes.

Next, open the *InAppPurchaseViewController.m* implementation file, and add the following bold code to complete your setup of the inappObserver property, UIButton, and the buyInApp method.

```
#import "InAppPurchaseViewController.h"

@implementation InAppPurchaseViewController
@synthesize inappObserver;
@synthesize inappButton;

- (void)viewDidLoad {

    inappObserver = [[InAppPurchaseObserver alloc] init];

    [super viewDidLoad];
}

// When the buy button is clicked, start In-App Purchase process.
-(IBAction)buyInApp:(id)sender {
```

```
      // Interact with StoreKit here.
}

- (void)didReceiveMemoryWarning {

    [super didReceiveMemoryWarning];
}

- (void)viewDidUnload {
    // Release any retained subviews of the main view.
    // e.g. self.myOutlet = nil;
}

- (void)dealloc {
    [inappButton release];
    [inappObserver release];
    [super dealloc];
}

@end
```

After saving those changes, launch *InAppPurchaseViewController.xib* in Interface Builder. Add a Rounded Rect Button to the View, and wire up its Touch Up Inside connector to the File Owner's buyInApp connector. Then wire the File Owner's inappButton outlet to the Rounded Rect Button. Also add a label with **Purchase Additional Features** as the text, and change the button's default title to read **None Available** (see Figure 8–17). Make sure to disable the button by unchecking the Enabled property. This will all make sense when we start interacting with Store Kit.

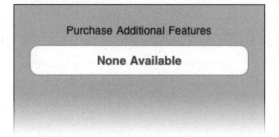

Figure 8–17. *Setting up our simple example in Interface Builder. Uncheck the button's Enabled property.*

Getting In-App Purchase Up and Running

Now that you're finished building and wiring up your basic UI, it's time to have some fun with Store Kit. In only five steps, you'll have In-App Purchase up and running in your application!

Step 1: Does the Consumer Allow In-App Purchase?

Since users can disable the In-App Purchase feature in their device settings, you'll want to check that an In-App Purchase can be made before doing anything else. After you've saved your changes in Interface Builder, go back to Xcode, and open the *InAppPurchaseViewController.m* implementation file again. Add the following new bold code to viewDidLoad:

```
- (void)viewDidLoad {

    inappObserver = [[InAppPurchaseObserver alloc] init];

    if ([SKPaymentQueue canMakePayments]) {
        // Yes, In-App Purchase is enabled on this device!
        // Proceed to fetch available In-App Purchase items.

    } else {
        // Notify user that In-App Purchase is disabled via button text.
        [inappButton setTitle:@"In-App Purchase is Disabled"
forState:UIControlStateNormal];
        inappButton.enabled = NO;
    }

    [super viewDidLoad];
}
```

Here, a quick call is being made to the canMakePayments method in Store Kit's SKPaymentQueue class. If a Yes value is returned, then the In-App Purchase feature is allowed on that device, and the App Store is accessible. If a No is returned, you can notify the users that they have In-App Purchase disabled via the button's Title label. Remember that the initial state of the button was set to disabled in Interface Builder, so just leave it disabled for now, simply using it to communicate information to the user.

Step 2: Fetch Available In-App Purchase Items

With the In-App Purchase feature accessible, you can now check the App Store for the availability of your item. Your application must already know the related In-App Purchase product ID before performing this check.

If you are offering only one or two In-App Purchase items and don't plan on adding more, the easiest approach is to store your In-App Purchase product IDs within your app. Of course, any time you add a new In-App Purchase product ID to your app, you'll need to make it available to customers as an update, which will require submitting your app again for review/approval.

Since iTunes Connect requires In-App Purchase product IDs to be unique, don't preassign nonexistent IDs in your parent app with plans to create those IDs in iTunes Connect at some point in the future. That strategy could backfire on you if some other developer takes ownership of that product ID before you get a chance to create it in iTunes Connect.

Of course, you could plan ahead by creating all your known In-App Purchase items in iTunes Connect now and simply mark them as Pending Developer Approval. That way, you'll know the product IDs to include in your application binary, and when you're ready to make those future In-App Purchase items available to consumers, you can submit them for approval.

If you want the flexibility to add new In-App Purchase items without requiring a new build of your app, you'll need to use the server-based In-App Purchase model (discussed earlier in this chapter), where your app can fetch all related product IDs from your server. As you learned, Store Kit does not provide any infrastructure for this, so it's your responsibility to configure the app to talk to your server. Although this requires extra work on your part, it is the recommended method for retrieving a large number of product IDs, especially if you're constantly adding new In-App Purchase items. Apple's approval process is too time-consuming to continuously submit a new app update every time you release new purchasable add-on content.

The related In-App Purchase items will need to be approved and ready for sale in the App Store before customers can purchase them within your app. Before the items are approved, they are available to only your Test User account within your parent app's development build.

Once your app has retrieved the In-App Purchase product ID—in this example, you're using only one—proceed to request that product from the App Store to ensure that it's currently available for purchase.

```
- (void)viewDidLoad {

    inappObserver = [[InAppPurchaseObserver alloc] init];

    if ([SKPaymentQueue canMakePayments]) {
        // Yes, In-App Purchase is enabled on this device!
        // Proceed to fetch available In-App Purchase items.

        // Replace "Your IAP Product ID" with your actual In-App Purchase Product ID,
        // fetched from either a remote server or stored locally within your app.
        SKProductsRequest *prodRequest= [[SKProductsRequest alloc]
initWithProductIdentifiers: [NSSet setWithObject: @"Your IAP Product ID"]];
        prodRequest.delegate = self;
        [prodRequest start];

    } else {
        // Notify user that In-App Purchase is disabled via button text.
        [inappButton setTitle:@"In-App Purchase is Disabled"
forState:UIControlStateNormal];
        inappButton.enabled = NO;
    }

    [super viewDidLoad];
}
```

Of the new code added (in bold) to *InAppPurchaseViewController.m*'s viewDidLoad, you'll need to replace the placeholder string "Your IAP Product ID" with your own actual In-App Purchase product ID. For example, the In-App Purchase product ID of the $1.99 Premium Pack for our fictional Breadcrumbs app is breadcrumbs.premiumpack (as shown in Figure 8–15).

And remember that SKProductsRequestDelegate code you added to the header file a while back? By assigning InAppPurchaseViewController as the SKProductsRequest delegate, you can simply state self for the Delegate property. The Store Kit will then return a response to this delegate. To receive that response, add the following code to the *InAppPurchaseViewController.m* file:

```
// StoreKit returns a response from an SKProductsRequest.
- (void)productsRequest:(SKProductsRequest *)request
didReceiveResponse:(SKProductsResponse *)response {

    // Populate the inappBuy button with the received product info.
    SKProduct *validProduct = nil;
    int count = [response.products count];
    if (count>0) {
        validProduct = [response.products objectAtIndex:0];
    }
    if (!validProduct) {
        [inappButton setTitle:@"No Products Available" forState:UIControlStateNormal];
        inappButton.enabled = NO;
        return;
    }

    NSString *buttonText = [[NSString alloc] initWithFormat:@"%@ - Buy %@",
validProduct.localizedTitle, validProduct.price];
    [inappButton setTitle:buttonText forState:UIControlStateNormal];
    inappButton.enabled = YES;
    [buttonText release];
}
```

Store Kit responds with an array of available In-App Purchase products. Since you have only one here, you populate the inappBuy button with the product's localized title and price (see Figure 8–18). If you're interested in also displaying the localized description, that can be accessed via the localizedDescription property. Don't forget to enable the button via code now that it's displaying a valid In-App Purchase item.

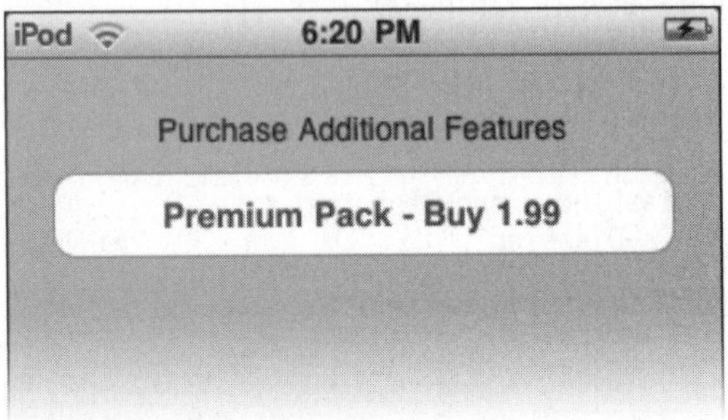

Figure 8–18. *The Store Kit replies to the product request with information about the available In-App Purchase item. The example code then populates the button with the item's localized title and price.*

Why bother checking for the In-App Purchase item through the Store Kit if you already know the product ID? This vital step ensures that your application does not try to sell an item that is not currently available in the App Store. For example, what if you submitted both your application and an In-App Purchase item for review at the same time, but only your iOS app was approved? Forcing your application to first check for the availability of the In-App Purchase item before listing it will prevent potential customer purchase issues. Never assume. Always perform this check before displaying any items for sale within your app.

If you successfully set up an In-App Purchase item in iTunes Connect and yet your app encounters problems retrieving that item data as a valid product, make sure your application's bundle identifier in its plist file matches the parent app's bundle ID assigned to your In-App Purchase item in iTunes Connect.

Do not discard that In-App Purchase product ID after using it for the product request. It will come in handy again soon. If the user taps the buy button, you'll need that product ID to submit a purchase request to Store Kit.

Step 3: Request a Purchase

Tapping the buy button in the example fires the buyInApp method in the *InAppPurchaseViewController.m* file. So, the next step is to handle that action by sending a payment request to Store Kit.

```
// When the buy button is clicked, start In-App Purchase process.
-(IBAction)buyInApp:(id)sender {

    // Replace "Your IAP Product ID" with your actual In-App Purchase Product ID.
    SKPayment *paymentRequest = [SKPayment paymentWithProductIdentifier: @"Your IAP
Product ID"];

    // Assign an Observer class to the SKPaymentTransactionObserver,
    // so that it can monitor the transaction status.
    [[SKPaymentQueue defaultQueue] addTransactionObserver:inappObserver];

    // Request a purchase of the selected item.
    [[SKPaymentQueue defaultQueue] addPayment:paymentRequest];
}
```

After creating an SKPayment instance with the In-App Purchase product ID of the item the user wants to buy, you'll need to assign an observer class to the SKPaymentQueue's transaction observer. This is where your InAppPurchaseObserver class comes into play. Remember how the inappObserver property was created to reference that class? By assigning inappObserver as the SKPaymentTransactionObserver, your project's InAppPurchaseObserver class can monitor the transaction status of the SKPaymentQueue after a payment request has been sent to it.

Since payment transactions are not lost when the app quits, you may want to assign your observer to the payment queue when your app launches, so that any existing transactions can resume being monitored and processed the next time your app is run. Why would this be important? One possible scenario is that the user receives a phone call in the middle of making a purchase. After the call, when the user returns to your app, the transaction can be resumed.

When the payment request is delivered, the App Store prompts the user to confirm the purchase and then enter an iTunes account login. When testing your own app in this sandbox environment, this is where you select Use Existing Account and enter your Test User account e-mail address and password (see Figure 8–19).

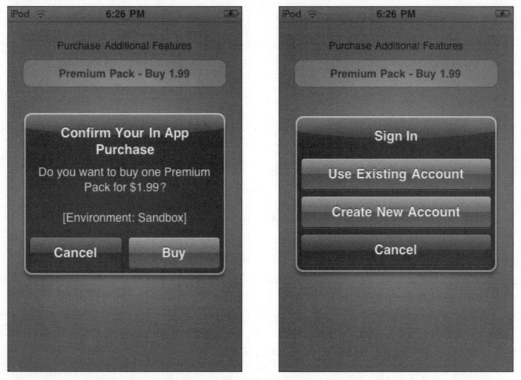

Figure 8–19. *You're asked to confirm your purchase request (left). After selecting the Buy button, you're then prompted to sign in as a Test User via the Use Existing Account button (right).*

Step 4: Receive Payment Status

After the user either cancels or confirms the purchase, the transaction status is sent back to your InAppPurchaseObserver class. Now it's time to add code to that class to handle this job. Open the *InAppPurchaseObserver.h* header file, and update the code as follows:

```
#import <Foundation/Foundation.h>
#import <StoreKit/StoreKit.h>

@interface InAppPurchaseObserver : NSObject <SKPaymentTransactionObserver> {

}

- (void)paymentQueue:(SKPaymentQueue *)queue updatedTransactions:(NSArray
*)transactions;

@end
```

As you'll notice, the bold code imports the Store Kit framework and assigns this NSObject subclass to be an SKPaymentTransactionObserver. With that in place, along with a reference to paymentQueue, save and close that header file.

To receive payment transaction status updates, your *InAppPurchaseObserver.m* implementation file should include the following code:

```
#import "InAppPurchaseObserver.h"
#import "InAppPurchaseViewController.h"

@implementation InAppPurchaseObserver

// The transaction status of the SKPaymentQueue is sent here.
- (void)paymentQueue:(SKPaymentQueue *)queue updatedTransactions:(NSArray *)transactions
{
    for(SKPaymentTransaction *transaction in transactions) {
        switch (transaction.transactionState) {

            case SKPaymentTransactionStatePurchasing:
                // Item is still in the process of being purchased.
                break;

            case SKPaymentTransactionStatePurchased:
                // Item was successfully purchased!
                break;

            case SKPaymentTransactionStateRestored:
                // Verified that user has already paid for this item.
                // Ideal for restoring item across all devices of this customer.
                break;

            case SKPaymentTransactionStateFailed:
                // Purchase was either cancelled by user or an error occurred.

                if (transaction.error.code != SKErrorPaymentCancelled) {
                    // A transaction error occurred, so notify user.
                }
                break;
        }
    }
}

@end
```

Within the paymentQueue status receiver, you can check the current state of the transaction. As noted in the previous code, SKPaymentTransactionStatePurchasing means the purchase is still in progress, so there's nothing for you to do yet. You'll want to pay close attention to the return of SKPaymentTransactionStatePurchased or SKPaymentTransactionStateRestored, since that will signal the need for your app to unlock or download the purchased content (see Figure 8–20).

Figure 8–20. *If the In-App Purchase transaction was successful, the App Store presents a thank-you message and returns SKPaymentTransactionStatePurchased to the paymentQueue receiver.*

SKPaymentTransactionStateFailed is returned if either the purchase was canceled by the user or a transaction error occurred. If the user tapped the Cancel button (as indicated by SKErrorPaymentCancelled), the aborted purchase can be safely ignored. But if the transaction failed for some other reason, you should let the user know that the purchase was not completed.

Step 5: Provide Access to the Purchased Content

If the transaction status received proves to be SKPaymentTransactionStatePurchased, this confirms that the user's purchase was successful. This is the point where you should reward the customer by immediately providing access to the purchased content. As you've learned, you have the option to either unlock the item within your app or download the content from a remote server. After the purchased content has been successfully delivered to the user, the last thing you'll need to do is remove the transaction from the payment queue by calling finishTransaction:

```
- (void)paymentQueue:(SKPaymentQueue *)queue updatedTransactions:(NSArray *)transactions
{
    for(SKPaymentTransaction *transaction in transactions) {
        switch (transaction.transactionState) {
```

```
        case SKPaymentTransactionStatePurchasing:
            // Item is still in the process of being purchased.
            break;

        case SKPaymentTransactionStatePurchased:
            // Item was successfully purchased!

            // --- UNLOCK FEATURE OR DOWNLOAD CONTENT HERE ---
            // The purchased item ID is accessible via
            // transaction.payment.productIdentifier

            // After customer has successfully received purchased content,
            // remove the finished transaction from the payment queue.
            [[SKPaymentQueue defaultQueue] finishTransaction: transaction];
            break;

        case SKPaymentTransactionStateRestored:
            // Verified that user has already paid for this item.
            // Ideal for restoring item across all devices of this customer.

            // --- UNLOCK FEATURE OR DOWNLOAD CONTENT HERE ---
            // The purchased item ID is accessible via
            // transaction.payment.productIdentifier

            // After customer has restored purchased content on this device,
            // remove the finished transaction from the payment queue.
            [[SKPaymentQueue defaultQueue] finishTransaction: transaction];
            break;

        case SKPaymentTransactionStateFailed:
            // Purchase was either cancelled by user or an error occurred.

            if (transaction.error.code != SKErrorPaymentCancelled) {
                // A transaction error occurred, so notify user.
            }
            // Finished transactions should be removed from the payment queue.
            [[SKPaymentQueue defaultQueue] finishTransaction: transaction];
            break;
        }
    }
}
```

Since transactions are persistent, removing the finished transaction from the payment queue is very important. You'll notice from the bold code that this is done not only after a successful transaction, but also after a failed transaction. But do this only after you're finished retrieving the information you need from the transaction.

In the case of a successful transaction, you'll want to capture the ID of the purchased item via transaction.payment.productIdentifier before removing the transaction. This will tell you the specific In-App Purchase product that should be provided to the user, which is especially useful if your application offers multiple in-app items for sale. You should store this ID somewhere in your app (such as in a plist file), so that it can keep track of which items have already been purchased and ensure that content remains readily accessible the next time the user runs your app.

The app's preferences file is a good place to store purchased product IDs, since an app's preferences are backed up when users sync their devices with their computer via iTunes. For Non-consumable and valid subscription items, your customers should have access to their purchased items every time they run your app.

If purchased content is downloaded from your server, you'll also want to grab the `transaction.transactionReceipt` before removing the transaction from the payment queue. Your server will need to receive this receipt data so that it can verify its authenticity with the App Store before authorizing the download request from your app.

Last, but not least, is the transaction status for `SKPaymentTransactionStateRestored`. This is usually returned when a restore request has been sent to the payment queue.

Restoring Paid Content

At first glance, ensuring that purchases are accessible on all compatible devices owned by a customer may sound like a fairly daunting task, but the Store Kit provides support for automating much of this for you. For Auto-renewable Subscriptions and Non-consumable In-App Purchase items, you can send a restore request to the payment queue by calling the following:

```
[[SKPaymentQueue defaultQueue] restoreCompletedTransactions];
```

The result is returned as `SKPaymentTransactionStateRestored` to the `paymentQueue` receiver in your transaction observer class. In the example project, the `paymentQueue` is located in the *InAppPurchaseObserver.m* file. Just as with a normal in-app item purchase, you can check the product IDs in the restored transaction record, and then provide the customer with access to these paid items. The main difference with restored transactions is that the user is not billed again. The items are already paid for, so this method is simply identifying which in-app items your application should make available to the user.

Likewise, if customers accidentally attempt to purchase a Non-consumable item that they've already bought, the result is returned as `SKPaymentTransactionStatePurchased`, but there is no charge for the transaction. After you've provided access to the user's purchased items, you should remove the transaction from the payment queue.

Unfortunately, the older Subscriptions type and Consumable item transactions are not restored by Store Kit. To restore those types, you'll need to employ the server-based In-App Purchase model and keep records of the original purchase transactions on your own server. Then your server's web applications can orchestrate the restoration of those items to your customer's devices.

No matter what you have to do on the back end to support this, you should make the restoration process as convenient and simple as possible for your users. Many developers accomplish this by including a Restore Purchased Content button in a logical location within their apps. A visually appealing example is The Iconfactory's Astronut game, which provides this feature on its level-selection screen with great effect (see Figure 8–21).

Figure 8–21. *The Iconfactory's Astronut game provides a convenient Restore Previous Purchase button to restore a customer's purchased content.*

Digging for Gold

Between the in-app advertising opportunities discussed in Chapter 7 and the new business models explored in this chapter with In-App Purchase, there are many ways to make money on the iOS platform beyond just traditional app sales.

This chapter has provided you with a good starting point for understanding and using In-App Purchase within your applications. For an in-depth look at the entire Store Kit API, I highly recommend reading the related iOS SDK documentation. Log into the iOS Dev Center, and then check out these resources:

- *In-App Purchase Programming Guide*
  (http://developer.apple.com/library/ios/#documentation/
  NetworkingInternet/Conceptual/StoreKitGuide/)

- *Store Kit Framework Reference*
  (http://developer.apple.com/library/ios/#documentation/StoreKit/
  Reference/StoreKit_Collection/)

Chapter 9

Testing and Usability: Putting Your Best Foot Forward

As you've read about the various techniques for improving your app's marketability from within the app itself, you've probably noticed a running theme throughout this book: your app needs to rock! Having a great app idea is not enough. So, what sells? Beautiful, intuitive interfaces that are easy to use and provide functionality that works as intended.

No amount of marketing and publicity will help a poorly conceived app. Buggy performance and rough edges in usability can quickly ruin your app's reputation, prompting negative word-of-mouth, bad reviews, and disastrous customer ratings in the App Store.

Before any release, especially your initial 1.0 launch, implementing a thorough testing process should be a key step in your development cycle. This chapter will touch on the merits of providing built-in help, provisioning apps for on-device testing, and receiving valuable feedback from beta testers.

Preventing the Majority of One-Star Reviews

On the surface, many of the negative customer reviews in the App Store appear to be complaining about nothing more than pricing. There are countless reviews stating that after purchasing the app, the user felt it was not worth the price. Those kinds of comments seem quite petty if the app costs only a few dollars or less, but it's important to understand why those customers feel cheated.

Sure, there will always be those unique individuals who shout from the rooftops about pricing, no matter how good of an app you delivered. But for a large portion of disgruntled customers, there is an underlying principle in effect. For them, it's not really about the money—their morning latte from Starbucks costs more than the app. Rather, it has everything to do with their purchase satisfaction.

After reading the App Store description and browsing the screenshots, a customer will download an app with specific expectations in mind. Whether right or wrong, if those expectations are not met, frustration sets in—even if the app was free! Obviously, some expectations are bound to be unreasonable, and you won't be able to make everyone happy, but there are steps you can take to minimize the number of unsatisfied customers, as you'll learn in this chapter.

Avoiding Common Pitfalls

Here are the two biggest factors that contribute to user frustration:

- Poor performance
- Lack of usability

The good news is that you can fix these two showstoppers before unleashing your app into the wild.

Of course, no one *wants* to release buggy software that's hard to use. Although avoiding poor performance and usability problems may seem plainly obvious to you, it's amazing just how many App Store apps fall victim to those very issues. So, how does this happen? It's easier than you might think, if you're working in an isolated bubble where you're the sole developer and the only tester.

Even if you actively use Instruments (included in Apple's development tools download) and Xcode's Build and Analyze feature to weed out bugs and memory leaks, that's not enough.

Unfortunately, way too many developers don't take the time to extensively test an app across multiple devices and users before submitting the app to the App Store. An app may run fine in your iOS Simulator, but how about on an actual iPhone, iPad, and iPod touch? A number of performance, memory, and usability issues can be discovered only by testing your app on the device itself. In the Simulator, your app may run fast on your mighty Mac with high-speed broadband Internet connectivity, but the true performance test is running on the slower wireless network and processor of a real iOS device.

And don't forget that the iOS Simulator has a much larger display size than the device's compact screen. On a big Mac monitor, an app's interface design can look deceptively large, but it may shrink dramatically on a tiny, high-resolution iPhone screen. UI elements can appear quite functional in the iOS Simulator, but then when testing on the iPhone's small screen, you may find that custom buttons are too small and close together, making accurate finger taps extremely difficult.

Apple rejects almost 60 percent of app submissions at least once. The handful of high-profile rejections that you've read about in the various tech blogs have become news fodder because of vague or ridiculous rejection reasons. However, most of the daily rejections—the ones that don't make headlines—are simply apps that fail to work or fall prey to bugs and crashes while being reviewed. So, it's important that you take the time to test your app not only in the iOS Simulator, but also on as many devices as possible.

If you're a solo, independent developer, you may not have access to all the iOS-powered hardware models, such as the original iPhone, iPhone 3G and 3GS, iPhone 4, iPad, and iPod touch, but it's a worthy investment to have more than one testing device at your disposal. I test apps on an iPod touch, an original iPhone, an iPad, and an iPhone 4. This allows me to check app compatibility on older hardware and iOS 3, as well as on the latest processors, Retina display, and iOS 4.

To accommodate the broadest possible audience, you should consider targeting the lowest common denominator. If an app's Internet-related functionality performs well on the original iPhone's slower EDGE network, then it can only be that much faster on the newer 3GS in the iPhone 4. For memory-intensive apps, it's recommended that you test on an older iPhone model that's limited to a smaller amount of available RAM. And if you plan on making your app backward-compatible with older iOS versions, I recommend using test devices with those versions installed, such as a few different iPod touch models.

Have you let anyone else test-drive your app? If not, then it's imperative that you do! Recruiting beta testers to evaluate your app is one of the most effective ways to unearth hard-to-find bugs and other critical issues. As the app's creator, you've lived with this app through months of laborious design and development. Its completion is your pride and joy. You're too close to it, which means that you might miss glaring problems that others will see. Subconsciously, you might not want to find any faults, since that will mean delaying the release. But when it comes to the harsh frenzy of the App Store, ignorance is not bliss.

Beta testing is not only about squashing bugs. Everyone approaches an app with a unique mind-set and varying expectations. You know your own app inside and out, so naturally, its design seems intuitive to you. However, for others who are unfamiliar with it, figuring out how to use it may prove much more elusive.

Also, the way someone else uses your app may be vastly different from how you intended it to be used. This is important knowledge that will help you fill usability holes and also reveal new target markets for your app that you had not previously considered. For example, a once generic note-taking app may evolve into a more clearly defined journal-writing tool after discovering the specific needs expressed by beta testers.

If you're new to on-device testing or beta testing, then keep reading, because both topics are covered in detail later in this chapter.

Soliciting Direct Feedback

Including an in-app mechanism for customers to easily send you feedback directly can help alleviate many of those negative app store postings. Remember how we integrated In-App Email into an example project in Chapter 5? Even though that was for providing users with a Tell A Friend feature, that same In-App Email functionality can be employed for soliciting direct feedback from customers.

Giving users a dedicated channel for e-mailing you from within your app provides a huge level of convenience for your customers. Don't assume that users will take the time to hunt down the support page on your web site, especially if they are using their iPhone, iPad, or iPod touch (away from their computer). The most convenient avenue to express their opinion is to simply post it as a review on the App Store—unless you give them an easier and quicker method directly within your app!

PumpOne's FitnessBuilder includes a nice example of an in-app feedback form. By making this form accessible from an Ask button on the app's main screen, the developers have set up a remarkably easy way for customers to submit direct feedback from within the app itself (see Figure 9–1).

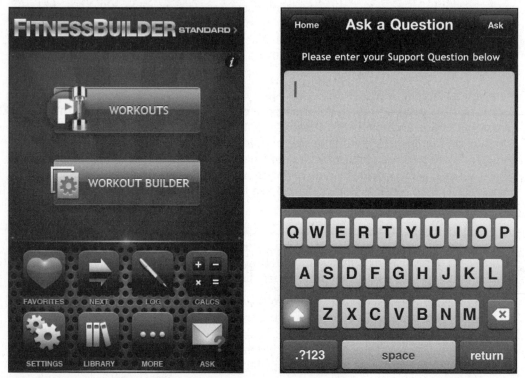

Figure 9–1. *PumpOne's FitnessBuilder provides a convenient in-app feedback form, easily accessible from the Ask button on the app's main screen.*

So, if you're interested in adding direct feedback functionality to your own app, where do you start? Check out Chapter 5's Tell A Friend example project. It should be easy enough to modify that In-App Email code for use as an in-app feedback form. If you would rather not build your own solution, third-party alternatives are available, such as Crittercism (http://www.crittercism.com/).

If you also offer a free app or a lite version of your paid app, it's just as important (if not more important) to add an in-app feedback form to that version as well. With no barrier to entry for free and lite apps, their availability invites a much broader audience of users, most simply curious and wanting to kick the tires. Without the vested interest in the app that paid customers have, those users tend to be harsher critics. Free and lite apps generally receive lower App Store ratings than their paid-version counterparts. With this in mind, your goal is to get users to submit their feedback directly to you within the app, instead of publicly posting their negative rants online in the App Store.

By providing an in-app feedback form, you're letting users know that their voice matters to you. If given the choice to either communicate directly with the app developer or just wait and hope the developer sees their App Store review, odds are they will choose the in-app feedback form, especially if they are seriously interested in seeing the app improve and evolve. This won't stop that minority of loud users who simply like to complain about everything from their online soapbox in the App Store, but it will help reduce the number of negative App Store reviews that are nothing more than feature requests and support questions.

But won't an in-app e-mail form also funnel positive feedback directly to you, instead of having it posted publicly on the App Store, where it can help promote sales? Sure, you may find a little of that happening, but you can always reply to those customers via e-mail, thanking them and politely asking whether they would be willing to post their positive comments in the App Store. If they love your app, more often than not, they will be flattered by the request and help you out.

Establishing a direct connection with your customers is always a win-win for everyone involved. If customers are rooting for your personal success as an independent developer, there's a stronger likelihood that they will evangelize your app in their own interactions online with friends via Twitter, Facebook, and so on.

Preventing User Frustration with In-App Help

A major cause of user frustration is the inability to figure out how your app works. In a desktop computer world, people have grown accustomed to massive, complex software applications that require bible-sized manuals.

In a mobile environment, where apps are often operated with one free hand (and sometimes only a single thumb), users expect apps to have intuitive interfaces that can be quickly learned at a glance. The iOS SDK helps in that regard by providing a universal set of native UI controls for common functions. If you've used a navigation controller in one app, then you'll know how to use it in all other iPhone apps.

For most mobile apps, if a manual is required to explain how to use even the most basic functions, you should seriously consider rethinking your current interface design. Users should be able to download your app and immediately begin playing with the core functionality without being told how to use it. But with that said, figuring out how to operate even the most intuitive, simple UI may not be obvious to everyone. To play it safe, it's never a bad idea to provide a built-in demo or tutorial to help guide those users in need of assistance.

Games often require instructions on how to activate various controls and commands. The more sophisticated productivity apps frequently need to reveal advanced tips and tricks for power users. In these situations, it's important to make this information easily accessible within your app. Don't just post it on your web site or support site, assuming users will find their way there. If customers have gotten to that point, they're already frustrated from searching high and low for the instructions you seem to be keeping well hidden from them. Also keep in mind that your app may be used on an airplane or away from a wireless connection, so including documentation within your app will prove much more convenient for your users.

Including in-app guides will also help reduce the amount of time you spend on customer support, which in turn saves you money (and countless headaches). If users can easily find the answers to their questions within your app, there will be fewer support requests for you to deal with. And if you're an independent developer, you know that the less time you need to spend fielding customer support queries, the more time you have to do actual programming.

There are four common types of in-app help that you can employ in your iOS application:

- On-screen tips
- Instructional videos
- Visual demos
- Text-based help

We'll look at the pros and cons of each approach, so that you can decide which type best suits your app. Whichever method you choose, including some form of in-app help can only improve your app's overall user experience.

Planting Knowledge Seeds with On-Screen Tips

Let's say your app is easy to use and does not require a dedicated help screen or tutorial, but it does include a few advanced power features. Displaying on-screen tips in a UIAlertView pop-up is a great way to quickly educate users.

Upon launch, the popular e-book reader app, Stanza, displays a helpful tip (see Figure 9–2). The app automatically chooses a random tip each time the app launches. A user can opt to see more tips by tapping the Show Next Tip button or choose Dismiss to begin enjoying the app.

Figure 9–2. *Upon launch, the Stanza e-book reader displays helpful on-screen tips for using the app. There are convenient options to either disable tips or show more tips.*

Notice that there is also a Disable Tips button. This is a critical option that allows power users who are already familiar with all of the tips to easily deactivate the startup alert before it becomes annoying. The tips feature can be turned on and off in the app's Settings panel, but why make the user search for that? Allowing users to quickly disable tips with a simple tap will prevent them from becoming frustrated with something that is supposed to be nothing but helpful.

Instructional Videos: The Double-Edged Sword

For many games (and even apps), a video showing the actual game in action is often the easiest way to explain how to play it. Although this is highly effective, there are some drawbacks.

Because of the typical file size of a video clip, you won't want to include it in your app's download for fear of bloating your mobile app to an unreasonable size. This leaves you with two main options:

- Upload the video to a video-sharing site like YouTube.
- Host the video on your own web server.

Since many developers upload trailers and instructional clips to video-sharing sites to help promote their app, an easy solution is to simply link to one of those "how to play" videos from a button within the app. There are a couple problems with this approach, however.

Most video-sharing sites use Flash video, which the iOS platform does not currently support. You can use YouTube, because its videos are dynamically converted from Flash video into the iOS-compatible H.264 video format. But then you must make sure your app is not linking to the video's YouTube page, forcing the video to load in either the YouTube app or the Mobile Safari browser, which takes users out of your app. Since users were not aware they had left the app to begin with, they may not understand why they are not returned to the app after viewing the video. Yes, I know that directing all traffic to that YouTube video page will increase the number of viewings and your YouTube ranking, but in this case, user experience should trump your online social marketing efforts.

Whenever possible, you should load the media file directly so that it plays in the native iOS movie player controller. When the clip finishes playing or the user taps the controller's Done button, the user is automatically returned to your app. This provides a seamless transition, enabling consumers to instantly begin using the app after watching the how-to video. The popular contact data-sharing app, Bump, does this well with the brief, instructional video on its About screen (see Figure 9–3).

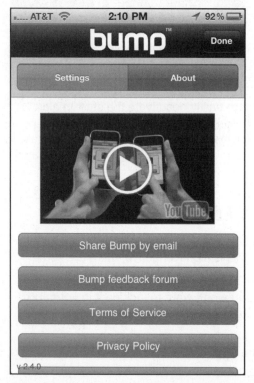

Figure 9–3. *Tapping the video thumbnail in Bump's About screen will play the how-to video in the iOS movie player controller. When the clip is finished, users are automatically returned to the app.*

Of course, producing an instructional video requires some digital filmmaking chops, but if you're a game developer, then it's practically a marketing requirement these days. It seems like every iPhone and iPad game has a slick video trailer for promotional purposes. Creating another video that explains how to play it may prove equally important.

Show, Don't Tell, with Visual Demos

You know the old saying "A picture is worth a thousand words." It rings just as true when teaching people how to use your app. Although a video is great, a visual demo made up of static images or short animations can be just as effective. Since these kinds of demos are typically constructed as a brief slide show of screenshots or illustrations, they're usually much smaller in size than a video file, which means they load faster and use less memory—important factors to consider when building mobile apps.

The popular Convertbot app boasts a beautiful and unique interface, but since it doesn't use familiar UIKit controls, how to use it may not be apparent at first glance. The developers, Tapbots, solve this issue by asking users upon first launch if they would like to view a quick demo. If the prompt is dismissed, the demo can always be accessed through the Info panel.

Convertbot has one of the best demos I've seen in an iOS app. Instead of loading the demo into a different view, the app's actual main interface is shown full screen, performing actions on autopilot with pop-up balloons describing how the different UI elements work and what steps to take to perform specific unit conversions (see Figure 9–4).

Another great example is the demonstration in Rovio's Angry Birds. When first launching the game, users are given the option to view a quick how-to guide (see Figure 9–5). Showing only detailed pictures without words, these visual instructions translate effortlessly into any language and age group.

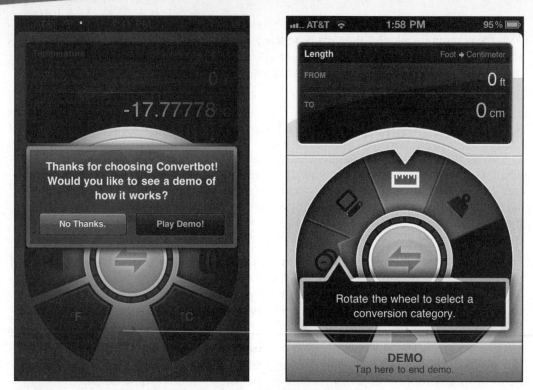

Figure 9–4. *Convertbot includes a very effective demo. Placing the main interface on autopilot, it shows you how to use the unique UI elements with pop-up balloon descriptions.*

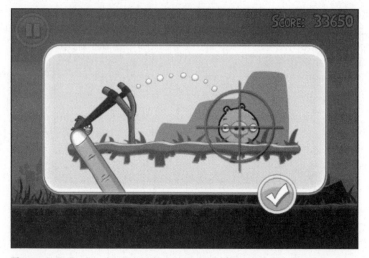

Figure 9–5. *By showing only pictures, Angry Birds' game-play instructions are easily accessible by any language and age group.*

The only drawback to constructing an effective in-app demo is the time and development energy required. Crafting a tutorial demo as a series of illustrations or modified screenshots with instructional annotations can often be a lot easier than creating a video, especially if your film-editing skills are limited. You could write a very simple slide show view controller to run through the PNG screenshots. If you have an app that would benefit from an embedded demo, then it's well worth the effort.

Providing Mobile Manuals with Text-based Help

Although simple pictures can often suffice to explain game play, many productivity and lifestyle apps require more extensive instructions for using advanced features and services. If other types of in-app help are not applicable, and you really need to provide comprehensive documentation, then good old-fashioned text-based help might be your only answer.

But don't settle for plain text. Present the information in an appealing format, following these basic guidelines:

- Quickly explain steps in fewer words by organizing text into sections with bullet points.

- Use larger font sizes with a bold style to reflect topic titles.

- Insert screenshots or illustrations as visual aids to the text.

The popular fitness app, RunKeeper Pro, accomplishes this with the help guide presented on its About screen. Since the content is organized into sections with styled text, numbered lists, and cropped screenshots, the instructions are easy to understand and read quickly (see Figure 9–6).

Figure 9–6. *RunKeeper Pro's text-based help is presented in a styled and organized manner, which is attractive and easy to read.*

Don't worry! There's no need to tackle the complexities of Core Text just to display the kind of stylized help shown in Figure 9–6. With a UIWebView, you can use HTML to display styled text and images!

A Little HTML Goes a Long Way

The beauty of HTML is that it's easy to create and maintain. Just add a UIWebView to your help view controller and have it load the HTML page or HTML string you want displayed. You can even include the HTML help page within your compiled app so that there's nothing to fetch remotely—perfect for devices that are not connected to the Internet, such as an iPad without Wi-Fi or an iPhone in airplane mode. And during development, modifying the documentation requires only a few simple text changes to the HTML—no need to fiddle with Objective-C code.

For apps that require a constant Internet connection for their core functionality, the help panel's UIWebView could just as easily load an URL of an external web site. This gives you the flexibility to update your help content without needing to modify or recompile the actual iOS app.

Remotely hosting the help content is especially useful if you receive a lot of feedback from users. You can continuously update your help page with additional answers to frequently asked questions, improving the support within your existing iOS app. This also allows you to maintain a single source of help content on your web server, which can be accessed by multiple platforms. A different set of CSS styles can be employed depending on whether that same help content is rendered in a desktop web browser, an iPhone, an iPad, or some other mobile device.

With many users accessing your in-app help with single thumb taps on small screens, take great care to keep the help content tightly organized and easy to navigate. If you're building a sophisticated productivity app that requires extensive documentation, one long scrolling screen of text can be a little unwieldy. Break it up into smaller topics. This list of help topics can be presented as a UITableView. Selecting a topic loads a new screen that displays that topic's HTML page of text and images in a UIWebView.

If you would rather not create your own infrastructure of a navigation controller with multiple UITableViews and UIWebView screens, an alternative is to use a third-party mobile web framework within a single UIWebView.

Building In-App Help with Mobile Web Frameworks

Most developers groan at the thought of writing documentation of any kind, And if you lack web-design skills, then needing to create a set of HTML pages makes matters even worse. Fortunately, there are some amazing third-party iOS web kit frameworks that you can use to streamline this process. Here are just a few:

- iUI, an iPhone UI web framework (http://code.google.com/p/iui/)

- Sencha Touch, a feature-rich mobile JavaScript framework (http://www.sencha.com/products/touch/)

- jQTouch, a jQuery plug-in for iPhone web development (http://www.jqtouch.com/)

- iWebKit, an iPhone web site toolkit (http://snippetspace.com/projects/iwebkit/)

- WebApp.Net, an iPhone web development framework (http://webapp-net.com/)

- Magic Framework, an iPhone HTML5 framework (http://www.jeffmcfadden.com/projects/Magic%20Framework/)

- SaFire, an iPhone web app framework (http://code.rememberthisguy.com/safire/)

- UiUIKit, a universal iPhone UI kit (http://code.google.com/p/iphone-universal/)

Not only are these toolkits specifically optimized for iOS screen sizes, but they also provide time-saving templates that mimic native UI controls and behavior. This is beneficial for two major reasons:

- The web design looks like an iOS interface, so it blends well with the rest of your app.

- The UI is familiar, so there's absolutely no learning curve for the user.

An instant help system that works like an iOS app! All you need to do is write the text.

So, which framework should you use? They all have their own unique benefits and strengths, so check out their web sites to see which one best suits your specific needs.

All of the frameworks include full source code and are available as free downloads. Usage rights can vary, so be sure to read their licensing terms before adding a third-party web framework to your app.

Provisioning: Setting Up a Development Device

When you need to test features that are not supported in the iOS Simulator, such as the accelerometer, multitouch gestures, and In-App Purchase, you should run your app on an actual iPhone, iPad, or iPod touch.

For preliminary testing during development, Vimov's ingenious iSimulate iPhone app and SDK can wirelessly send the GPS location and multitouch, accelerometer, and compass events to the iOS Simulator from an iPhone or iPod touch on the same Wi-Fi network. This can greatly reduce the amount of time spent on testing, since running apps in the iOS Simulator is much faster than installing apps on a test device. Learn more about iSimulate at http://www.vimov.com/isimulate/.

Even if you don't use the specific features that require running on an actual mobile device, it's highly recommended to test and debug your app on several iOS devices to ensure that everything works as intended *before* submission to the App Store. In order to do that, you need to set up a developer certificate and provisioning profile to authorize your device.

Thoroughly testing your project on actual mobile hardware is a crucial factor in the potential success of your application. Yet many developers avoid this task because Apple's provisioning process can appear complicated. Perform a quick search through the popular developer forums, and you'll find dozens (if not hundreds) of posts from frustrated programmers who have been unable to get this working correctly.

If you're never done this before, setting up a test device can be quite daunting. Here's a step-by-step walk-through to help demystify the process.

Step 1: Establish Your Test Device in Xcode Organizer

First, you'll need to assign an iPhone, iPad, or iPod touch as a test device within Xcode Organizer. Using the 30-pin USB cable that came with the device, plug it into your Mac. This action will typically cause iTunes to launch. If iTunes' preferences are configured to automatically sync the device upon connection, then simply wait for the synchronizing to finish. Once completed, open Xcode and choose **Window ➤ Organizer**.

When the Xcode Organizer window appears, you should see your connected device listed in the left pane. Select that device, and in the main pane's Summary tab, you should see device-related information. To designate the selected device for testing in Xcode, click the Use for Development button (see Figure 9–7). To authenticate the request, you may be asked to provide your iOS Dev Center login and password, if you have not done so previously.

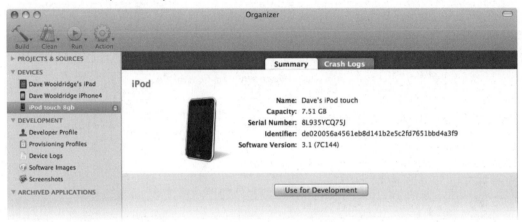

Figure 9–7. *Designate the selected device for testing in Xcode Organizer by clicking the Use for Development button.*

It's perfectly fine to use your primary iPhone as a development device. Even after clicking the Use for Development button, that device will still operate like a normal iPhone. Just remember to always back up the device's data when synchronizing in iTunes. That way, if anything goes wrong during testing, you can always restore the device's operating system, applications, and settings in iTunes with the last saved backup.

After finishing this step, do not quit Xcode Organizer, since we'll be referring to it again later in the provisioning process. One essential bit of information that will be needed is the 40-character device identifier, which is listed here in the device's Summary tab. This is referred to as the *unique device identifier* (UDID).

Step 2: Acquire Your Development Certificate

Next, you'll need to request a certificate. Launch the Keychain Access application, located on your Mac at */Applications/Utilities/Keychain Access*.

In the Keychain Access utility, open the Preferences window by choosing **Keychain Access ➤ Preferences...** and select the Certificates tab. Make sure Online Certificate Status Protocol (OSCP) and Certificate Revocation List (CRL) are both set to Off before closing the Preferences window.

Now, select **Keychain Access ➤ Certificate Assistant ➤ Request a Certificate from a Certificate Authority** from the menu. In the Certificate Assistant window that appears, enter your iOS

Developer Program e-mail address and a name for your certificate (see Figure 9–8). In this example, I simply used my full name, but I could have just as easily used a more descriptive label, like Dave Dev Key. The Request is option should be set to Saved to disk. Click the Continue button, and Keychain Access will generate and save your certificate request file to your hard drive. If you chose your desktop as the location, you should see a new file there called *CertificateSigningRequest.certSigningRequest*.

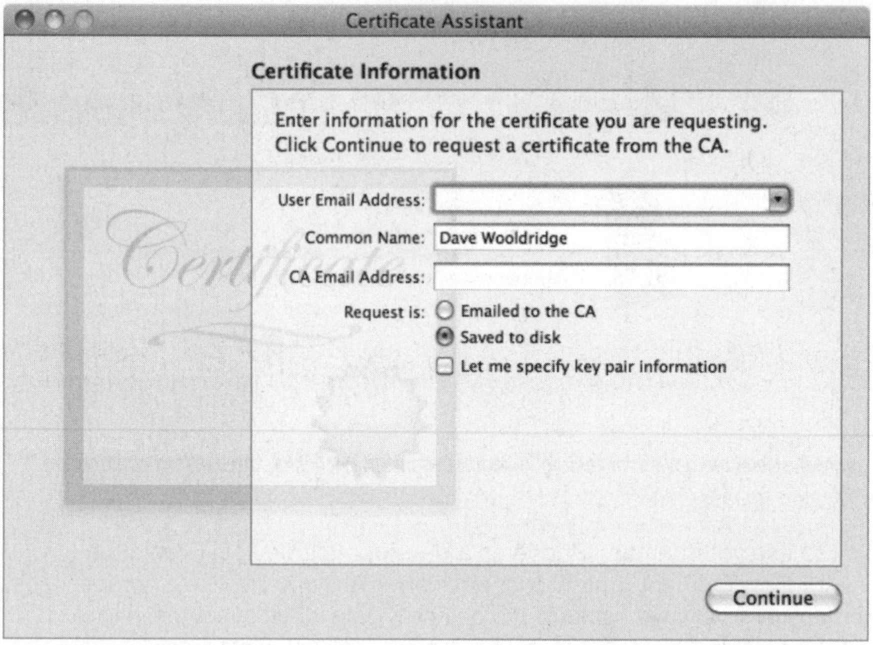

Figure 9–8. *Generate a certificate-signing request file from the Keychain Access application on your Mac.*

Open your web browser and log in to the iOS Dev Center at `http://developer.apple.com/devcenter/ios/`. Then navigate to the iOS Provisioning Portal by clicking its respective link in the right column.

On the main Provisioning Portal page, select Certificates in the left column. Within the Development tab, click the Request Certificate button and upload your *CertificateSigningRequest.certSigningRequest* file to the online system. Once your team admin (you, in most individual cases) approves the certificate request, your new development certificate will be available for download from this Certificates section (see Figure 9–9).

Figure 9–9. *Download your development certificate to your Mac desktop.*

VERIFY THAT APPLE'S WWDR CERTIFICATE IS INSTALLED

When you initially signed up for the iOS Developer Program online, one of the first things you might have done was to download and install Apple's Worldwide Developer Relations (WWDR) certificate. If you don't yet have Apple's WWDR certificate in your Mac's keychain, you'll need to take care of that *before* installing your development certificate.

Directly below the download link for your development certificate in the iOS Provisioning Portal, look for the text "If you do not have the WWDR intermediate certificate installed, click here to download now" (see Figure 9–9). Click that link. When prompted, choose to save the *AppleWWDRCA.cer* file to your desktop. Next, double-click that downloaded file. A dialog box will appear asking if you would like to add this certificate to your Mac's keychain. Make sure the login keychain is selected, and then click the Add button.

Download the *developer_identity.cer* file to your Mac desktop. Double-click that downloaded .cer file, which will launch the Keychain Access application (if it's not already open). Keychain Access will display a dialog box, asking if you would like to add the certificate to a keychain. Make sure the dialog box's keychain menu is set to login, and then click the Add button.

In the Keys category of the main Keychain Access window, verify that your private and public keys are now paired together with your development certificate to ensure it is properly configured on your Mac. In this example, my Dave Wooldridge key (which was created when I generated a certificate-signing request under the same name) is now paired with my imported development certificate (see Figure 9–10).

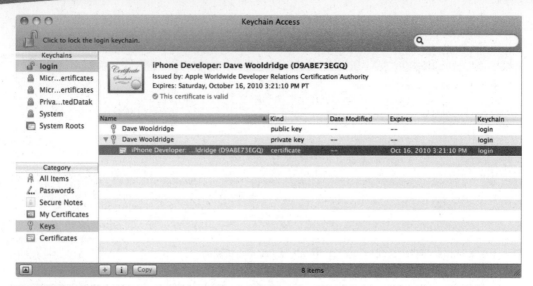

Figure 9–10. *Verify that your imported development certificate has been paired with your developer key in Keychain Access.*

With the developer certificate installed, you can now quit the Keychain Access application and return to the iOS Provisioning Portal in your web browser.

Step 3: Register Your Device ID

In the iOS Provisioning Portal, select Devices from the left column, and then within the Manage tab, click the Add Devices button. This web form is where you enter the name and ID of your test device. The device name can be any name you want, but make it descriptive enough to differentiate it from other device names you plan to add. Referring to your selected device in Xcode Organizer, copy the 40-character device identifier, and paste it into the Device ID field (see Figure 9–11).

For standard iOS Developer Program members, Apple allows you to assign up to 100 devices for development and testing purposes. A hundred may seem like a lot at first glance, but as you gather beta testers for multiple apps, that number will eventually seem rather limiting, so use these slots wisely.

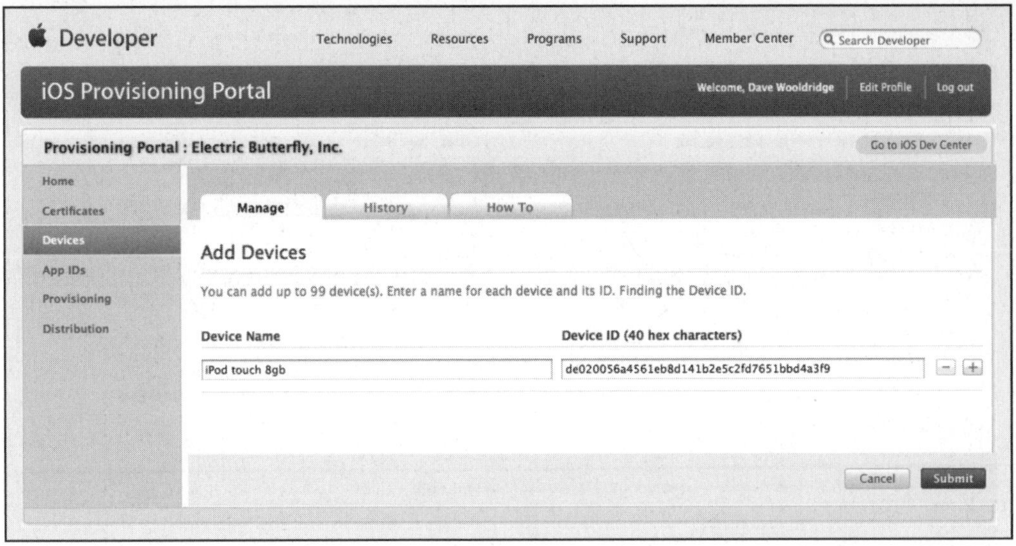

Figure 9–11. *The device ID should be your test device's 40-character device identifier listed in Xcode Organizer.*

Step 4: Create an App ID

With your test device's ID registered, navigate to the App IDs section of the iOS Provisioning Portal. Within the Manage tab, click the New App ID button. On the web form that appears, enter a name in the Description field (see Figure 9–12). This can be any name you want. It is the name of the app ID listing in the iOS Provisioning Portal, so use a unique description that makes it distinguishable from other app IDs you create.

The Bundle Seed ID (App ID Prefix) value is dynamically generated by Apple, but you should set the Bundle Identifier (App ID Suffix) value to be the same as the one listed in your Xcode project's Info *.plist* file. For example, in our fictional Breadcrumbs app, the bundle identifier is the reverse-domain name com.ebutterfly.breadcrumbs (see Figure 9–12).

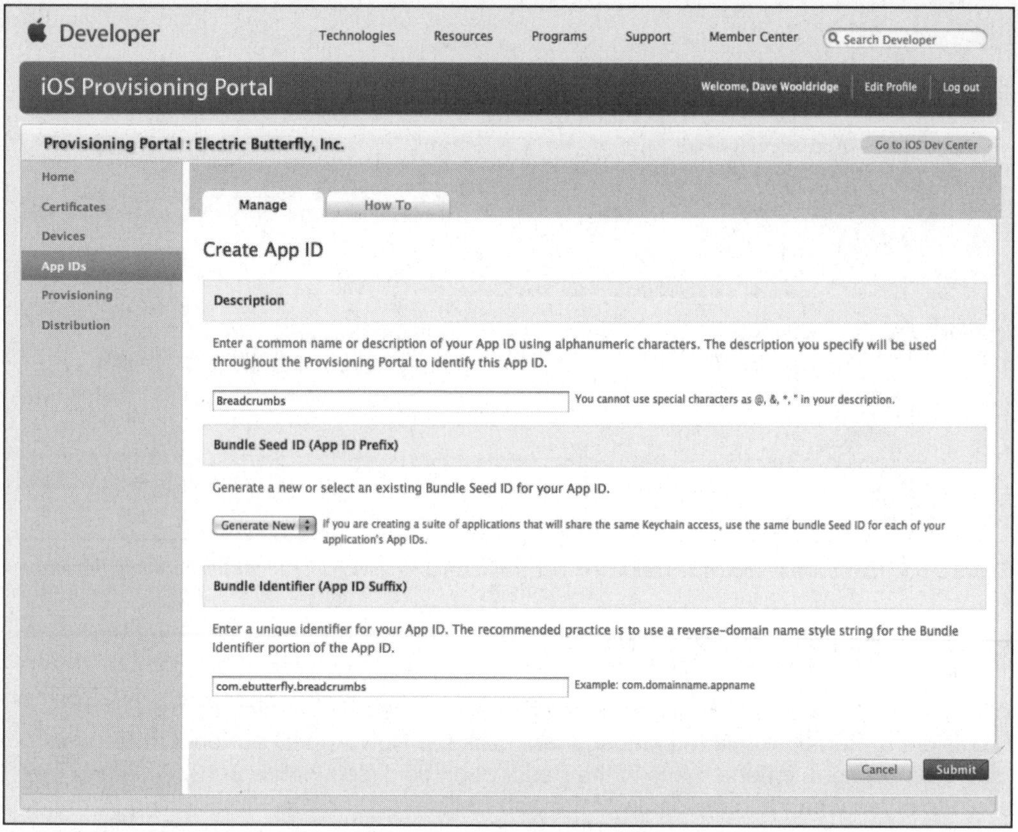

Figure 9–12. *Create an explicit app ID with an app-specific bundle identifier.*

After submitting your new app ID, you should see it displayed in your list of app IDs in the Manage tab (see Figure 9–13). Notice that your explicit app ID can be configured for testing push notifications, In-App Purchase, and Game Center. That's because it contains an app-specific bundle identifier, which is required for your app to properly communicate with those Apple services.

Figure 9–13. *An explicit app ID can be configured for testing push notifications, In-App Purchase, and Game Center.*

The provisioning profiles generated from Apple's handy Development Provisioning Assistant wizard and Xcode's Automatic Device Provisioning are convenient for testing apps on a device because they use a wildcard app ID. Instead of assigning an app-specific bundle identifier, an asterisk (*) is used as a wildcard placeholder. This way, the related provisioning profile can be used to test any app on a device, regardless of its bundle identifier.

As you'll notice from the disabled options of TestApp in Figure 9–13, the major limitation to wildcard app IDs is that they cannot be used for testing app-specific push notifications, In-App Purchase, and Game Center.

This is the reason we're working through the extra steps to create an explicit app ID and provisioning profile that can be used for testing any iOS feature on your device.

Step 5: Generate and Install Your Provisioning Profile

Now we're finally ready to generate a provisioning profile. This is where it all comes together.

Select Provisioning from the left column of the iOS Provisioning Portal. Within the Development tab, click the New Profile button. On the web form that loads, give the provisioning profile a unique name, such as Breadcrumbs Dev Profile (see Figure 9–14).

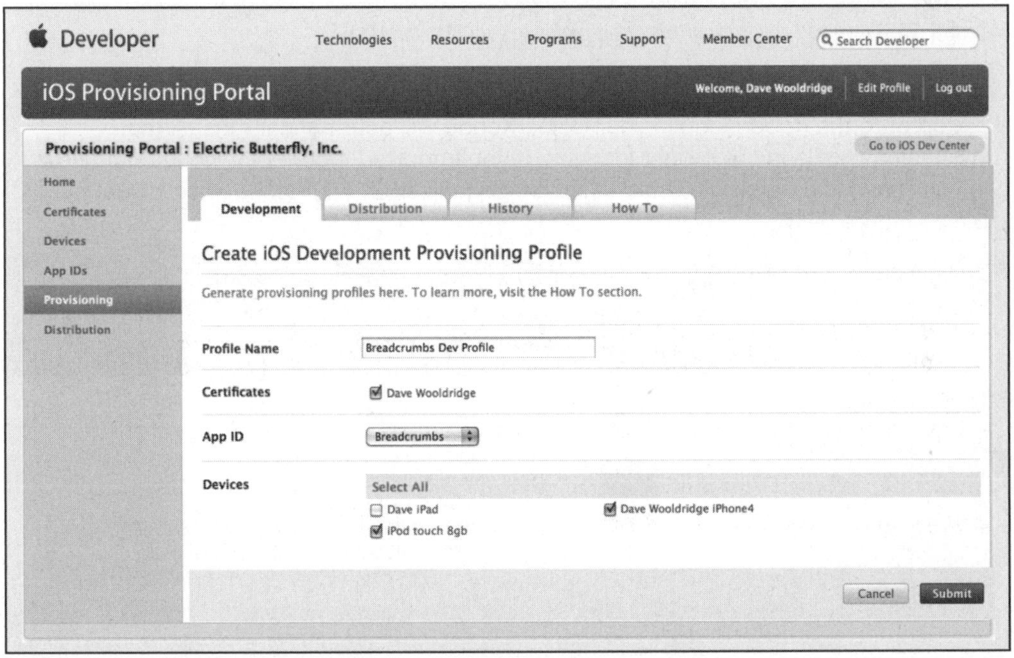

Figure 9–14. *Using the online Development Provisioning Assistant to generate your provisioning profile.*

If you've done everything correctly up to this point, you should see your developer certificate, app ID, and device IDs listed on that form as well. Select the appropriate entries for each field, and then click the Submit button (see Figure 9–14).

After your provisioning profile has been generated, you'll be prompted to download it from your list of provisioning profiles (see Figure 9–15). Download the *.mobileprovision* file to your Mac desktop.

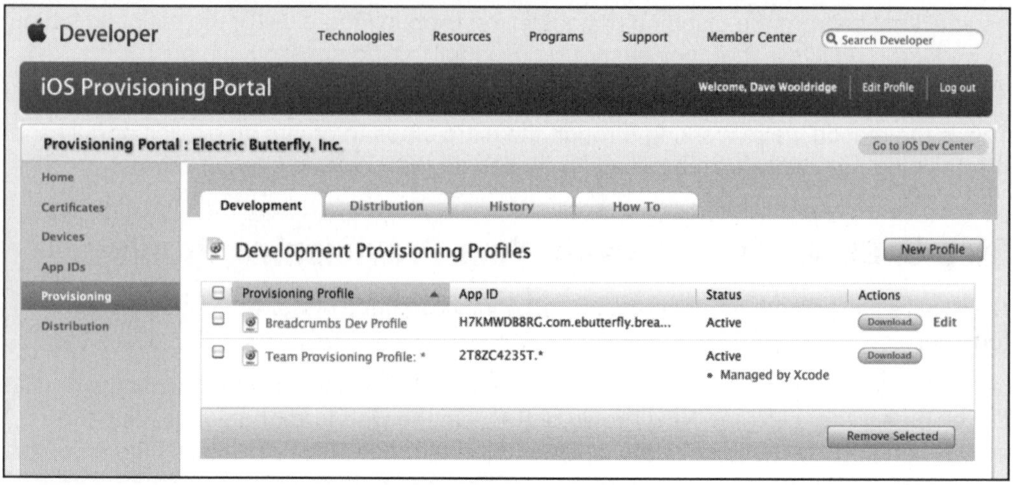

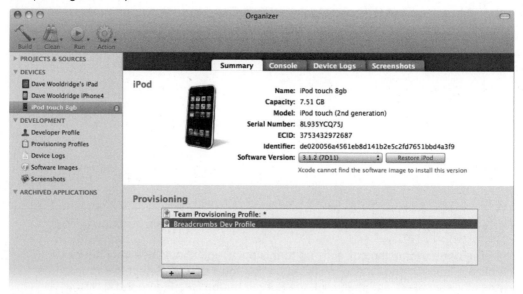

Figure 9–15. *Download your new provisioning profile to your Mac desktop.*

With your test device still connected to your Mac, drag the *.mobileprovision* file from the desktop onto the Xcode icon in your Dock. Xcode will automatically install that provisioning profile in the proper location. If you imported it correctly, you should now see your provisioning profile listed in Xcode Organizer on your test device's Summary tab (see Figure 9–16).

Figure 9–16. *If your provisioning profile was installed successfully, you should see it listed in Xcode Organizer on your test device's Summary tab.*

Step 6: Run Your Xcode Project on Your Test Device

Now that you have the proper provisioning profile and certificates in place, you can finally start testing your app on the connected device. Open your Xcode project, and in the top-left corner of the main project window, choose Device from the Overview drop-down menu.

Before you can run your project, you'll need to modify the build settings to specify your new provisioning profile. Select the Target app within the Groups & Files pane and click the blue Info button in the toolbar menu. In the Target Info window that appears, choose the Build tab, and scroll down to the Any iOS listing under Code Signing Identity. Select your desired development provisioning profile from the pop-up menu (see Figure 9–17).

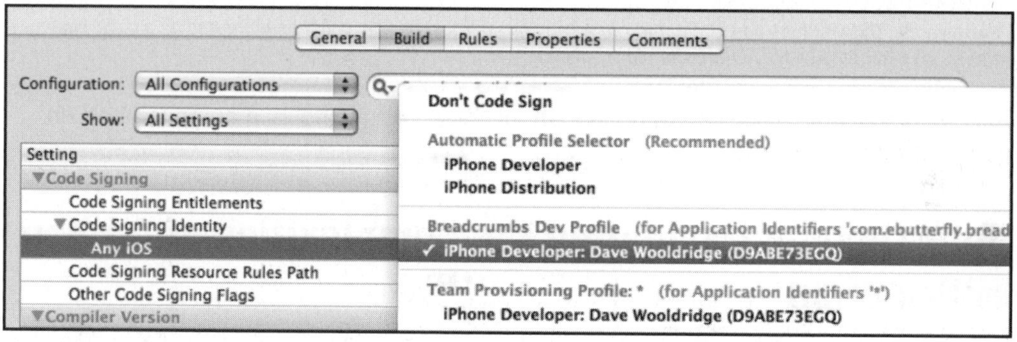

Figure 9–17. *Assign a specific provisioning profile to your Xcode project for device testing.*

As your last task, switch over to the Properties tab in the Target Info window, and enter your app ID's bundle identifier in the Identifier field. For the example in Figure 9–18, the app ID bundle identifier for our fictional Breadcrumbs app is com.ebutterfly.breadcrumbs, and it is also listed as such in the Xcode project's Info .plist file.

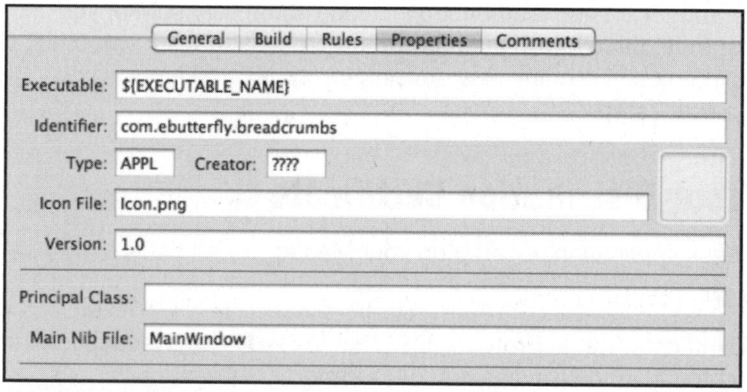

Figure 9–18. *Input your app ID's bundle ID in the Target Properties tab's Identifier field.*

When you click the Build and Run button, Xcode will compile the app and send it via USB to the test device, where it will be installed and run. The first time you attempt this, you'll be prompted by a code-signing dialog box, requesting to use your developer key (see Figure 9–19). Click the Always Allow button to proceed.

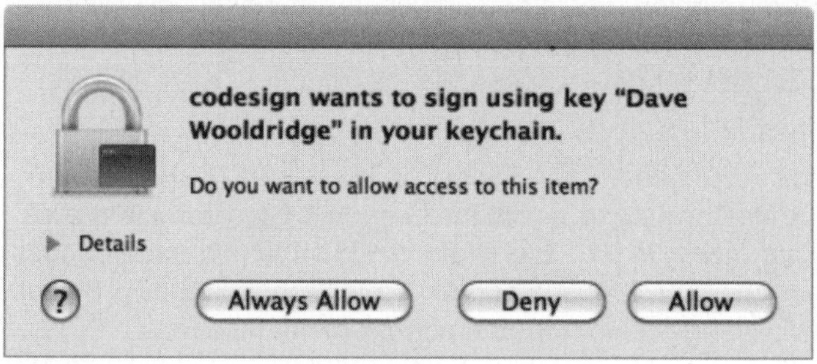

Figure 9–19. *The first time you attempt to run an app on your test device, you'll be prompted by a code-signing request, so click the Always Allow button to proceed.*

And we have liftoff! Your Xcode project should now be running as a compiled app on your test device.

Beta Testing: Navigating the Complexities of Ad Hoc Distribution

Even more important than your own testing in the iOS Simulator and on an actual device is having multiple people test your app. After performing extensive tests of your own, it's highly recommended that you round up a group of volunteers who are willing to beta-test your application before release in the App Store.

We've gone over the steps for setting up certificates and provisioning profiles for testing on your own iOS device. Many of the steps required to set up ad hoc distribution for multiple beta testers will seem quite similar, with only a few exceptions. But make no mistake, configuring your app for ad hoc distribution includes some very subtle, yet important, extra tasks that must be followed in order for the process to work smoothly. This is yet another stumbling block for many new developers, so let's take our time walking through each and every step.

Step 1: Acquire Your Distribution Certificate

Launch the Keychain Access application, located on your Mac at

`/Applications/Utilities/Keychain Access.`

First, make sure Online Certificate Status Protocol (OSCP) and Certificate Revocation List (CRL) are both still set to Off in the Keychain Access Preferences window's Certificates tab.

Then, select **Keychain Access ➤ Certificate Assistant ➤ Request a Certificate from a Certificate Authority** from the menu. In the Certificate Assistant window that appears, enter the e-mail address and exact name listed for you in your iOS Developer Program account (see Figure 9–20).

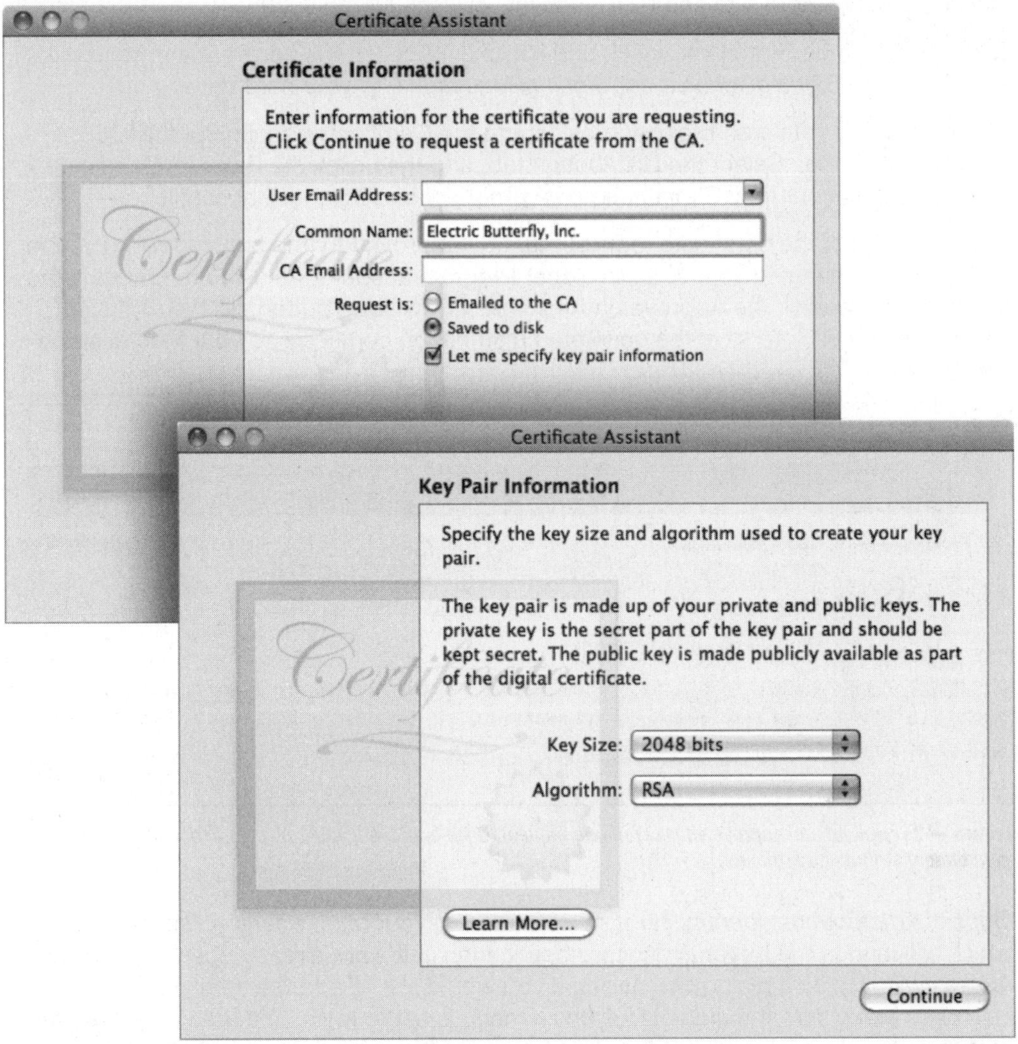

Figure 9–20. *Your distribution certificate request must include the same name and e-mail address as assigned to your iOS Developer Program account. You must specify the Key Size and Algorithm settings as 2048 bits and RSA, respectively.*

Since this request is for your official distribution certificate, which will be used for both ad hoc distribution and App Store distribution, the e-mail and name must match up identically to your iOS Developer Program credentials. For example, my company name, Electric Butterfly, Inc., is the official name in my account, so that's what I used for this form. The Request is option should be set to Saved to disk.

There's one more thing that makes this request different from the one previously made during the development certificate process. Make sure "Let me specify key pair information" is checked. Because that box is checked, when you click the Continue button, the Certificate Assistant will ask you to assign the key size and algorithm, which should be set to 2048 bits and RSA, respectively (see Figure 9–20).

Click the Continue button yet again, and Keychain Access will generate and save the new *CertificateSigningRequest.certSigningRequest* file to your hard drive.

Moving back to your web browser, navigate to the Certificates section of the iOS Provisioning Portal. Select the Distribution tab, and then click the Request Certificate button. Upload your new *CertificateSigningRequest.certSigningRequest* file.

Once submitted, the certificate request must be approved by the team admin. If you're the only one managing your iOS Developer Program account, then you're probably the team admin, so click the Approve button. Now a Download button will be displayed, which you can click to save the generated distribution certificate to your Mac desktop (see Figure 9–21).

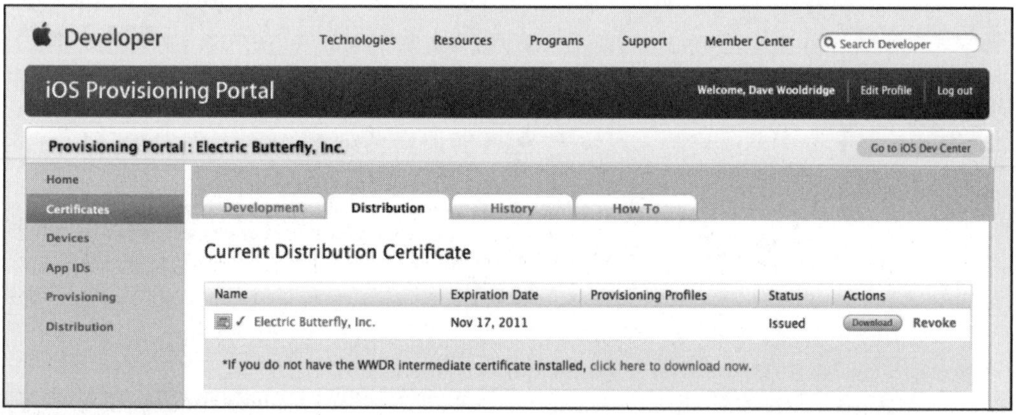

Figure 9–21. *Upload and approve your certificate request. Once approved, you'll be able to download the generated distribution certificate.*

Once the *distribution_identity.cer* is downloaded to your Mac, double-click the file, which will launch the Keychain Access application (if it's not already open). Keychain Access will display a dialog box asking if you would like to add the certificate to a keychain. Make sure the dialog's keychain menu is set to login, and then click the Add button. In the Keys category of the main Keychain Access window, verify that your private and public keys are now paired together with your distribution certificate to ensure it is properly configured on your Mac. In this example, my Electric Butterfly, Inc. key (which was created when I generated a certificate-signing request under the same name) is now paired with my imported distribution certificate (see Figure 9–22).

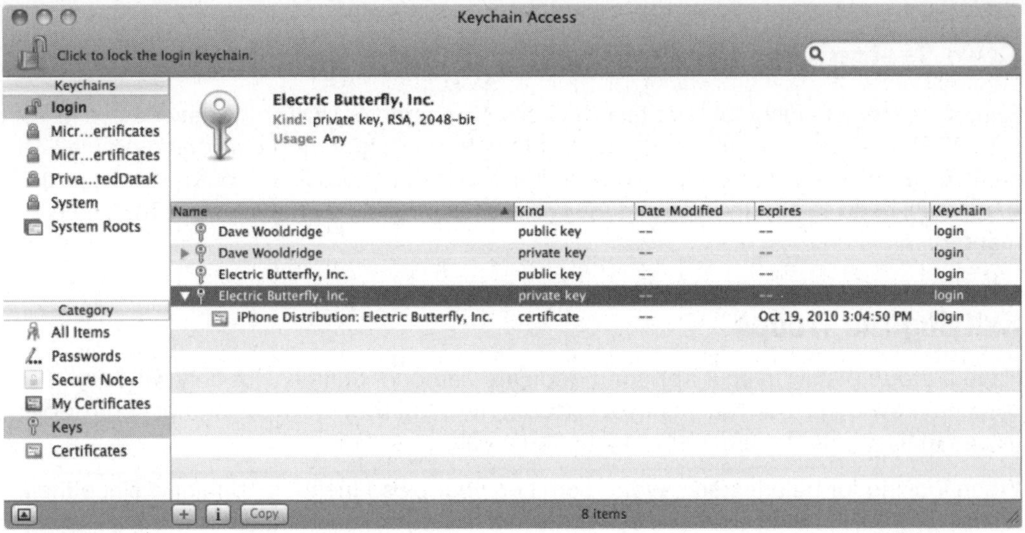

Figure 9–22. *Verify that your imported distribution certificate has been paired with the correct private key in Keychain Access.*

Do not install distribution certificates for multiple iOS Developer Program accounts into the same keychain. Doing so will cause problems in Xcode. If you're compiling and submitting iOS apps for clients, then create a separate Mac OS X user account for each distribution certificate you need to install. You can do all your development within your primary Mac user account, but to compile for distribution, you should switch to the user account that has that client's distribution certificate installed.

EXPORT YOUR DISTRIBUTION PRIVATE KEY FOR SAFEKEEPING

Your distribution private key is required by Xcode to sign compiled app binaries. Without the proper code signing, the application cannot be uploaded to the App Store, nor will it work with ad hoc testing. This private key cannot be reproduced, so it is imperative that you export it and save the file in a special place, just in case you need to restore it at a later date when switching to a new Mac or reinstalling the operating system.

To export your distribution private key, select it from the Keys section of Keychain Access. In the Figure 9–22 example, my distribution private key is selected. Then choose File ➤ Export Items. Save the file in Personal Information Exchange (*.p12*) format, which requires you to assign a password.

If you ever need to reinstall this private key, simply double-click the exported *.p12* file and enter your password. Keychain Access will take care of the rest.

Step 2: Register the Device IDs of Your Beta Testers

Remember registering your own test device's 40-character UDID as a new device ID in the iOS Provisioning Portal in order to create your development provisioning profile? The same holds true when creating a distribution provisioning profile, so before you can do that, you'll need to add the UDID of every beta tester as a new device ID in the same manner.

Rallying the Troops

Have a group play with your app for a dedicated amount of time. Not only will they discover new bugs that you've never encountered, but they will also stumble on usability issues that may not be apparent to you, the creator.

When looking for beta testers, avoid recruiting your close friends and family, since their feedback will not be as objective as you would like. More often than not, they will give only positive comments—you won't get the harsh truth you need at this juncture.

And don't just get fellow developers to test your app. Also recruit a fresh set of nontechnical eyes to run the app through its paces. People who are not familiar with programming offer a very valuable, objective viewpoint, and they will most likely be a closer representation of your app's target audience. Just be prepared to ask a lot of questions to extract the pertinent bits.

Often, nontechnical users will know when they don't like something, but they may not initially understand why it bothers them. It may take a great deal of patience on your part to get them to properly communicate their reasoning behind a reported issue.

On the flip side, developers speak your language, so they can easily describe problems on a very technical level, and may even suggest ways to fix them. But since developers are attuned to navigating through even the most nonintuitive interfaces, they may not recognize usability issues that would trouble a newbie.

Your best bet is to gather a diverse group of beta testers that is composed of developers, power users, and nontechnical, casual users.

Since quality beta testing requires a fair amount of dedicated time from a participant, you should offer some form of payment as an incentive for providing a satisfactory amount of feedback. It does not need to be cash. For developers on a shoestring budget, the reward can be a free copy of the app you're testing or a free license to another related product you sell. Just make sure to carefully outline exactly what a beta tester is required to complete to earn the free goods. A good barter system will be a win-win situation for everyone involved. You get valuable feedback, and the testers get free swag and software.

So, beyond your own pool of developer friends, where can you find additional beta testers? Imangi Studios (creators of Harbor Master) and other popular game developers recruit many of their beta testers from popular gaming sites, such as the Touch Arcade forums. It's not uncommon to see online queries from companies looking for beta-test volunteers posted on blogs, Facebook, and Twitter.

Collecting a UDID from Every Beta Tester

Most users won't know where to locate the UDID on their iPhone, iPad, or iPod touch. You can tell the user to follow these steps:

1. Sync your device with iTunes.

2. Select the device's Summary tab to display its properties.

3. If the serial number is listed, click it to toggle the listing to show the identifier (UDID).

4. Choose Edit   Copy from the Edit menu to copy that 40-character UDID to the clipboard. (Even though the user won't be able to select the text of the UDID in iTunes, the Copy command will copy it to the clipboard.)

5. Paste it into an e-mail message and send it to the developer (you).

If that's too complicated, simply have the user download Erica Sadun's free Ad Hoc Helper app from the App Store. Once installed on the test device, running the app generates an e-mail containing the device's UDID, which the user can send to you.

After receiving all your beta testers' UDIDs, simply register them online in the Devices section of the iOS Provisioning Portal, using the same form you submitted earlier when registering your own test devices.

Many developers employ a naming scheme to help keep their Devices list organized. Instead of just the beta tester's first and last name, I highly recommend including the tester's device model as well, such as "Joe Smith iPhone 4" or "Jane Walker iPad."

Unfortunately, you need to know who all of your beta testers are before you generate your distribution provisioning profile, since every beta tester's device ID must be tied to that profile. If you need to insert additional device IDs later, that will require you to generate a new distribution provisioning profile, and then redistribute the updated profile and app. It's a very laborious, time-consuming process, so it's best not to need to go through that more than once.

> **NOTE:** A major drawback to Apple's current system is that a standard iOS Developer Program account is limited to only 100 devices per membership year. That may seem like a lot, but in reality, if you're developing several apps and each one has its own group of beta testers, it's actually pretty easy to max out your device ID allotment. You do have the option to delete old unused device IDs from the portal, but they will still count toward your device ID total within that membership year. So with that said, take care to use your device ID slots wisely. Whenever possible, register only the device IDs of beta testers you know will provide quality feedback.

Step 3: Generate and Install an Ad Hoc Distribution Provisioning Profile

Jumping back to the iOS Provisioning Portal in your web browser, select the Distribution tab within the Provisioning section. Then click the New Profile button.

In the form that's presented, be sure to choose Ad Hoc as the distribution method. Select the appropriate app ID for your application, and verify that the distribution certificate is assigned correctly. Enter a profile name that reflects the nature of this provisioning profile. When testing multiple applications, including the name of the app along with a reference to the distribution stage (Ad Hoc or App Store) in the Profile Name field helps keep the collection of profiles organized.

Last, but not least, you'll need to select all of the beta tester device IDs that should be included in this provisioning profile (see Figure 9–23). If a specific beta tester's device ID is not embedded in the provisioning profile, that person will not be able to install and run the app on their device. Any accidental omissions will force you to create and install a new, updated provisioning profile, so carefully review the selected devices before clicking the Submit button.

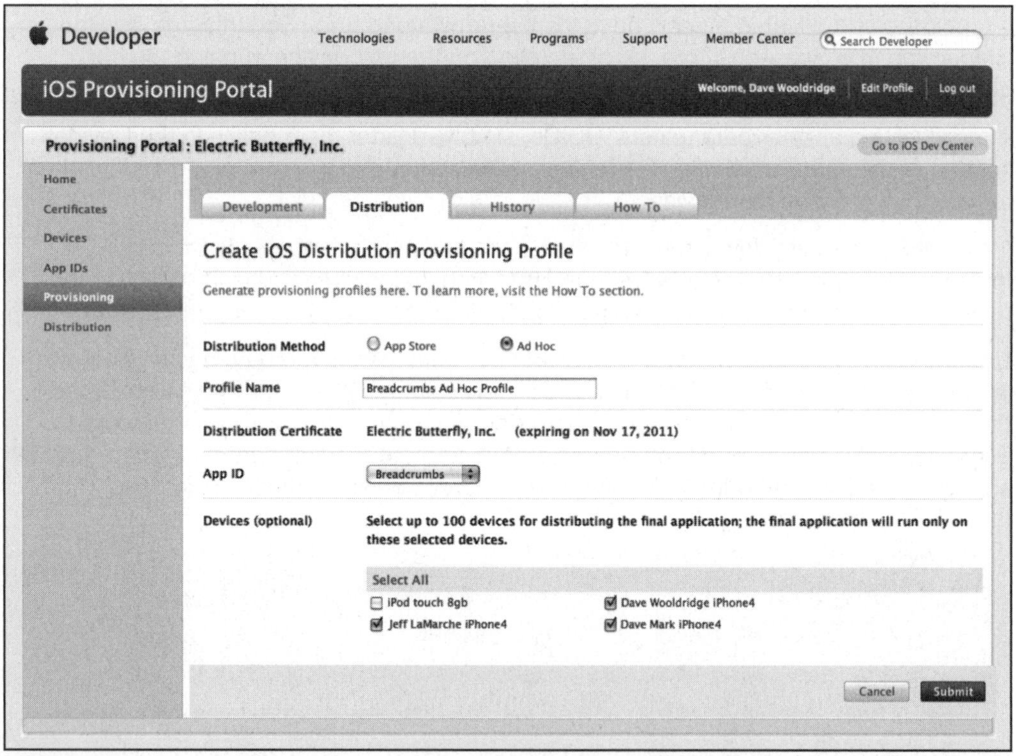

Figure 9–23. *Carefully select all the device IDs of your beta testers before generating the distribution provisioning profile.*

When your distribution provisioning profile has been generated and can be found in the Distribution tab's list of provisioning profiles, click the Download button to save the *.mobileprovision* file to your hard drive. With your test device still connected to your Mac, drag the *.mobileprovision* file onto the Xcode icon in your Dock. Xcode will automatically install that provisioning profile in the proper location.

Save a copy of that distribution provisioning profile that you stored on your hard drive. You'll need to include that *.mobileprovision* file with the compiled app you deliver to your beta testers.

Step 4: Configure Your App for Ad Hoc Distribution

Now that you have the distribution certificate and provisioning profile in place, the next step is to configure your Xcode project for ad hoc distribution. Fire up your project in Xcode, but before you do anything, ensure that you've added a 57 × 57 pixel *icon.png* file and a 114 × 114 pixel *icon@2x.png* file (for Retina display) to the project. Beyond the fact that you may encounter distribution build errors without an icon, visual impressions count even in the beta-testing stage, so including a beautiful app icon is important.

In the main Xcode project window, select the project name at the top of the Groups & Files pane, and then click the Info button in the toolbar. Within the Configurations tab of the Info window, duplicate the existing Release configuration, naming the copy **Distribution** (see Figure 9–24).

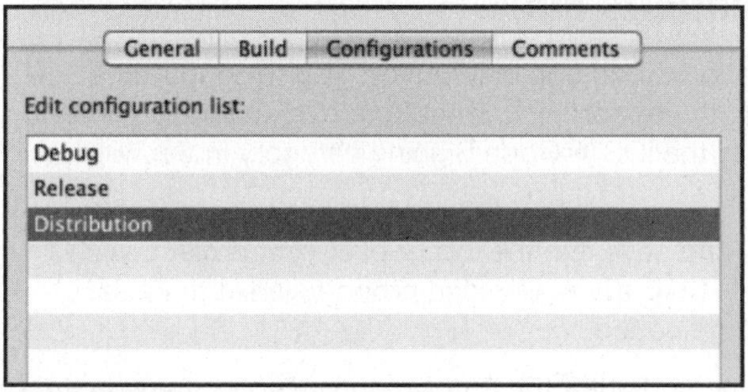

Figure 9–24. *Within the Xcode Project's Info window, duplicate the Release configuration and name it Distribution.*

Close the project's Info window. Now select the Target app within the Groups & Files pane, and click the toolbar's Info button again. In the new Target Info window that appears, navigate to the Build tab, and choose Distribution from the Configuration drop-down menu. Scroll down to the Any iOS field below the Code Signing Identity row, and assign it to your new distribution provisioning profile (see Figure 9–25). Even though your development provisioning profile may also be listed in the pop-up menu, it's critical that the distribution provisioning profile is selected, since that is the only one that will work with ad hoc distribution.

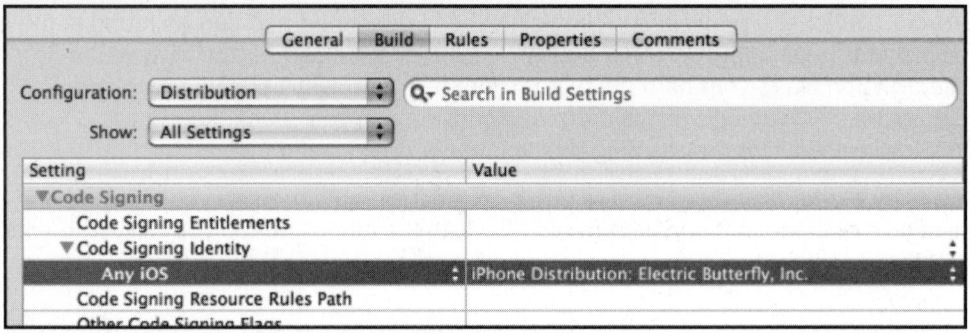

Figure 9–25. *Modify your Target's Build tab to reflect the Distribution configuration and your distribution provisioning profile.*

Jump over to the Properties tab, and enter your app ID's bundle identifier in the Identifier field, which should be the same as the bundle identifier listed in your Xcode project's Info *.plist* file. Again, as an example, the Breadcrumbs bundle identifier is com.ebutterfly.breadcrumbs.

With all of that completed, go back to the main Xcode project window. From the drop-down menu in the top-left corner, select Distribution as the Active Configuration and Device as the Active SDK.

Step 5: Create the Entitlements File

Before you can compile your application for ad hoc distribution, you need to add a special code-signing *Entitlements* file to your project. From Xcode, choose File ➤ New File, and then select Entitlements from the iOS ➤ Code Signing category in the window that appears (see Figure 9–26).

Name the new file *Entitlements.plist*, and save it in the top level of your project. With it selected in Xcode, make sure the `get-task-allow` Boolean property is set to False (unchecked), and then resave the file if needed.

Finally, reopen the Target Info window, and enter the *Entitlements.plist* file name in the Code Signing Entitlements field of the Build tab.

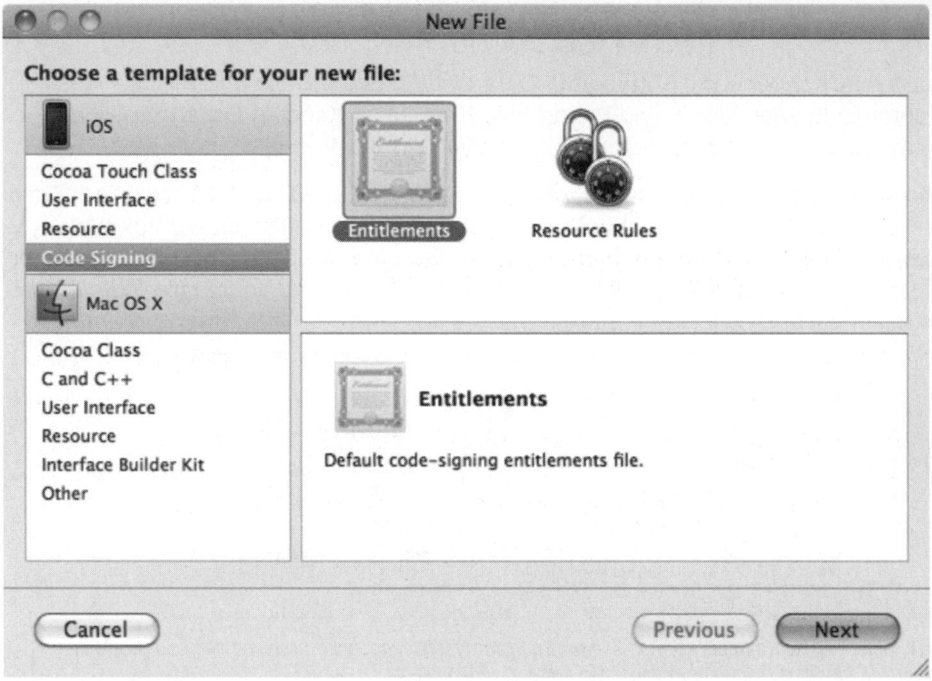

Figure 9–26. *Add a special code-signing Entitlements file to your Xcode project.*

Step 6: Compile Your iOS App

After making all the described changes to your project, save it. Then select **Build ➤ Build and Archive**. If you've configured everything correctly, your app should compile successfully.

The first time you build the app with your distribution provisioning profile, a code-signing dialog box will appear, asking you to grant code-signing permission. Simply click the Always Allow button.

Build and Archive checks your app during the compilation process to ensure that it's code-signed properly and references the correct provisioning profile.

If build errors arise that are related to the project settings, retrace your steps to ensure that you've followed every single task outlined in these instructions, no matter how insignificant it may seem. Build errors can often be caused by the smallest mistakes, such as a misspelled bundle identifier or a mismarked check box. If problems persist, and you've ruled out code bugs and faulty configuration settings, then clean out your project's build directory, reopen the project in Xcode, and try another build attempt.

Once you've successfully compiled your app, take a moment to revel in the accomplishment. Preparing your application for ad hoc distribution is a fairly tedious process, so making it this far deserves a pat on the back.

Step 7: Distribute Your App to the Beta Testers

Now you're ready to send the app to your beta testers! Since Build and Archive was used to compile the app, you'll find the archived version in Xcode's Organizer window. In the left pane of Xcode Organizer, select Archived Applications.

In the applications list that's displayed, choose the ad hoc build you just compiled. Then at the bottom of the screen, click the Share Application button. The dialog box that appears will ask you to assign the distribution provisioning profile for this app. Xcode will actually package your compiled app and provisioning profile into an *.ipa* file that you can either e-mail or save to disk (see Figure 9–27).

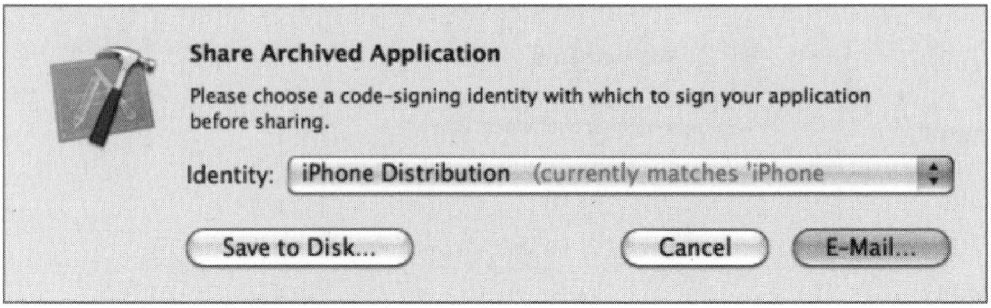

Share Archived Application

Please choose a code-signing identity with which to sign your application before sharing.

Identity: | iPhone Distribution　(currently matches 'iPhone　　　　▲▼

(Save to Disk...)　　　　　(Cancel)　(E–Mail...)

Figure 9–27. *Selecting Share Application in Xcode Organizer will package your archived app and provisioning profile into an .ipa file for distributing to your beta testers.*

For beta testers to install your app, their device should already be mounted in iTunes (connected via USB). They will need to drag the *.ipa* file and the *.mobileprovision* file into iTunes. Mac users can simply drag the files onto the iTunes icon in the Dock. Windows users should drag the files into the Library or Apps in the main iTunes window. If they perform a sync, your app and related provisioning profile should appear on their device, ready to run. Let the beta testing begin!

Wireless Distribution to Beta Testers

Forcing beta testers to deal with importing an app package into the desktop iTunes just to sync an ad hoc version onto their mobile devices has always been annoying for developers and often problematic for newbie beta testers. Fortunately, iOS 4 introduced a little-known new method for distributing your ad hoc builds wirelessly. Yup, that's right—no more syncing with iTunes just to install a beta version.

In iOS 4 and higher, Apple supports over-the-air installation of iOS apps, which means you can download and install an ad hoc app build and its related provisioning file by tapping an HTTP link on a web page or in an e-mail. This feature was originally promoted as a benefit to Enterprise iOS Developer Program members, but it seems to work just as well for standard program members, too.

Unfortunately, this new over-the-air feature does not bypass the need for all the ad hoc distribution steps we previously walked through. You still must collect your beta testers' device IDs, create an ad hoc distribution provisioning profile, and configure your Xcode project accordingly. In fact, preparing your app for over-the-air distribution requires a few more extra steps, which are explained in detail on Alex Okafor's excellent developer blog, Parade of Rain, at `http://www.paradeofrain.com/2010/11/taking-the-pain-out-of-ad-hoc-testing/`.

But before you attempt to replicate that setup, there is an easier way, and it's free! Enter TestFlight, an amazing new service that offers over-the-air beta distribution without the extra hassles. TestFlight also helps you to organize your beta-testing efforts with an online dashboard that lets you invite and manage beta testers, as well as track beta testing across multiple apps. With a brilliantly designed web site and service, TestFlight has made the process incredibly painless for both developers and beta testers. Remarkably, for the foreseeable future, TestFlight is free, so I highly recommend checking it out at `http://www.testflightapp.com/`.

Although this new wireless distribution method is convenient, it's supported on only iOS 4 and higher, so if you need to distribute your app to iOS 3 beta testers, they will need to use the old-fashioned method of dragging your app binary and provisioning profile into the desktop iTunes to sync with their connected iOS device.

Sitting Pretty

This was, by far, one of the most instruction-heavy chapters in the book. Since both provisioning and ad hoc distribution have proven to be such challenging topics for many new iOS developers, I hope the thorough explanations helped clarify the process for anyone struggling with these two tasks.

It won't matter how brilliant your app idea is if it's poorly executed. I can't emphasize enough the importance of your app's overall user experience as one of the primary factors in its potential success. On-device testing and group-managed beta testing should be mandatory steps in every application's development cycle.

Chapter 10

Get the Party Started! Creating a Prerelease Buzz

Development completed? Check. Testing completed? Check. Ready for the App Store? Almost.

After months of hard work to finish your application, I know you're eager to release it to the world, but don't jump the gun just yet. You still need to accomplish a few very important tasks.

Before submitting your iOS app to the App Store, you want to start generating some prerelease buzz through a carefully crafted online presence. This chapter will explore the best ways to stir up some excitement and anticipation for your app by promoting it on your web site, blogs, and social networking sites, such as Twitter and Facebook.

The Final Countdown: Preparing for Liftoff

I know what you're thinking: "Why can't I simply take care of building my app's web site and prerelease buzz while the app is being reviewed by Apple? Since the App Store can take weeks to approve or reject an application, that should give me enough time, right?" Don't count on it. Even if your app review takes longer than the average 7-day to 14-day turnaround, that's still not enough time to cultivate a large online following and effective web presence.

Just your luck, when you actually rely on Apple's app review team to take a long time, that will undoubtedly be the one occasion your app sails through to approval within only a few days. That would leave you unprepared, without your app's web site and social marketing plan in place.

Invest the Time to Find Your Audience

Even though developing an attractive web site always takes longer than you think it will, if you were really pressed for time, you could probably construct a decent site in only a matter of days (with a little web-design expertise). But what does require a much longer gestation period is the job of growing your online audience. Marketing requires an audience, so you need to invest the time to find yours.

This audience usually consists of not only influential bloggers and journalists, but also your own Twitter followers, Facebook friends, LinkedIn connections, blog readers, and e-mail newsletter subscribers. To a social media newbie, this may all seem a little overwhelming, but don't worry. Later in this chapter, I'll explain how to take advantage of these powerful tools and relationships in extensive detail.

If you don't yet have a Twitter account, a Facebook fan page, or a good rapport with high-profile bloggers and journalists, it's never too soon to get the ball rolling. How early should you start? It usually takes a few months to acquire a decent number of followers on Twitter and Facebook, so you should dive into the social media sea at least three months before you plan on submitting your app to the App Store. Some developers start tweeting about their forthcoming iPhone and iPad apps while still in development. The goal here is to amass your own social information network for easily distributing news about your iOS applications. So the earlier you start, the better.

Just be careful not to give away too much information during this prerelease campaign. You don't want to prematurely expose your poker hand to your competitors (yes, they are watching). Also, if you inundate your online audience with a blitz of overhyped marketing messages long before your app is released, you risk losing a large portion of your followers before launch day. No one likes an overzealous, aggressive salesperson who clutters their Twitter streams and e-mail inboxes with too much marketing noise. It's all about gently stoking the fire, building anticipation and interest. Simply whet their appetite, leaving them wanting for more—be a tease!

Craft Your Elevator Pitch

To effectively explain the features and benefits of your forthcoming app in a quick and concise manner, you should write several versions of your app description. Each variation should be limited to a specific length for different uses. Don't mistake this exercise for writing a full-blown press release. You'll have plenty of time to do that later for your app's actual release. For now, think much shorter.

I typically write three versions at this stage: a one-sentence description, a single-paragraph description, and then one that's a few paragraphs long. Not only does that provide me with an app description size that's appropriate for almost any need, but it also helps me fine-tune my marketing message. When forced to explain your app in only a few sentences, you need to cut out the fat, leaving only the key selling points that would appeal to potential customers.

The old term *elevator pitch* refers to the ability to sell someone on an idea in the short amount of time it takes to ride an elevator. This concept applies to almost every industry. When pitching a movie treatment, a screenwriter may have no more than a brief moment to convince a studio executive of its merits. A publisher may discard a book submission if it fails to captivate him in the first few pages. In a radio commercial, an advertiser may have only 15 seconds to grab the listener's attention. Promoting an iOS app in the fast-paced world of technology is no different.

Often, you have only a minute or two to describe your app to an influential journalist. Hot-tech blogs are flooded with press releases and queries about new mobile apps every day, so what makes yours so special? Whether it's read in an e-mail or quickly explained at a conference, after only a few sentences, you want that journalist to instantly "get it" and want to write about your app.

To start off, think of an effective caption that describes your app in only a few words. For our fictional Breadcrumbs app example, we've established the caption "Parked Car Locator." Sure, it's basic, but in only three words, we've said what the app does. And with the 140-character limit imposed by Twitter, short is sweet. Now with the general functionality covered by the caption, the Breadcrumbs description can focus on the primary features and benefits, as well as the key differentiator that sets this app apart from its competition.

Remember our discussion of determining your application's differentiator in Chapter 2? Here's where it starts to pay dividends for you. Not only will it help attract customers, but it will also assist you in capturing the attention of the media in this prerelease stage. When describing your app to journalists and bloggers, you never want them to ask "Why?" With the many existing parked-car locators in the App Store, why should anyone care about your app? If you've crafted your pitch successfully, you've already answered that question, describing how your app is the first parked-car locator to implement augmented reality using the iPhone's built-in camera. Augmented reality in mobile apps has recently been a hot topic in the news, so that's the hook. And the media loves a good hook.

Just make sure that any claim you make is true before including it in your pitch. You don't want to announce your app as the first augmented reality-based parked-car locator if an existing iOS app has already staked that claim. As always, do your homework first, making sure to do plenty of research online and in the App Store.

Ad-supported blogs and news sites need to continuously draw in readers to satisfy sponsors, and in order to do that, there's an insatiable demand to publish fascinating, topical stories. If your pitch fails to interest the press, you'll want to rethink your strategy. Later in this chapter, I'll touch on when and how to communicate with the press to establish important relationships and jump-start some prerelease publicity.

Another advantage to crafting your elevator pitch now is that it will help you write a better App Store description when you're ready to submit your app to Apple. I've seen too many long-winded App Store descriptions that scroll for days to explain a simple game concept. Those lengthy descriptions actually do the apps a disservice, since no one will spend the time reading them.

Like your elevator pitch, your App Store description should be brief and concise, with bulleted key features and a few highlighted testimonial quotes (and even award mentions). It should quickly tell readers what your app does and why they should buy it. Anything more is just noise that gets in the way of your sales pitch.

Gather Additional Prerelease Marketing Materials

Beyond having short and long text descriptions of your app, you should also have the following items prepared for use in your marketing campaigns (both prerelease and postrelease):

- Company logo (high-resolution)
- App icon (high-resolution)
- App logo (high-resolution)
- Screenshots
- Video trailer
- Dedicated web presence

These items will come in handy for not only your own web site and social media efforts, but also for the press if requested by journalists and bloggers.

Company Logo

No matter what kind of products you develop, you should always have a high-resolution version of your logo available, just in case the press requests it. Many companies actually include a "press room" page on their web site or a download link to a press kit so that their company information and logo are available 24/7.

Technology is a global industry, so reporters and bloggers from various time zones may be interested in writing about your company or product. They may be on a tight deadline and can't wait until you read your e-mail in the morning. Providing a press kit or company logo download on your web site will help make their job easier!

Although most media coverage may be online, don't discount the needs of print magazines and newspapers. Make sure your company logo is a scalable, vector-based image and saved as an EPS file. Or at the very least, it's a large 300 dpi bitmap image saved in a lossless compression format, such as TIFF or PNG. That will ensure maximum flexibility for any use.

If you're a publisher who partnered with a third-party development company to create the application, you'll also want to have the other party's logo available. This would be a good time to check your contracts to see whether the third party also requires its logos and/or names included in all press coverage about your iOS app.

App Icon and Logo

You should have a high-resolution icon and logo for your iOS app. Ideally, you took my advice in Chapter 4 to design your app icon at a high resolution for various press and marketing purposes.

Scalable, vector-based EPS files are always nice, but large 300 dpi bitmap files (like PNG or TIFF) can work just as well. If you're saving your icon or logo as a PNG file, ensure that the background is transparent. If you're saving it as a TIFF or high-quality JPEG, use a default white background.

Since most of your media coverage and marketing efforts will focus primarily on your new app, and not necessarily your company itself, the 300 dpi print-ready versions of your app's icon and logo will prove much more important than any of your other logos. You'll also find high-resolution app-branding graphics useful when designing other related elements, such as your app's web site and the background image for your Twitter profile. And on the off chance that Apple requests an ultra-large app icon for inclusion in its print advertisements, Worldwide Developers Conference wall banner, or (gasp!) a TV commercial, you'll have one ready at your fingertips (and you can thank me later).

Screenshots

Having a few good screenshots of your app in action may seem fairly obvious, but it's amazing just how many bad screenshots I've encountered in the App Store and online at various developer web sites and app review blogs. Don't just run your app and take some random screenshots of the main views. The screenshots you unveil to the world should be stellar examples of your app, showing off just how much fun or productive it is to use it.

If your app is a notebook-style writing tool, don't show me an empty, unused list. And don't show me a few test notes with generic titles like "Note 1" or "Example 1." If I'm a writer looking for a tool like that, I want to see it being used to its full potential. Create some authentic-looking documents inside your app's notes list, like "My Novel Outline," "Research for Tech Article," and "Tuesday Meeting Notes." The app needs to look valuable and worthy of purchase.

In the real estate market, *staging* helps sell houses. Some prospective buyers have trouble envisioning what an empty house would look like with their own furniture in it, so they walk away, believing it's not really a good fit for their needs. Staging is the act of filling that house with appealing furniture and interior design nuances to help those people better visualize the possibilities. "See, this is what your house could look like! Nice, right?"

You need to take the same staging approach with your iPhone and iPad app screenshots. This does not mean faking your screenshots in any way. Just spend some time actively using the app yourself, setting up a scenario within your app that would make for a visually enticing screenshot. This "in-action" screen should help potential buyers immediately see the value in purchasing your app. Although this applies well to productivity and utility apps, it's also a good rule of thumb for all other types of apps, such as games. Don't just show any example of game play. If it's a first-person shooter, show the player in the middle of heavy combat, racking up a high score. Showcase the fun!

Video Trailer

Producing an engaging video trailer for your app is something every iOS developer should seriously consider. Some apps are hard to describe through static images alone. Providing an actual video walk-through of the app in a slick, movie-style video trailer—complete with title treatments, visual effects, and music—is a very powerful marketing tool. Captivating video trailers on YouTube have helped hundreds of iPhone games become best sellers.

Depending on the kind of app you've developed, producing a trailer now may be a tad premature for your prerelease marketing efforts. Since you haven't submitted your app to Apple's review team, you have no idea if you'll be required to change major portions in order to receive an approval. A video trailer floating out there on YouTube and other video-sharing sites should be representative of the actual final application that will be in the App Store.

If you do plan on creating a video trailer for your app, I definitely recommend completing it before your app is released, so that it can help boost awareness from the very beginning. Two compelling reasons to produce your own video trailer are control and convenience. Without a video trailer, some app review sites may choose to shoot their own video walk-through, which may not show your app in its best light. By providing them with your own video trailer, you retain control of how your app will be presented visually. And by alleviating the need for reviewers to shoot a video, you've just made it that much more convenient for them to write a review of your app.

Using a video camera to film the app running on your iPhone or iPad is a huge undertaking that often produces poor results if not done properly. There are many requirements when taking this approach—such as capturing the right lighting, ensuring the device's screen is always in focus, and keeping your hands from shaking—which are much harder to achieve than you might think. Unless you're a professional filmmaker or have access to one, this is not the ideal path.

Most developers rely on screen-capture software to record video of their apps running in the iOS Simulator. This provides a high-quality solution that is easy to implement.

If you want to enhance the look and capabilities of the iOS Simulator, a few third-party software products are worth exploring:

- To emulate support for GPS location, multitouch gestures, the accelerometer, and the compass, check out Vimov's clever iSimulate iPhone app and SDK (http://www.vimov.com/isimulate/). It wirelessly sends those events to the iOS Simulator from an iPhone or iPod touch device on the same Wi-Fi network.

- To customize the look of the iOS Simulator's home screen and improve the visibility of the cursor with a translucent white dot, try SimFinger (http://blog.atebits.com/2009/03/not-your-average-iphone-screencast/). atebits offers this utility as donationware.

- If you would rather use an actual finger image as a cursor replacement in the iOS Simulator, you'll like Wonder Warp Software's PhoneFinger (http://www.wonderwarp.com/phonefinger/), which is also available as donationware.

Once you have the iOS Simulator optimized, you'll need to find a screen-capture utility for recording the video. Here are several options to evaluate:

- ScreenFlow (http://www.telestream.net/screen-flow/)

- iShowU HD (http://www.shinywhitebox.com/ishowuhd/main.html)

- Sound Stage (http://soundstageapp.com/)

- Screenium (http://www.syniumsoftware.com/screenium/)

- Snapz Pro X (http://www.ambrosiasw.com/utilities/snapzprox/)

- Camtasia for Mac (http://www.techsmith.com/camtasia/)

- Voila (http://www.globaldelight.com/voila/)

Some popular choices among iOS developers are Telestream's ScreenFlow, shinywhitebox's iShowU HD, and New Leaders' Sound Stage. Some of the screencasting products available offer an all-in-one, comprehensive recording and editing solution. If you choose a tool that provides only screen recording, you'll also need a third-party editor like Apple's iMovie or Final Cut Pro to turn the footage into a polished video trailer.

It's up to you to create a compelling video trailer, so take the time to not only plan the recorded walk-through of your app in the iOS Simulator, but also to script any audio voice-over tracks. Don't forget to add some music to set the tone—making sure to use licensed or royalty-free music. Since the trailer may be played on various video-sharing sites and app-review sites, always incorporate your app's icon and logo within the video to help reinforce its brand identity.

If producing a video trailer falls far outside your comfort zone, don't think twice about hiring a professional editor. An amateurish video can definitely taint consumer perception of your app's quality. When possible, don't cut corners on production value.

An image is worth a thousand words, but the impact of video can be even more effective in building anticipation for your forthcoming iOS app or game. Just be careful not to release the video trailer too far in advance of your app's release. Since Apple's app review process can often take longer than expected, you don't want to overhype your app prematurely, only to lose that momentum long before the app becomes available in the App Store.

Dedicated Web Presence

Last, but not least, you need a web site or dedicated web page for your app. Providing a central online destination for both consumers and the press to access additional information is a powerful tool that every software developer should embrace. Next, we'll take a look at what constitutes a good web site for promoting an iPhone or iPad app.

Your iOS App Deserves a Well-Designed Web Site

You'll need a web site and online support up and running for your app before it becomes available in the App Store, so why not take advantage of its promotional power while drumming up excitement during the prerelease phase? Since your application is not in the App Store yet, your site should be the primary URL where all interested parties are directed. And even after your app is released, a custom-designed web site (when done right) can be a much more effective sales tool than the limited content found in App Store product pages.

Having a strong web presence should be mandatory for every iOS developer, regardless of the fact that the App Store is a closed system. The App Store includes direct external links to a developer's web site and support site from an app's product page. Consumers interested in your application may visit your web site before making a purchase decision, looking for additional information, a video trailer, or an animated tutorial. They may also want to check whether you're a legitimate business that offers customer support. When people buy your app, in a small sense, it's an investment in your company, so they like to know you're going to be around awhile.

You don't want any technical glitches or missed opportunities to ruin the heightened exposure that surrounds your app's actual release in the App Store. By getting all of your "ducks in a row" now, you'll be able to navigate through any web issues that may arise long before your app's debut.

Web Hosting

If you don't yet have a web site, the first step is to set up an account with one of the many web-hosting companies available. Just do a quick Google search for *web hosting*, and you'll see there's no shortage of companies. Most of them offer very affordable hosting packages, but the real trick is to find one that meets your specific needs.

Ask fellow developers who they recommend for web hosting. It's important to inquire about their experiences with server uptime and customer service. Does their site ever go offline for long periods of time? Does their provider offer 24/7 support and resolve server issues quickly?

Format Wars: Blogs vs. Custom Sites

Once you have web hosting established, the next question that arises is, "Should I create a traditional web site or use a blog instead?" Although a blog is certainly easier to update and maintain, there are distinct disadvantages to the blog format as your primary site in this particular situation. Every developer should have a blog to easily announce updates and news, but it should be connected to static web pages that you can custom design to promote your app without being limited to the blog post structure.

If you're comfortable building web sites, I recommend creating a custom site for your app. If web development is not your thing, and you would rather use a blog platform such as WordPress, be sure it supports the addition of static pages. You need that so your app can have its own set of permanent pages for screenshots, videos, support, and other typical marketing elements. For all you WordPress fans out there, Cory Shaw created an excellent WordPress Theme called AppifyWP, which provides time-saving, optimized page templates for promoting your iPhone and iPad apps. Check it out at http://appifywp.com/.

Most of the successful iOS developers have dedicated web sites for their apps, and if they also have blogs, their respective sites link to them. One of the rare exceptions is Bolt Creative's Pocket God site, which consists entirely of a blog, hosted free on Blogger at http://pocketgod.blogspot.com/. In the unique case of Pocket God, the developers are updating the app with new episodes so frequently that the blog format works well for them, allowing them to easily post new information for fans every few days. For most apps and games, updates are much less frequent, so a blog should be secondary to a primary application web site.

Domain Name Benefits

In Chapter 2, I mentioned the importance of registering a domain name for your iOS app web site, so you've already done that, right? I won't rehash that prior discussion, but I will reveal one more reason why a unique domain name for your app can be very valuable.

The length of your web site URL may not appear relevant in the desktop version of iTunes or the iPad version of the App Store, since the actual URL is hidden behind a text-based link or a button, respectively. For example, the URL for the popular Plants vs. Zombies game, by PopCap Games, Inc., is http://www.popcap.com/games/pvz, but on the Plants vs. Zombies App Store page on the iPad, all you see is an active link button titled Developer Web Site (see Figure 10–1).

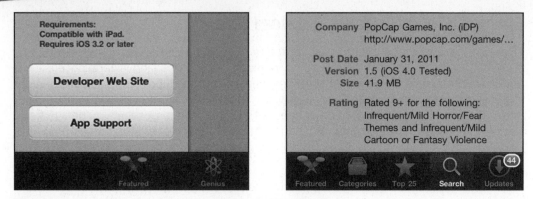

Figure 10–1. *Long URLs don't matter in the desktop version of iTunes or the iPad App Store (left), but truncation issues arise when displayed in the iPhone version of the App Store (right).*

The problem lies in how Apple lists the same web site link in the iPhone version of the App Store, in which the actual URL is displayed. On such a narrow mobile screen, a long URL is truncated (see Figure 10–1). And since the URL is merely listed and not provided as an active link, the user may have a difficult time guessing what the full URL should be. This may seem like a minor nitpick, but according to AdMob, more than 90 percent of iPhone users browse and purchase from the App Store on their mobile devices. So, the ability to easily access your web site in Mobile Safari is a lot more important than many developers realize (I'll talk about this in more detail later in this chapter).

If you already have an existing web site for your company, or you currently maintain one central site for all your software products, most likely you've organized your site to assign each app to its own directory. For example, Streaming Colour Studios has its iOS games categorized this way. The Dapple game's web page is located at `http://www.streamingcolour.com/games/dapple/`. Although that URL seems simple enough, it would definitely be truncated in the iPhone version of the App Store. To avoid that issue, the developer Owen Goss registered the domain name `dapplegame.com`. Not only does this shorter domain name fit nicely when displayed in the iPhone's App Store (see Figure 10–2), but it's also a much easier URL for users to remember when they see it listed in marketing materials and advertisements.

Figure 10–2. *Instead of using the long company URL of its official Dapple web page, Streaming Colour Studios opted to use a much shorter app-specific domain name.*

Don't worry—this does not require you to maintain two separate sites and hosting bills: one for your company and one for your app. Most domain registrars offer web-forwarding services, so that you can easily set your app URL to redirect to any directory or page within your existing company web site. That's what Streaming Colour Studios does. The URL `http://www.dapplegame.com/` simply redirects to the actual Dapple web page at `http://www.streamingcolour.com/games/dapple/`.

Another option is to use *subdomains*. Instead of using nested directories within its site at `http://www.smule.com/`, Smule uses a unique subdomain for each of its products. For example, the Ocarina app's web page is located at `http://ocarina.smule.com/`, and the I Am T-Pain web page is at `http://iamtpain.smule.com/`. This enables Smule to display short, easy-to-remember app URLs, while maintaining only one central company web site. And it does all this without the expense of registering additional domain names and web-forwarding fees.

SEO Tactics

Search engine optimization (SEO) is a vast topic, one that has birthed a cottage industry of SEO consultants, seminars, and books. Here, let's tackle the basics you should know for your app's web site.

> **TIP:** If you would like to learn more about SEO, check out the free *SEO Starter Guide* from Google: `http://www.google.com/webmasters/docs/search-engine-optimization-starter-guide.pdf`.

`<title>` Tag

The `<title>` tag, which is located within the `<head>` tag in your HTML code, displays the title of the page in the web browser's top title bar. Although that may seem fairly useless, `<title>` is actually quite an important tag when it comes to search engines and social media.

The `<title>` tag is the primary link headline displayed in search engine results. Let's use the fictional Breadcrumbs app as an example:

`<title>Breadcrumbs - Parked Car Locator App for the iPhone</title>`

Notice how I incorporated not only the app's name and caption, but also that it's an iPhone app. It's important to use strategic keywords in your title to help improve your ranking in the search results. When that page is listed in Google's search engine results, users will immediately know what it is by the link headline alone.

If you take advantage of one of the many free sharing services available (such as AddThis and ShareThis) to enable site visitors to share that web page with their friends, their JavaScript code that you've pasted into your HTML simply grabs that page's `<title>` tag on the fly as part of the message that's being sent along with the page's

URL. With this mind, it's always a good idea to keep the character count well below 140 characters to promote easy retweeting on Twitter.

description and keywords Meta Tags

Although the description and keywords meta tags are not required, they should never be seen as optional. Also located within the HTML <head> tag, they are important elements that most search engines analyze when crawling your site:

- The keywords <meta> tag helps provide context as to the subject of your web page.

- The description <meta> tag is often used as the text description that is displayed directly below the title link headline in search engine results.

Here's an example of the syntax:

```
<meta name="description" content="Easily find your car in crowded parking lots with
Breadcrumbs, now available in the iPhone App Store">
<meta name="keywords" content="iPhone, App Store, GPS, car finder, car locator, mobile,
augmented reality, map, directions, lost car, parking, app">
```

To prevent your description from appearing truncated in search engine results, try to limit its length to no more than 25 to 30 words.

You can include a lot more words in your keywords <meta> tag, but be very careful to include only keywords that are relevant to that web page. Don't try to "game" the system by including popular search terms that are unrelated in the hopes of getting broader exposure. That's so 1998. These days, modern search engines employ extremely sophisticated algorithms that compare your meta keywords with the keywords in your main body text. Any discrepancies found will penalize your current search engine page ranking.

Not sure which keywords to use for optimal results? Try using Google's AdWords keyword tool (https://adwords.google.com/select/KeywordToolExternal). Although it was designed to help advertisers refine their ad campaign keywords, it can also help you determine the value of search keywords so that your keywords <meta> tag is loaded with the most optimized words.

Keyword-Rich Text

As with the keywords <meta> tag, make sure the visible text within the main body of your web page contains optimized keywords to help improve your search engine rankings. If your app currently has several competitors, check out their web sites to see which keywords they're using and how they rank in the search engines. Your goal is to place just as high, if not better than them, in the search engine results for similar keywords.

Make sure all of your web images include the alt text parameter, so that search engines can still read their intended description. It's also a good idea to appropriately name your image files. For example, a search engine-optimized buy button might look like this:

```
<img src="images/buy.jpg" alt="Buy Now at the App Store" width="200" height="60"
border="0">
```

Try to avoid using Adobe Flash on your web site whenever possible. Although it's a great web technology, it poses two serious problems for iOS app developers:

- The iOS native browser, Mobile Safari, does not currently support Flash. It renders Flash objects as broken when viewed on an iPhone, iPad, or iPod touch.

- Some search engines have trouble properly searching Flash-based SWF files, so embedded text keywords may not be indexed.

If you want to use the popular Flash video format on your site, you'll want to read more about how to do that in the "Why Site Compatibility with Mobile Safari Is So Important" section later in this chapter.

Keyword-Friendly URLs

Following the theme of strategically named image files, if your app-specific domain name redirects to your existing company web site, you should also try to use strategically named directories and files in your URLs. For example, using a web site naming structure like this:

```
http://www.mywebsite.com/iphone/breadcrumbs/
```

will help your site rank much higher in search results than a nondescript URL like this:

```
http://www.mywebsite.com/sw/0901/page01.html
```

Maintaining Valid Links

Make sure to place default index pages within all subdirectories to prevent both users and search engine spiders from encountering 404 errors or "Forbidden Directory" warnings. Broken URLs can dramatically affect how your site is indexed in the major search engines.

XML Sitemap

The XML Sitemap is a standard introduced by Google several years ago. It enables you to submit an XML Sitemap file to Google, Yahoo!, and Microsoft Bing. The XML listing includes entries for all of the web page URLs in your site that you want indexed by these search engines. Within the XML, you can specify the priority (importance) of each page, the last date it was modified, and the frequency rate of changes.

This site map helps Google, Yahoo!, and Bing discover pages on your web site that their search bots may not have found during their crawling process. If you add or delete pages from your site, simply update the XML Sitemap file, and then resubmit it to Google and others for indexing.

To get started, visit Google's free Webmaster Tools site
(http://www.google.com/webmasters/tools/) to learn how to create and submit your
own XML Sitemap file. Google even provides helpful reports on any crawling issues
found, as well as identifying any meta tag issues.

Never seen an XML Sitemap file before? Here's a short example:

```
<?xml version="1.0" encoding="UTF-8"?><urlset
xmlns="http://www.sitemaps.org/schemas/sitemap/0.9">
    <url><loc>http://www.ebutterfly.com/</loc><lastmod>2010-9-
30</lastmod><changefreq>weekly</changefreq><priority>1.0</priority></url>
    <url><loc>http://www.ebutterfly.com/books/devsketchbook/</loc><lastmod>2010-9-
30</lastmod><changefreq>monthly</changefreq><priority>0.9</priority></url>
    <url><loc>http://www.ebutterfly.com/books/iphonebusiness/</loc><lastmod>2010-9-
30</lastmod><changefreq>monthly</changefreq><priority>0.9</priority></url>
    <url><loc>http://www.ebutterfly.com/company/</loc><lastmod>2010-9-
30</lastmod><changefreq>monthly</changefreq><priority>0.6</priority></url>
</urlset>
```

See how simple the syntax is? Within the main parent `urlset` tag, each child `<url>` tag
contains the information for a different, unique URL in my web site. (Although keep in
mind that my real XML Sitemap file is actually much larger.)

If you're not comfortable crafting your own XML code within a text editor, you may
prefer to use a site-map automation tool. Here are a few:

- XML Sitemap (http://xmlsitemap.com/)

- XML-Sitemaps.com (http://www.xml-sitemaps.com/)

- RAGE Sitemap Automator for Mac OS X
  (http://www.ragesw.com/products/googlesitemap.html)

After creating your XML Sitemap file, submit it to the major search engines that support
this standard:

- Google (http://www.google.com/webmasters/tools/)

- Yahoo! (http://siteexplorer.search.yahoo.com/submit)

- Bing (http://www.bing.com/toolbox/webmasters/)

Tracking Web Site Traffic

In Chapter 7, I stressed the value of tracking iOS app usage via third-party app
analytics, such as Flurry. And it is equally beneficial to do the same with your web site.
Tracking site traffic can shed light on where visitors are originating from, the browser
versions they're using, when and how many people are viewing your site, which web
pages and links are the most popular, and much more.

By monitoring when peak traffic hours occur for your site, combined with which days of
the week generate the most downloads for your app in the App Store, you can best
determine the optimal times to announce limited sale offers and related app news. On

the flip side, site traffic statistics can also help pinpoint design weaknesses by listing which pages are responsible for the most visitor exits (leaving your site).

Since English is a globally accepted language, your English-based app can achieve success in Apple's various regional App Stores. But if you're interested in producing localized versions of your app to increase sales in countries outside your own, which languages should you target first? Good web site traffic statistics can tell you which countries your visitors are from. Beyond the United States, are a large percentage of your site visitors coming from Italy, France, or Germany? Or maybe Japan and China? The combination of your international App Store downloads/sales reports and web site traffic statistics can help you determine on which countries to focus your translation efforts.

Most web-hosting companies offer traffic tracking as part of their package. If your web host does not include traffic statistics (or if its bundled solution lacks robust features), check out the available third-party analytics services. Many of them are either free or very low cost. Here are a few of the popular offerings:

- Google Analytics (http://www.google.com/analytics/)
- Site Meter (http://www.sitemeter.com/)
- Mint (http://haveamint.com/)

If you're already using Google Analytics for Mobile Apps within your iOS application, then setting up the free Google Analytics for your web site should be a no-brainer! Being able to monitor both your web site and iOS app usage statistics within the same web-based dashboard is a highly convenient and powerful solution.

Anatomy of an iOS App Web Site

Now you're ready to design your application's web page, but what elements should you include? Here's a list of common ingredients to consider:

- Consistent brand identity, displaying your app icon and name/logo
- Caption and/or quick-pitch description
- Apple's App Store identity badge
- Buy button
- Pricing
- Screenshots and video
- Additional details, such as features, benefits, requirements, testimonials, and reviews
- A sharing mechanism to easily share your page URL with others via social media, such as Twitter and Facebook
- A community built with a blog, RSS, and e-mail newsletter
- Customer support and contact information

- Company identity
- Links to cross-promote your other products
- Download extras (optional)

Although this may seem like a long list of elements, the really effective sites present the information in a very clean, simple layout that is easy for visitors to read. If you've evaluated the web sites for your favorite iOS apps and games, you've seen many (if not all) of these items already.

Figure 10–3 provides a conceptual mock-up of how all these components can be integrated into a single web page. After evaluating several leading iOS app web sites, this example outline will appear quite familiar.

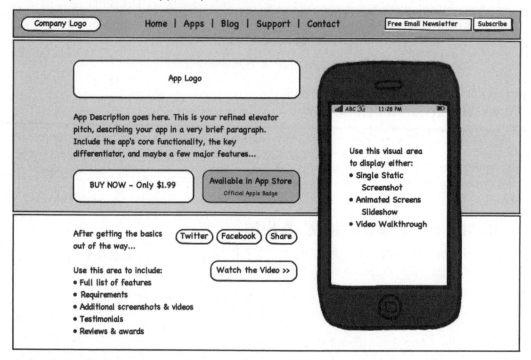

Figure 10–3. *This web page mock-up demonstrates how to integrate the essential content into a clean, easy-to-read layout (designed with Balsamiq Mockups, http://balsamiq.com/products/mockups/)*

Unlike a printed page, a web page can scroll vertically, so it can contain more content. The trick is to avoid overwhelming the user with too much information all at once. This is achieved by placing only the most important "quick-pitch" data front and center at the top of the screen. Those users interested in reading more can scroll down the page for additional details. This enables you to space out the content so that the design can "breathe" on the page.

If the top portion of your page is overcrowded, it will appear cluttered, making it difficult to read. By keeping the design simple, you make the page much easier for the human eye to quickly scan and process. A product-based web site is little more than an online marketing brochure, so it must convey its message quickly and efficiently. The Web is a very visual medium, so don't weigh down the page with too much text. Of course, you want to include enough rich, related keywords to successfully describe the app to both consumers and search engines, but it's important to draw in visitors with appealing imagery.

Now that you've had an overview, let's take a closer look at each of the elements your web site should contain.

App Brand Identity

The bare-bones mock-up shown in Figure 10–3 could serve as the layout for almost any iPhone app or game web page. What will make it unique to your application will be the visuals you incorporate. The web imagery should directly reflect your application's icon and interface theme. Brand consistency is key.

Always, always, always display your app's icon! The icon visually represents your product in the App Store, so you need to reinforce that same imagery on your web site. The goal is to condition consumers to associate that icon with your application's name and functionality. Whenever they see that icon in the App Store, you want them to immediately recognize it. That's why I recommended incorporating the app icon into the overall logo design in Chapter 4. And likewise, the app icon should also be a prominent part of your web page design.

As an example, I've designed a fake web page for the fictional Breadcrumbs app, based on the generic layout from Figure 10–3. As you can see from Figure 10–4, the page structure is identical to the mock-up outline, but the unique branding in the underlying design theme sets it apart.

Figure 10–4. *Based on the mock-up shown in Figure 10–3, this Breadcrumbs web page reinforces the app's brand identity.*

Notice how the app's icon is an integrated part of the Breadcrumbs logo in Figure 10–4. The branding is further supported by using the icon's blue sky horizon as the web page's background image.

The nice thing about the Internet is that its accessibility truly equalizes the playing field for developers. You may not have the massive marketing budgets of the big publishers, but if you're skilled at using Adobe Photoshop and a web page editor, you can make your site look just as impressive.

Don't worry if your graphics experience is limited. You can design an amazing site with only a few key visuals. Just look at the web page for Shiny Development's Balloons! app at http://balloonsapp.com/ (see Figure 10–5). Although the page design is fairly minimal with black text on a solid white background, the app's primary art of floating balloons is very bold and eye-catching. It's the only imagery on the page, yet the simplicity of it strongly reinforces the established brand identity and nonverbally communicates ease of use, both of which are vital to the success of a social media app.

Figure 10–5. *You don't have to be a Photoshop guru to build an attractive web site. With only one central image in the background, the simplicity of Shiny Development's web site for its Balloons! app is eye-catching and effective.*

Even though the Balloons! app icon is not displayed next to the logo, it is integrated into the Get Balloons! buy button. If you click the button, that red balloon is the same one you'll see in the icon listed in the App Store.

Like the design of your app's interface, the look and feel of the corresponding web site should be appealing. If you hired a professional designer to create your app's icon and logo, you should consider contracting that same person to also generate visuals for your web site and all other promotional needs, so that your branding remains consistent across all of your marketing materials.

The Quick Pitch: What Is It and Why Should I Care?

Remember when I talked about crafting your elevator pitch earlier in this chapter? You'll want to place this at the top of your web page, typically below your app name. This will quickly inform visitors what your app does and how it can benefit them. Your app may be packed with tons of great features, but don't overwhelm the reader by listing them all at once. That will only make the page feel cluttered and top-heavy.

In Figure 10–5, only a short caption and a few sentences are displayed within the main Balloons! visual. Within seconds, you have a broad grasp of what this app does and the potential fun you could have using it. That's the hook that draws you in, motivating you to keep reading. To learn more, simply scroll down the page for a comprehensive list of features.

App Store Identity Badge

The most common element you'll see on most iPhone and iPad app-related web sites is the official App Store identity badge that's labeled "Available on the App Store." To obtain this graphic, you'll need to visit Apple's App Store Resource Center at `http://developer.apple.com/appstore/resources/marketing/`. You'll see the identity badge displayed within the App Store Badging and Artwork section.

You'll need to download and sign the App Marketing Artwork License Agreement form and mail it back to Apple. Although the identity badge and iOS device graphics download links are already provided there, before using any of those images, be sure to download and read the *App Marketing and Identity Guidelines for Developers* PDF. This document explains the rules for how to properly use the App Store identity badge and the authorized iPhone and iPad images. Since Apple reserves the right to revoke permission to use the supplied graphics if you fail to follow the guidelines, it's in your best interest to read that document and make sure you understand how to remain compliant.

The graphics downloads include both web and print resolutions of the badge, as well as several different versions of iPhone, iPad, and iPod touch images in layered Photoshop PSD files. This gives you the flexibility to use these graphics within all your marketing materials.

Buy Button

Although the App Store identity badge is typically linked from your web site to your app's product page in the App Store, don't rely on it as your sole buy button. Some people may see it only as an official badge, not understanding that it actually links to the App Store. Since the primary goal of your web site is to sell more units of your app, you should also include a dedicated buy button to help drive traffic to the App Store.

In our fictional Breadcrumbs web page example (see Figure 10–4), the large Buy Now button uses the same high-contrast red color as the icon's red car, so that it really "pops" as a prominent, eye-catching element.

Any time you're linking to the App Store, don't forget to use an iTunes affiliate link so that you can earn extra revenue from all the sales you're sending Apple's way. (You did join the free iTunes Affiliate Program after reading Chapter 6, right?)

Pricing

Including the app's price on your web site seems to be a highly debated topic among iOS developers. Some believe that stating the price may deter people from clicking through to the App Store, while others believe the price can actually help drive sales. Although there are valid points to both arguments, I think stating the price in all your marketing materials, including your site, will help sales more than it could possibly hurt.

If you're constantly experimenting with different price points to improve your app's position in the App Store's top sales charts, then I can understand your reluctance to display the fluctuating price on your web site. But this is a venture you're attempting to grow into a successful business, so it's worth every minute of extra time it takes to frequently update pricing on your web site. And if your app is on sale, surely you want the world to know about it.

If you're selling your app in more than one regional App Store, try to be conscientious of the currency in those countries. Many app-related web sites display the price in both US dollars and euros to accommodate the majority of their target audience. FutureTap took this idea one step further. Since its Where To? app is available in several languages, it has localized its web site, with pricing and text descriptions translated for every major region the app supports. If you visit `http://www.futuretap.com/home/whereto-en/`, you'll see tabs along the left side of the screen, each one representing a different country flag. Click a flag icon to display the translated product page and pricing for that country. In Figure 10–6, the English product page displays the price in US dollars, and the French product page shows the equivalent price in euros.

Figure 10–6. *FutureTap's web site for its Where To? app displays the price in the appropriate currency for each localized product page, such as US dollars for the English description and euros for the French description.*

For best results, display your app's price either within the buy button (as shown in the Breadcrumbs example in Figure 10–4) or near the iPhone or iPad image on your web page (like FutureTap does in Figure 10–6). You cannot include the price on or within the App Store identity badge, because Apple's guidelines specifically prohibit modifying that logo.

Screenshots and Video

Besides designing the web page to emulate your app's brand identity, the other crucial visuals are screenshots and video of your app in action. To make a purchase decision, people need to see what your application looks like and how it works. Outside a free trial version of the software, the best way to do that is through screenshots and video simulations.

Interested bloggers and journalists may pull content from your site when writing a review, so it's always a good idea to include both video and screenshots whenever possible. If you have not yet finished producing your app's video trailer, then at the very least, include some high-quality screenshots.

Although most developers display their app's primary screenshot within a large iPhone or iPad image on their web pages, the more effective sites actually embed video or an animated slide show of screenshots within the iOS device image. This is very engaging, giving the user a much more immersive representation of your app's functionality or game play. FutureTap does this on its Where To? web site (see Figure 10–6). Every few seconds, a different screenshot slides into view within the displayed iPhone. If you want to go back to a particular screen, it has even included iOS-centric page "dot" markers for manually stepping to a specific image.

To achieve a similar effect, you can use JavaScript code to run through a slide show of static screenshots within the iPhone or iPad image frame. Not a JavaScript guru? No problem. Plenty of great slide show scripts are available online, many of which are free. Just search the Web for *JavaScript image slide show*, or check out the nice collection of JavaScript solutions at these sites:

- Dynamic Drive (http://www.dynamicdrive.com/)
- Hot Scripts (http://www.hotscripts.com/)

Some of the slide show scripts offer such smooth transition effects between images that the slide show almost plays like a movie, without the overhead of a large video download.

The iPhone displayed on the Put Things Off web site at http://putthingsoff.com/ showcases an embedded QuickTime video. Click the play symbol, and the video will load and play right there within the iPhone frame, simulating the Put Things Off app in action (see Figure 10–7). The combination of the video and simple four-step text instructions emphasizes just how easy the app is to use.

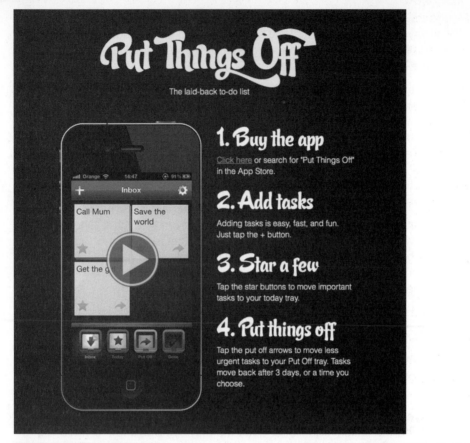

Figure 10–7. *The embedded video and the brief four-step instructions on the Put Things Off web site spotlight the app's ease of use.*

This eye-catching technique creates the illusion that the iPhone graphic is running the app live within your web browser. To maintain that illusion, set the HTML QuickTime code's `controller` parameter to `false` to ensure that the playback controller bar is invisible. You should set the `bgcolor` parameter to #000000 (black) to avoid any unsightly borders around the video frame. You may also want to assign the `autoplay` and `loop` parameters to `true`, so that the video begins playing immediately when the web page loads and continues to loop endlessly. To learn about the dozens of other QuickTime parameters for customizing video playback, as well as the best method for embedding a QuickTime video within a web page, check out Apple's official *HTML Scripting Guide for QuickTime* at `http://developer.apple.com/library/safari/#documentation/QuickTime/Conceptual/QTScripting_HTML/QTScripting_HTML_AIntroduction/Introduction.html`.

If you have produced a video trailer for your app, you'll want to also upload it to the major video-sharing sites like YouTube to benefit from the additional exposure of their massive audiences and social media sharing features. But don't be a lazy web designer and simply link directly to your video page on YouTube or Vimeo. It may be tempting to do this in the hopes of increasing your video's view count (and popularity ranking), but that would pull visitors away from your site. Your goal should be to keep users engaged within your site so that your buy button is always only a click away. You can achieve this by simply embedding the video in your own web page. Even if your video trailer plays more like a commercial than pure simulation, so it would not make sense framed within a large iPhone or iPad graphic, it still should be viewable within your own site.

For example, on your YouTube video page, there is an Embed button that allows you to copy and paste a short snippet of HTML code into your own web pages.

Be sure to customize the embed code that YouTube generates with both the "Include related videos" option and the "Use old embed code" option turned off. The old embed code that YouTube used to employ would play only the Flash video format, which is not supported on iOS devices. The new embed code supports both Flash and HTML5 video, depending on the browser that loads the video. This enables iPhone, iPad, and iPod touch users to view your video, since the YouTube embed code will automatically switch to the HTML5 video format within Mobile Safari.

Additional Details

The lower half of your app's web page is an ideal area to include additional text such as a comprehensive list of features, benefits, requirements, and even quotes from testimonials and reviews.

Most people lead very busy lives, and the trend is toward increasingly short attention spans. Don't expect anyone to take the time to read long, dense paragraphs of information. Organize the data into easy-to-read bullet points.

Social Media

I'll be talking at length about growing your social media presence later in this chapter, but one major way to draw new followers to your social network identities is to heavily promote them on your web site.

Looking at the blogs and web sites for most iOS developers, you'll notice that a vast majority of them display button links to their Twitter and Facebook Pages in the hopes you'll follow them there. The icons for both of those social media titans are very well known, so you could opt to display only their linked icons if you prefer a more space-saving approach, as shown in the fictional Breadcrumbs web page (Figure 10–4).

Another icon button you may have noticed in Figure 10–4 is the little green sharing emblem. You don't just want people to follow you, but you also want them to share your web site URL with their friends and family. As I've said before, word-of-mouth is one of the most powerful marketing forces that social media provides. People trust their friends, so recommendations that come to them via word-of-mouth are a much more powerful sales tool than any advertising or self-promotion you do yourself.

In previous chapters, I've shown you how to build support for Twitter, Facebook, and Tell A Friend functionality within your app. Your web site should also offer those same features, but thanks to some wonderful third-party services, you don't need to write a single line of code! These services provide custom "share" widgets that can be easily installed on your web pages by copying and pasting their supplied code snippet, which typically consists of only a few lines of JavaScript. Here are a few of these services, which you may recognize from their use on millions of web sites:

- AddThis (http://www.addthis.com/)

- ShareThis (http://sharethis.com/)

- AddToAny (http://www.addtoany.com/)

The beauty of these share buttons is that they give your site visitors the ability to bookmark or share a specific URL with dozens of popular social media sites, such as Twitter, Facebook, Digg, Delicious, StumbleUpon, LinkedIn, MySpace, Slashdot, Reddit, Technorati, and many others. You can even "tell a friend" via e-mail. Their share buttons are small and compact, for easy placement anywhere on your web pages. Hover your mouse over the button, and a drop-down menu appears with sharing options (see Figure 10–8).

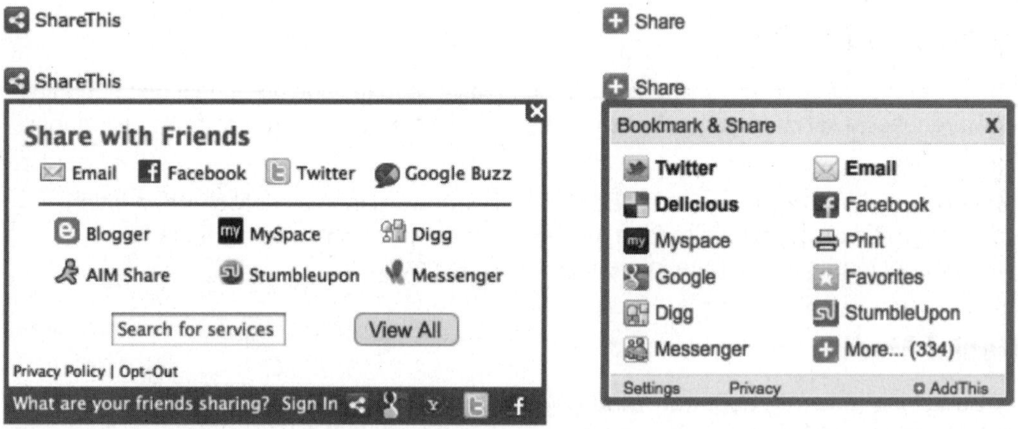

Figure 10–8. *The default button offerings from ShareThis (left) and AddThis (right) provide comprehensive drop-down menus for convenient URL sharing.*

Don't like their default button choices? Some of these sharing services even let you use your own custom button image. This enables you to better integrate their service into your site's existing design, such as in the Breadcrumbs example (Figure 10–4), where I modified the share icon to match the same dimensions as the accompanying Twitter and Facebook icons for visual consistency.

You can easily grab the needed code from these sharing services and be on your way. However, if you want to track the performance of your share buttons, I recommend signing up for a free account with these services. As with web site analytics, you'll be able to log in to your AddThis or ShareThis account to monitor which of your web pages are being bookmarked and shared the most, as well as which social media sites they are sharing with. This is very valuable information to have. Knowing which social networking sites your visitors use regularly can help you determine where to focus your own online marketing efforts.

If the majority of your web audience is using a specific social media site, such as Facebook, you may be interested in targeting your share button to that site, rather than the "everything but the kitchen sink" approach of third-party share services like AddThis. If you read a lot of blogs, you've undoubtedly seen the popular Twitter, Facebook Like, and Digg buttons (see Figure 10–9).

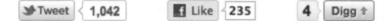

Figure 10–9. *Targeted sharing buttons provided by Twitter, Facebook, and Digg dramatically increase URL sharing, but visible counters can also reveal unpopular web pages.*

These high-profile buttons reduce the sharing task down to a single targeted click, which results in a greater number of URLs shared. The easier you make sharing for your site visitors, the more they'll do it.

If your web page is popular and racks up a nice large number in the share counter, as shown in Figure 10–9's Tweet button (on the far left), your content looks that much more attractive to new visitors, making them eager to share the page as well.

But on the flip side is the inevitable disadvantage that visible counter will have for new or rarely visited sites. Clocking in at an excruciatingly low number of retweets is frustrating enough, but to have it advertised to everyone who visits your web page is just downright embarrassing. And no one likes to hang around the unpopular kids.

If your site is still struggling to increase traffic, you may want to use all-in-one sharing aggregators like ShareThis, until you're able to drum up higher numbers.

So, if your web site already enjoys a healthy stream of traffic, high-impact, targeted share buttons are worthy additions. Here are a few, all of which are easily installed on your web page or blog by copying and pasting a small snippet of JavaScript code:

- Tweet Button (http://twitter.com/about/resources/tweetbutton)
- Facebook Like Button (http://developers.facebook.com/docs/reference/plugins/like/)
- Smart Digg Button (http://about.digg.com/downloads/button/smart)

Whichever share button options you decide to use, be sure your web pages have HTML <title> tags that are short enough to easily retweet. If your site visitors are forced to edit your title text in order to share it via Twitter, odds are they will abandon the URL share attempt, not wanting to be bothered with the extra effort required.

So, what's an appropriate title length? Twitter limits tweets to no more than 140 characters, but even that's too long for your title, since your retweet will need to also include your web page's URL. Reserving space for the URL, let's see how many characters remain for the actual title text.

For the sake of this example, we'll walk through constructing a viable web page title for the fictional Breadcrumbs app—one that is easily retweetable. The web site URL of `http://www.breadcrumbsapp.com/` is short, but Twitter may automatically convert it into a shorter URL using its built-in URL-shortening feature. You'll want to track the number of click-throughs coming from that tweet, so instead of relying on Twitter's native URL shortener, set up your own free account at a URL-shortener service like Bit.ly (`http://bit.ly/`) and provide your own shortened URL. This way, you'll reduce the number of characters needed for the URL, and you'll be able to monitor the link's popularity via Bit.ly's analytics.

With a shortened Bit.ly URL weighing in at approximately 20 characters (`http://bit.ly/3EmvfN`), that leaves us with 120 characters to avoid exceeding Twitter's 140-character limit. To safely account for any additional comments that users want to add to the tweet (such as "Cool app!"), let's craft a title that's 100 characters or less.

"Breadcrumbs for iPhone - Never misplace your car again with this new parked car locator app!" is only 92 characters, so that will work! The web page's HTML `<title>` tag now reads as follows:

```
<title>Breadcrumbs for iPhone - Never misplace your car again with this new parked car
locator app!</title>
```

This produces the following 113-character share message:

```
Breadcrumbs for iPhone - Never misplace your car again with this new parked car locator
app! http://bit.ly/3EmvfN
```

Perfect! Our web page's `<title>` tag includes important keyword phrases like *iPhone app* and *car locator* for proper search engine positioning, yet it's short enough to promote URL sharing across the popular social networking sites. This may all seem like a lot of attention paid to trivial minutiae, but it's this level of detail that can turn an ordinary web site into a powerful marketing tool.

Your Blog and RSS Feed

Most of you already maintain a blog for posting news about software releases and development updates. And if you don't, then you really should! It's a great way to grow a readership, drawing users to your site. Don't have much to say? That's OK, because you don't need to make it a daily journal.

A blog establishes a direct connection between you and your customers, where readers can stay on top of your latest news and post comments. For those of you new to blogs, I'll be discussing the community-building power of blogs later in this chapter.

For now, if you do maintain a blog for discussing software development or iOS news, make sure that your app-related web site includes a direct link to it. Beyond Twitter and Facebook, you want site visitors to know that your blog is yet one more available resource for staying informed about your app.

Since most blog software, such as WordPress, automatically generates RSS feeds for the latest blog entries, many bloggers are not placing much emphasis on their feed, beyond offering the obligatory link for interested subscribers. Although exciting new platforms like Twitter have seemingly cooled the popularity of this XML-based standard, RSS is still a very powerful mechanism for distributing information. To really leverage RSS for your own marketing needs, I highly recommend signing up for Google's free FeedBurner service at `http://www.feedburner.com/`.

At first glance, FeedBurner may appear to be just a glorified analytics service, tracking who is subscribing to your RSS feed and which browsers or client apps are being used to read it. Although RSS statistics monitoring is very useful, FeedBurner is really so much more than that.

One of FeedBurner's features is FeedFlare, which inserts social media links within your feed. So with a single click, RSS subscribers can actually share individual posts on Digg, Delicious, Facebook, and other social networking sites. On top of that, FeedBurner will automatically send ping notifications to all major feed aggregators and search engines when you've posted a new blog entry.

The service also provides JavaScript widgets for easily publishing feed content in HTML form on any web site, which is perfect for third-party sites interested in syndicating your blog content without the hassles of parsing XML. Although some bloggers may be wary of who repurposes their content, you're using your blog and RSS feed to market your iOS app, so the more locations your feed is syndicated, the more exposure your app receives. It's a win-win situation for you, since your primary goal is to drive as much traffic as possible to your product page in the App Store.

But the most valuable feature by far is FeedBurner's free Email Subscriptions service. This enables your site visitors to receive your blog posts via e-mail. Think about that for a moment. Instead of installing and maintaining complicated mailing list software on your own server for managing subscribers and sending out broadcast e-mail messages, FeedBurner does all of that for you. And you don't even need to waste time configuring a SQL database and constructing e-mail templates. Just post a blog entry. It gets added to your RSS feed, which in turn gets sent out via e-mail to your e-mail subscribers. And did I already mention it's free? You can even customize the e-mail messages with your own logo and font styles. And with the simple copy-and-paste Email Subscription HTML form code that FeedBurner provides, people can easily subscribe from within your own web site.

But what if you don't want every single blog post to be sent out to your mailing list? What if you need more control over the design of the e-mail messages? And how about importing existing mailing lists from previous marketing campaigns? To serve those needs, you'll need a more robust e-mail marketing solution.

E-mail News Mailing List

Would you like to send news, announcements, and special offers directly to your customers via e-mail? If you're like me, you may not want to be bothered with monkeying with your own mailing list software and the maintenance headaches that come with aggressive spam filters, SQL database security to keep out hackers, and other time-consuming nuisances. Fortunately, some easy-to-use yet affordable third-party e-mail marketing services can take care of all the heavy lifting.

E-mail marketing services handle tasks like the following:

- Maintain your mailing list databases and e-mail campaigns on their secure servers

- Support custom HTML e-mail messages

- List imports and exports

- Provide extensive web-based admin sites with comprehensive analytics reports for each campaign

- Produce custom HTML form code for you to copy and paste into your own web site for visitors to easily subscribe

These services have "whitelist" agreements with the major Internet service providers (ISPs) and e-mail vendors to help prevent your campaigns from getting eaten by server-side spam filters. This alone makes these third-party services a better option than installing your own PHP/MySQL solution.

Hundreds of e-mail marketing companies exist, but here's a select group of services that have proven popular with software developers:

- Campaign Monitor (http://www.campaignmonitor.com/)

- MailChimp (http://www.mailchimp.com/)

- Constant Contact (http://www.constantcontact.com/)

- iContact (http://www.icontact.com/)

- StreamSend (http://www.streamsend.com/)

- Vertical Response (http://www.verticalresponse.com/)

I've had the most experience with Campaign Monitor, which offers complete design control over the look and feel of your e-mail blasts. The thing I like best about Campaign Monitor is that you only pay per e-mail campaign; there's no monthly fee. So, if I don't send out an e-mail campaign this month, then I pay nothing. When I do send out a campaign, the rate is affordable. This is a great solution for developers with large mailing lists who send out very few e-mail messages.

MailChimp offers its service free for low-volume accounts of fewer than 2,000 subscribers. It gives you the ability to upgrade to larger-capacity plans as your subscriber base grows. MailChimp also offers ChimpKit, an Objective-C wrapper for the MailChimp API, which enables you to provide an e-mail newsletter sign-up form directly within your iOS app!

Whether you choose the free FeedBurner Email Subscriptions or a more comprehensive e-mail marketing solution, let your site visitors know that unsubscribe links are located at the bottom of every e-mail newsletter for their convenience.

It's also important to include a link to a privacy policy somewhere on your web site. People are tired of dealing with spam, so they've become wary of giving out their e-mail address. A simple privacy policy statement can reassure site visitors that you won't be selling or sharing their e-mail addresses with anyone. If you're not sure how to word it, perform an online search for *privacy policy*. You'll find hundreds of samples. Just be sure to adhere to whatever privacy policy you set to avoid liability issues. Beyond the fact that most countries now have strict antispam laws in effect, the wrath of negative word-of-mouth from angry subscribers can be even more damaging to your business.

Why bother with e-mail newsletters at all if they are so troublesome? With overly aggressive spam filters, is it still an effective delivery mechanism? True, a fair percentage of your recipients may never see your e-mail because of hungry junk mail filters. But e-mail is still a very powerful pipeline to communicate news.

Although you may be tempted to post announcements only on Twitter, Facebook, or your blog, you're reliant on users to follow you there and religiously monitor your latest news. That places the responsibility on your audience, and although you may be vigilant about reading every tweet and Facebook update, most people are not. Why risk the possibility of your important posts being overlooked?

There are still a lot of consumers who prefer a more passive approach. They would rather have requested information delivered to them directly than be forced to go find it for themselves. It's all about providing as many communication options as possible on your web site, so that anyone interested in your iOS app can receive related news in the format or platform of their choice.

Customer Support and Contact Information

Even though I'll be talking more about customer support options in Chapter 11, here I will mention that you should always link to your support page from your app's main web site. At the very least, give site visitors some way to contact you—whether by e-mail or an HTML form.

Even though the desktop version of iTunes and the iPad version of the App Store supply a dedicated active link to your support site from your product's App Store page, that's not the case in the iPhone version of the App Store. The App Store on the iPhone lists only the web site URL for a selected application (see Figure 10–1). And with more than 90 percent of all iPhone and iPod touch users browsing and downloading apps directly from their device, if they encounter a support issue, they'll look up your web site in Mobile Safari in the hopes of finding online assistance. So, make life easier for both you and your customers by having your support page easily accessible from your app's web site.

Company Identity

This may seem obvious if your app's web page is part of your existing company site, but if you're an independent developer who decides to build a stand-alone web site for just your iOS app, don't forget to include your own business name and an About page.

If you're building only a cheap 99-cent novelty app that will soon be forgotten three months from now, then establishing a company identity may not matter (and if that were the case, you probably wouldn't be reading this book). But if you've developed a rock-solid, niche application that sells for more than the average app price (such as $3.99 or higher), consumers will want to know you're a serious developer with plans to support the app for the long haul before making their purchase decision.

When people buy a higher-priced app, especially one that they may come to rely on daily, they're really investing in the product's future. You want your web site to exude a prosperous and confident professionalism. Seeing your business logo and reading your company/developer bio online can help give your customers peace of mind.

Cross-Promotion of Your Other Products

Are you trying to sell multiple software applications? If you're driving traffic to your web site to promote a new iOS app, take advantage of this opportunity to also spotlight some of your other products, especially if they're apps that would appeal to this same audience. That's what Tap Tap Tap does at `http://www.taptaptap.com/`.

Tap Tap Tap's web site was designed with cross-promotion as a central factor. Using a clever sushi menu theme, app icons for all of the products sit on a virtual wood table. Select an app, and its icon slides forward, revealing a full description, screenshots, video demos, and other related information. But the other app icons remain visible on the left. Click another, and the current app icon slides back into place, while the new selection slides forward (see Figure 10–10). This is all done within the same screen. It's an elegant, animated design that was achieved with a sophisticated mix of Cascading Style Sheets (CSS) and JavaScript—no Flash.

Figure 10–10. *Tap Tap Tap utilizes a clever web site design that cross-promotes all of its iPhone apps within a single screen.*

You can also cross-promote other products and services. Even though people came to your site interested in an iPhone or iPad app, they surely have other interests that may involve books, desktop software, related consulting services, and so on. But be very careful not to overpromote those other items, or you run the risk of appearing too ad-centric, pimping out your iOS app as bait. Also keep in mind that you don't want to distract site visitors from your primary goal: convincing them to buy your iOS application in the App Store!

Downloadable Extras

People love freebies! And offering up fun downloads on your web site is an easy way to promote your app. For example, you might include Twitter avatar images, desktop backgrounds, and iPhone and iPad wallpaper.

But just because you created a freebie does not necessarily mean your site visitors will want it. Since these are essentially digital advertisements for your product, you need to make them visually compelling enough for people to look at every time they turn on their computer or mobile device. People don't want to stare at interface components or company logos, so if you're promoting a productivity app, these kinds of image-based freebies may not be a good fit. But if your app is a game with cool scenery and characters, then the game's visuals may lend itself quite well to promotional downloads like avatar icons and digital wallpaper.

Before Selling, Start Collecting

Your iOS app is not yet live in the App Store, so including a buy button and App Store identity badge on your site (as in the Breadcrumbs example shown in Figure 10–4) is a tad premature. Although it is good to have those two images designed and ready to go, you'll want to leave them off your web page for now.

During this prerelease stage, use your web site to grow your online audience. You could keep it simple and just ask people to follow you on Twitter or visit your Facebook Page to stay informed on the latest news about your forthcoming iOS app. But if you're not yet a known developer, there may not be a compelling reason for people to follow you. They may just decide to check your site later. Of course, in time, memory fades, and they may not remember to come back. By placing the ball in their court, you're risking the loss of those potential app sales.

Here's where offering that free e-mail newsletter can really benefit your prerelease marketing efforts. Interested site visitors can subscribe, and then a month later after they have forgotten about your app, you can send them an e-mail announcing its availability in the App Store!

Don't rely on the small subscription link located in your navigation menu or in another section of the site. Replacing the buy button and App Store identity badge, position the subscription form front and center on your app's web page. Invite visitors to submit their e-mail address to be the first notified when your application becomes available in the App Store (see Figure 10–11).

Figure 10–11. *During the prerelease stage, replace the buy button and App Store identity badge with a Notify Me When It's Available e-mail subscription form.*

What's convenient about this strategy is that nothing else on the web page must be moved or modified. Once your app is live in the App Store, you can easily swap out that prominent Notify Me… e-mail form, adding back the buy button and App Store identity badge (as in Figure 10–4).

Why Site Compatibility with Mobile Safari Is So Important

AdMob reported that a whopping 93 percent of iPhone users browse and purchase apps directly from the App Store on their mobile devices, while only a meager 7 percent do so from the desktop version of iTunes. Since it's highly possible that consumers may check out your app's official site before making a purchase decision, it's in your best interest to make sure your web site is compatible with the Mobile Safari browser in iOS.

Mobile Safari uses the powerful WebKit engine under the hood, so it has extensive support for JavaScript, CSS, and other modern web standards. In practice, most sites actually render quite well in Mobile Safari. But you can use a few optimization tricks to make your site even more enjoyable for iOS users:

- Control page scale with the `viewport` meta tag.

- Detect the platform from the browser's user agent.

- Work around Mobile Safari's lack of Flash support.

- Enhance home screen bookmarking.

"I'm Ready for My Close-up, Mr. Viewport"

The majority of web developers design page layouts based on average desktop screen dimensions. To accommodate the typical widths of most web sites, Mobile Safari's default zoom is set at a screen width of 980 pixels. This enables all web sites to fit nicely within the Mobile Safari browser window when initially loaded.

Viewing web sites in landscape mode on the large screen of an iPad feels identical to a desktop web browser, but the same can't be said for the smaller screen of an iPhone or iPod touch. In portrait mode, the browser window is quite narrow, so the pages are scaled down quite a bit, making the text practically illegible. To read the content and tap text links, users are forced to pinch the screen to zoom in closer.

But what if you want to design your web site to accommodate the unique dimensions of the Mobile Safari browser on the iPhone and iPod touch, alleviating the need to manually pinch zoom?

Consider Tap Tap Tap's web page layout, which is only a little wider than 600 pixels (see Figure 10–10). It's designed to display well in both the wide-screen format of desktop computer browsers and the narrow portrait mode of the iPhone's Mobile Safari. Yet Mobile Safari's default screen scale of 980 pixels wide would still render the page's main content as a tiny object centered in the screen, with a large unused margin of black background color on both sides. The solution is an HTML tag called `viewport`. Within the `<head>` tag of Tap Tap Tap's web page at `http://www.taptaptap.com/` is the following meta tag:

```
<meta name="viewport" content="width=device-width" />
```

The `viewport` tag is acknowledged by Mobile Safari but is ignored by all other browsers, so it will affect your site display only on iOS devices with small screens. Assigning the `content` parameter to `width=device-width` tells Mobile Safari to appropriately scale the page content's width to match the browser's width. This makes Tap Tap Tap's web site appear iPhone-optimized and easy to read (see Figure 10–12). It affects only the amount of zoom and page positioning that's applied. The web page's original aspect ratio remains unaltered.

Figure 10–12. *Tap Tap Tap sets the viewport tag's width to match the device width, which enhances its web site's appearance and readability within Mobile Safari on the iPhone and iPod touch.*

Several other `viewport` properties can be assigned to affect the scaling and a user's zoom capabilities, all of which are documented by Apple online at http://developer.apple.com/library/safari/#documentation/appleapplications/refe rence/safarihtmlref/Articles/MetaTags.html.If you're looking for greater control over the viewport's width than is offered by setting the `device-width` value, you can set the `width` property to a specific number of pixels. How might this come in handy?

Let's say your page's background imagery is an integrated part of the overall design. With the `viewport` tag set to `width=device-width`, the foreground web content will fill the screen; little to no margin space will remain to reveal the background image. If your main content is 400 pixels wide (and centered on the page), and you would like to see at least 50 pixels of background image on both the left and right sides of the screen, set your viewport tag to the following:

```
<meta name="viewport" content="width=500">
```

NOTE: I did notice that Tap Tap Tap's cool JavaScript-driven app icon animations don't slide as well in Mobile Safari; they're flawlessly smooth in the Mac OS X version of Safari. I'm not knocking the beautiful page design, but rather pointing out a common problem that plagues quite a few iOS-related web sites. Even though both browsers use WebKit, there are subtle differences in JavaScript and CSS support. When using complex scripts or third-party web frameworks in your site, be sure to test your code in Mobile Safari to ensure that the viewing experience is similar on both desktop computers and mobile devices.

If you need help debugging your web page within Mobile Safari, turn on the Debug Console located in Safari's Developer panel within the iOS Settings app. Mobile Safari's Debug Console is a huge time-saver, as it pinpoints errors and recommends optimization tips.

Using Browser Detection to Deliver Targeted Content

For software publishers who develop apps and games for several different platforms, it may not be appropriate to modify their main web site to accommodate just one of them. A perfect example of this is PopCap Games, which produces games for Mac, PC, Web, Nintendo, Xbox, PlayStation, and even various mobile devices such as the iPhone and iPad.

To promote all of its latest games and supported platforms within a single site, PopCap Games must take advantage of the wide-screen real estate of desktop web browsers, which probably account for the majority of their site traffic. The main PopCaps.com home page would be quite difficult to navigate and read when scaled down to fit within the iPhone's Mobile Safari browser window (see Figure 10–13). Instead of trying to dynamically alter the existing site design on the fly based on the browser accessing it, PopCap uses a simple redirect to send iPhone users to a special mobile-optimized web site that showcases only its iPhone games. Within Mobile Safari, visiting http://www.popcap.com/ automatically redirects you to http://www.popcap.com/iphone/ (see Figure 10–13).

Figure 10–13. *The PopCap Games main home page caters to several platforms and would be hard to read on a small mobile screen (left), so iPhone users are automatically redirected to a special iPhone-centric site (right).*

This simple redirect trick is achieved by first detecting the browser's user agent. Here's what Mobile Safari's user agent looks like from an iPhone 4 running iOS 4.2.1:

```
Mozilla/5.0 (iPhone; U; CPU iPhone OS 4_2_1 like Mac OS X; en-us) AppleWebKit/533.17.9
(KHTML, like Gecko) Version/5.0.2 Mobile/8C148 Safari/6533.18.5
```

Here's Mobile Safari's user agent from an iPod touch running iOS 3.1:

```
Mozilla/5.0 (iPod; U; CPU iPhone OS 3_1 like Mac OS X; en-us) AppleWebKit/528.18 (KHTML,
like Gecko) Version/4.0 Mobile/7C144 Safari/528.16
```

And here's Mobile Safari's user agent from an iPad running iOS 4.2.1:

```
Mozilla/5.0 (iPad; U; CPU OS 4_2_1 like Mac OS X; en-us) AppleWebKit/533.17.9 (KHTML,
like Gecko) Version/5.0.2 Mobile/8C148 Safari/6533.18.5
```

The browser's user agent can be accessed from any modern web scripting language. If the user agent description reveals the user's browser is from the iPhone or iPod touch, your web code can send the user to a different URL. If the user agent is from any other platform or device (such as a Mac or iPad), then do nothing, remaining on the current web page. Let's take a look at how to program this in JavaScript and PHP with only a few lines of code.

JavaScript for Browser Detection

Place the following code within the <head> tag in your HTML page. This will cause the redirect to happen for Mobile Safari users before the rest of the page finishes loading, which will make the transition fast and seamless.

```
<script type="text/javascript">
<!--
var os = navigator.userAgent.toLowerCase();
if (os.indexOf('iphone')!=-1) {
    window.location.href = "http://www.mywebsite.com/iphone/";
}
// -->
</script>
```

In JavaScript, the user agent is accessed via navigator.userAgent. Although Mobile Safari's current user agent in both the iPhone and iPod touch references iPhone, it's best to convert the entire string to all lowercase letters using JavaScript's toLowerCase() function. This ensures the code will always work, even if Apple ever switches the case in the future.

Once you have the user agent string in lowercase format, use the indexOf() function to search for *iphone*, since *iPhone OS* is listed by both the iPhone and iPod touch (but not the iPad). An integer position of the first occurrence of that word is returned. If that search term is not found, then -1 is returned. If any other number is returned, that signals a match for either the iPhone or iPod touch, so the JavaScript code redirects the browser to the URL location of your iPhone-optimized web page.

PHP for Browser Detection

For this example, you must place the following PHP code at the very top of the HTML page, before even the <html> tag. This PHP code needs to run before any HTML code is executed.

```
<?
$os = $_SERVER['HTTP_USER_AGENT'];
if (stristr($os, 'iphone')) {
    header("Location: http://www.mywebsite.com/iphone/");
    exit;
}
?>
```

In PHP, the user agent is retrieved from the HTTP_USER_AGENT property in the $_SERVER array. Similar to how the JavaScript version works, this PHP code uses the case-insensitive stristr() function to search the user agent string for an occurrence of *iphone*. If the search term is not found, then stristr() returns False, and the rest of the web page continues to load. But if the word *iphone* is found, then the PHP redirects the identified iPhone or iPod touch Mobile Safari browser to your dedicated iPhone site URL.

After calling the redirect via the header() function, you should include the exit() function, which will prevent the rest of that HTML page from loading while the redirect is being processed.

Dynamically Replacing Flash with iOS-Compatible Content

What if you don't need to redirect to a separate iPhone-centric site, but merely want to replace a single web element—such as a Flash video—for your web page to be iOS-compliant? You can also apply the browser user agent detection technique here.

Since Flash is not supported in Mobile Safari, if your web site includes a Flash video or Flash animation, you'll want to provide an alternative replacement (such as QuickTime-compatible video or an HTML5-driven animation, respectively) for viewing on iOS devices.

This content swap can be done dynamically on your web page with only minor tweaks to the JavaScript and PHP browser-detection examples.

JavaScript for Flash Replacement

Place the following JavaScript code anywhere in your web page where you need to switch between two content formats based on the browser model. As in the previous JavaScript example, retrieve the user agent and check it for the presence of *iphone* and *ipad* (since you want to identify iPads, too). If either word is found, then the page is being viewed with Mobile Safari, so display an iOS-compatible format. If some other web browser is being used from a computer, then it's safe to load a Flash file instead.

```
<script type="text/javascript">
<!--
var os = navigator.userAgent.toLowerCase();
if (os.indexOf('iphone')!=-1 || os.indexOf('ipad')!=-1) {

    // Yes, viewed by Mobile Safari, so show iOS-compatible web content.
    document.write("Place QuickTime or HTML5 code here");
}
else {
    // No, some other browser, so load Flash file instead.
    document.write("Place Flash HTML Object/Embed code here");
}
// -->
</script>
```

PHP for Flash Replacement

You can place the following PHP code anywhere in your web page where you need to swap content based on the browser being used. If the PHP determines the user agent is from Mobile Safari, then it will display iOS-compatible web content. If the user agent reveals some other web browser, then you can load a Flash file.

```
<?
$os = $_SERVER['HTTP_USER_AGENT'];
if (stristr($os, 'iphone') || stristr($os, 'ipad')) {
?>
    <!-- Yes, viewed by Mobile Safari, so show iOS-compatible web content. -->
<?
}
```

```
else {
?>
    <!-- No, some other browser, so place Flash HTML Object/Embed code here. -->
<?
}
?>
```

Of course, if you don't have a specific need to use Flash on your web site, the easiest solution is to simply use a QuickTime-compatible format for all your web-based videos. Anyone who has an iOS device is required to have the desktop version of iTunes on their computer for device synchronizing. Since QuickTime is installed with iTunes, even Windows users will be able to watch your web site's QuickTime videos.

Home Screen Bookmarking Made Beautiful

You can make it easy for loyal fans who visit your site frequently to add a web site bookmark to their iOS home screens.

When bookmarking a URL in Mobile Safari, one of the options is Add to Home Screen, which saves the bookmark as an app icon on your iOS device's home screen. Tap the icon, and it displays that web site in Mobile Safari. By default, a thumbnail snapshot of your web page is displayed as the app icon, but that shrunken thumbnail is so small that the site is probably unrecognizable.

Fortunately, you don't have to settle for that.

You can design your own custom image for display as a home screen bookmark icon. As with an iPhone or iPad app icon, do not add rounded corners or the glossy bevel, since iOS will automatically add those effects to the icon. Just create and save the icon in PNG format for each iOS screen resolution size:

- Older iPhone and iPod touch: 57 × 57 pixels

- iPad: 72 × 72 pixels

- Retina display iPhone and iPod touch: 114 × 114 pixels

The default 57 × 57 pixel icon should be named *apple-touch-icon.png*, but the other two files can be named whatever you want (such as *apple-touch-icon-72px.png* and *apple-touch-icon-114px.png*). Then upload those PNG images to your web site's root directory, and add the following lines of HTML code within the <head> tag of your web page:

```
<link rel="apple-touch-icon" media="screen and (resolution: 163dpi)" href="apple-touch-icon.png" />

<link rel="apple-touch-icon" media="screen and (resolution: 132dpi)" href="apple-touch-icon-72px.png" />

<link rel="apple-touch-icon" media="screen and (resolution: 326dpi)" href="apple-touch-icon-114px.png" />
```

The user's device resolution will determine which icon size is used for the home screen web site bookmark. This is important to avoid saving a blurry, small icon on a higher-resolution device.

If the URL points to a dedicated web site for your iOS app, then don't use your application's existing icon, since that might prove confusing to customers who have both icons on their home screen. Instead, use an alternate image so that users can easily differentiate between your app icon and your web site bookmark icon. If the URL points to your company site that showcases several apps, assigning your company logo as the bookmark icon is a good branding choice.

Let's Make Some Noise: The Power of Blogs, Twitter, and Social Networks

Now that your web site is ready, you finally have an online destination for promoting the forthcoming release of your iOS app. But the only way anyone will know about your new web site is if you get out there and start building your online audience.

Cultivating an Online Community

Although important, submitting your web site URL and XML Sitemap file to the major search engines is not enough. Don't wait for the masses to find you. Go out and find them. You want to start conversations and get people talking about your new app.

By focusing your initial marketing efforts on Twitter, Facebook, and other popular social networks, you can leverage their word-of-mouth power to drive interested consumers to your web site. Since your app is not yet available in the App Store, this prerelease stage is all about building awareness and anticipation for the product.

I will warn you in advance that diving into the world of social media can be very time-consuming. If you already actively use Twitter or Facebook, you know what I'm talking about. Be prepared to dedicate at least one hour every day to online marketing. If done right, your interactions should feel less like business and more like community building, establishing meaningful connections with a global audience.

Carving out an hour or more each day for online marketing can seem like an overwhelming concept, but to succeed in the App Store, it's worth every second. And the punch line is that this is all free, grassroots advertising. There's no cost to join any of these social networks, so the only investment is your time.

It's important to remember that the only way any of this works is if you treat your audience with respect. If you tweet and blog only about press releases and sales pitches, no one will want to follow you. To grow your audience requires posting about things that people want to read.

The top social media sites are Facebook and Twitter. With third-party iOS frameworks available for Twitter and Facebook, it should come as no surprise that these are the two most widely embraced social networks within the iOS community. So, it makes sense to concentrate most of your energy on these two sites.

Blogging

As I've already mentioned, maintaining a blog is an essential element in driving traffic to your web site. Your iOS app's main web page probably won't change often, since it primarily serves to educate people on what your app is and why they should buy your app. Your blog, on the other hand, is the central online engine for posting all your announcements, special offers, and news updates.

You just posted a new video trailer or some screenshots? Blog about it. Your app has been submitted to the App Store review team? Blog about it. Your app won an award or has been reviewed by another site? Blog about it. Have an interesting story to share about your development experience? Yes, you guessed right—blog about it.

Syndicating Your Blog Content

Every time you publish a new blog entry, the related RSS feed is updated, along with feed reader subscribers and any site that syndicates your blog content. You should also post a link to the new blog entry on Twitter, Facebook, Digg, Delicious, and all other major social media sites that could push web traffic your way and increase awareness of your app.

Don't assume everyone who visits your site will subscribe to your blog's RSS feed or e-mail alerts (see the "Anatomy of an iOS App Web Site" section for details on FeedBurner's e-mail subscriptions). Some people prefer to receive news through other services, such as Twitter.

If the thought of needing to manually post your blog update on each and every one of your social network accounts sounds tedious, you can use one of the free blog services that automate this task.

You can configure Posterous, Tumblr, and TypePad to automatically syndicate your blog entries to your Twitter and Facebook accounts, as well as several other sites. And you can even set Tumblr to autopost your tweets on your blog, retrieved from your Twitter RSS feed.

If you currently have a blog with a different service, such as WordPress, Blogger, LiveJournal, or MovableType, you can still automate the posting of your blog entries into Facebook. Later in this chapter, I'll explain how to easily syndicate your blog's RSS feed into your Facebook account.

Inviting Comments

The one feature that really makes a blog come alive is the inclusion of commenting. Giving your readers a voice turns your blog from a read-only article into a vibrant two-way conversation. By encouraging interaction, your blog readers will become much more loyal and supportive. Even if they disagree with one of your posts, they are still talking about it and linking to it. When building a community, not everyone is going to have the same opinion, which is fine—that's what keeps the conversation interesting.

Unfortunately, the amount of spam that ends up clogging up the comments section of many blogs can be quite annoying. To help eliminate spam that comes from automated bots, make sure to use a blog service with CAPTCHA web forms and spam filters to ensure that posted comments are from actual humans. You may also want to monitor posted comments frequently and remove questionable ones via the blog's admin dashboard. Yes, that can be time-consuming, but it's ultimately worth the effort to offer a true blogging environment.

Although some people opt to hold their conversations on a Facebook Page to avoid anonymous spam, the convenience of blog comments is that no account is required. There's no barrier to entry. Readers don't need to join a social network or log in to any system. They just fill out the comment form and click the submit button.

Host Your Own Blog or Use a Third-Party Blog Service?

If you're comfortable with installing and modifying blog software, such as the open source download from WordPress, on your own web server, you'll have the power to customize every aspect of the blog to suit your specific needs.

If you would rather not deal with configuring MySQL databases, installing security update patches, and editing PHP files, consider using one of the many free blog services previously mentioned. They automatically update the blog software on their servers and offer state-of-the-art antispam tools for managing comments. You can also customize the look and feel of your blog to match your web site's existing page design if desired. For example, I use Blogger to remotely host my company blog, but the template was customized to mimic the same design as my Electric Butterfly web site, for a seamless transition between the two.

Twitter

Since a large percentage of iPhone, iPad, and iPod touch users are on Twitter, that's one social network you really can't afford to avoid. If you don't already have a presence on Twitter, before we go any further, do yourself a favor and sign up for a free account now (go to http://twitter.com/).

Although you can easily access Twitter from a web browser on both your computer and mobile device, you may prefer using a dedicated client app for staying on top of your Twitter world. Popular favorites are Twitterrific, Echofon, TweetDeck, and Twitter's official iOS app. To explore all the available options for Mac, Windows, Linux, and iOS, check out oneforty's comprehensive Twitter apps directory at http://oneforty.com/.

Twitter's microblogging/messaging is not only a great way to communicate with your customers in real time on everything from support issues to feature requests, but it's also a very accepted platform for promoting your iOS apps and games. And on top of that, many of the major app review sites and news bloggers keep tabs on related trends and topics within the Twittersphere, so your tweets may attract additional press coverage for your apps!

According to the report "Winning iPhone Strategies," written by Jonathan Deamer and Katie Lips at Kisky Netmedia and supported by Northwest Vision and Media (http://www.scribd.com/winningiphonestrategies), the fourth most influential method of app discovery for iPhone users is recommendations on Twitter, just below the top three: word-of-mouth, online reviews, and browsing the App Store. This reinforces the importance of Twitter as a powerful marketing tool for iOS developers.

Managing Twitter Accounts

When establishing your existence on Twitter, you should decide how you want to use the service.

Some developers create a Twitter account for themselves and a separate account for their iOS app. This allows them to use the app-focused account for posting related news and fielding support queries, while their own personal account is used for tweeting about other products or miscellaneous, nonbusiness items. Some organizations have one account that is dedicated to company news, and then assign separate accounts to each employee of the company. These two approaches work well if your venture is composed of more than one developer or if you want to reserve one Twitter account for only personal use.

If you're a solo developer, you may find it much easier to consolidate your efforts into a single Twitter account. And with a few iOS apps under your belt, cross-promoting them within a single Twitter feed can be very beneficial. This is especially helpful if one of your apps becomes popular and brings you a lot of Twitter followers, because you'll have a large audience that is eager to hear about any other products you release.

Gaining Followers

"Followers" are those users who choose to follow your Twitter stream, which means your tweets will show up in their timeline (a stream of posts from the people they follow). The more followers you accrue, the larger your audience becomes.

And since growing your audience is the main marketing objective here, how does one get more followers?

Ah, that is probably the most frequently asked question regarding Twitter.

Sure, a lot of third-party services promise to boost your number of followers if you agree to follow the people they request, but that's the wrong avenue to take. It's not about getting just anyone and everyone to follow you in exchange for following them. True, your audience will grow exponentially with that kind of tactic, but quantity does not necessarily equal quality. Typically, those people care about only one thing: increasing their own follower count. You're just a number to them. Most (if not all) of them don't really care what you have to say—they may not even own an iOS device.

Don't worry about how many people follow you. Focus on growing a good-quality audience, one genuinely interested in iOS apps. Let's look at a few ways you can make that happen.

- **Who you follow matters.** Building an audience starts with you. Search Twitter for the people who influence you most—your favorite app developers, publishers, bloggers, journalists, friends, and peers. Whenever they post something of value related to your views, then retweet it. They may notice your occasional retweets and reply to you. There's absolutely nothing wrong with being on the radar of influential people! Who knows, they may even follow you back. And even if they don't, who you follow says a lot about you. People who stumble on your Twitter profile may look at who you follow before deciding whether to follow you themselves.

- **Follow your fans.** Create a connection with loyal followers by showing them a little love in return. Nothing is more complimentary than reciprocity in following. Now that doesn't mean you need to follow everyone who follows you, but if their tweets interest you, it is the ultimate gesture of thanks.

- **Engage your community.** If people reach out to you on Twitter with comments or questions, always answer them. Twitter is not about talking *at* people. It's about talking *to* people. Having public conversations on Twitter can not only draw others into the discussion, but it also shows a personal touch, proving you're not an automated spambot that spews out only marketing messages. If you feel that your Twitter stream is becoming dominated by a single conversation, you may want to follow the person and continue the discussion via direct messages, to avoid alienating any of your other followers. If people are being rude, you do have the option to block them, but that should always be a last resort. More often than not, people just want to be heard. By following you, they have agreed to listen to your voice, so it's only fair that you listen to theirs as well.

- **Quality content is king!** Don't just tweet about your app nonstop with an endless barrage of links to reviews and announcements. No one will follow if you post only marketing spam 24/7. And that's probably a surefire way to lose whatever followers you do have. Give people a reason to follow you. Your tweets should portray a genuine voice that's entertaining and informative. Like a blog, your Twitter posts should reflect your personality and even your opinions (as long as they are not offensive or counterproductive to your marketing mission). And if you publish a blog post, then tweet about it with a link! Followers will evangelize and retweet people, not corporate entities, so let them see the person behind the product.

■ **Stay true to your voice.** To retain your followers, it's important to stay on topic. If you're known for tweeting about iOS game development, then spending a solid month talking about nothing but house renovations will quickly decimate your follower count. They followed you to learn from your valued game programming expertise, not to trudge through hundreds of tweets about laying new tile in the bathroom. It's good to share personal events in your life, especially if your audience has similar interests, but those posts should be sprinkled among your primary topic tweets. Staying focused on only one or two themes will also help attract new followers. If someone is searching Twitter for *iPhone dev* to learn and network with fellow programmers, and they stumble on one of your tweets, they will most likely follow you only if the majority of your other posts are also related to iOS development.

■ **Retweet!** If someone posts something that you feel your audience would enjoy, retweet it. Twitter is built on the spirit of karma. What goes around comes around. Spend the time promoting other people's tweets more than you promote yourself, and you'll cultivate a deeper bond with your followers. They may even retweet *your* posts more often to return the favor. Remember that this isn't about finding people you can merely talk at, but rather building synergy within the community. And when people do retweet you or promote one of your links, take a moment to thank them. It's a small gesture, but it goes a long way. If your followers know their support is appreciated, they are more likely to retweet your posts again in the future.

■ **Time your tweets.** Very few people monitor Twitter all day long. And then there's that damn sleep thing that gets in the way every night. Unless your followers are using a client app that keeps track of their current reading position in the timeline, they may miss some of your posts. Of course, it's always that perfect tweet you spent ten minutes crafting or the all-important product announcement that you've been planning for weeks. We all live in different time zones with different schedules, so your timing is essential. Sending out a tweet at 8 a.m. from Los Angeles would cover quite a few territories during daylight hours. For example, it would be 10 a.m. in Chicago; 11 a.m. in New York; 4 p.m. in London; and 5 p.m. in Paris, Berlin, and Rome. Twitter allows you to repeat a tweet every eight hours, so if the same message was sent out again at 5 p.m. from Los Angeles, it would be 8 a.m. in Hong Kong, 9 a.m. in Tokyo, and 11 a.m. in Sydney, Australia. Since some of your followers will see *all* your tweets, don't make a habit of repeating posts multiple times. If it starts smelling like spam, you're liable to lose followers. But a rare repeated tweet every once in awhile for special announcements is tolerable and can be very effective in reaching more people.

Customizing Your Profile

Twitter offers a nice selection of background images and colors to beautify your account pages. Although the colors are easy enough to modify, don't settle for the same default themes seen on countless profiles. Be unique and personalize your page with your own custom background image and avatar picture. Take advantage of this free marketing opportunity to visually showcase your iOS app and brand identity!

Regarding your avatar picture, if you maintain two Twitter accounts—one for your company and one for your own personal use—you'll most likely want to differentiate the two by using a corporate logo for the company profile and a photo of yourself for the personal profile. For an independent developer using a single Twitter account, I highly recommend using a photo of yourself as the profile picture. Even though you'll be tweeting about your software products and iOS news, a photo adds a personal touch. People like to see who they are following.

When I first joined Twitter, I listed Electric Butterfly as the profile name and uploaded my company logo as the avatar picture. I didn't tweet that much, and in return, few people followed me. After a couple months of seeing how other people operated on Twitter, I decided to follow their lead. I switched the profile name to Dave Wooldridge and replaced the avatar with my photo. After I provided a human face and name to my Twitter presence, and made a conscious effort to tweet more frequently, my follower count began to rapidly increase.

Although all Twitter clients support the display of avatar pictures, a person's background image is seen only when visiting the profile page on Twitter.com. Even then, when viewing the Twitter site on the iPad, the main content is scaled to fill the width of the Mobile Safari screen, obscuring the background image. And on the iPhone, Mobile Safari loads a mobile-optimized version of Twitter, which excludes custom backgrounds. But none of that minimizes the importance of customizing your profile's background image. Many people will check out your profile page from a desktop web browser before deciding whether to follow you.

In the Design section of Twitter's Settings page, you can upload your own custom background image file. Since this is a valuable piece of screen real estate, the background should be designed to effectively promote your company or iOS app, without being hidden by the main Twitter content centered within the browser. To accommodate most common screen dimensions, this requires a design theme that's planted in the top-left corner and extends outward to the right and down. Take a look at several custom backgrounds. Check out the great collection from real Twitter accounts at the fun site http://twitterbackgroundsgallery.com/, and you'll see what I mean.

With large monitors with high resolutions of 1,280 × 800, 1,900 × 1,200, or even higher, it's recommended that your background image be at least 1,600 pixels wide. Since web browsers are not usually maximized full width on such large screens, that size should work fine. But web pages scroll down, so the chances are greater that a web browser's height may span from top to bottom on the screen. For best results, set your image height to a minimum of 1,300 pixels.

If your image fades to the same solid color as the background color, then the image can be much shorter. When Twitter's Tile Background setting is left unchecked, the background color will show through where the image ends, but with the color the same, it will appear seamless to the viewer. This is the approach used in the example background image designed to promote the fictional Breadcrumbs app (see Figure 10–

14). The background image is only 700 pixels tall, yet because the background color is set to the same brown as the ground beneath the car, it creates the illusion that the ground continues far below it.

Figure 10–14. *A Twitter background image design for the fictional Breadcrumbs app, leaving plenty of empty space for the main Twitter page content that will be centered on the screen.*

Looking at Figure 10–14, notice that the iPhone app graphics are positioned in the far-top-left area, leaving the rest of the image fairly empty, with nothing but the simple horizon line and the navigational breadcrumbs leading off the screen. This was done intentionally so that there is ample room for the main Twitter page content that will be displayed in the center of the browser screen. The trick is to create something unique and compelling, without being visually overpowering.

Based on average screen sizes, I recommend limiting your primary design elements to 180 pixels wide by 660 pixels tall in the top-left corner of the background image. Confining your main graphics to that safe area helps prevent your background visual from being obscured by the Twitter page content (see Figure 10–15). Since Twitter's content area is fairly wide, you may want to try limiting your design area's width to less than 180 pixels to accommodate smaller screens, such as laptops.

Figure 10–15. *Limiting your primary graphics to 180 pixels wide (or less) in the top-left corner ensures that imagery won't be obscured by the main Twitter content when viewed on most desktop computer screens.*

For those of you who think the inclusion of the iPhone app's site URL in Figure 10–15's background is a little too much, let me be the first to say it really is quite effective. Not because everyone seems to be doing it (they are), but because it actually works!

After changing my own Twitter background image to promote a few of my Electric Butterfly products with web site domain names listed, I began receiving a lot more tweets asking about those products. I also saw a significant increase in traffic to those URLs. I was surprised by this, since you can't add active hyperlinks to a Twitter background image, which means that people are forced to manually type that URL into their browser to visit that site. But if followers are curious enough, they'll do it, especially if the URL is short and easy to remember (yet another reason for registering a dedicated domain name for your app's web site).

Last, but not least, when customizing your Twitter profile, don't forget to add some brief information about yourself and your app to the Bio field and your site's URL in the Web field. People want to know who you are and what you do. I personally won't follow anyone who leaves those fields blank. And the beauty of your profile's bio text and web URL is that they are accessible in all Twitter client apps and web browsers—even those that don't support Twitter's custom background images.

Keywords and Hashtags

Before you dash off your next tweet, it's important to know that the wording of your message can greatly impact its success in reaching the right audience. You want to use words that are quickly identified by readers scanning the timeline and searching Twitter for specific keywords.

For example, if you're talking about your iPhone app in a tweet, don't refer to it as a generic "app." You know it's an iPhone or iPad app, but those new to you, who came via a retweet or Twitter search, may not know which platform your app supports. Most people will search for *iPhone* or *iPad*, so always include the supported device name in product-related tweets.

Don't assume everyone knows what your app does. If you're tweeting the iTunes App Store link of your application, don't just post the app name and URL. I know the limit is 140 characters, but I'm sure you have a few more characters to spare (especially when using a URL-shortener service like Bit.ly, as discussed earlier in the chapter). Don't be vague. Oh, it's a parked-car locator for the iPhone? Ah, I could use one of those. And you were kind enough to state "(iTunes)" after the URL, warning me that the link will launch iTunes on my computer. Very convenient and respectful.

Besides crafting your tweet with appropriate keywords, hashtags can also be included. *Hashtags* are keywords that are preceded with a number (#) symbol. What makes them special is that Twitter and most third-party clients display hashtags as active text links.

Click a hashtag, and a group of recent tweets that include that same hashtag are listed. It's a great way to increase the discoverability of your tweets by including them in popular hashtag groups. People who don't follow you or even know your Twitter ID can stumble on your tweets from a hashtag list.

Just be careful not to overuse hashtags. Don't insert a hashtag in every tweet, and certainly don't #pollute a #single #tweet with #multiple #hashtags, or else your posts will be hard to read and look like spam.

For those select few tweets that are important enough to warrant a little extra exposure, convert one of the keywords into a hashtag. If none of your words is a popular tag, then tack on the desired hashtag to the end of your tweet. For example, when I post valuable links that would benefit fellow iPhone developers, I often add the known hashtag #iphonedev.

To help pinpoint existing hashtags and popular search keywords, check out these handy resources:

- Twitter Search (http://search.twitter.com/)
- Hashtags .org (http://hashtags.org/)
- What the Trend (http://www.whatthetrend.com/)

Twitter Lists

Lists represent yet one more reason that the number of followers you have isn't as important as it once was. Within your account on Twitter, you can create a new list and give it a unique name. Since Twitter assigns a domain name to it—such as http://twitter.com/ebutterfly/iphonedev—it's best to use a name without spaces.

Lists provide a way to organize people into groups, making it easier to follow particular topics. The reason lists chip away the importance of followers is that you can follow a list without following all the people in the list. And you can create a list of people you don't follow.

Some app developers have created lists of their favorite iOS-related Twitterers, including fellow developers, review sites, and bloggers. It's a great way to see a daily snapshot of the iOS developer community. A lot of developers follow the lists of other developers as a way to connect with the major influencers.

Creating your own lists can bring new followers to it, so make sure you include yourself in your own lists. That's something many people tend to forget to do.

If you've compiled a great list and submitted to the major Twitter list directories like Listorious, newcomers will possibly follow your list and maybe also your own Twitter account. It's yet another way to get discovered on Twitter and reach a larger audience with your tweets.

Don't just create iOS-related lists. If your app is related to a specific subject such as music or writing, create a list for that topic. By creating such lists, you can attract new followers who are interested in those subjects. If they own an iOS device, then your tweets within those lists will expose your app to potential customers who may not have known about it.

If someone adds you to their list, it means they think your tweets provide enough value to warrant being part of a select group. Be sure to thank them for the kind gesture. And likewise, if someone follows your list, thank them for it. In such an impersonal online world, you might be surprised how much goodwill can be exchanged with a simple "thank you."

Managing the Pipeline

Everything you post on Twitter (not counting retweets) should drive traffic back to your web site. That includes any photos or videos you tweet.

It's true that many of the Twitter client apps make it extremely easy to upload photos from your iPhone camera to media-sharing sites like Flickr, TwitPic, and yfrog, but that's not an optimal use of your tweets. If people are interested enough to check out cool screenshots or video play from your app, you should be hosting those media files on your own web site, within web pages that provide additional information about your product.

Even if you're showing very early alpha screenshots that you don't want published on your main web site, just link to a stand-alone page on your server that serves as a sneak preview for your tweets. This way, you get to control the message and content on the page. Plus, it can be designed to reflect your app's visual branding, rather than the generic pages of third-party media-sharing sites.

Remember when I mentioned that you should set up a free account with one of the URL shortening services like Bit.ly, so that you can track the click-throughs and retweets of the links you post on Twitter? If you experiment with two different ways to word a tweet about your iOS app, use two different Bit.ly URLs, so that you can track which word phrasing was more successful in click-throughs. This will help you refine your marketing messages as effective, eye-catching tweets!

For those of you ready to dive deeper into the Twitterverse with advanced management tools, check out oneforty's vast directory of third-party applications and services for tracking unfollows, Twitter marketing campaigns, follower locations, spam filters, and much more. There really is quite an amazing cottage industry of businesses out there based on Twitter—too many to list here. Some of them are less useful than others, so tread carefully.

Facebook

The Facebook SDK for iOS is widely used in the app development world. Facebook logins are just as common as Twitter in today's mobile apps and games. If you don't have a Facebook account already, you'll want to sign up for one at `http://www.facebook.com/`, and use that for personal interactions with friends and colleagues.

Although Facebook has made it extremely easy to interface with its API from within an iOS project, your marketing efforts within the social networking site itself need to be formulated a little differently than they are in Twitter. Since it's all about growing your audience, all of the same rules of etiquette discussed for Twitter also apply to Facebook. The difference here is that while you can mix personal and business tweets within a single Twitter account, it's recommended to separate the two in Facebook.

With Twitter, you can choose not to follow everyone who follows you, but not so with Facebook. If someone adds you as a friend in Facebook and you approve the request, that person is automatically added to your friends list as well. For this reason, you'll want to create a Facebook Page for your business. For those people interested in following your iOS app news and updates, they can simply "like" your Facebook Page. This provides you with a way to grow your audience without being forced to add each and every one of them to your own personal friends list, since those followers are instead added to your Facebook Page's list of fans.

Creating a Facebook Page

Setting up a Facebook Page for your product or business is a great way to connect with people on the world's most popular social networking site. The only requirement is that you must be the owner or official representative of the business or product reflected in the page you're creating.

Unlike with Twitter, members are not able to search for keywords in posts. Facebook's search engine is limited to searching for member names. With only a personal Facebook account under your own name, you won't be listed in Facebook searches for your iOS app name or business name. But with a Facebook Page for your app or company, related Facebook searches will find it.

To create a Facebook Page, you must have a personal Facebook account, since that is the account assigned as the page's administrator. If you plan on creating more than one app, I recommend building a fan base under one company Facebook Page, rather than several separate accounts for each iPhone or iPad app. One centralized page will not only be easier to manage, but it will also allow you to cross-promote your products to the same audience.

Sign in to your personal Facebook account, and then visit the official Create a Page URL at http://www.facebook.com/pages/create.php.

From the options provided, select Company, Organization, or Institution to create a page for your business, or Brand or Product to create a page for a specific app. You're then prompted to assign the appropriate category for your new page. If you're setting up a page for your app development business, you will most likely select Computers/Technology as your category. If you're building an app page under Brand or Product, your category should be Software.

Once the new Facebook Page is built, add your company description to the Info tab, and add your logo or app icon to the page's main picture. Then post information about your app, including development news, updates, and special offers. You can even post sneak preview screenshots of upcoming new features to get fans excited about a future release.

Connecting with Fans

Now that your Facebook Page is up and running, it's time to spread the word about it, encouraging people to click the Like button to become a fan of your page! To get one of those cool Facebook domain names assigned to your page—such as http://www.facebook.com/iTunes—at least 25 people must like your page.

There's absolutely nothing wrong with appealing to your existing blog and Twitter audience. Let them know that you have a new dedicated Facebook Page, and invite them to show support by clicking the Like button. As expected, Facebook even provides an affordable way to advertise your page throughout its network to gain new fans.

When communicating with your fans, post status updates, notes, photos, links, and more to your Facebook Page's Wall. People who have liked your page will see your posts in their own Facebook newsfeeds. Occasionally, you may need to broadcast an important announcement to the inbox of every fan. To do that, click your page's Edit Info link, then from within the Edit Info's Marketing tab, click Send an Update. Remember that no one likes to receive a barrage of press releases and marketing messages, so to retain your fans, try not to abuse this direct line of communication.

To break up the stream of app-related marketing posts on your Wall, try to sprinkle in a variety of related news, photos, and videos that might also be of interest to your fans. If people post comments on your Wall, reply back to create a sense of community within your Facebook Page.

TRACKING THE PERFORMANCE OF YOUR FACEBOOK MARKETING EFFORTS

Facebook offers its own free analytics service, Facebook Insights, for Facebook Pages and Facebook developers. When logged in to your Facebook Page as an Admin, click the View Insights link in the far-right column to view metrics about your Facebook Page.

Tracking the visitor traffic can be especially helpful if you're running a Facebook ad or directing people to your Facebook Page from other marketing materials.

Importing Your Blog, Outputting to Twitter

By extending your marketing reach across more and more social networks, the first concern is time. Posting the same content across multiple sites, such as your blog, Twitter, and Facebook, can be very time-consuming. Fortunately, a recent trend in social media is the ability to syndicate content across networks to make publishing more convenient. Post your news in one place, and it gets published on multiple sites.

As I've mentioned earlier, several blog sites, like Tumblr and Posterous, enable users to autoupdate Twitter and Facebook with links to their new blog posts. Facebook also offers a way to do this with its own Import a Blog feature.

Do you want your new blog posts to automatically be published on your Facebook Page? Just follow these steps:

1. From your Facebook Page's profile, type **Notes** into the search field.

2. From the dynamic drop-down menu of results, select the Facebook Notes app.

3. On the Notes page, choose Edit Import Settings from the left column. You'll be prompted to provide your blog's RSS feed URL (see Figure 10–16). Enter a URL and click Start Importing.

Once you've followed these steps, Facebook will automatically post your new blog entries to your Facebook Page's notes.

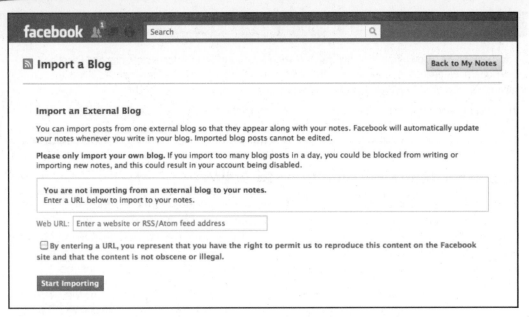

Figure 10–16. *Submit your blog's RSS feed URL to autoimport blog posts into Facebook as notes.*

If you want your Facebook posts to be automatically tweeted on Twitter, Facebook offers support for that at `http://www.facebook.com/twitter` (see Figure 10–17). When linking your Twitter account to your Facebook Page, you can opt to share everything you post on Facebook or elect to share only specific kinds of posts, such as status updates and notes.

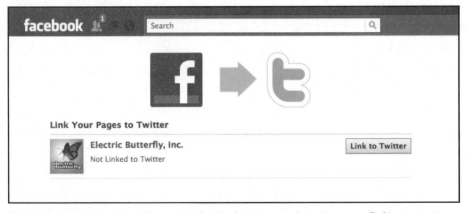

Figure 10–17. *Facebook provides support for sharing your page's posts on your Twitter account.*

In reverse, you can also publish your tweets as status updates on your Facebook Page by installing Andy Young's handy Facebook application Selective Tweets (`http://www.facebook.com/selectivetwitter`). This application is much more powerful than importing your Twitter RSS feed as a blog, because it allows you to choose which specific tweets are posted on your Facebook Page by marking them with the special #fb hashtag. This prevents nonbusiness tweets from accidentally sneaking into your company's Facebook Page. For the Selective Tweets application to work, your Twitter account's tweets must not be protected.

Other Social Networks and Bookmarking Sites

Obviously, Twitter and Facebook are not the only social media giants in town. Depending on the kind of app or game you've developed, some of the other sites may offer a more targeted demographic.

Although Myspace may have been dethroned by the current king, Facebook, Myspace is still a popular social networking site in the music community. Countless new artists have been discovered via Myspace, moving on to lucrative record deals and high-profile music careers. If your app is music-related, then the Myspace music crowd may just be the perfect audience for you to reach. Time to unveil your own Myspace profile page to network with other music lovers and promote your iOS app!

If your app appeals to businesses, you'll definitely want to get connected on LinkedIn. Besides including a link to your app's web site on your LinkedIn profile, the popular business network hosts thousands of active discussion groups. Pick the groups that best match your app's target audience, and promote it by posting app-related information and links to your blog articles. This is a great way to reach business executives who may not have found your iOS app on their own in the crowded App Store.

LinkedIn also makes it easy to publish your Twitter posts on your LinkedIn page. Activate your Twitter account on your LinkedIn profile, and then append either the #in or #li hashtag to your tweets for those select messages to also be published as LinkedIn status updates.

For additional exposure, don't forget to submit your blog posts and published web articles to sites that specialize in sharing news and social bookmarking, like Digg, Delicious, Technorati, Reddit, and StumbleUpon.

Commenting on Forums, Groups, and Blogs

Do a little research to find online forums, message boards, and blogs related to your iOS app's target audience. If it's a music app, explore the most popular music forums and groups. If it's a writing app, investigate which sites are the most popular hangouts for authors. Since you developed an app for a particular niche market, it's a safe assumption you know a little something about the topic. Put your knowledge to good use by offering help on related special-interest forums or posting comments on blogs.

Yes, I'm creating extra work for you, but with good reason. Don't ever post anonymously on those sites. Most forums, groups, and even blogs support member logins to make frequent posting more convenient and secure. When requested, sign up as a free member and enter all the profile information. You want your presence on those sites visibly identifiable with a name, URL link, and photo.

Some blogs use third-party avatar systems like Gravatar. It's worth having a Gravatar profile already registered and ready to use. If signatures are supported, then use that small bit of HTML-savvy space to promote your app and web site.

See where I'm going with this? Every time you post a comment to a forum thread or blog article, your photo, your name, your web site link, and a subtle app reference are always represented. As long as you don't abuse your presence by spamming blatant sales pitches for your app, it's a win-win situation for everyone. In helping others, you're also increasing awareness of your forthcoming iOS app, simply by referencing it in your member URL and signature.

But Not Too Much Noise: Maintaining a Professional Reputation

Because of the high volume of informal conversations that occurs on social media sites like Twitter and Facebook, it's often easy to forget that the things you say are not just between you and the participants—they can be read by literally everyone within your network. And in the case of Twitter, anyone can visit your profile page and read your tweets, whether they follow you or not. Your online actions play out on a very public, global stage.

While being personable is encouraged, you're still representing your product and/or company. Your online behavior should be respectful, knowing that the things you say and link to make lasting impressions with potential customers worldwide. If you feel this advice is painfully obvious and shouldn't warrant a mention, then you're one step ahead of the game. You may have enough business savvy to recognize this, but you might be surprised by just how many professional developers are oblivious to the overall image they project.

Over the years, I've seen developer web sites that promote their software products alongside their online shrines to pro wrestling stars and the sexy Cylon babes from *Battlestar Galactica*! Yeah, you know who you are. It's fine if you're still in college and operate your software business out of the garage, but the world does not need to know this. In fact, you want your web site and your social media accounts to project a professional image that instills confidence in consumers. They want to know that by purchasing your app, they're investing in a developer who will continue to update and support the product. If they suspect it's nothing more than a hobby for you, you run the risk of missing out on those potential sales. Without faith in you, how can they have faith in your product?

Here are a few guidelines to consider:

- **Portray yourself as a professional.** Always portray a professional image of how you want to be seen. It doesn't matter if you're 18 or 68, fresh out of high school or recently retired. The Internet equalizes the playing field. The visual design of your web site, the kind of content it offers, and the way you present yourself to others via e-mail, tweets, and blog posts paints a vivid picture of you and how you do business. It's not about projecting a false illusion, but rather showcasing your true self in a professional light.

- **NSFW? Not appropriate to post!** If you're using your blog and social media accounts to promote your iOS app and business, don't curse or post jokes, funny photos, or videos that others might find offensive. Just because you tack on the warning NSFW (not suitable for work) doesn't make it acceptable. What you find funny, others may find wildly offensive. And those are potential sales you just lost. I hate to be a killjoy. We all want to have fun, but the goal is to sell more apps, right?

- **Don't mix business with politics or religion.** The two topics that elicit the strongest reactions from people are politics and religion. Whatever your viewpoint, there is always someone just as passionate on the opposing side. It's a conversation you can't win. If you're using social networks like Twitter and Facebook to promote your forthcoming iOS app, taking advantage of your audience by preaching your own political or religious agenda is the quickest way to alienate potential customers.

- **Keep your emotions in check.** Don't ever tweet, comment, or post blog entries in anger. Even though you can usually delete most items after the fact, copies of them linger on the Web to haunt you for years to come. You may have deleted that nasty blog post, but all of your blog's e-mail subscribers still have it sitting in their inboxes. And don't forget the elephant memory of Google's cache. Your online rants can live on indefinitely in Google's search databases.

- **Two wrongs don't make a right.** If someone says something negative about your app or your blog posts, don't lash back with venom. Talking trash about someone—especially online where everything is logged, cached, and archived—can win you a defamation lawsuit. You laugh, but it has happened. Protect your reputation and your personal assets by taking the high road.

- **Customers come first.** Customers may not always be right, but they should always be given your utmost respect and attention. Reply to every e-mail and tweet you receive in a prompt and courteous manner. There's no such thing as a stupid question, only stupid answers. OK, so maybe there are stupid questions, and some customers may get on your nerves. But if you embarrass a person in any way with sarcastic public replies on Twitter, you may have lost more than one customer—that's someone who may now warn friends and family to avoid your products. Be willing to go out of your way to make your customers happy. If they feel valued, they will reward you with their loyalty.

Everyone Loves a Winner: Collecting Prerelease Press and Testimonials

Although growing the prerelease buzz via social media is important, you should also start reaching out to influential journalists and bloggers who you hope will cover your app's forthcoming launch announcement and publish a review.

As I've said before, if you don't have the patience or time to dedicate to prerelease publicity, then it may be worth hiring a third-party firm that specializes in mobile app marketing. After searching Google for *iPhone app marketing*, you'll see there are many choices. If you do go that route, do your homework and talk to several of them to find the one that can meet your needs and budget.

Preparing a Hit List

Whether you hire a third-party publicist or do it yourself, you'll need to have a few marketing materials ready at your fingertips. Luckily, these are elements I've discussed earlier in this book, so you should already have them prepared:

- Company logo
- Your iOS app's icon and logo
- The app description—the quick elevator pitch and full list of features
- A few stunning screenshots that best represent your app
- A dedicated web page for your app
- A video trailer showcasing your app

Most tech journalists will be publishing coverage online, but in the event that your app attracts interest from a print magazine or newspaper, be sure to have ready high-resolution images of your company logo and iOS app icon/logo.

Getting your app's web site completed before you reach out to the press is vital, since journalists will ask for your web site URL.

Additionally, if you produced a video trailer, be sure to upload it to a video-sharing site like YouTube, so that online publications can easily embed the video in their news articles.

It's time to do a little research online. To receive news coverage from the most influential press sources, you need to know which tech sites and journalists would be interested in writing about your particular app. Prepare a hit list of people you should contact. Take note of their target audience and what they specialize in writing about. There's no point spending valuable time pitching your app to a mobile games site if it's not a game. If the site has never covered productivity apps in the past, it's probably not looking to start now. Conserve your efforts and focus only on those select people who will be interested in your app's category.

Establishing Relationships

When performing competitive research in Chapter 2, you explored dozens of app review sites. Those sites will prove important once again when you want them to review your application after it becomes available in the App Store.

And don't forget about the various tech sites and magazines that cover iPhone and iPad news. Even the ones that don't post press releases may be interested in writing about your app if it provides a unique feature or service that is deemed newsworthy and would directly benefit their readers.

I'll discuss acquiring media news exposure and reviews for your iOS app extensively in Chapter 12. However, at this point, if you don't have an existing relationship with any prominent tech journalists and bloggers, now is the time to introduce yourself. You don't want to cold-call them when your app is released. That's too late, wasting valuable time with introductions when your marketing engine should be moving at full speed.

During this prerelease stage, establish a connection with the people on your press hit list. Target the most important ones first, gradually making your way through the list.

Although the contacts' phone numbers may be listed on their respective web sites, don't call them first. Introduce yourself initially through e-mail, so that they can read about your company and your forthcoming app at their convenience.

Remember that most journalists are under a deadline to write several articles each day, so their time is very limited. Don't expect an instantaneous response. It may take them several days or even a week to reply to your e-mail, so patience is key here. This is yet another reason to begin the process a good month or so before your application goes live in the App Store.

Even if some journalists ignore your queries, do not—under any circumstances— bombard their voice mail or e-mail inboxes with an onslaught of repeated messages. With more than 300,000 apps in the App Store, you're not the only iOS developer looking for press coverage. There's nothing wrong with being persistent, but no one likes being spammed either.

Another good way to make journalists and influential bloggers aware of you is to follow them on Twitter. Since Twitter has become a major news source for the press, your tweets will not only increase awareness of your app with potential customers, but may also attract the attention of the press, generating requests for interviews and app reviews. Follow your favorite tech journalists, and they may just follow you back!

One of the reasons it's so crucial that your app's web site and screenshots are stunning visuals is to make you stand out from the overwhelming pile of queries from other developers. An eye-catching web site linked from a tweet and a killer screenshot posted on a popular iPhone forum have been known to kick-start a good dose of press coverage and word-of-mouth.

The tech press deals with thousands of developers and publishers of applications and games for several different platforms. Don't assume that those journalists who have reported on your products in the past will remember you when you send out a new press release. Reintroduce yourself before sending that release, thanking them for their previous coverage as a reminder before mentioning your impending new app.

Be conscious of their busy writing schedules and deadlines by asking about editorial calendars and how much advance notice they need in order to run a story or review during a given time period. This is especially important when dealing with the print world. Online bloggers can usually turn around articles within days, but print magazines typically have a three-month lead time.

Offering Exclusives and Advance Ad Hoc Builds to Secure Coverage

If you have something new and exciting to offer, journalists will want to be the first to break the news. They will have more interest in covering your story if it's an exclusive. Obviously, you can't offer everyone an exclusive, so if you do provide a special sneak preview of your app in the form of a video clip, a screenshot, or even an early beta version, make sure it's with a major publication that pulls in a large audience.

Having a few key bloggers play with your app before its release can work in your favor. If they enjoy your app, they are more likely to talk about it. If they love your app, they may even become unofficial evangelists for it, providing you with amazing quotes that you can include in your press release and on your web site.

Most reviewers and bloggers are accustomed to receiving apps via ad hoc distribution, so when beta-testing your app, don't forget to reserve a few of your allotted device slots for prerelease press coverage. Many iPhone-savvy journalists even include their device's UDID in their contact vCard or online bio. This is handy, since you'll need to set up a device ID for them in your iOS Provisioning Portal. Yes, configuring and providing ad hoc builds of your app for a select group of influential press members can be a hassle, but the potential publicity is well worth it. If you're sending a beta version, be sure to make them aware of that fact, so that they don't judge it as the final app release.

Even though the app may change or encounter unexpected delays during Apple's review process, some tech sites don't respect embargoes. So, even if you stress the importance of holding back the publication of their app review until its release in the App Store, your wishes may not always be granted.

Since you can't always control when reviews are published, it's vital that you don't send out ad hoc builds to tech sites too far in advance. You certainly don't want to oversaturate the market with tons of press coverage long before the actual release—that's simply a waste of publicity that would be of greater benefit postrelease. People generally have short memories when it comes to software products. The majority of your publicity should take place when it can do you the most good—when consumers can instantly buy the app they just read about.

With that said, it's always nice to have some winning testimonials in place from respected tech sites before your application is released. This way, when your app goes live in the App Store, it won't seem like such an unknown entity. Based on the prerelease buzz and the endorsements plastered on your web site, your new app will appear that much more appealing to consumers. Everyone loves a winner.

Passing the Baton

This was one of the longer chapters in the book, but ultimately one of the most important when it comes to marketing yourself and your app online.

With your prerelease marketing efforts in full swing, it's now time to place your iOS application in the good hands of Apple's app review team. Next up, I'll walk through the dreaded app-submission process. You've read the horror stories posted online of long review times and disheartening rejections, but don't let that discourage you. The sooner you work through Apple's app review process and get approved, the sooner you can start selling in the App Store. So, take a deep breath, and turn the page.

Chapter 11

Keys to the Kingdom: The App Store Submission Process

After months of extensive planning, development, and testing, you're finally ready to submit your iOS application to the App Store! Congratulations on all your hard work! Your beta testers love your app, but will Apple's app review team give it a thumbs-up?

This chapter will walk you through the app submission process in iTunes Connect. If you've followed Apple's guidelines, chances are good that your app submission will go smoothly. Just remember that more than 300,000 apps have already been approved, far outweighing the number of rejected apps.

Your product page in the App Store is the world's gateway to your app, so its presentation is essential in properly communicating the value of your app. Before submitting your app in iTunes Connect, you will need to have a few items ready for the online submission form. It's worth taking the time up-front to craft the following:

- Your app's title
- An enticing app description
- Eye-catching screenshots
- An optimized keywords list
- A pricing strategy

These elements will influence not only Apple's app review team, but also your product's marketability in the App Store.

The Politics of Pricing

One of the most important things you'll need to determine before submitting your app is the selling price. With most of the apps in the App Store's Top 25 priced at only 99 cents, don't assume that's the magic price point for your app. There are actually quite a few factors to consider before settling on a price.

Analyzing Similar Apps

Having already researched your competition (as discussed in Chapter 2), you should know the prices and feature sets of similar apps. Although keeping your price below that of competitive apps may seem like the obvious move, don't sell yourself short just yet.

If your app does not offer an attractive differentiator, such as an enhanced UI or killer feature, then you may be forced to price your app below similar apps, especially if they already enjoy a successful run of sales and positive customer reviews. But if you did your competitive homework, this shouldn't be an issue, right?

If your app *does* bring a much desired feature that sets it apart from the competition, you may be able to do quite well in the App Store with the same price or even a higher price. If you feel similar apps selling at $1.99 will quickly copy your unique killer feature, then maintaining the same $1.99 price point might be the answer. But if you think the feature may remain exclusive to your app—for whatever reason, such as technical difficulty or licensing deals—you may be able to charge $2.99 or a slighter higher price.

If you've stumbled upon an untapped market where your app does not currently have any competitors, then it really comes down to determining how much your product is worth to potential customers. Usually, the more niche market it serves, the higher price threshold it can bear. For example, apps that cater to scientists, doctors, or sales reps are often priced at the higher end of the spectrum, ranging anywhere from $6.99 to $99. You'll want to research the particular field your app specializes in to help calculate how much potential customers would be willing to spend on such a mobile application, based on the benefits it provides. You certainly don't want to gouge your customers, but at the same time, you don't want to leave money behind on the table either.

Room to Maneuver

Productivity apps experience a longer life span than fly-by-night, hit-driven apps, so pricing can be a little easier to determine. But for games and novelty apps that don't benefit from that same longevity, ranking high in the App Store charts immediately after launch is usually the goal. Although most of those hit-driven apps debut at the rock-bottom price of 99 cents in the hopes of propelling them into the Top 100, you should think twice before employing this same pricing strategy.

Setting the price at 99 cents upon release is a nice impulse-buy incentive, but what happens when the initial sales boost from your launch publicity efforts eventually tapers off? When awareness and sales later drop (and at some point, they will), that's the time you'll want to rejuvenate your presence in the App Store with a limited-time sale offer. But with your app already priced at the minimum 99 cents, you have no room to maneuver. But with an app price of $1.99 or higher, you'll have room to offer a special discount sale when needed to keep your momentum going in the App Store.

Games often receive complaints from consumers when released with a price tag higher than 99 cents, but don't let the vocal few sway you. If you've built a high-quality game, then complaints aside, your profits will benefit from the higher price. Although most higher-priced games are from big publishers like Electronic Arts and Gameloft, many small, independent developers have also found success—for example, Semi Secret Software's Canabalt at $2.99.

With your app priced at only 99 cents, you need to sell a lot of copies to make any decent money, especially after Apple takes its 30 percent cut. This usually requires ranking in the Top 25, with your business model relying on the boosted sales volume. And if you can get there, the visible exposure of the Top 25 can increase your sales exponentially, making the low 99–cent price worthwhile.

If you can rank high—that's the gamble. Since there's no guarantee your app will make it to the Top 25, or even the Top 100, pricing it at 99 cents is very risky if you end up selling fewer copies than expected. When you charge an app price of $1.99 or higher, you don't need to sell as many units to make just as much money, which in turn makes the App Store ranking less vital to your app's profitability.

Let's say your app manages to sell only 10,000 units over the course of several months:

- 10,000 × $0.99 = $9,900 – $2,970 (Apple's 30%) = $6,930
- 10,000 × $1.99 = $19,900 – $5,970 (Apple's 30%) = $13,930

With disappointing overall sales, a $1.99 or higher price can still provide respectable sales numbers, and may even recoup the product's initial development costs. A 99–cent price drastically reduces your profit margin by half!

Sustaining a Long-Term Business

Since you've purchased this book, it's probably a safe bet that you're looking to make money from your mobile app development. And you're not just looking to bank on a single app, but ideally build a profitable business producing several iOS apps. To accomplish this, you must price your apps not only to be competitive with other similar apps, but also to provide enough revenue to pay for the actual development costs of each app and run your business. To help determine your pricing, you should first figure out what your business needs to earn each year to survive.

As a fledgling business, your operating overhead may appear to be very low. Like many independent developers, you could be working from home and doing all of the design, programming, marketing, accounting, and other business tasks yourself. This is a common formula that has worked for many iOS app developers. But when calculating your financial needs, don't focus on only immediate expenses such as advertising, web hosting, Internet access, telephone lines, health insurance, food, and your mortgage/rent. It's important to place a value on your time as well. You don't want to merely "get by." Your plan should be to profit from all your hard work, earning enough money to not only fund your next app project, but also to reward your efforts with a little luxury.

As an example, let's say your iOS app will cost $5,000 to develop. That assumes you're doing all the UI design and programming work yourself, with a small budget to license graphics, music, or other services. To put food on the table and pay all of your bills, let's assume your monthly overhead is $4,000. If you plan on producing three apps within a year, your total development budget and annual living expenses will be approximately $63,000. To give yourself a little breathing room in case of additional expenses and unexpected emergencies, let's round up to $70,000.

- $70,000 / $0.69 ($0.99 – Apple's 30%) = 101,449 apps sold

- $70,000 / $1.39 ($1.99 – Apple's 30%) = 50,360 apps sold

- $70,000 / $2.09 ($2.99 – Apple's 30%) = 33,493 apps sold

To generate $70,000 in annual revenue, your three 99–cent apps would need to sell 101,449 copies before the year's end! Easy enough if your three apps are best sellers, sitting comfortably within the App Store's Top 100. But if they are ranked outside the Top 100, then charging only 99 cents per app may not get you anywhere close to your annual $70,000 revenue goal. And if you're coming from the world of desktop software development and consulting, you're probably used to making quite a bit more than that per year.

Just do the math. You'll quickly see how selling apps for only 99 cents requires them to be best sellers with no margin for failure.

What if you manage a small in-house team of designers and programmers, or outsource development to a third-party company? Then the development costs for your app project will mostly likely exceed $10,000 or $20,000. I'm being conservative here, as some apps and games can cost more than $100,000 to develop. It just depends on the project's complexity and the overhead of your staff and related expenses.

Looking to support your business with an annual revenue stream of at least $300,000?

- $300,000 / $0.69 ($0.99 – Apple's 30%) = 434,783 apps sold

- $300,000 / $1.39 ($1.99 – Apple's 30%) = 215,827 apps sold

- $300,000 / $2.09 ($2.99 – Apple's 30%) = 143,541 apps sold

That's a lot of apps you'll need to sell per year at only 99 cents each! You'll either need a bona fide hit or to work much harder to release a larger collection of apps that can be generating revenue. Just remember that the more apps you produce, the more money you spend on development, which in turn raises your overhead.

Just because you've read about hit games like Angry Birds and Cut the Rope selling millions of copies, don't assume that selling 500,000 apps is an easy goal to achieve. Sure, it would be great, and we all hope to hit the jackpot with a best-selling app. But when calculating your development budget and app pricing, keep in mind that most apps sell only a few thousand copies during their lifetime in the App Store. You'll need to work very hard as it is to ensure your app is more successful than the rest of the pack, so don't make your job any more difficult by pricing your app too low.

Perceived Value and Consumer Resistance

Are you starting to understand the great risk involved with the 99–cent price point? Your revenue earnings are not the only potential victim if your app does not sell well. There also seems to be a direct correlation between price and ratings, but not in the direction you would expect. The lower your price, the lower your customer ratings may sink.

It's true that if your app is priced too high, consumers will lash out with negative ratings in the App Store. So, the cheaper your app is, then the better the reviews, right? Not necessarily. A lower price brings a broader audience of customers, many of whom acquired it as an impulse buy. After paying just 99 cents, you wouldn't think anyone would complain, but complain they do. Quite a few users out there have unreasonably high expectations for what they will get for 99 cents. Many of them have been spoiled by the wealth of great 99-cent games. The popular strategy of dropping app prices to only 99 cents in an attempt to boost volume sales and rank higher on the App Store charts seems to have cultivated a distorted perception of app worth among consumers.

In 2009, Hog Bay Software's Jesse Grosjean decided to experiment with the pricing of his acclaimed WriteRoom app, dropping from the regular $4.99 price down to free (for a weekend) and then 99 cents. The test was to see whether the limited free offer and then the later subtle increase to 99 cents would spur enough of a boost in overall sales volume to make up for the decreased profit per sale. Although sales did increase, they eventually tapered off again—proof that for the longevity of this niche productivity app, the higher price ultimately generated more revenue in the long haul.

Jesse Grosjean had planned to end up at a lower price point such as $1.99 or $2.99, but during the sales experiment, he watched WriteRoom's App Store star ratings "go from mostly fours and fives to evenly distributed between five and one star." Even though the cheaper pricing did increase the number of new users, it also yielded a perception that users were overall less satisfied. The experiment revealed a lot about App Store behavior. After the sale ended, Jesse opted to return to his original $4.99 price tag.

At a higher price, you may attract fewer customers, but they buy your app because they genuinely want it. Then they have a vested interest in the app's survival and success, so their posted App Store ratings tend to reflect a more positive tone. A higher price can also give your app a greater perceived value. Psychologically, many people relate price to quality, believing that you get what you pay for.

So if 99 cents is too low for a large percentage of apps, then what price is too high? It is generally believed that apps ranging from $0.99 to $1.99 are perceived as impulse buys. A price of $2.99 seems to be the threshold that causes people to think and evaluate the app with a higher degree of scrutiny before making a purchase decision. Real resistance kicks in at $4.99 and higher, which requires a particularly high-quality game or app with strong features. There are a handful of best-in-class apps that have prospered at the higher end of the price spectrum, such as The Omni Group's OmniFocus at $19.99 and Cultured Code's Things at $9.99.

One of my favorite games, Firemint's Real Racing, was originally launched at $9.99 to great fanfare. To sustain continued sales after several months of release, Firemint eventually dropped the price to $6.99 and then again to $4.99. This has enabled Firemint to extend the product's life span and remain competitive among the new releases in the App Store without sacrificing too much revenue.

When the highly anticipated sequel, Real Racing 2 was released, Firemint tried once again with a $9.99 price tag. It initially did quite well, taking advantage of those early adopters and loyal fans who couldn't wait to play it. But sales eventually began to slowly decline, and Firemint reduced the price to $6.99 to help maintain its position on the App Store charts.

Real Racing is *not* one of those games that can be developed for only a few thousand dollars. It's a state-of-the-art virtual racing game that required a large development budget and many months of programming. It should be priced accordingly, reinforcing the perceived value. The reduced price of $4.99 for Real Racing and $6.99 for Real Racing 2 seems like a steal for those consumers who were hesitant to buy those games at $9.99. Yet the games still retain a profitable price tag to help support continued development of updates and new games.

iPad apps appear to command a much higher average price than iPhone apps. With its larger tablet screen, consumers perceive the iPad as more of a mobile computing replacement for netbooks and laptops, so there's a belief that iPad apps are more powerful and feature-rich. This raises the overall price threshold, where an iPad version of an app can fetch at least one of two more dollars (if not more) than its iPhone counterpart. For example, the best-selling Angry Birds game is only 99 cents on the iPhone, yet Angry Birds HD for the iPad does quite well at $4.99.

While you can certainly make more money per app sale on the iPad, it's still a smaller audience than that of the iPhone and iPod touch. Even at a lower price point, an iPhone app can still make more total revenue than its iPad counterpart due to sheer sales volume. But that's only relevant if you offer two separate versions of your app: one for the iPhone and one for the iPad.

A universal app is designed for both the iPhone and the iPad, yet is assigned only one price. A lot of work goes into optimizing an app's UI for both devices. So, unless you have a good reason to price your universal app at 99 cents, it's in your best interest to go with a higher price based on the perceived value, your competitors, and what the market will bear for that category.

Just keep in mind that once your app has been released in the App Store, it's much easier to later reduce your price than to increase your price. After a few weeks of sales, if you're experiencing a lot of pushback from consumers over your app price, you can always experiment with sale prices or permanent price drops. But if you already established a set low price, raising the price at a later date can often cause friction with consumers who are angered by the increase.

Improving App Discovery: The Art of Keywords and Names

An app's description in the App Store used to be searchable, which allowed developers to fill their app descriptions with tons of optimized keywords and text phrases. It was also a source of abuse, because many developers tried to "game" the system by including competitor app names and irrelevant, popular keywords in their descriptions in the hopes of ranking better in search results. In the summer of 2009, Apple changed the iTunes search algorithm to prevent this kind of misuse. In its place, Apple introduced keywords, which developers can assign to their submitted applications.

Now, the only elements that are searchable in the App Store are your app's name, keywords, and company name. Because of this change, it's more important than ever that your app's submitted name and keywords are search engine-optimized to improve your app's visibility in related App Store searches.

Assigning Keywords

iTunes Connect limits the Keywords field to only 100 characters, so make every keyword count!

Keywords can be single words or multiword phrases. For best results, Apple recommends separating multiple keywords with commas.

Since your company name listed with your application is already searchable in the App Store, there is absolutely no need to include it in the Keywords field. Doing so is only a waste of your precious 100 characters.

Although the Keywords feature may seem a lot more limiting than the lengthy text blocks of app descriptions, Apple has done you a small favor by making keywords hidden from public view. This prevents your competitors from easily copying all of your keywords! Of course, it's a double-edged sword, in that you don't have easy access to their keywords either.

Since the keywords you select play such a crucial role in your app's discovery in the App Store, it's important to do a lot of search experiments of your own to find out which apps are included in the search results based on certain search queries. I mentioned this in Chapter 2 when discussing the benefits of researching your competition before developing your app.

Your goal is to build a list of keywords that you think would benefit your app's visibility in consumer searches. Sure, you'll want to include keywords that work for your competition, but you'll also want to use a thesaurus to figure out *all* the possible keywords related to your app's feature set. You want to cover all the keywords that users might possibly search for. If you find a few terms that seem like intuitive queries and are not used by your competition, those may be valuable keywords to include. The fewer similar apps that appear in a user's search results, the less competition you have when the user decides which listed items to explore.

Here are some guidelines for picking keywords:

- **Use relevant keywords.** Stick to relevant keywords for best results. If you're selling a niche app, such as a writing tool or parked-car locator, it might seem like a good idea to include popular terms such as *fart* or *bikini* in an attempt to push your app in front of a broader audience, but that strategy won't help you in the App Store. Not only do unrelated keywords hurt your search relevancy—lowering your search ranking in your actual genre—but including them is also a good way to get your app flagged by Apple during the review process.

APP REJECTION WARNING: Keywords cannot contain words or phrases that are irrelevant, offensive, or refer to other products, brands, and registered trademarks. Don't try to be clever by including the names of competitive apps in your keywords list. And be very careful not to include trademarked names or celebrity names that you do not have licensed permission to use. Doing so will only get your app rejected! For example, if your app is an independent movie listings guide, including keywords like *Moviefone*, *Netflix*, *Fandango*, or even actor names could get your app booted from the App Store. Apple says that "improper use of keywords is the fourth most common reason for App Store rejections."

- **Avoid overly common keywords.** Common, generalized keywords will produce a huge list of search results, making it much more difficult for your app to be discovered. Honing in on more specific keywords that will produce fewer search results will not only improve your search relevancy, but will also make it easier for your app to be included closer to the top of the search results list. For example, if your app is a flying game that requires users to navigate a spaceship through a three-dimensional maze of stars and planets, don't use general keywords like *game* or *fun*, which basically describes every game in the App Store. Narrow your keywords to more specific terms that game lovers might search for, such as *spaceship* and *mission*.

- **Avoid repetition.** Since you're limited to only 100 characters, don't repeat the same words in both your app name and keywords, since both are included in App Store searches. For example, if your app name includes the word *spaceship*, there's no need to waste valuable characters by including *spaceship* in your keywords.

- **Cover all your regions.** If you've localized your app to more than one language, it's important to include localized keywords in the Localization section of iTunes Connect for *every* region your app supports. If you've decided to make your application available in both English and German App Stores, you'll want to submit keywords in both English and German, so that your app is searchable in those related, regional App Stores.

Take special care in crafting your list of keywords before submitting them in iTunes Connect. You will be able to edit them again only upon uploading a new binary app version or if your app has been rejected and needs to be reviewed again. This precaution is in place so that Apple can approve your keywords during the app review process. It prevents the keywords system from being gamed or abused by developers. It also makes it vital that the keywords list submitted is perfectly optimized and free of typos, since you won't be able to go back and revise your keywords until the next time your app is officially reviewed by Apple.

> **TIP:** Still not sure what keywords to use for optimal results? As mentioned in Chapter 10, Google's AdWords keyword tool (`https://adwords.google.com/select/KeywordToolExternal`) can be a helpful resource. Although Google designed that web tool to help people refine their SEO plans and ad campaigns, it can also help you identify and compare the popularity of specific keywords. The data is not App Store-related, but it does give you a good idea of what people are searching for online as it relates to your app's subject matter. For those of you having trouble pinpointing strategic keywords via App Store searches, Google's keyword tool provides much better answers than simply making wild guesses on your own.

The Name Game

In Chapter 2, I stressed how important it is that your app name be short enough to display in its entirety on iOS' home screen without being truncated. Having a short app name also serves you well when displayed in search results in the App Store. A shorter app name ensures that the entire name is displayed without being truncated. Tap Tap Tap's Voices and Convert app names are very easy to read, leaving room to add a descriptive caption to the title (see Figure 11–1).

Figure 11–1. *With Voices and Convert, Tap Tap Tap kept its app names short for easy readability, and added descriptive, keyword-rich captions to their name titles in the App Store.*

That's right, your application's name in the App Store isn't limited to only the app name itself. It's perfectly acceptable to add a descriptive caption to the App Name field. Just be sure your app's name comes first, followed by any additional descriptive text, so that the actual name will always be visible when listed in search results. It's fine that the embedded caption shown in Figure 11–1 is truncated, since it will be displayed in full on the app's product page (after tapping the selection in the list). The simple app names Convert and Voices are listed in the App Store as follows:

- Convert—the unit calculator

- Voices—fun voice changing!

That added caption—usually separated from the preceding app name with a simple hyphen or colon—helps describe the application's core functionality. This eye-catching trick not only draws the viewer's attention, but also lets the viewer know what your app does without needing to first read the lengthy description. Since it would appear that not many people actually take the time to read long app descriptions anymore, this extended app title can really benefit your marketing efforts.

The other major benefit of this extended name technique is that it gives you the opportunity to fill the searchable App Name field with related keywords! As an example, consider "Convert—the unit calculator" and one of its competitors by Tapbots, "Convertbot—The Amazing Unit Converter":

- If a user searches the App Store for *convert*, both Convert and Convertbot are listed in the search results, because both of them include that term in their app names.

- If a user searches for *calculator* or *unit calculator*, only Convert appears in the search results, since its app title includes those terms as part of its extended name. (It appears that Convertbot's keywords are not optimized for *unit calculator* or *calculator*.)

- If a user searches for *converter*, Convertbot is included in the search results, whereas Convert is not.

Keep in mind that the app name you choose for display within the App Store can be edited only when submitting a new app binary for review or if your app was rejected and requires resubmission. Like your keywords, your app name is subject to Apple's review team to ensure that no one tries to abuse the opportunity with unlicensed trademarks or irrelevant and inappropriate words. So, all of the same rules apply here as they do for submitted keywords. Attempts to cheat the system will prevent your app from being approved.

Treat the app name as a marketing extension of your related keywords. When your keywords list and the app name are working together in unison with highly optimized words and phrases, you're increasing the chances of your product being discovered in the overcrowded App Store.

Perfecting the Sales Pitch of Your App Description

Although a product's App Store description is not searchable, it does still serve as a primary marketing tool for users who are interested in learning more about your app. Someone has gotten as far as viewing your product page in the App Store, and this is your one shot to convince that person why his life is not complete until he has purchased your app! The three influential elements on your product page are the description, the screenshots, and the customer reviews. We'll be exploring all of these items in this chapter, starting with the anatomy of a good app description.

What Is It?

If you're not using an extended app name (and you should), or if it's still not obvious what your app's primary function is, then the very first thing you should include in your description is a brief explanation of what your app does and why people should buy it. Remember my Chapter 10 discussion of "the quick pitch" on your app's web site? This is no different.

Just as with your web site, visitors to your App Store product page will take only a few seconds to scan the description and screenshots to see whether the app captures their interest. Your job is to make sure to provide enough of a sales hook that they are motivated to continue reading.

Although the iPhone version of the App Store displays the full app description on product pages, the iPad and desktop iTunes versions of the App Store display only the first three or four lines of text, with a More link to reveal the rest. Unless users are captivated by your screenshots, odds are good they won't take the time to click that More link. With this in mind, it's more important than ever to optimize your app summary into a couple of brief sentences placed at the very top of your description text, so that it will be included on your app's product page. If that brief text summary interests users, they will most likely click the More link to view your complete list of features and benefits.

Awards and Testimonials

Ideally, when you were generating a little prerelease buzz (covered in Chapter 10), you managed to get a few prominent media reviewers to check out your app and provide you with some choice quotes. When your app is new in the App Store, you'll have very few (if any) customer reviews posted, so it's best to include a few winning testimonials in your app description to help convince consumers of the app's quality. And even when your app does receive a lot of customer ratings, there's nothing more influential than praise from respected bloggers and magazines. This is also a perfect place to mention any awards your app has won.

It may be tempting to place eye-catching awards and testimonials at the very top of your app description, but not at the expense of your quick-pitch app summary. If a stellar quote or an award-winning reference can be included along with your app summary within the few lines of text that are visible in the iPad and desktop iTunes versions of the App Store, then great! But if those accolades use up too much space at the top, and your app summary is truncated (by the More link), that could pose a problem. Consumers may not care that your app won an award if they don't know what it does or how it could benefit them.

App Features and Benefits

Most people won't bother reading dense blocks of text, so don't describe your app's features in long paragraphs. Break it up into brief sections for easy eye-scanning. Better yet, if you have a lot of features to mention, structure it as an easy-to-read bulleted list instead.

Don't ramble on, listing every single last detail about the app. Less is more. Space and attention spans are limited, so consolidate your list to just the major features and benefits. This includes the core features that consumers are looking for, as well as the differentiating factors that set your app apart from the competition. If you think a specific feature is a key selling point, then it belongs in this list.

It's vital to understand the difference between *features* and *benefits*, so that you can craft a more effective app description:

- Features represent functionality in the app or game.

- Benefits illustrate how that functionality can improve your happiness, lifestyle, productivity, and so on.

For example, a writing app's ability to synchronize documents via Dropbox is a feature. The benefit is that it allows you to continue working on your novel from any device or location that can log in to the online Dropbox service.

Putting It All Together

For best results across all the various versions of the App Store, organize your app description elements into the following top-to-bottom sequence:

- App summary
- Awards and testimonials
- Features and benefits

After reading the previous sections, it should come as no surprise that the app summary should be placed at the very top of your App Store description. This is your quick pitch that explains what your app is. As I've emphasized, this brief text should always be visible; clicking the More link should not be required to read the summary.

If your app description requires quite a bit of scrolling to read it in its entirety, then it's too long. You don't want a potential customer's attention to stray. If you've included a lot of accolades, try cutting them down to only a few of the most influential awards and testimonials. And if your features and benefits are not already listed as brief bullet points, doing so can also reduce the amount of space your description consumes.

> **APP REJECTION WARNING:** Do not include pricing in your app description, name, or icon. The App Store caters to many regional languages and currencies, so displaying a static, text-based price is prohibited. If your English app description mentioned a price in US dollars, that could cause confusion among customers in the UK App Store, since the dynamic buy button lists the app's price in British pounds. To avoid App Store rejection, you can promote limited-time sale offers in your app description without mentioning a specific currency. For example, if your $1.99 app is currently on sale for only 99 cents, you could refer to the sale as "Half Off" or a "50% Discount."

Before submitting your app description, be sure to proofread it using a good spell checker! I cannot stress this enough. Nothing says unprofessional like typos and misspellings! You want to compete with the big boys like Electronic Arts and Gameloft? Then you need to double-check everything you write *before* it gets uploaded into iTunes Connect. Afraid you'll miss something? Then have a few friends proofread the description as well.

Make sure that your description is easy to understand and does not in any way misrepresent your app's true functionality. Don't forget that this description is not only read by consumers in the App Store. First it's read by an Apple reviewer. If something in your app description is ambiguous or misleading, or if the reviewer couldn't locate one of your listed features in the short time the app is being reviewed, it could cause the approval process to be delayed or even result in a rejection, with a request for further clarification. Remember that you can modify your description with additional information after your app has been approved.

A Picture Is Worth a Thousand Words: The Importance of Screenshots

Since the App Store does not currently support the inclusion of video demos, the only way an interested consumer can immediately see what your app looks like is via the screenshots on your product page.

Don't assume people will take the time to download your app just because you offer a free or lite version, or that they will jump to YouTube or your web site to view a video trailer. They are already browsing in the App Store, so they may not bother visiting other sites, especially if they are busy (and most people are). Your App Store product page needs to convince people to download the app, and probably the most influential element on that page will be your screenshots.

With so much riding on the visuals, it's imperative that you upload screenshots that best promote your app's core functionality and quality. If it's a game, then your screenshots better scream fun and excitement! If it's a productivity app, then your screenshots need to emphasize just how much better someone's life is going to be when using this app. Your screenshots need to have impact!

Choosing the Primary Screenshot

The first screenshot that is shown is the most important. It may be the only screenshot consumers see if they opt not to tap/scroll through the rest of the screenshots. So, make sure this primary screenshot is the one that best describes your app visually. Someone viewing it should immediately understand the general concept, without needing to read the description or load the other screenshots. This *is* the picture that's worth a thousand words!

Take some time to explore the App Store product pages of popular apps and games. Analyze the first primary screenshot for each one, especially similar apps that will compete with yours. When you see a screenshot that catches your eye, try to determine what it is that makes the image an effective graphic.

On the surface, it may appear that the winning attributes are simply a stunning interface design, but look closer. Many of the best primary screenshots are ones that have been set up to look good! No, I don't mean Photoshop enhancements. I'm talking about showing the app in action! If it's a to-do list app, don't show a new, empty list. Fill it with tasks that your target audience can relate to, demonstrating just how productive and time-saving it could be for them. If it's a space battle game, display the key fun factors like laser guns firing and alien crafts exploding. You want the reaction to be, "Wow, that looks exciting…I must buy it now!"

The goal is not necessarily about packing in as much action as possible into your screenshots. A compelling primary screenshot is one that instantly attracts your eye and successfully describes the core functionality in a single visual.

The App Store product page for Retro Dreamer's Sneezies game displays a great example of an effective primary screenshot (see Figure 11–2). Without reading the app description, this visual gives me a good idea of what kind of game play it offers. At first glance, it appears the goal is to free the Sneezies from their floating bubbles. Sure enough, the app summary in the description reads, "Touch the screen to drop a burst of sneezing powder into the field of floating Sneezies and watch as they sneeze themselves out of their bubbles. Try to initiate a chain reaction to rescue as many Sneezies as you can in this family fun puzzle game." The screenshot even shows the sneezing powder in action, with a couple Sneezies freed from their bubbles and parachuting to safety.

The Sneezies screenshot showcases the core game objective without cluttering the screen with too much activity. It looks like pure fun, without appearing too difficult for players of all ages to grasp the basics.

Figure 11–2. *Sneezies by Retro Dreamer (published by Chillingo). Without reading the app description, this primary screenshot tells me quite a lot about the game play and looks like pure fun!*

It may seem obvious to show a game in action, but the same strategy should also be employed with other kinds of apps. The primary screenshot of Rogue Sheep's Postage in Figure 11–3 (left) provides a beautiful example of the digital postcards you can create and send. The primary screenshot for Imagam's iFiles (on the right in Figure 11–3) showcases many of its file management and export features simply by displaying its custom pop-up menu above a populated file list. Screenshots of actual app activity visually demonstrate to users how those apps could benefit their own lives or help them become more productive.

Figure 11–3. *The primary screenshots of Rogue Sheep's Postage (left) and Imagam's iFiles (right) visually showcase many of their features and benefits within a single image.*

Apple recommends removing the status bar from your screenshots, but looking around the App Store, it's apparent that advice is not always heeded.

Apple also recommends capturing screenshots directly from an iPhone, iPad, or iPod touch, instead of the iOS Simulator. To do this, when you're ready to take the shot, hold down the device's Home button and Power button at the same time. The screenshot is saved to the device's Photo Library. Although you could easily e-mail the screenshot from the device's Photo Library to your desktop computer, you can also sync the device with your desktop iTunes, and launch the Mac's iPhoto application to import the saved PNG screenshot.

An alternative option is to capture screenshots from a connected device within the Screenshots tab of the Xcode Organizer window. From there, they can then be dragged to the Mac desktop as PNG files.

When a Screenshot Is More Than a Screenshot

Even though Apple refers to them as screenshots, this feature is not limited to the literal definition. If your app's core functionality takes advantage of the accelerometer or special multitouch gestures, then it's perfectly acceptable to show a photo of an actual person using the app on an iOS device.

Smule's Ocarina app, which turns your iPhone into a musical instrument, uses the primary screenshot to display a photo of how to "play" the app using the device's mic and multitouch screen (see Figure 11–4). This photo does a much better job at describing the unique app than an actual screenshot could show. Since the user's fingers obscure portions of the app's interface, Smule smartly included the Ocarina logo in the photo to reinforce the app name and branding.

Figure 11–4. *Because of the Smule Ocarina app's use of the iPhone's mic and multitouch functionality, displaying a photo of a user in action is a much more effective primary image than an actual screenshot.*

What if you've built a productivity app that is so packed full of features that a simple screen capture simply does not do it justice? Not to worry. There's no rule forbidding the inclusion of text in your screenshots if it helps explain how your app works.

A model example of text usage is the primary screenshot for Groups from Guided Ways Technologies Ltd. (on the left in Figure 11–5). It complements the embedded interface view with additional text and icons to visually promote a vast array of key features. It also boasts a nice recommendation from O'Reilly.

Another example is the primary screenshot for Newtoy's Words with Friends (on the right in Figure 11–5). It showcases a few core features and an impressive accolade from *Wired Magazine*. It also displays a few different iOS devices running the app, visually promoting the fact that its social game play is compatible with a variety of hardware models, so all your friends can join in on the fun.

Figure 11–5. *The primary screenshot for Groups by Guided Ways Technologies Ltd. (left) uses text and icons to visually promote a vast array of key features. The one for Newtoy's Words with Friends (right) showcases core features, an impressive accolade from Wired Magazine, and its compatibility with several iOS device models.*

If you do include text in your screenshots and you offer localized versions of your app in multiple regional App Stores, don't forget to also localize your screenshots accordingly. Before capturing the screenshots, set the preferred language on the device, which can be located in the Settings app at **General ➤ International ➤ Language**. If you're creating a custom image (such as the ones shown in Figure 11–5), be sure to translate the text correctly. Online web translator bots such as Google Translate can sometimes generate incorrect phrasing or syntax. To avoid confusion or even possibly offending someone with the wrong word, you might want to consult with a professional translator. When your localized screenshots are ready, simply upload them to the corresponding app language version in iTunes Connect.

APP REJECTION WARNING: Apple's review team will reject your app submission if any of the provided screenshots include an iAd test advertisement or display inappropriate content that does not adhere to the 4+ age rating policy. If your app displays iAd banners, then hide the banner view when capturing the screenshot. And if your app includes content for older audiences, be sure it's not visible in your screenshots. In other words, don't show mature media content or violent game play.

Preparing Your Application Binary for the App Store

After learning the configuration process for ad hoc distribution (detailed in Chapter 9), you'll be happy to know that compiling your iOS app for distribution in the App Store is almost the same process. The only difference is the provisioning profile you assign to your application in Xcode.

Have you finished beta-testing and tweaking your app? Are you ready to compile the master version for the App Store? Here's a rundown of the steps to prepare the application binary that you'll upload to iTunes Connect.

Step 1: Verify Your Distribution Certificate Is Still Installed

To compile your app for ad hoc distribution, you needed to generate your distribution certificate from the iOS Provisioning Portal and install it in your Mac's Keychain system. This distribution certificate is also used when compiling for App Store distribution, so take a moment to ensure that it is still installed properly. Launch the Keychain Access application, located on your Mac at */Applications/Utilities/Keychain Access*.

In the dialog box that's displayed, select login from the Keychains list and Keys from the Category list. In the list of keys, simply double-check that your private key is still paired with your distribution certificate. In the example in Figure 11–6, my Electric Butterfly, Inc. key (which was previously created for ad hoc distribution) is paired with my imported distribution certificate. If your distribution certificate is not paired with the appropriate key in a similar manner, then revisit step 1 of the ad hoc distribution process described in Chapter 9 before continuing.

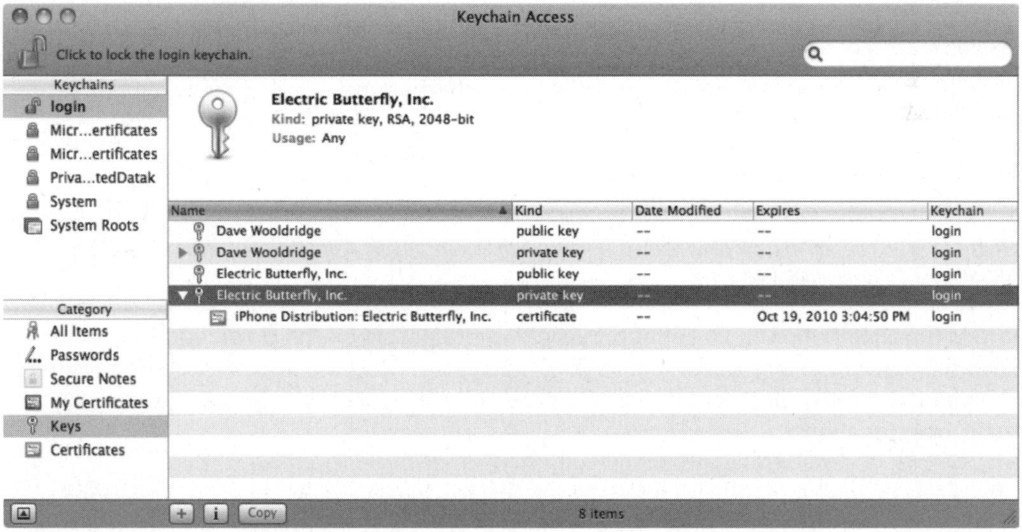

Figure 11–6. *Verify that your distribution certificate is still paired with the correct private key in Keychain Access.*

Step 2: Generate and Install an App Store Distribution Provisioning Profile

Log in to the iOS Dev Center online, click the iOS Provisioning Portal link in the top-right corner of the page, and then within the main Provisioning Portal page, navigate to the Provisioning section. Select the Distribution tab, and click the New Profile button.

In the form that's presented, be sure to choose App Store as the distribution method. Select the appropriate app ID for your application, and verify that the distribution certificate is assigned correctly. For easy reference, enter a profile name that includes the app's name and reflects the specific purpose of this provisioning profile, such as Breadcrumbs App Store Profile (see Figure 11–7). It's important that your App Store provisioning profile is named differently from your ad hoc distribution provisioning profile, so that they are easily identifiable when listed in Xcode. Choose Submit to generate your App Store distribution provisioning profile.

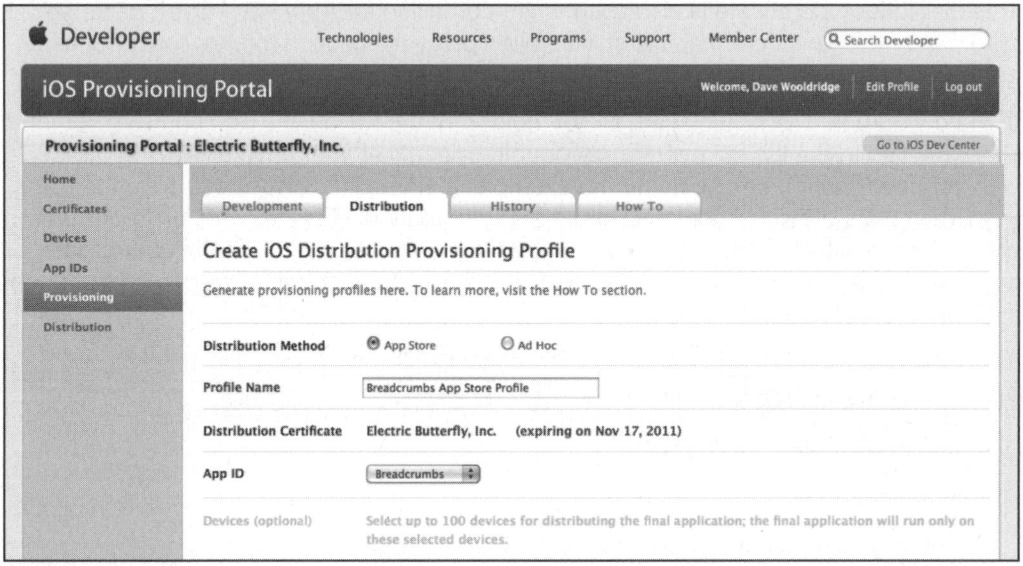

Figure 11–7. *Since you're done beta-testing, it's time to generate an App Store distribution provisioning profile in the online iOS Provisioning Portal site.*

Within the Distribution tab's list of provisioning profiles, click the download button to save this new *.mobileprovision* file to your hard drive. Drag the *.mobileprovision* file onto the Xcode icon in your Dock. Xcode will automatically install that provisioning profile in the proper location.

Step 3: Configure Your Xcode Project for App Store Distribution

Now with the proper provisioning profile in place, the next step is to open your project in Xcode and configure it for App Store distribution. In the main Xcode project window, select the project name at the top of the Groups & Files pane, and then click the Info button in the toolbar. Within the Configurations tab of the Info window, verify that you still have a Distribution configuration listed (which you should have already created during Chapter 9's ad hoc distribution stage). If you don't have one, then duplicate the existing Release configuration, naming the copy Distribution. Now close that Info window.

Next, select the Target app within the Groups & Files pane, and click the toolbar's Info button again. In the new Target Info window that appears, navigate to the Build tab, and double-check that the Configuration drop-down menu is set to Distribution. Scroll down to the Any iOS field below the Code Signing Identity row, and assign it to your new App Store distribution provisioning profile. Even though your ad hoc distribution provisioning profile may also be listed in the pop-up menu, it's critical that your App Store distribution provisioning profile is selected (see Figure 11–8).

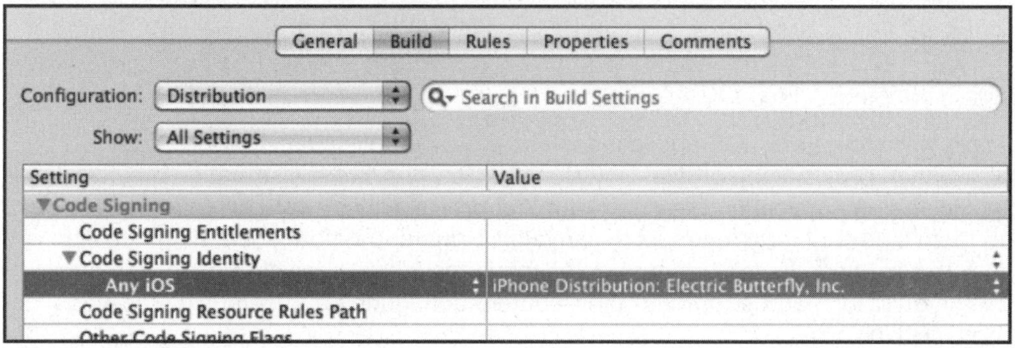

Figure 11–8. *Modify your Target's Build tab, assigning your new App Store distribution provisioning profile to the Any iOS Code Signing Identity.*

Switch to the Properties tab, and verify that the correct app ID bundle identifier is in the Identifier field. It should be the same as the bundle identifier listed in your Xcode project's Info *.plist* file (such as the example ID com.ebutterfly.breadcrumbs).

With all of that completed, the last step is to navigate to the main Xcode project window and ensure that the drop-down menu in the top-left corner has Device and Distribution selected for the Active SDK and Active Configuration settings, respectively.

Step 4: Compile Your iOS App

Now you're ready to compile your Xcode project! App Store distribution does not require your project to include an *Entitlements* file, as it does for ad hoc distribution, so save your project. Next, select Build ➤ Build and Archive. If you've configured everything correctly, your app should compile successfully.

If you get build errors that are related to the project settings, retrace your steps to ensure that you've followed every single task outlined here, no matter how insignificant it may seem. Build errors can often be caused by the smallest mistakes, such as a misspelled bundle identifier or a mismarked check box. If problems persist and you've ruled out code bugs and faulty configuration settings, clean out your project's build directory, reopen the project in Xcode, and try another build attempt.

> **APP REJECTION WARNING:** Do not utilize undocumented private Apple APIs in your app. Apple has rejected dozens of apps for tapping into private iOS APIs that are not officially sanctioned for public use. The app review team is rumored to be using a static analyzer tool to ferret out calls to restricted, private APIs. So, even if your app includes the code but doesn't execute it, your app may still get flagged for the code presence alone. To avoid App Store rejection, stick with the authorized APIs.

Apple will accept only iOS applications that were compiled with an App Store distribution provisioning profile. Unfortunately, an App Store distribution provisioning profile and an application compiled with that profile will not work on your test devices, so there's no way for you to test this version of the app before submitting it to Apple. With this in mind, it's important to do as much testing as possible—keeping a close eye on build logs and error messages—before configuring and compiling for App Store distribution.

After you've compiled it using the **Build and Archive** option, you'll find the app in Xcode's Organizer window. In the left pane of Xcode Organizer, select Archived Applications, and you should see your newly compiled app in the applications list that's displayed. With the app selected, you'll notice a Submit to iTunes Connect button at the bottom of the Xcode Organizer screen. But hold up! Don't click that button yet.

Before submitting your app binary, you first need to create your app's listing with required metadata in iTunes Connect, which I'll show you how to do shortly. The very last step in the submission process will be uploading your app binary, so we'll revisit Xcode Organizer again very soon.

Ensuring Apple Has Processed Your Contracts and Payment Settings

Before submitting your app, make sure all of Apple's required contracts, tax forms, and banking information have been properly submitted and processed. As I mentioned way back in Chapter 1, this process can often take a fair amount of time, so it's best to get it taken care of while you're in the initial stages of development. That way, when you're ready to submit your application to the App Store, there's no lingering paperwork holding you back.

To check your current status, log in to iTunes Connect at `http://itunesconnect.apple.com/`, and on the main page of iTunes Connect, visit the section called Contracts, Tax, and Banking to view the contracts you currently have in effect. As discussed in Chapter 1, you should have the Free Applications contract already activated by default, which allows you to submit free iOS apps to the App Store. To submit paid apps to the App Store, you should have already requested a Paid Applications contract and completed the related banking and tax forms. Without that information submitted, Apple is unable to pay you any revenue you earn from app sales. Instead, it will hold your accrued earnings in trust until the required forms have been processed.

Are We There Yet? Submitting Your App in iTunes Connect

After months of development and testing, you probably can't believe that you've finally arrived at this point: ready to submit your application to the App Store. It's a moment filled with both excitement and trepidation, uncertain as to the fate of your product in the hands of Apple's app review team. But not to fear, you've planned your application very carefully, methodically following all of Apple's guidelines, so you should be in good shape. Now you're ready to take the plunge.

Plan on adding your new app in iTunes Connect on a day when you have plenty of time to dedicate to this process. There are several screens of online forms to complete, so you'll want to patiently work through each section at a relaxed pace to avoid making any careless mistakes or typos.

> **NOTE:** You can add a new application listing in iTunes Connect without submitting it to the App Store. In fact, you'll need to do this in advance to test certain features, such as In-App Purchase. Your app will not be submitted to Apple's app review team until you've completed the very last step of uploading your app binary. If you've already created a listing for your app in iTunes Connect (based on these instructions) for In-App Purchase testing in Chapter 8 and you're ready for App Store submission, you can skip ahead to the section titled "Step 5: Upload Your App Icon and Screenshots."

Step 1: Create a New App Entry

Ready? Great, let's do this! Head over to the Manage Your Applications section of iTunes Connect. Click the blue Add New App button in the top-left corner of the Manage Your Applications page (see Figure 11–9).

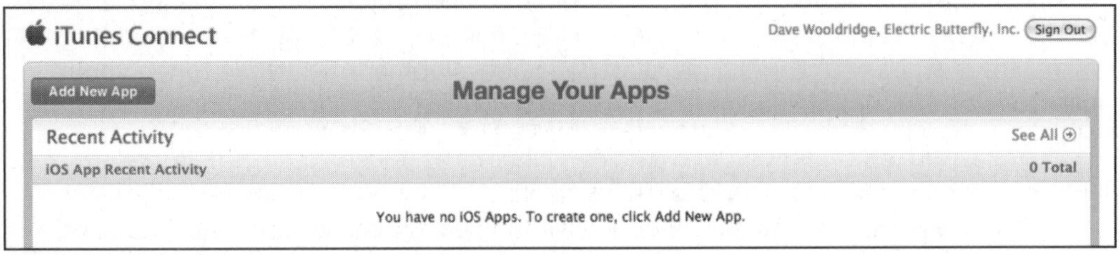

Figure 11–9. *In the Manage Your Applications section of iTunes Connect, click the Add New App button to get started.*

Company Name and Primary Language

If this is your very first iOS app submission, the first screen will ask you to provide your official company name and your application's primary language. *Please note that this information cannot be changed later, so do not make any mistakes on this page!*

The company name you submit should be the name you want listed in the App Store as the official developer of your application. Because of my own paranoia about proper code signing and App Store settings, *I recommend using the same company/developer name* across all of the following items to avoid any potential issues:

- Your iOS Developer Program account

- Your iOS distribution certificate

- Your iTunes Connect/App Store company name

I use my company name, Electric Butterfly, Inc., for all three of those items, making sure the spelling and punctuation are always consistent.

As for the primary language setting, this is the language that you'll use to enter all of your application data during this submission process. For example, if you choose English from the drop-down menu, the rest of the online forms will require your information to be in English. After you've created your app listing in iTunes Connect, you'll have an opportunity to add support for additional languages, such as French, German, Japanese, and so on.

Clicking the Continue button will send you to the next screen, where you will enter some initial app information.

App Information

Let's examine each of the three form elements on the App Information screen (see Figure 11–10) to better understand what's required:

- **App Name:** The submitted name can be up to 255 characters long. As discussed earlier in this chapter, this field is not limited to only your app's binary name or display name. Using an extended app name with a caption (like Tap Tap Tap's "Convert—the unit calculator") is recommended. But your app's actual name should be included in that caption (preferably first). If your App Store name and your app's display name on an iOS device's home screen are too dissimilar, that may cause confusion among consumers, as well as possibly raise a red flag during the app review process.

- **SKU Number:** This field is often the source of the most confusion for iOS developers, since Apple does not provide much explanation as to the correct format or syntax of this string. Contrary to popular belief, there is no defined template or numbering system for the SKU attribute. Even calling it a SKU *number* is somewhat misleading, in that it does not need to consist of numeric characters. Your app's SKU is never shown to customers and never publicly listed in the App Store. Basically, the SKU is an internal, unique ID for your app in iTunes Connect. It's often convenient to use an easily recognizable name, rather than a string of only numbers, especially if you have related In-App Purchase items. For example, our fictional Breadcrumbs app's SKU is breadcrumbs, and its In-App Purchase Premium Pack SKU is breadcrumbs.premiumpack. The SKU is independent of the version number, so it does not change with every version update. In fact, once submitted, that SKU number can never be modified, so pick a good identifying name that works for you. Also, if you opt to delete an existing app listing, that SKU can never be reused.

- **Bundle ID:** Your app ID should already be listed in iTunes Connect after configuring provisioning profiles for the app, so simply select it from the pull-down menu.

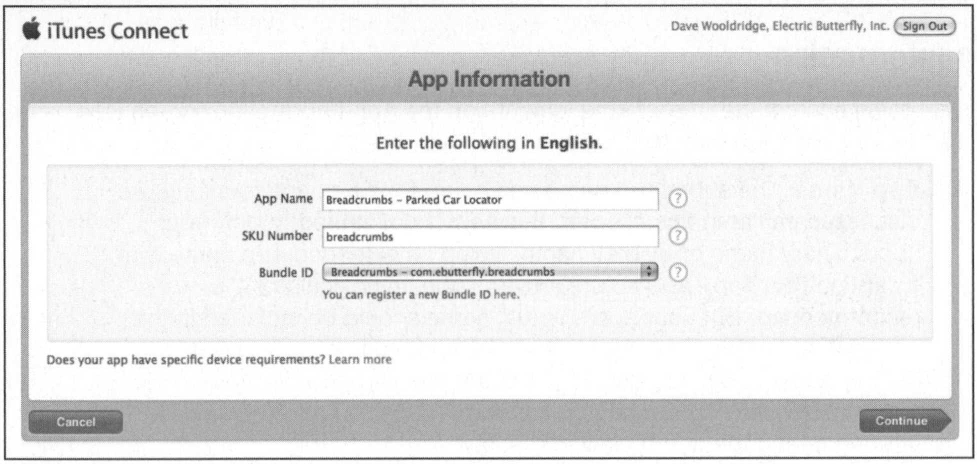

Figure 11–10. *The App Information form requires a unique app name and SKU, along with your app's bundle ID.*

To avoid consumer confusion in the marketplace, no two apps in the App Store can have the same app name or SKU. If the system reports that either of your requested choices is already taken (even if that other app has not been approved for sale in the App Store), you'll be forced to provide a different app name or SKU.

You may not have a way to capture a "taken" app name for use as your App Store name, but you can append a keyword-rich caption to your name to work around the issue. You want to go this route only if there is no other app available (or soon to be available) in the App Store with the same name. Identical app names could cause confusion in the marketplace, with consumers unsure as to which one is your app—especially if both apps provide similar functionality.

Even though your added caption makes your submitted name technically unique in the system, the app's actual name is still essentially the same as the others in the eyes of consumers. This could also lead to lawsuits if your app name is infringing on an existing trademarked application name in the App Store. If you already trademarked your app's name, then the law is on your side (at least in your country). This is why you must perform adequate competitive research and create a unique name (see Chapter 2). Avoiding common words for your app name can prevent these kinds of problems from occurring.

CAUTION: Since every app name and SKU must be unique, Apple has taken measures to prevent name squatting—the act of creating an app listing in iTunes Connect simply to keep other developers from obtaining that name. After adding an app to iTunes Connect, you'll have only 120 days to upload an app binary (which submits the app for App Store review). If the 120 days lapses without an uploaded app binary, the app name will then be removed from your account, making it available for another developer. So, if you've created an app listing in order to test specific features like In-App Purchase, make sure you complete your development and submit your app binary before that 120-day expiration date.

At the very bottom of the App Information screen, you'll notice a brief reminder from Apple about specifying device requirements. Special device requirements are those that require hardware-related features, such as GPS, network access, the built-in camera, or the accelerometer. You undoubtedly already learned how to define those device requirements via the UIRequiredDeviceCapabilities key in your app's *Info.plist* file when you read Apple's *iOS Application Programming Guide*. If you haven't yet done that, then you'll want to make the necessary modifications when compiling your app for submission to the App Store.

As in the previous screen, once these fields are submitted, they cannot be changed, so it's vital that you do not misspell anything.

When you've finished entering your app information, click the Continue button to proceed to the next screen.

Step 2: Set the Availability Date and Pricing

The Rights and Pricing screen presents options to choose your app's availability date, price tier, and other selling options (see Figure 11–11).

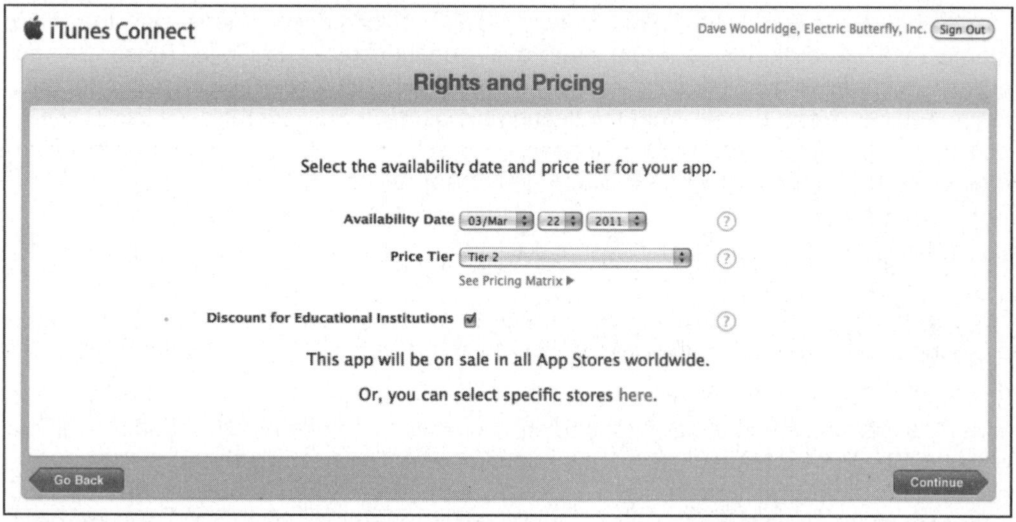

Figure 11–11. *Set your app's availability date and price tier on the Rights and Pricing page.*

Availability Date

The Availability Date setting has proven to be one of the more frustrating elements of the app submission process. Within the main category pages of the App Store, consumers have the ability to sort the list by release date, which is a great source of exposure for new app releases.

Once upon a time, developers used to be able to make quick changes to the availability date after being notified that their app had been approved, which allowed them to control when their app appeared in that valuable list. This enabled developers to closely time the launch of press releases with the product's visibility in the App Store's new releases list. Unfortunately, Apple has since made changes to the release date reflected in the App Store, rendering that little trick obsolete. Now, the actual release date of your app is the date it is approved by Apple.

So then why does Apple provide developers with an option to set the availability date? This still gives you control over when your app goes live in the App Store. For example, if Apple approves your app on March 1, but you would prefer to debut in the App Store on March 22 to coincide with your press release and marketing efforts, then set the availability date for March 22. But keep in mind that the app's release date in the App Store will state March 1, so you'll have missed that initial exposure in the new releases list, since newer releases will have already pushed your app much farther down the list.

If appearing near the top of that new releases list is more important to you than a preplanned launch date, then set your availability date to a distant day in the future (such as a few months ahead), way beyond the estimated approval date. Unless your app's review process takes an abnormally long time, Apple's approval date will typically be earlier than your future release date. Then after you've completed the submission, set your iTunes Connect user profile's preferences to notify you via e-mail when your app status changes to Ready for Sale. This way, if you regularly check your e-mail, the moment you're notified of your app's approval, you can quickly log in to iTunes Connect and change your availability date to Apple's approved date. It then will instantly appear in the App Store and benefit from the fleeting exposure in the new releases list. This e-mail notification also serves as a nice head's up, so you can send out your press release closely following the product's availability in the App Store.

Price Tier

For paid applications, you'll also need to choose a price tier. Since regional App Stores support various currencies, the drop-down menu forces you to choose a tier instead of an actual price.

When you choose a tier, the corresponding pricing is automatically displayed. And if you click the See Pricing Matrix link, a table appears, revealing not only the currency conversions in several regions, but also what your proceeds would be after Apple subtracts its 30 percent fee.

Educational Discounts and Regional Availability

By default, your application will be available worldwide, unless you choose to select only specific individual countries. You can also elect to participate in Apple's educational discount program, which enables educational institutions to purchase volume quantities of your app at a discount of 50 percent of the App Store price.

Clicking the Continue button on the Rights and Pricing page will bring you to the Version Information page.

Step 3: Submit Your App's Metadata

Of all the forms in the app submission process, you'll probably spend the most time on the Version Information page, specifying all of your app's metadata (see Figure 11–12). Fortunately, you should have already prepared many of the requested elements, such as the app description, keywords, and web site URL.

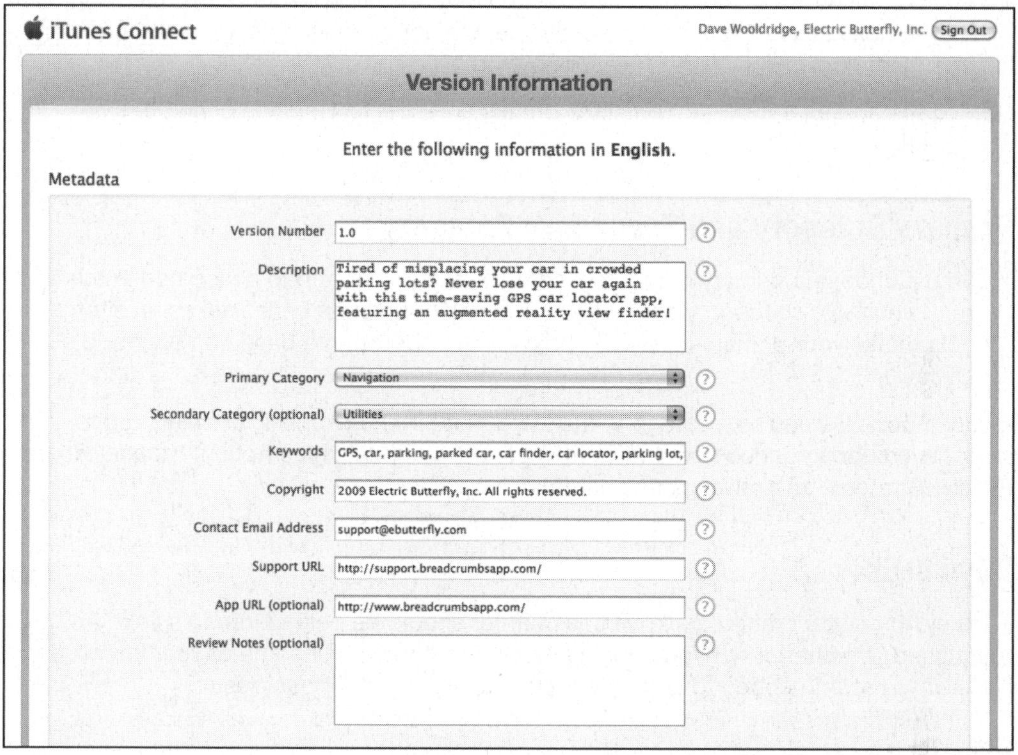

Figure 11–12. *Of all the screens in the submission process, the Version Information page is by far the longest, but fortunately, you should already have many of these items prepared, such as the app description, keywords, and web site URL.*

As you can see from Figure 11–12, it's quite a long form, so let's take a closer look at each item.

Version Number

This is a fairly self-explanatory field, listing your app's version number, such as 1.0 or 1.3.1. You should use the same version number as the value listed in your application *Info.plist* file's `CFBundleVersion` property, so avoid including alpha characters such as "Beta 1."

Discrepancies between your actual app binary version and the version number you enter in this field might cause delays or problems during the app review process.

Description

The description you painstakingly wrote earlier in this chapter should be pasted into this field. Just remember that the desktop iTunes and the iPad versions of the App Store initially display only the first few lines of text, with a More link to read the rest of it. This makes those first few lines of text very important, so be sure to use that limited space wisely, explaining what your app does. Since you are allowed a generous maximum of 4,000 characters, use the rest of the available characters to list features and benefits, awards, testimonials, and other key selling points.

HTML tags are not supported, but lines breaks and special Unicode characters are acceptable.

Primary Category and Secondary Category

You must choose a primary category where you want your app to be located in the App Store. Selecting a secondary category is optional, but can be beneficial as an alternative if Apple thinks your primary category choice is not appropriate based on your app's functionality.

If you choose Games as a category, then two more menus appear, allowing you to select two subcategories from the Games parent group, such as Action, Arcade, Board, Puzzle, Strategy, and other game genres.

Keywords

The keywords you crafted earlier in this chapter should be pasted into this field. As I've mentioned, whether or not you're using multiword phrases for some of your keywords, it's always recommended to separate them with commas for best results.

Copyright

List your copyright line as you want it displayed in the App Store. There's no need to include the © symbol, since the App Store automatically places it before your copyright line. So, for example, submitting the line "2009 Electric Butterfly, Inc. All rights reserved." would appear in the App Store as: "© 2009 Electric Butterfly, Inc. All rights reserved."

Contact Email Address

Apple requires you to supply a contact e-mail address, but it won't be posted in the App Store. It is only for Apple's internal team in the event they need to contact you during the review process or while your app resides in the App Store.

Support URL

Apple requires all developers to provide an online support URL for each app listed in the App Store. Even though the desktop iTunes and iPad versions of the App Store include your support URL as an active link on your product's App Store page, the iPhone version of the App Store includes only your app URL. With this in mind, you'll want to make sure your support page is also easily accessible from your app's web site.

It's important that your support URL points to a valid source for contacting you, since Apple will check its existence during the app review process. At the very least, give site visitors some way to contact you directly, whether by an e-mail link or by an HTML feedback form (if you would rather hide your e-mail address from spambots).

To help reduce the flood of support queries and provide 24/7 assistance even when you're offline, it's always a good idea to post a list of frequently asked questions (FAQs), especially if you find yourself answering the same e-mail questions repeatedly. For iOS apps that enjoy an active and vibrant user community, self-hosting an online forum, such as the popular open source phpBB (`http://www.phpbb.com/`), might be a beneficial addition to your support site.

If you don't have the time or skill set to build your own custom support offerings, there are some amazing ready-made, third-party services available at very affordable monthly rates. Here are a few options:

- Get Satisfaction (`http://getsatisfaction.com/`)
- Tender Support (`http://tenderapp.com/`)
- UserVoice (`http://uservoice.com/`)
- Zendesk (`http://www.zendesk.com/`)

AN ADDITIONAL NOTE ABOUT SUPPORT

Even after providing an extensive support site, if you find too many customers misusing the App Store's Customer Reviews section as a place to post feature requests and bug reports, it may be helpful to add some support information to your app description text. Anything you can do to redirect users to your support site may help reduce the number of unnecessary one-star reviews that are nothing more than feature wish lists! But never reprimand customers who do that. Phrase it in a positive manner that persuades customers into believing your support site is the best and fastest method of receiving quality assistance.

For example, you could insert additional wording at the bottom of your app description text that reads: "For quick support assistance, please contact us directly at `http://support.breadcrumbsapp.com/` -OR- e-mail us at `support@breadcrumbsapp.com`." And if you prefer connecting with users via Twitter, you can also add your Twitter URL to that sentence.

Basically, the more customer care options you provide, the greater chance you have of reducing the clutter of support-related posts in the App Store's customer reviews (which in turn, may help boost your app's overall customer star rating).

App URL

I discussed the importance of maintaining a dedicated web site for your iOS app in Chapter 10, so even though the App URL field is optional, you *should* include your site URL here. Not doing so will only hurt your app's marketability down the road, especially now that the application URL link is displayed so prominently in the App Store.

Review Notes

Most developers won't need to fill out this optional field, but if there are unique features in your app that you worry the reviewers may misinterpret or have trouble accessing, including some additional notes here may help expedite the review process.

If your app requires creating a user account or logging in to a password-protected web service, you'll want to provide a test account or login credentials that Apple can use during the review process. Those login features are definitely tested by the app review team, so if you forget to provide this information in the Review Notes field, reviewers will request this login data from you, delaying the approval process. Some apps have even been flat out rejected based on the inability of app reviewers to successfully log in to a test account or a members-only web service from within an app. So even if you do supply the required information in this field, be sure to first test that it's a working, valid login.

Be careful that whatever text you include here is clear and concise. The last thing you want is for your app to be rejected because the extra notes you added here proved to be more confusing than helpful.

Step 4: Assign a Rating to Your App

Scrolling down the Version Information page, the second section refers to the intended age rating for your app. Here, you're presented with a survey-style list of questions that you must answer (see Figure 11–13). Apple requires all iOS apps to be assigned a content-related age rating so that the iOS parental controls can filter out specified age-appropriate applications when children access the App Store.

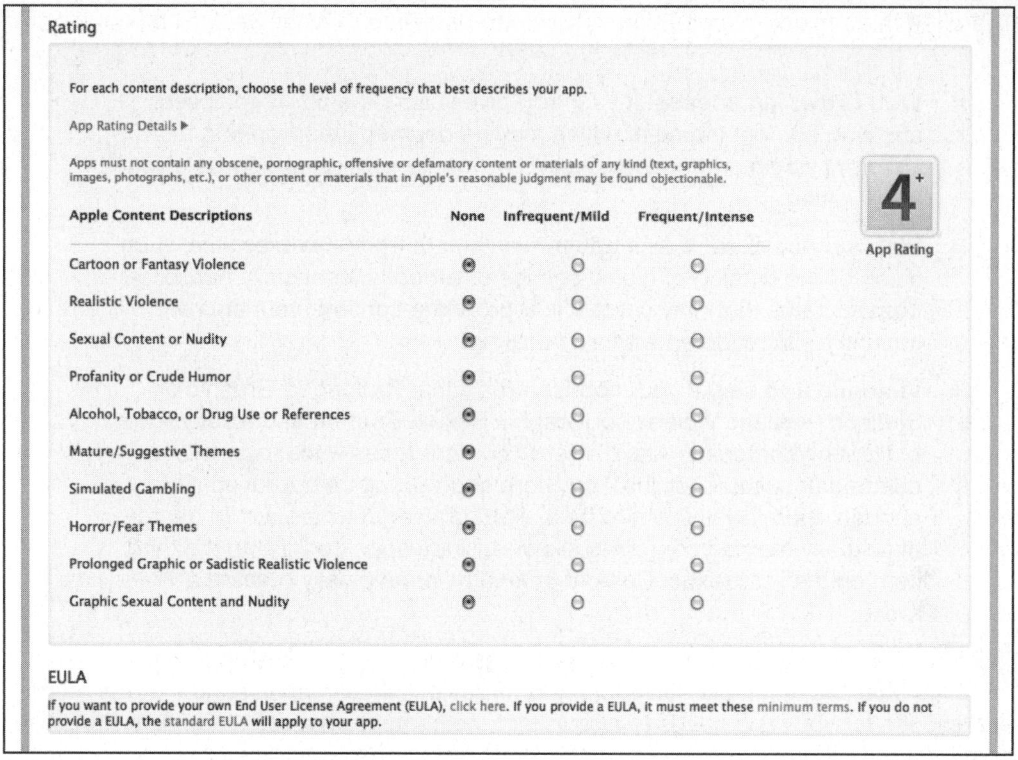

Rating

For each content description, choose the level of frequency that best describes your app.

App Rating Details ▶

Apps must not contain any obscene, pornographic, offensive or defamatory content or materials of any kind (text, graphics, images, photographs, etc.), or other content or materials that in Apple's reasonable judgment may be found objectionable.

Apple Content Descriptions	None	Infrequent/Mild	Frequent/Intense
Cartoon or Fantasy Violence	◉	○	○
Realistic Violence	◉	○	○
Sexual Content or Nudity	◉	○	○
Profanity or Crude Humor	◉	○	○
Alcohol, Tobacco, or Drug Use or References	◉	○	○
Mature/Suggestive Themes	◉	○	○
Simulated Gambling	◉	○	○
Horror/Fear Themes	◉	○	○
Prolonged Graphic or Sadistic Realistic Violence	◉	○	○
Graphic Sexual Content and Nudity	◉	○	○

4+

App Rating

EULA

If you want to provide your own End User License Agreement (EULA), click here. If you provide a EULA, it must meet these minimum terms. If you do not provide a EULA, the standard EULA will apply to your app.

Figure 11–13. *Answering None to all of the content questions dynamically displays an age rating of 4+, labeling the application as suitable for both kids and adults.*

The possible age ratings are 4+, 9+, 12+, and 17+. As illustrated in Figure 11–13, answering None to all of the content questions will dynamically display an age rating of 4+. Experiment with various Infrequent/Mild and Frequent/Intense answers for some of the content types, and you'll see the displayed rating change to 9+, 12+, or even 17+.

It's in your best interest to answer truthfully, selecting a rating that's appropriate for your app. Even if your submitted 12+ rating consists of only a few Infrequent/Mild answers, if Apple's review team thinks your app requires a more restrictive rating of 17+, it can and will reclassify your rating before approving it for sale in the App Store.

Ratings may seem subjective, especially with vague, generalized content types like Mature/Suggestive Themes, which can mean different things to different people. Nonetheless, Apple takes its ratings system very seriously, so there's not much wiggle room to complain if you don't like the approved rating your app has been given.

There are three major ratings-related factors to be aware of when designing your iOS app:

- **Web browsing access**: If your app gives users the ability to access any web content (some of which may be deemed inappropriate for children) via an embedded `UIWebView`, your app will probably be given a 17+ rating.

- **Web service data**: If your app retrieves data from a web service, such as an online catalog of digital comics or e-books, especially public domain items that may contain inappropriate content, your app will most likely be saddled with a 17+ rating.

- **Violence and sex**: If your app features either Prolonged Graphic or Sadistic Realistic Violence or Graphic Sexual Content and Nudity—the bottom two criteria in Apple's list of content types—your app will be deemed unsuitable for the App Store and will not be approved. Oddly enough, there does seem to be a slight gray area where a mild degree of sexually themed content is allowed, since apps containing the third item on the list, Sexual Content or Nudity, are typically granted a 17+ rating.

Take great care when answering the ten ratings questions, because they cannot be modified after the app has been submitted for review. Also keep in mind that the rating you choose for your app needs to also reflect the content of all related In-App Purchase items.

Directly below the Rating section is a small reference to the EULA. By default, if you do not provide your own EULA, then Apple's standard App Store EULA will be applied to your application. This appears to be the EULA that most iOS developers choose to adopt. However, if reading about end-user agreements in Michael Schneider's Chapter 3 leads you to believe that specific features in your app warrant a custom EULA, then Apple does allow you to upload your own, as long as it meets Apple's minimum terms. Since Apple needs to review custom EULAs upon submission, that option could potentially slow down the approval process.

Step 5: Upload Your App Icon and Screenshots

Continuing to scroll down the long Version Information page, the next section you'll encounter is called Images. This is where you upload your large 512 × 512 pixel app icon and your screenshots. To upload a particular element, click the related Choose File button below it to select the file from your hard drive (see Figure 11–14).

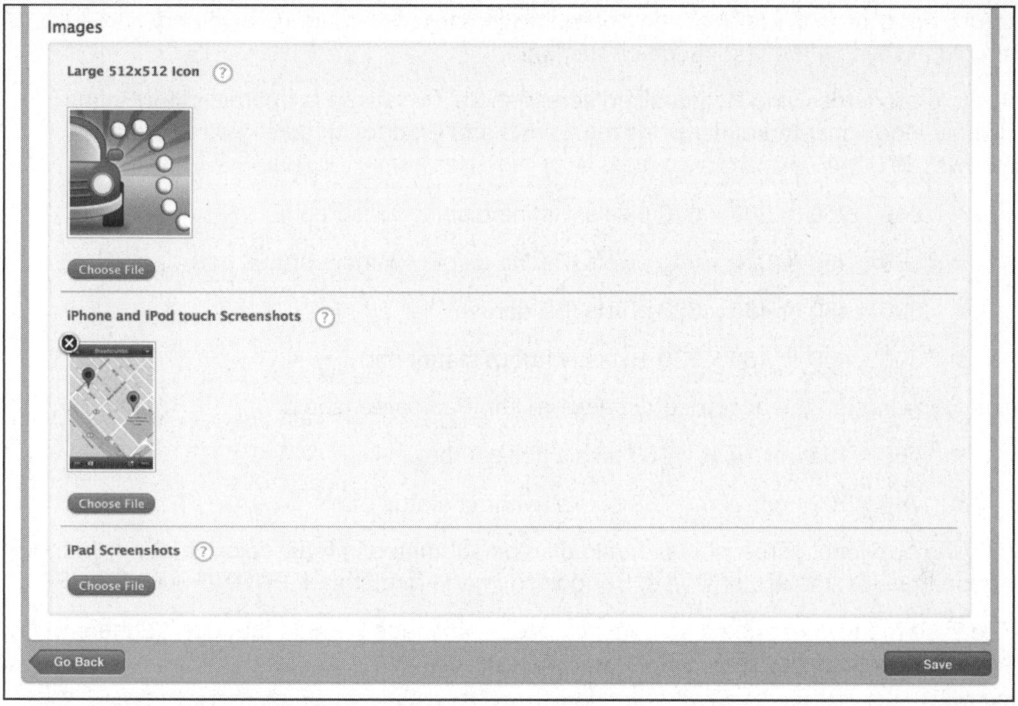

Figure 11–14. *The Images section of the Version Information page allows you to choose and upload your large 512 × 512 pixel app icon and your app screenshots for display in the App Store.*

App Store Icon

Since I discussed the need for creating a large, high-quality 512 × 512 pixel app icon way back in Chapter 4, you should already have this icon file prepared and ready to upload. Note that this large icon must be the same design as the app icon compiled in your iOS application. Submitting app icons that are not identical in design will quickly earn you a rejection letter.

The 512 × 512 pixel icon should be delivered as a flat, square PNG image with a 72 dpi resolution and RGB color mode. Do not include layers, masks, or transparencies of any kind.

And this is the most important rule: do not add rounded corners or the beveled gloss yourself. The App Store automatically adds those icon effects dynamically, but will honor the custom setting of the `UIPrerenderedIcon` key in your application's *Info.plist* file.

App Screenshots

When submitting your screenshots, they do not need to be uploaded in any particular order. Once uploaded, you should see them displayed as thumbnails in the Images section. To place them in a specific sequence for the App Store, simply use your mouse to drag-and-drop the image thumbnails into the desired order. Your primary screenshot should always be the first image on the left.

Apple prefers receiving Retina-sized screenshots if your app is optimized for Retina display. The accepted dimensions for iPhone and iPod touch screenshots are as follows:

- 640 × 960 or 960 × 640 pixels (Retina display full screen)
- 600 × 960 or 920 × 640 pixels (Retina display without status bar)
- 320 × 480 or 480 × 320 pixels (full screen)
- 300 × 480 or 460 × 320 pixels (without status bar)

The following are the accepted dimensions for iPad screenshots:

- 768 × 1024 or 1024 × 768 pixels (full screen)
- 748 × 1024 or 1004 × 768 pixels (without status bar)

Like the app icon, screenshots should also be submitted in RGB color at 72 dpi with no transparencies, masks, or layers. Supported image formats are PNG, JPEG, and TIFF.

The system may not accept screenshot sizes and image formats that don't adhere to Apple's specifications.

> **NOTE:** If you're creating an app listing in iTunes Connect so that you can test certain features like In-App Purchase, then screenshots are not required to finish the process. After you've uploaded your 512 × 512 app icon, simply click the Save button. You can always go back and upload your screenshots to the app listing in iTunes Connect when you're ready to submit your application for App Store review.

Once you've completed the Version Information page, click the Save button to finish creating your app listing.

Your New App Listing in iTunes Connect

Now when visiting the Manage Your Applications section of iTunes Connect, you should see your new app listing displayed. Clicking the app's icon will take you to its main summary page (see Figure 11–15).

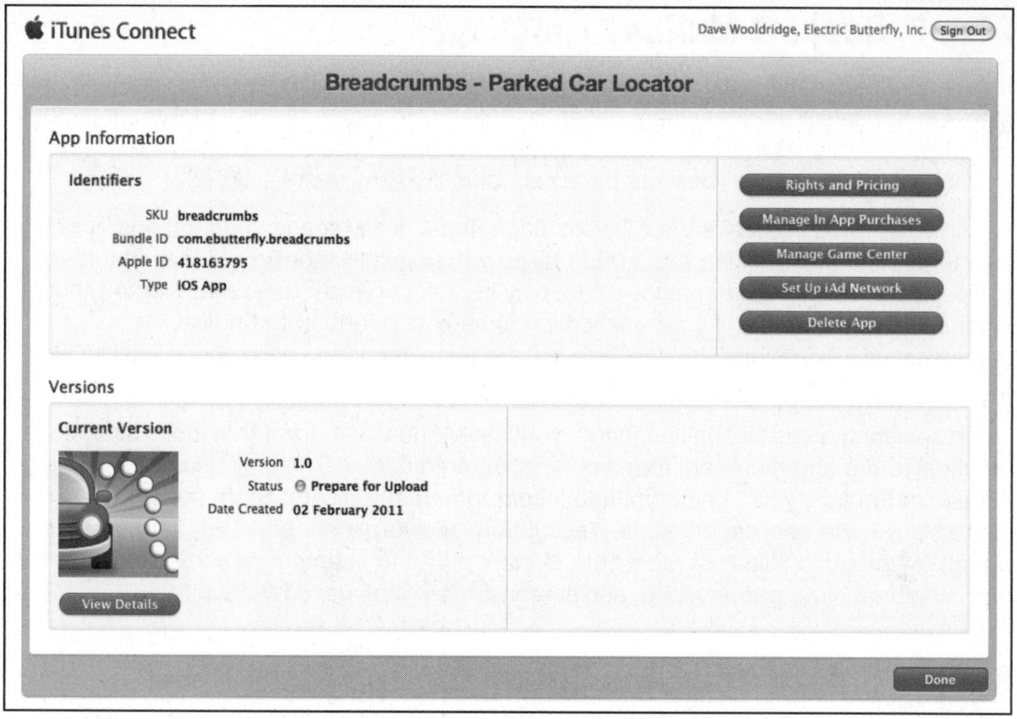

Figure 11–15. *Your new app listing's main summary page in iTunes Connect*

On the app's summary page, you can manage any related In-App Purchase items and other attributes. Click the View Details button if you need to access and edit metadata or screenshots before submitting your app binary for review (see Figure 11–16).

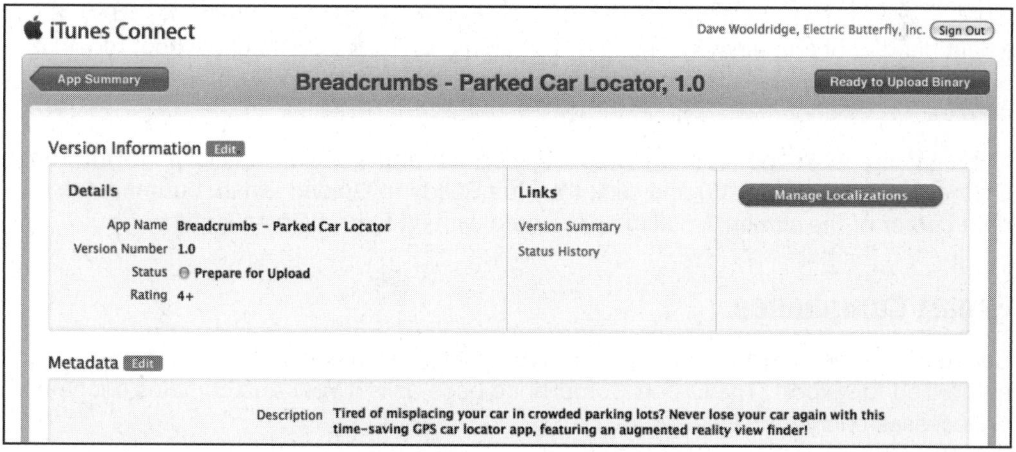

Figure 11–16. *Visit the View Details page (accessible from your app's main summary page) to edit various attributes before submitting your app binary for review.*

Step 6: Support Multiple Languages

If your application currently supports your primary language only, then you can skip this step. Do not select additional languages in iTunes Connect until your application actually includes localized support for those languages. Those of you who did provide support for multiple languages in your app binary shouldn't go anywhere just yet!

Within your app summary's View Details page, there is a Manage Localizations button (see Figure 11–16). Clicking that button takes you to localizations page that enables you to designate additional languages for display in regional App Stores that support those languages. For example, if your application already supports both English and Japanese, you would add Japanese as an additional language here. Since English was the primary language you selected back in step 1, there's no need to add English.

Upon selecting an additional language, you'll see a new web form that looks almost identical to the app metadata form you encountered earlier. The only difference is that instead of English, you'll be submitting localized content for App Store metadata elements like the application name, description, keywords, support URL, and even an option to upload localized screenshots. If you opt not to submit new screenshots for the new language, your primary language screenshots will be used by default.

Step 7: Upload Your App Binary for App Store Review

Earlier in this chapter, you compiled your application for App Store distribution. Now that you've just finished adding your app listing to iTunes Connect, the very last step in the App Store submission process is to upload your app binary.

Before you continue, take a moment to meticulously review the listed details in your iTunes Connect app summary, checking very carefully for any errors or typos. Once you upload your app binary, it will be added to the queue for Apple to review, and only a select handful of app elements can be later edited in iTunes Connect (without requiring an updated submission). In other words, now is the time to make sure everything is correct!

If everything looks good, then proceed to your app's View Details page in iTunes Connect (see Figure 11–16) and click the blue Ready to Upload Binary button in the top-right corner of the screen. You'll be presented with an Export Compliance page.

Export Compliance

Because of current export laws, any products that contain encryption need to be authorized for export. The Export Compliance page asks if your app contains encryption or accesses encryption (see Figure 11–17).

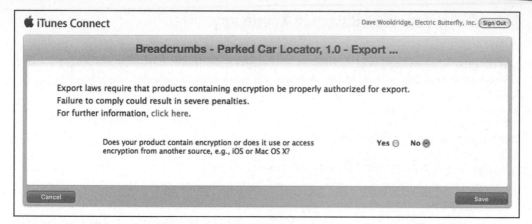

Figure 11–17. *Before you can upload your app binary, iTunes Connect requires you to answer an export compliance question.*

If the answer is No, you can move along—just click the Save button.

If the answer is Yes, then a few more encryption questions will appear, requiring answers before you can proceed. Based on how you answer those additional questions, you may be asked to upload a copy of your Commodity Classification Automated Tracking System (CCATS) document.

Since Export Compliance must review and approve your CCATS file before your application can be made available in the App Store, be prepared for a longer than normal app review period if a CCATS document is required. If you've never heard of CCATS before, odds are good your app does not fall into this category.

Waiting for Upload App Status

Now that you've imitated a request to upload your app binary, you app's status in iTunes Connect should have changed from Prepare for Upload to Waiting for Upload (see Figure 11–18).

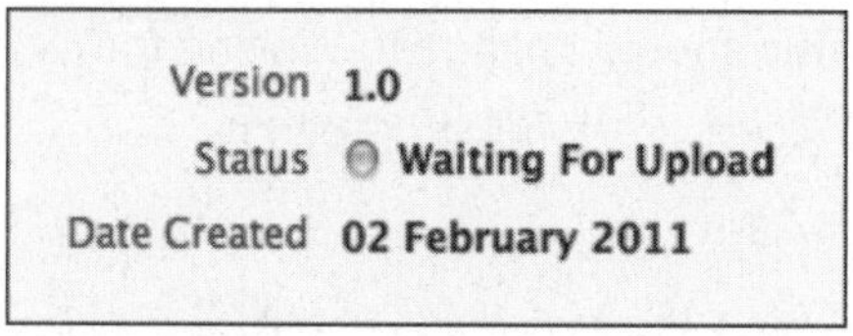

Version **1.0**
Status ◉ **Waiting For Upload**
Date Created **02 February 2011**

Figure 11–18. *Your app status changing to Waiting for Upload signals that iTunes Connect is now ready to receive your app binary upload.*

You won't be able to successfully upload your app binary until your app status is Waiting for Upload. Once that's verified on your app's main summary page in iTunes Connect, you can finally go back to Xcode Organizer.

Submitting Your App Binary in Xcode Organizer

Remember when you compiled your app with Xcode's **Build and Archive** option earlier in this chapter? Make sure your compiled app is still selected in the Archived Applications section of Xcode Organizer. At the bottom of the window, you should see three buttons (see Figure 11–19).

Figure 11–19. *When iTunes Connect is waiting for your binary upload, you can validate and submit your application for App Store review within Xcode Organizer.*

NOTE: An alternate method of uploading your app binary is via the Application Loader utility that's included in the Xcode developer tools download. In various places in Apple's documentation, you're directed to use Application Loader for uploading your app binary to iTunes Connect. While that's certainly a valid option, most iOS developers recommend compiling your app with Xcode's **Build and Archive** option and uploading your app binary through the latest version of Xcode Organizer.

First, click the Validate Application button. This performs the same validation tests that Apple will run during the review process. If it notifies you of any problems with your app binary, take this opportunity to fix the issues and recompile before submitting your app to Apple.

After passing the validation checks, you can now click the Submit Application to iTunes Connect button. You'll be asked to provide your iTunes Connect login and password to complete the submission request.

And that's it! Once the upload finishes, your app status should change to Waiting for Review.

Developer Rejected Status

If you discover a problem or need to edit certain assets that are untouchable when in the submission queue, then you can pull the app from review by clicking the app listing's Reject Binary button in iTunes Connect. This will change your app's status to Developer Rejected.

When you're ready, you'll need to resubmit a new app binary, which will start the review process from the very beginning. Obviously, you would do this only when in dire need.

In Review Status

When your app is being reviewed by Apple, the status changes to In Review. If you were required to upload a CCATS document, you may see the status Waiting for Export Compliance while your CCATS is being evaluated.

Ready for Sale Status

If your status reads Ready for Sale, then your app has been approved! Time to celebrate the momentous occasion!

MANAGING YOUR OWN EXPECTATIONS

Tom Petty was never wiser when singing "the waiting is the hardest part." You've worked so hard to get to this point that, even if the app review process ends up being much shorter than expected, the slow passing of time until Apple's confirmation arrives can feel excruciatingly long. Patience, Grasshopper. It's best not to dwell on it. Instead, give yourself a project to keep you occupied.

Have you finished creating all of your marketing materials, such as your press release and video trailer? And how about researching and connecting with potential media sites for reviews and press opportunities, as discussed in Chapter 10?

If you've taken care of your marketing tasks, then that's great! You'll be ready to rock when your app does become available in the App Store. But that's still no excuse to idly sit, feverishly watching the clock. There's no time like the present to dive into developing your next application or begin working on new features for the existing app. Just whatever you do, keep busy, and the time will fly.

Getting App Status Notifications

Those of you who would rather not log in to iTunes Connect a million times a day, obsessing over when that status message will change, can elect to have status updates sent to you directly via e-mail. Within your iTunes Connect user profile, simply opt in to receive status update e-mail by modifying the settings in the Notifications tab (see Figure 11–20).

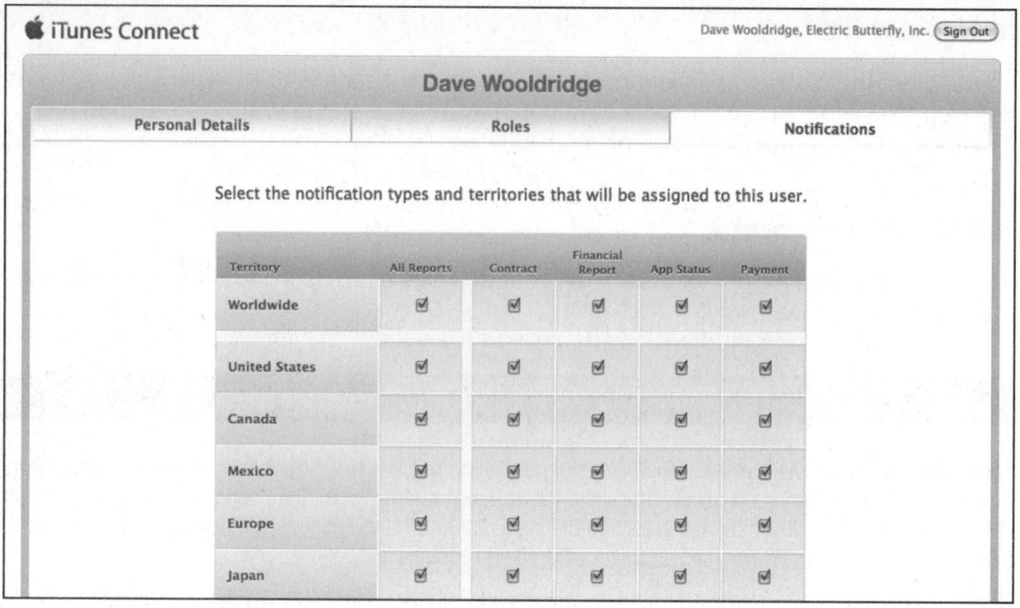

Figure 11–20. *Request to receive e-mail notifications when your app's status changes by updating the Notifications tab in your iTunes Connect user profile.*

But if you're paranoid that you might miss that all-important e-mail notification, Apple also provides a handy Status History feature. On your app listing's main summary page in iTunes Connect, click the Status History link to see which stages of the review process have already transpired, as well as when specific actions happened and who initiated them (you or Apple).

TIP: In an effort to provide greater transparency and streamlined communication, Apple also created the News and Announcements for Apple Developers site at `http://developer.apple.com/news/` as an online resource for app submission tips, iOS Dev Program updates, SDK news, and recommended programming techniques. This web site even posts the latest turnaround time for app reviews, such as "Percentage of iOS submissions reviewed within the last 7 days: 80% of new apps and 92% of app updates."

Try, Try Again: Dealing with App Store Rejections

We all cross our fingers, desperately hoping not to receive the dreaded Rejected notice, but if your submitted iOS app is rejected by Apple, do not despair. Although painfully frustrating, it is not the end of the world. The nice thing about software is that it can always be modified and resubmitted!

In the rejection letter that Apple sends, the reviewers usually explain why your app was rejected, and if you're lucky, they sometimes even provide suggestions on how to remedy the issue. For simple things, such as inappropriate icons or the incorrect usage of a UI element, making the necessary adjustments should be a no-brainer.

It doesn't matter whether or not you agree with the reason for rejection. The important thing is that you make the requested fixes and resubmit your application. Fortunately, there's no limit to how many times you can resubmit an app, so get back on that horse and keep trying. You've come this far, and you shouldn't let a tiny dispute prevent you from making money in the App Store.

For major rejection issues that are not so easily remedied, it's important to remain calm and deal with this as a professional business owner. I know that just the idea of several months of your life being thrown out the window because of an unacceptable app is enough to drive any person into a screaming frenzy. Your first instinct may be to write a scathing blog post in an effort to rally the troops behind your cause. Social media networks like Twitter make it entirely too easy to gather an angry mob of online followers, but raging against the machine won't endear you to Apple or the app review team. Yes, they do read blog posts and news sites. Although it might feel personally satisfying to have TechCrunch report on how you're yet another victim of app rejection, that won't help you get into the App Store.

And if Apple's rejection was completely justified because your application violates its established terms and conditions, you really don't have a good reason to complain. Your loud rants will only make you look unprofessional in the eyes of your peers: the developer community. And it certainly won't win you any points with consumers who read your blog or follow you on Twitter.

If you feel that you have a legitimate reason for considering your app rejection unjust, then talk to Apple about it. Try to establish a dialogue with the app reviewers who evaluated your app. If that doesn't work, then you can submit an appeal to the official App Review Board at
`http://developer.apple.com/appstore/resources/approval/contact.html`. Always state your case in a thoughtful, clear manner to help the reviewers understand your reasoning. Several app rejections have been overturned because of persuasive developer arguments and a quick reevaluation.

No one has said the app review process is perfect. Just remember that the App Store is still a relatively new marketplace—one that grew in size much faster than Apple (or anyone else) ever anticipated. It's easy to get upset over rejection, but with more than 300,000 apps flooding the App Store and more than 15,000 app submissions each week, Apple's overworked review team is merely trying to do its job as best it can under such remarkable pressure.

Mistakes do happen, but Apple is constantly working to improve the process. Although that kind of sentiment may make me sound like a glorified fanboy, please don't misinterpret my intentions. As a developer myself, I certainly get frustrated if my creativity and ambition are limited by the restrictions of the business world, but then I remember that it *is* a business. If I want to be a part of it, solving problems with etiquette and professionalism is the only way to truly succeed in the long run.

Apple holds the keys to the kingdom, so if you hope to someday thrive in the App Store, it's in your best interest to maintain a good working relationship with the company and its review team.

Approved! Making It to the Promised Land

So that miraculous day has finally come. Your app has been approved and is now available in the App Store! Congratulations! It is indeed a worthy achievement that can bring you much success, especially if you've taken all the necessary steps to effectively market your app.

Checking on your application's performance in the App Store is as simple as logging in to iTunes Connect to review reported sales and downloads on either a weekly or daily basis. *Beware: tracking sales can be utterly addictive and destroy your daily productivity level.* iTunes Connect also issues monthly financial reports that summarize your app sales and earned revenue.

Analyzing Your App Store Sales Statistics

The sales and trends reports in iTunes Connect include a lot of data for analyzing your product's life cycle and sales performance in the marketplace. But what if you're looking for more assistance and additional features like the following?

- Tracking your App Store statistics from a desktop application or mobile device

- Custom graphing your statistics to better educate your own marketing efforts

- Automating the task of retrieving and analyzing sales and download data (when you forget to do it yourself)

Third-party tools and web-based services can provide such capabilities. There's definitely a solution out there that will mesh well with your workflow. Although this may not be an exhaustive list, here are some options to explore:

- Apple's iTunes Connect Mobile
  (http://itunes.com/apps/iTunesConnectMobile) is a universal iPhone and iPad app that is free to download from the App Store and gives you direct access to your iTunes Connect sales and trend data. Regardless if you employ other services such as appFigures or App Annie, this free mobile Apple app is a convenient way to track your app's sales from anywhere.

- appFigures (http://www.appfigures.com/) is a popular web-based solution that supports the automated importing of your iTunes Connect sales reports, presenting the data in dynamic graphs and charts. Beyond tracking sales, trends, App Store rankings, and reviews, appFigures will also automatically e-mail you report summaries every day. You can choose either a free Basic account or upgrade to access all Premium features. Although appFigures' web reports are iOS-compatible (when viewed in Mobile Safari), there is also a third-party native iPhone app for accessing your appFigures account: appTrends by David Knell, available in the App Store.

- App Annie (http://www.appannie.com/), dubbed "Your App Nanny," is a comprehensive app sales tracking and trend analytics web service. It offers many of the same features as appFigures, as well as historical App Store rankings data on all apps. Its attractive online dashboard interface can be accessed and viewed from either your desktop web browser or iPad's Mobile Safari.

- AppSales Mobile (https://github.com/omz/AppSales-Mobile) is an iPhone app that downloads and analyzes your iTunes Connect sales reports. Since it's available as open source from GitHub, you'll need to compile the project in Xcode and run it as a debug build in order to use it. But it gives you the flexibility to customize, compile, and install the software on your own mobile iOS devices to suit your own needs.

- AppStar (http://www.damabia.com/appstar.php), Damabia's Mac OS X application, is a comprehensive desktop solution for tracking your iTunes Connect sales and trends reports, Apple's monthly financial sales reports, and App Store chart rankings and app reviews. It also provides you with a built-in interface for organizing all of your app icons, screenshots, and marketing materials in one place. A ten-day fully functional demo of AppStar is available for download.

- AppStore Clerk (http://blog.fieryferret.com/2008/10/appstore-clerk.html) is a free Mac OS X application that parses your sales reports and displays your app downloads in a simple, easy-to-read spreadsheet table. It may not include the advanced graphing features of other solutions listed here, but it's generously offered as freeware (and the developer even provides the source code as well).

- AppViz (http://www.ideaswarm.com/products/appviz/), by Ideaswarm, is a beautifully designed Mac OS X application that can download your iTunes Connect sales data, as well as import reports that you've already downloaded to your hard drive. Like most of the other tools in this list, it can analyze and track your sales and downloads in visual graphs to reveal trends. It also monitors multiple apps and accounts, App Store category ranking, and customer reviews, plus sales tracking for your In-App Purchase products. A trial version of this popular, feature-rich desktop app is available for download.

- Distimo Monitor (`https://monitor.distimo.com/`), like appFigures and App Annie, is an extensive web-based app sales tracking tool. What sets this solution apart from many of the other offerings listed here is that Distimo Monitor supports all major app stores, such as Apple's App Store, Google's Android Market, BlackBerry's App World, and so on—perfect for cross-platform mobile developers.

- Heartbeat (`http://www.heartbeatapp.com/`), a service of Mobclix, is a very slick, remotely hosted web application that offers an extensive suite of sales tracking, trends, crash report monitoring, usage stats, App Store rankings, revenue payment management, and more. If you're looking for a comprehensive tool for managing your entire App Store business, then sign up for a Mobclix account to take advantage of the free Heartbeat.

- MyAppSales (`https://github.com/Cocoanetics/MyAppSales`) is a convenient iPhone app like AppSales Mobile, but it offers quite a few more features because of the creator Oliver Drobnik's active development. Even though MyAppSales is now available as open source, allowing you to compile and run this feature-packed app on your own iOS devices, donations are still welcome and appreciated by Oliver.

- Prismo (`http://positiveteam.com/products/prismo/mac/`), Positive Team's Mac OS X application, boasts a clean and simplified iTunes-style interface design. It supports the automatic download of reports from iTunes Connect, as well as tracking the ranking and sales of your iPhone apps and In-App Purchase products. A 30-day trial of Prismo is available for download.

Beyond the solutions already mentioned here, don't forget to also check out the many App Store ranking tools that were profiled in Chapter 2, such as APPlyzer and David Frampton's excellent (and free) MajicRank.

Rev Your Engines

You're in the App Store…now what? No, it's not time to take a break. I know you're tired from months of development, but you need to capitalize on the short-lived momentum surrounding your app's launch! Chapter 12 cranks up the publicity engine to increase consumer awareness of your app's availability.

Increasing Awareness for Your iOS App

Your app has been approved and is available for sale in the App Store, so now what? First, I would like to congratulate you on this milestone achievement! If you've worked your way through the entire book and finally have an application listed in the App Store, that in itself is quite an accomplishment. Only fellow developers truly know how much hard work and dedication goes into launching a new software product. After months of meticulously planning and programming your app, you deserve to celebrate. Although you would probably love nothing more than to take a much needed vacation at this point, unfortunately, you can't rest yet.

It's time to rev up the publicity engine to increase consumer awareness of your app's availability. Even if you implemented the various business strategies from previous chapters, and your prerelease marketing efforts resulted in an initial sales surge, there's still vital work to be done. It's your job to ensure that your iOS application does not get buried amid the thousands of new apps flooding into the App Store. This chapter reveals how to craft effective press releases, utilize promo codes, gain exposure through reviews and interviews, and sustain momentum in the App Store with promotions, giveaways, and carefully timed sale events.

Dedicating As Much Effort to Marketing Your App As You Put into Developing It

If your app was already available in the App Store when you bought this book and you decided to skip ahead to this chapter, I highly recommend reading Chapter 10 first. In fact, I insist. This chapter will prove much more useful to you *after* you've read Chapter 10.

Even though Chapter 10 is aimed at prerelease marketing, its primary goal is to help you build a solid foundation online. It covers establishing a web site presence, a social media following via Twitter and Facebook, and relationships with prominent bloggers and influential iOS app review sites. All of those elements will serve as the underlying backbone of your postrelease marketing efforts as well, so having them in place long before your app goes live in the App Store is crucial to your success.

Launching with a Supernova of Publicity

You want to capitalize on the initial visibility of your app's release in the App Store, so the trick is to get as many consumers and news outlets as possible talking about your app at the same time. Think of it as a supernova of publicity in the hopes of creating a snowball effect. You want consumers thinking, "Everyone is talking about that app, so it must be good!" With that in mind, when reading this chapter, don't tackle a single task each week. Read through all the topics, and then try to implement as many of them as possible at the same time, in the hopes of sustaining that buzz well beyond the initial release.

How much time should you dedicate to marketing your app? Initially, only one or two hours a day is *not* enough. Yes, I know you're eager to start developing that next great app idea, but before you dive into any future projects, your new 1.0 app release needs attention. You should be prepared to set aside the first two weeks to focus on nothing but promoting your new app. Request reviews, publicize your app on Twitter and Facebook, set up media interviews, post blog articles, submit your app for awards, and the list goes on. Once your marketing efforts start to pay off with an increase in sales and/or a rise in the App Store charts, you can gradually ease back into your normal work life, with only a couple hours a day spent on app marketing.

Unfortunately, there are no shortcuts in software marketing. For your iOS app to have a chance at becoming successful, you must be willing to invest just as much time and effort into promoting your app as you put into developing it.

Enlisting Help from the Pros

If you're not able to dedicate the necessary hours to postrelease marketing, then it's in your best interest to hire a third-party company to handle this job. Perform a search online for *iphone app marketing* or *iphone marketing agency*. You'll find hundreds of marketing and PR firms around the world that specialize in mobile product launches. Here are several agencies to give you an idea of some of the services available:

- Appency (http://www.appency.com/)
- Appular (http://appular.com/)
- App2Market (http://www.app2market.com/)
- Apalon App Marketing (http://www.apalon.com/iphone_marketing.html)
- Digital Automat (http://www.digitalautomat.com/)
- Mobility Public Relations (http://www.mobilitypr.com/)
- TriplePoint PR (http://www.triplepointpr.com/)

Of course, there are many more marketing agencies out there beyond the ones listed here. Depending on where you live, you may feel more comfortable hiring a local firm, so do several online searches to find one that meets your specific needs.

As I've said before, whenever you're hiring third-party consultants or companies, you should do ample research before selecting one. Not only should they be experts on the specific challenges of the App Store and marketing iOS apps, but their practices, policies, and performance should also be very transparent. Since they are representing your company and products, their actions are a reflection of you and your application.

For example, if an unscrupulous PR firm uses its own internal iTunes accounts to plant the same fake five-star reviews for all of its clients' apps in the App Store, it's only a matter of time before someone makes the connection and blows the whistle. Even if you were unaware that this was happening, ultimately, it's your reputation that gets tarnished.

Apple has even been known to remove from the App Store apps that have abused the customer review system. Obviously, most PR agencies take their ethical responsibility very seriously and never cross that line. I only mention this so that you do your homework and ask the right questions before choosing a mobile marketing firm to promote your iPhone or iPad app.

Depending on the level of services provided, an experienced third-party marketing agency will cost at least $1,000 (and possibly thousands more). If you're an independent developer who can't afford to outsource the marketing and publicity for your app, then you'll need to carve out the necessary time in your schedule to handle the job yourself. So, roll up your sleeves, and let's dive in!

> **TIP:** Know when people are talking about your app! Based on the latest relevant search results, Google Alerts is a fantastic free e-mail notification service that enables you to monitor when a specific name or topic is discussed online on web sites, blogs, and even Twitter. I highly recommend setting up Google Alerts to track your app name and company name. You can even use the service to keep tabs on your competitors! Sign up for free at `http://www.google.com/alerts`.

The Art of Crafting Effective Press Releases

Once your app becomes available in the App Store, you'll want to tell the world about it! Sure, notifying your followers on Twitter, Facebook, and your blog are important first steps. But you'll also want to announce the news on a grander scale to reach as many iPhone, iPad, and iPod touch users as possible. One way to accomplish this is to send out a press release to all the major technology and mobile news sites.

Even if you're a well-established developer in the Mac or iOS communities, don't assume that the major news outlets are watching your blog or Twitter posts. With the constant flood of tech news that comes across journalists' desks on a daily basis, your news needs to get their attention, so take the time to deliver important announcements directly to their e-mail inboxes.

Press releases are not limited to only new products. Send out a press release to announce anything that's newsworthy, such as new app versions and special limited-time sale offers and promotions.

The Essential Ingredients of a Press Release

So, how does one write an effective press release? Do not simply copy and paste the app announcement from your blog into an e-mail message!

Press releases consist of specific formatting. By following the standard rules and syntax for press releases, you'll be making it much easier for reporters to quickly scan your story for the pertinent facts.

> **NOTE:** Do you have to follow a standard press release format? No, some developers have found success with unique, clever announcements, but take great care to ensure that the press release remains easy to read and contains all of the necessary information. Sometimes "too creative" can backfire, such as a press release formatted in Objective-C code syntax, which would receive quite a bit of attention and admiration from developer blogs, but might prove extremely difficult for nonprogrammer journalists to decipher. If you have your heart set on creating a clever press release for select recipients, be sure to also prepare a normal one for those news sites that may not "get the joke" or are unable to accept nonstandard press releases.

Using Streaming Colour Studios' press release for Dapple as a visual example (see Figure 12–1), I'll walk you through each of the essential elements of a press release to convey the information that journalists need.

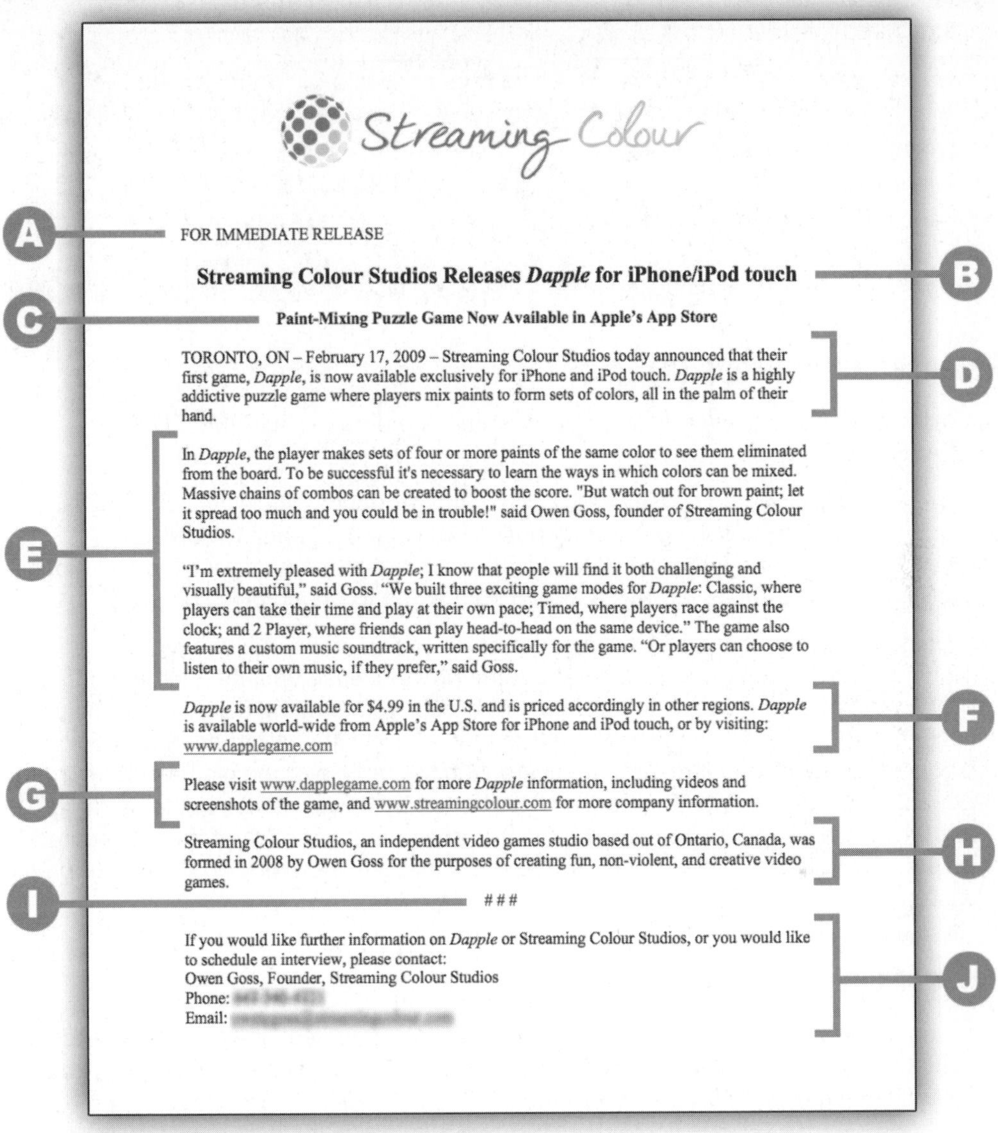

FOR IMMEDIATE RELEASE

Streaming Colour Studios Releases *Dapple* for iPhone/iPod touch

Paint-Mixing Puzzle Game Now Available in Apple's App Store

TORONTO, ON – February 17, 2009 – Streaming Colour Studios today announced that their first game, *Dapple*, is now available exclusively for iPhone and iPod touch. *Dapple* is a highly addictive puzzle game where players mix paints to form sets of colors, all in the palm of their hand.

In *Dapple*, the player makes sets of four or more paints of the same color to see them eliminated from the board. To be successful it's necessary to learn the ways in which colors can be mixed. Massive chains of combos can be created to boost the score. "But watch out for brown paint; let it spread too much and you could be in trouble!" said Owen Goss, founder of Streaming Colour Studios.

"I'm extremely pleased with *Dapple*; I know that people will find it both challenging and visually beautiful," said Goss. "We built three exciting game modes for *Dapple*: Classic, where players can take their time and play at their own pace; Timed, where players race against the clock; and 2 Player, where friends can play head-to-head on the same device." The game also features a custom music soundtrack, written specifically for the game. "Or players can choose to listen to their own music, if they prefer," said Goss.

Dapple is now available for $4.99 in the U.S. and is priced accordingly in other regions. *Dapple* is available world-wide from Apple's App Store for iPhone and iPod touch, or by visiting: www.dapplegame.com

Please visit www.dapplegame.com for more *Dapple* information, including videos and screenshots of the game, and www.streamingcolour.com for more company information.

Streaming Colour Studios, an independent video games studio based out of Ontario, Canada, was formed in 2008 by Owen Goss for the purposes of creating fun, non-violent, and creative video games.

###

If you would like further information on *Dapple* or Streaming Colour Studios, or you would like to schedule an interview, please contact:
Owen Goss, Founder, Streaming Colour Studios
Phone: [redacted]
Email: [redacted]

Figure 12–1. *Using Streaming Colour Studios' Dapple announcement as an example, this illustration pinpoints the essential ingredients for effective press releases.*

Referring to Figure 12–1, let's go over each component and its importance in the press release format.

> **CAUTION:** Those of you who think this press release stuff all seems like common sense are one step ahead of the game. You would be surprised at just how many developers forget to include vital information—such as pricing, a web site URL, and even contact information— in their press releases. How are journalists supposed to write a good story based on your new app announcement if they can't reach you with any additional questions they have? They won't. Incomplete press releases simply get discarded, and the media moves onto the next story. Don't let that happen to you!

Release Instructions (A)

Typically, if your app is already available, you use the phrase "FOR IMMEDIATE RELEASE" (in all caps).

If you're sending a press release in advance of the product's official launch and want the press to hold off on publishing the story until then, you could specify "UNDER EMBARGO UNTIL" and specify a date. Just be aware that many news sites and blogs actively ignore embargoes, always eager to be the first to break new stories.

If it's imperative that your announcement remains under wraps until the product is available, you may want to wait to send out the press release until the morning of the app's actual debut in the App Store. Some publicists recommend sending out the press release the night before. The problem is that many news sites report around the clock, and your press release just might get coverage in the middle of the night while your target audience is sleeping. Then the story is buried by newer stories in the morning. That's why it's a good idea to research the reporting habits of each of the iOS-related news sites and blogs. This will allow you to better gauge when to send them your press release.

Subject Line (B)

The most important element of your press release is the subject line. This title needs to capture the attention of anyone who reads it, whether it's the subject line of an e-mail or the headline of a hyperlink on a news site.

Traditionally, the subject line formula is "*company* releases *product* for *platform*," replacing *company*, *product*, and *platform* with your specifics. In Figure 12–1, this translates to "Streaming Colour Studios Releases Dapple for iPhone/iPod touch."

Never, never, never add marketing adjectives like "amazing" or "exciting" to the subject line. Doing so only makes your press release look like it was written by an amateur. Unlike your other marketing materials, a press release should stick to only the facts, without the flourish of marketing jargon. But at the same time, to compete with the hundreds of other press releases that arrive daily, your subject line should be both informative *and* captivating. If you're announcing a new version of an existing app that has previously won awards, it's perfectly acceptable to include "award-winning" in the subject line.

Since the goal is to grab the attention of the media, if the app name is not reflective of its unique, pioneering features, then adjust the subject line accordingly. Instead of saying "Electric Butterfly Releases XRayMed for the iPad," the subject might draw more attention if worded "Electric Butterfly Releases First X-Ray Reader App for the iPad." You can always mention your app's name in the summary line below the subject title. (And if you do boast of being first to market with a particular app or feature, be sure that's true!)

Summary Line (C)

This is the second most important element of your press release. If journalists are remotely intrigued by your subject line, this brief one-sentence summary will help determine whether they continue to read the rest of the press release. Many developers opt not to include this line, using only the subject line to lead into the introductory paragraph, but I highly recommend including a summary line to help deliver the basics even if the reader stops there.

In the case of the Dapple press release in Figure 12–1, the subject line and summary line together convey that Streaming Colour Studios released Dapple for iPhone and iPod touch and that this paint-mixing puzzle game is now available in Apple's App Store. If readers only bothered to read those two lines, they would still be aware of the most important information: what your app is and where to get it.

Introduction (D)

The first paragraph begins with your location and release date, followed by a rehash of your subject and summary lines. This introduction should be a single paragraph with only a couple sentences. It should state that your company announces the release of a specific product, what it is, who the target audience/platform is, and where it's available.

Description (E)

Remember when I talked about crafting an "elevator pitch" for your app description in Chapter 10? The next few paragraphs that follow the introductory paragraph are essentially your elevator pitch description without the flowery marketing adjectives.

The main body of your press release should explain in concise detail exactly what your app does, the features and benefits it provides, and why people should care. The press love to include quotes in the stories they run, so it's also a good idea to include a good quote from a senior executive of your company (you?) on why the product was created or how it represents an important milestone for your company.

Just remember that less is more. Unless your app represents some earth-shattering technology breakthrough that warrants a lengthy explanation, your press release should not be longer than one page. That means if you are using word processor software such as Microsoft Word to write your press release, the entire document should fit within a single 8.5 × 11-inch page with 1-inch margins.

Pricing and Availability (F)

The next text block should include your app's price, any specific device hardware or iOS version requirements, and where the app can be purchased. Since most iPhone and iPad apps are available in multiple countries, if the price is listed in dollars, then indicate that's the price in the US App Store and that the app is priced accordingly in other regions.

Most news sites cater to a global audience, so it's important to mention if your app is available worldwide in all of Apple's regional App Stores.

If you also offer a free lite version, be sure to include that information as well, so that interested readers can download it and try it risk-free.

Web Site URL and Additional Information (G)

Since a one-page press release can't possibly include everything about your new iOS app, it's absolutely crucial that you include a link to your app's web site or company web site. This gives interested consumers easy access to additional information, screenshots, and video demos.

If the press is interested in writing about your product, they will also visit your listed URLs to better familiarize themselves with your company. And that's yet another reason to make sure you have a professional, well-designed web site before your app is released.

About Your Company (H)

This last paragraph should describe your company. This is also a great place to briefly mention any relevant awards you've won and other well-known products you've produced. Journalists are consumers too, so if they recognize and admire your other software apps, they may be more inclined to write about your new product.

End of the Press Release (I)

The three hash symbols (###) centered on the page represent the end of the press release content. Anything that you include below that marker is regarded as information that should not be posted publically, such as your phone number and other media contact details.

Of course, for those automated news sites that simply post the exact e-mail announcement you send them, the entire message will be published, regardless of those markers. For those automated sites, be sure to omit any personal contact information that you don't want posted online for search engines to index and cache for all eternity.

Media Contact Information (J)

Always provide a way for the press to reach you. An e-mail address is a must, and a phone number is also recommended. Since international phone calls can be quite expensive, you may want to set up a Skype account or instant messaging account and list that in lieu of a phone number.

The more avenues you provide for reaching you, the better, so it can't hurt to also include your Twitter handle as well. If they like your app, they may just decide to follow you!

This section is also a great place to include download links for screenshot images, video trailers, an official press kit, and any other marketing materials that you've produced for your iOS app. Journalists don't have time to hunt through your web site for screenshots, so always include direct links to media resources.

And don't forget to state that you welcome all questions, interviews, and app reviews. Let the press know that you're openly accessible for additional inquiries and can provide promo codes for reviewing your app. (Promo codes are discussed a little later in this chapter.)

Translating Your Press Release

Most of the dominant iOS-related news sites are English-based. If English is not your native language, don't send them a press release in a foreign language. And certainly don't try converting your press release with an automated online tool like Google Translate. Either the journalists won't be able to translate it themselves or the autotranslated English will contain so much incorrect syntax and phrasing that it can render your announcement unreadable.

Hire a professional translator to convert your press release to proper English, and do likewise for translations from English to any other language. First impressions are everything when dealing with the press, so it's a worthy investment.

The Virtual 24/7 Press Room

Although you'll be sending out your press release to as many iOS-related news sites as possible, you'll also want to make your press release available on your web site or blog. You can't possibly reach everyone yourself. For those journalists who were not included in your initial e-mail list but discover your app on their own, provide access to your press release online. And don't just post it as an HTML page. Make it available as its own download that the press can save to their computers for later reference.

After looking at the Dapple press release in Figure 12–1, nicely formatted with a company logo letterhead and various font sizes and styles applied, you may be tempted to create something similar—and you should! This is easy enough to produce with most word processor software programs and makes your press release look that much more professional. Be sure to save the press release in several popular formats, such as DOC (Microsoft Word), RTF, and PDF to ensure that anyone can easily open and read the file.

Create a dedicated section on your web site for posting all your press releases. Make it easily accessible from anywhere in your site by including a link to it from your main navigation menu or footer menu. Most developers tend to call this section something intuitive and simple, such as "Press" or "Press Room," so that it's extremely easy to find.

Although providing a public archive of downloadable press releases online is great, don't stop there. Make it as easy as possible for journalists and reviewers to write about your iOS app by also including download links of screenshots, video trailers, app icons and logos, and even your company logo! Any materials that might prove useful to the press should be included in your virtual online press room. Streaming Colour Studios' online press page at `http://www.streamingcolour.com/press/` accomplishes this and more. It offers a convenient downloadable press kit for each iOS game that includes screenshots, an app icon, a company logo, and a press release—all compressed in a single zip archive. This press page also lists links to relevant awards, interviews, and app reviews to further spotlight its games.

Maintaining an online press section on your site will serve as a comprehensive resource for those journalists and bloggers who are interested in doing a story on your company or products, no matter their time zone. Reporters are often under tight deadlines, so your 24/7 virtual press room can help provide immediate answers, even when you're unavailable.

Of course, don't wait for the media to find your web site. A dedicated press section is a good resource to offer, but you'll definitely want to actively send out your press release to the prominent tech and mobile news sites as well.

Connecting with the Press

When contacting specific journalists and bloggers directly, your press release should not be the first correspondence they receive from you. As discussed in Chapter 10, you should have already initiated a dialogue with them during your prerelease marketing stage with a brief query, asking if they would be interested in an exclusive preview or reviewing the app. With introductions already established, those people will be much more receptive to your press release and future announcements. Obviously, you won't have time to formulate a connection with everyone, but you should do this for the most important, influential reporters and bloggers on your list.

Beyond your initial introduction, the other vital elements to master when communicating with the press are presentation, delivery logistics, and etiquette.

Formatting Your E-mail Announcement

A nicely formatted press release with your company logo looks great, but don't send that out as a PDF attached to an e-mail message that merely asks journalists to read the attachment. Not only is that a surefire way to have your e-mail ignored, but it's also a common flag for spam filters. If your e-mail address has not been whitelisted by the press members you're attempting to reach (yet another reason to establish a relationship with them beforehand), your e-mail with attachments may accidentally get marked as junk mail. And for those sites that automatically post press releases that are e-mailed to their mail bots, sending the press release in an e-mail attachment makes it close to impossible for their automated scripts to parse your announcement text.

Your e-mail should include your entire press release in the body of the message, with the subject headline as the e-mail's subject line. Don't format the text as styled rich text or as a fancy HTML e-mail. To enable journalists and mail bots to easily copy the press release, use the tried-and-true plain-text e-mail format.

Since word processors such as Microsoft Word tend to insert curly quotes, curly apostrophes, long dashes, and other special characters, you'll want to ensure your press release is converted to standard ASCII plain text. Although your e-mail application may support Unicode characters, many web sites still publish HTML pages with an ASCII text-related content type such as ISO-8859-1. News sites often copy and paste your text directly to the Web, without first converting it into HTML entities. If your press release contains special characters, it may be displayed online with strange question mark symbols representing the unrecognizable characters. This not only makes your press release look unprofessional, but it can also render it difficult to read.

For the same reasons that you should not include your press release as an e-mail attachment, do not include screenshots of your iOS app as attachments. If you know the journalist who is receiving your e-mail, then attaching one or two screenshots is perfectly acceptable. However, for most cases, you should include only direct URL links to your screenshots and video trailer. This provides immediate access to your screenshots and other press materials, without the issues that often plague e-mail attachments.

When listing URLs within your e-mail message, always include the full URL, complete with the http:// prefix. Most modern e-mail programs will dynamically display full http URLs as clickable links, but that's not always the case for partial URLs that start only with www.

Who to Notify?

Now that your press release e-mail is ready to go, to whom should you send it? Perform online searches for *iPhone news* and *iPhone app reviews* to find the sites and blogs that cover new iOS app announcements. If you're launching an iPad app, you may also want to search for iPad-related news sites (although most iPhone news sites cover all things iOS, including iPad). After scanning the search results, you'll quickly compile a list much more comprehensive than the collection of sites I've included in this book's appendix.

My list in the appendix consists of web sites that specialize in iPhone and iPad news and app reviews, and should serve as a good starting point. And since some of the major Mac and PC news sites also cover iOS app news, I've included a few of them there as well. That long list may seem daunting at first glance, but take the time to send your press release to as many relevant iOS news sites as possible. Remember that they won't all report on your new app release. The more sites you contact, the more potential coverage you'll get, compensating for any sites that ignore your e-mail.

Before sending press releases and app review requests to any web site or blog, first explore the site to learn about any special submission policies that are enforced and which staff members handle iOS app news and reviews. Don't send a press release or app review request to a site sight unseen. Doing so is not only a waste of your time, but it annoys those site administrators who don't cover mobile app news or your particular app genre. For example, don't send a press release or review inquiry for a productivity app to a games-only site like TouchArcade.com. You never want anyone in the media to perceive your submissions as ignorant spam. Do your research before contacting specific sites or individual writers.

If your app targets a specific niche market—such as writing, yoga, or golf—you should also make an effort to send your press release to related web sites and magazines in those fields. Those sites and magazines like to keep their readers informed on the latest related products. Even though not everyone will own an iPhone or iPad, targeted coverage in a specific field could help reach new customers who don't ordinarily visit tech sites.

Reaching the Masses

Not everyone you send a press release is going to post your announcement, but if you send it out to a large number of news outlets, you're bound to get some coverage. If your iOS app does not get mentioned on one of your favorite news sites, don't despair.

If you're having trouble reaching the right people or getting posted on mainstream sites like Google News (http://news.google.com/), you may want to enlist the assistance of a third-party press release distribution service that specializes in technology news. Perform an online search for press release distribution, and you'll find dozens of free and commercial services, such as the following:

- BeeSaved (http://beesaved.com/)

- Business Wire (http://www.businesswire.com/)

- Games Press (http://www.gamespress.com/)

- The Indie Press Release Service (http://www.gamerelease.net/)

- iSpreadNews (http://ispreadnews.com/)

- Newswire (http://www.newswire.net/)

- prMac (http://prmac.com/)

- PRWeb (http://www.prweb.com/)

- PR Newswire (http://www.prnewswire.com/)

- SoftPressRelease (http://www.softpressrelease.com/)

Before signing up for a specific service, verify that it will distribute your press release to the mainstream news outlets you want to target. But don't expect a service like this to be able to adequately reach smaller, niche iOS news sites—that may be a job best suited for you.

Reinforcing Relationships with a Thank-You

When journalists and bloggers do post stories or reviews on your new app, be sure to e-mail a personal thank-you to each one. Even if your press release didn't warrant a spot on their main news site but was just mentioned as a posted link on their Twitter account, that's still coverage that will drive additional traffic to your app's product page in the App Store. No matter how small, any publicity a third party gives your app is worthy of a thank-you.

Expressing your gratitude with a sincere e-mail note also helps strengthen your relationship with those journalists and bloggers. Creating a dialogue with them keeps those valuable connections open, so that you can continue sending new app announcements their way.

Issuing Promo Codes: Soliciting App Reviews on Influential Blogs and Review Sites

For those sites that post app reviews, you won't want to send them only a press release. You should also contact them about writing a review of your app, which requires a slightly modified pitch.

With more than 300,000 apps in the App Store, everyone wants their app reviewed, so how do you ensure that your app stands out from the crowd? This is where having an established relationship with prominent bloggers and app reviewers (as discussed in Chapter 10) can help move your app to the front of the queue. If you've already prepped them with sneak-preview screenshots and a video trailer of your app during your prerelease marketing efforts, and they were impressed, there's a good chance they will want to review your app when it's released.

Providing Review Materials

Your app review pitch should contain all the information from your press release, plus additional media materials such as a few screenshots, a video trailer, and the app's icon—basically all of the elements that you included on your web site's press page and/or downloadable press kit. Depending on the submission rules of each web site, reviewers may ask you to include screenshots and other app-related images as e-mail attachments or require URLs of your materials online. Some sites accept app review requests only through online web forms.

Here's a rundown of the materials that most app reviewers require:

- **Your elevator pitch:** Why should reviewers care about your app or game? They need to be sold on why your new app is important to their readers. That elevator pitch I talked about crafting in Chapter 10 is proving to be quite useful in almost all of your marketing efforts—your web site, App Store text, press release, and now app review requests! Use your elevator pitch to help construct an appealing e-mail subject line and app description. Those two elements need to convey your passion and excitement as the creator of the app. Reviewers are extremely busy, so brevity is key. Like your press release, your app description should be short. And always remember to include your app's price!

- **Three to five screenshots**: Don't inundate reviewers with too many screenshots. Pick three that best represent your app, and submit only those. If a site requires that you submit more than that, send the five screenshots that you had uploaded to the App Store, since those were obviously picked as the best representations of your app.

- **Video trailer**: If you've produced a video trailer that shows the app or game in action, *always* include a URL link for viewing that as well. As I mentioned in Chapter 10, pay close attention to production value, because your video trailer is a direct reflection of your app's quality. A well-produced video trailer can educate a reviewer in less than two minutes—less time than it would take to download and test-drive your app. This can often be the deciding factor on whether your app gets reviewed.

- **App icon and App Store URL**: Although some reviewers don't require your app icon image, you should always include a direct link to your app in the App Store. This enables them to check out your App Store listing and link to it from their review. Instead of copying the long, complicated URL from the App Store, it is often easier to provide Apple's shortened iTunes link format of `http://itunes.com/apps/APPNAME`, replacing `APPNAME` with your application's official App Store name. For example, the link to the popular Bump app is `http://itunes.com/apps/bump`. For those reviewers who do accept app icon images, submit the high-quality 512 × 512 pixel version for maximum flexibility.

- **App web site URL**: Definitely include a link to your app's web site so that reviewers can explore any additional online resources you offer. Don't be disappointed if a review does not link to your web site. The iTunes Affiliate Program is a major revenue source for many review sites, so typically the review will only direct readers to your app in the App Store via an affiliate link.

- **Contact information**: Just as with your press release, make sure to provide all your relevant contact information, such as your name, company name, e-mail address, phone number, Skype, IM, and Twitter. The more options you provide, the better. It's surprising just how many developers forget to include these vital details. If a reviewer can't reach you with additional questions, that alone could prevent a review from being written.

- **Promo code:** Many sites tell you not to include a promo code with your app review request, stating that if they're interested in reviewing the app after evaluating your submission, they will ask for a promo code. It's nice that they don't want to unnecessarily waste promo codes for apps they don't plan on reviewing, but here's a little secret. If you provide a promo code with your initial review request, you've made it incredibly convenient for them to download your app for free and try it immediately. Odds are they will use the supplied promo code, and your chances of getting reviewed just got a little better! Apple limits how many promo codes you can issue per app version, so you'll want to use your promo codes sparingly. Supply them with the initial submission only to the most popular and influential review sites.

Not sure what a promo code is? I explain what they are and how to acquire them in the following section.

Obtaining Promo Codes

Promo codes are special codes that you can use to provide someone with a free copy of your app. Promo codes work just like iTunes gift card codes and are redeemed in the same way. This is the easy and recommended way to provide journalists, bloggers, and app reviewers with a free download of your product.

A promo code is assigned to a specific item in the iTunes Store. In this case, that's your iOS application. If a user redeems a promo code provided by you, only the related app is downloaded free of charge. That promo code cannot be used to download any other item. And as with gift cards, once a promo code is redeemed, it can never be used again, which prevents piracy.

Promo codes are not tied to an individual's iTunes account, so treat them like cash. A promo code can be given to anyone you want.

Apple grants you only 50 promo codes per app update. So if you use up all 50 promo codes for your 1.0 version, you won't be able to request any more promo codes until after your next app update is uploaded and approved in the App Store.

Although 50 may sound like a lot, these promo codes will disappear much faster than you might expect. Everyone loves free apps, so a lot of people will ask you for promo codes, but use them sparingly.

Your first priority is making sure you have enough promo codes for the press and app reviews. After that, you can use remaining ones for giveaways and promotions. But I recommend always hanging onto a handful of promo codes, just in case an exciting app review or marketing opportunity presents itself down the road.

So, how do you obtain promo codes for your iOS app? As with everything else associated with your App Store products, promo codes are managed from Apple's iTunes Connect site. Log in to iTunes Connect at `http://itunesconnect.apple.com/` and within the Manage Your Applications section, select your app. Then navigate to your app's View Details page. From there, you can access the Promotional Codes screen and enter the number of promo codes you need (as long as you don't exceed your remaining balance of codes for that app update). If your allotment isn't yet depleted, simply return to iTunes Connect any time you need additional promo codes issued to you.

If you don't see a link or button for promo codes on your app's View Details page, that means the app has not yet been approved by Apple. Since promo codes are redeemed via iTunes, your app must be available for sale in the App Store before you can request promo codes for it.

If you want to send an advance copy of your app to someone to review before it's available in the App Store, then obviously you won't be able to issue a promo code. Your only option is to use ad hoc distribution to provide the app to that reviewer. Most, if not all, app review sites can provide their device IDs and will accept ad hoc distributed versions if they have agreed to do an advance review. And since sneak previews and exclusives for highly anticipated apps are greatly desired, they will gladly deal with the irritating complexity of ad hoc distribution and expiring provision profiles.

But keep in mind that you can register only 100 device IDs per year for all your apps combined, whereas Apple is much more generous with 50 promo codes per app update. If your app is already available in the App Store, don't waste your precious ad hoc device ID allotment. Issue promo codes instead, which are preferred by reviewers anyway.

Publicity Requires Planning and Patience

Just because you sent someone a promo code, don't assume that automatically grants you an app review. And even if a reviewer does eventually write about your app, it may not be within the timetable you anticipated. As I've mentioned, journalists and reviewers are extremely busy, receiving hundreds of new product releases and review requests every day. It may be days or even weeks before they reply to your inquiry, so be patient.

I know I'm starting to sound like a broken record, but this is yet another reason why establishing relationships with the press during your early prerelease marketing efforts is so important. Everything takes time, and publicity is no different, so plan ahead.

If an important app review site does not respond to your submission in a timely manner, whatever you do, never offer bribes, beg, or attempt to solicit sympathy. And, certainly, don't hassle them with a mind-numbing barrage of e-mail messages and phone calls.

Such behavior will not only ruin your chances at receiving coverage, but it may just get you and your company banned from the site.

You can preempt much of the mystery by asking two simple questions when you're initially contacting bloggers and reviewers:

- After receiving a new press release or app review inquiry, how long does it typically take for an article or review to be written and posted online?

- If I don't receive a response, may I check back with you in a week or two?

If you push too hard, you may not like the result. If you're dealing with a fellow developer with a popular app review blog and you're having trouble getting him to commit to writing a review, tread carefully. Keep in mind that the reason could be that he didn't like your app and is reluctant to write a negative review, because as a developer, he understands how much hard work went into its creation. If you continue to hound him, he may opt to publish the bad review just to get you off his back. And that certainly doesn't help you at all, so approach every potential opportunity with patience.

For those of you who are eager to speed up the app review process and move to the front of the line, a few sites out there offer expedited app reviews for a fee. For the record, I'm *not* a fan of buying reviews, especially since some of those sites won't write a review unless you agree to buy into their sponsorship or premium review packages. Due to my own disapproval of that tactic, I won't promote those site names here. They will be easy enough for you to spot when requesting app reviews. Granted, I understand that the ethical quandary is somewhat alleviated, since the fee promises only that a review will be written, with no guarantee that it will be positive. You could pay the fee and still receive a bad review.

If you're going to go down that path, why not pay for an unbiased review to be posted where it can reach the most eyeballs: in the App Store! Truevoo (http://www.truevoo.com/) offers just such a pay-per-review service, and you won't even need to waste any promo codes! It costs you only the price of your app plus a small service fee per review. When posted reviews show up in the App Store, the reviewers are then reimbursed the app cost, so they receive a free app for their efforts.

Even if you encourage happy customers to post App Store reviews, that won't help you the first day or two your app is available in the App Store. You'll be heavily promoting your app's release, driving as much traffic as possible to your product page in the App Store, and yet for the first couple days, it may have only a few customer reviews. Without a substantial number of reviews, consumers may be hesitant to buy your app. If your app has more than a dozen reviews in the App Store, that seems to change how it is perceived, causing people to be a little less reluctant to make a purchase.

If you have several friends or peers who would be willing to post a review, it's worth sacrificing ten promo codes to ensure that your app has a decent number of reviews in the App Store during those crucial first few days after its debut. You could also give away a few promo codes on AppGiveaway (http://www.appgiveaway.com/) or via your

Twitter and Facebook accounts in exchange for some App Store reviews. Just make sure the participants post honest, objective reviews. Having all five-star ratings on the very first day will look quite suspect!

Using Promotions and Giveaways to Improve App Discovery

Who doesn't love freebies? Giving away something of value is a great way to draw attention to your iOS app, especially if it's your app that's free! Temporarily reducing your app's price to free for a single day or a weekend can help boost it higher in the App Store's Top Free Apps charts, especially if you notify all the iOS-related news sites of this limited-time offer. Those sites love to report on price reductions and freebies, so the stunt should gain your app quite a bit of exposure. And if you partner with a popular giveaway site, such as the following services, the extra publicity should really improve your app's ranking and visibility in the App Store charts.

- FreeAppADay (http://www.freeappaday.com/) and its related FreeAppADay Store iPhone app (see Figure 12–2)

- OpenFeint's Free Game of the Day site (http://freegameoftheday.com/) and its related Game Channel iPhone app (see Figure 12–2)

- Free App Calendar (http://www.freeappcalendar.com/)

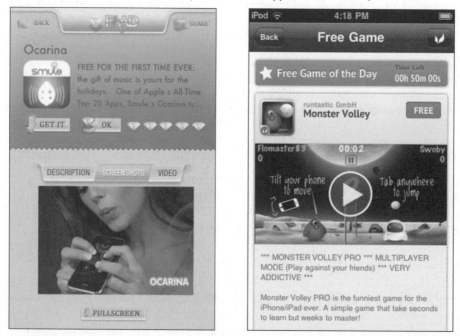

Figure 12–2. *Beyond the audience that visits their respective web sites, the FreeAppADay Store app (left) and OpenFeint's free Game Channel app (right) can promote your free app offer directly to mobile users.*

If you're scratching your head, wondering how you're supposed to profit by giving away your app, then you're not looking at the big picture. It's true that you won't be making any money from all those users who downloaded the app for free, and you won't see a huge spike in paid app sales after the free offer ends. So why do it? This strategy is all about the up-sell.

By removing the price barrier for a limited time, you may have thousands of new users take advantage of the free download. Those are new customers who probably would not have purchased your app. So, thousands of new users are discovering your app for the first time. If they enjoy the free app, you've just expanded your customer base with an opportunity to up-sell future In-App Purchase content and other new apps. Even if you were already doing that within a free lite version, there's a big difference in audience size. The lite version of your relatively unknown app may reach 50,000 users over the course of a few months, whereas a highly publicized weekend giveaway of your full paid version may add more than 100,000 new users to your existing customer base in only a matter of days.

This strategy works only if you have a way to eventually convert a large percentage of these new users into paying customers. Having In-App Purchase items available within your app or cross-promoting another paid app can make these kinds of free giveaway offers less risky.

Robert Szeleney partnered with FreeAppADay to offer his popular Rope'n'Fly game as a free App Store download for one day. He did this with the express intent of spreading awareness for the new sequel, Rope'n'Fly 2. He capitalized on the free download offer by promoting the sequel on the original game's main screen (see Figure 12–3), reaching a much larger audience in the process. This extra exposure helped propel Rope'n'Fly 2 into the App Store's Top 50 Paid Apps chart.

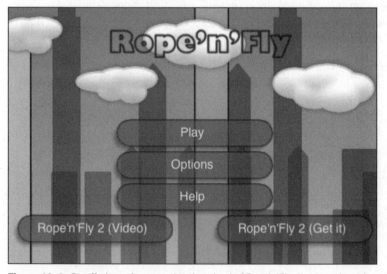

Figure 12–3. *By offering a free one-day download of Rope'n'Fly, the game's main screen helped promote the new paid sequel, Rope'n'Fly 2, to a much larger audience.*

If you currently have only one app available and do not have any plans to integrate In-App Purchase, then offering a limited-time free download will aid in app discovery and visibility within the App Store, but it may not improve your sales. Candy Cane was fortunate in that its gamble of giving away Fling! for a short time pushed the game to the number-one spot on the App Store's Top Free Apps chart. When Fling! returned to its normal price, the wave of positive word-of-mouth recommendations from users resulted in enough sales to catapult Fling! into the US Top 50 Paid Apps chart.

If you have faith in the quality of your app, then the limited-time free strategy may work for you, but it's risky. For most apps that try this approach, the developers see a slight bump in sales after the free offer ends, but it doesn't last long. Without a way to up-sell In-App Purchase items or cross-promote other products, it's often hard to justify this kind of freebie strategy.

If you're worried about cannibalizing potential app sales, then why not give away something else? That's what Tap Tap Tap did. To promote the launch of the voice-morphing app Voices, Tap Tap Tap partnered with Potion Factory to offer a free copy of its Voice Candy application for Mac OS X. To help promote the Voices iPhone app, consumers had to tweet about the special offer on Twitter in order to download their free copy of Voice Candy. Tap Tap Tap announced this "TweetBlast" promotion through MacHeist's e-mail database and Twitter feed, initially reaching almost 600,000 members. The word was spread via Twitter, and more and more people found their way to the web site. They then tweeted about it to receive the free Mac software.

Tap Tap Tap conducted a successful viral campaign that motivated tens of thousands of people to tweet about the offer, which resulted in hundreds of thousands of people checking out the Voices app. Besides providing the promotion details, the web site also beautifully showcased Tap Tap Tap's Voices app with demo videos and an App Store buy button (see Figure 12–4). And sure enough, the ploy worked. With an introductory price of only 99 cents, enough people purchased the app within the first few days that Voices skyrocketed to number one in the US Top Paid Apps chart.

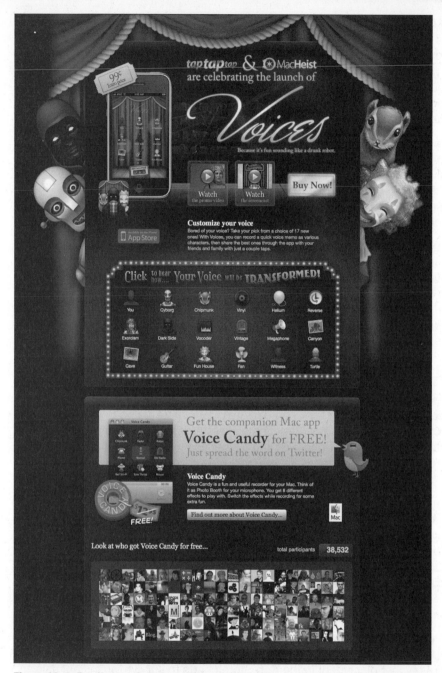

Figure 12–4. *By offering a free copy of Voice Candy for Mac to anyone who tweeted about the special promotion, Tap Tap Tap's clever TweetBlast campaign helped propel Voices to number one in the US App Store's Top Paid Apps chart.*

With Tap Tap Tap's John Casasanta being the creator of MacHeist, the company had unique access to an extremely large targeted audience. Obviously, most independent developers won't have mailing lists as large as MacHeist's list, but this kind of social media-based promotion can still work on a smaller level. If you followed my advice in Chapter 10 and have spent the past few months cultivating your own audience via Twitter, Facebook, e-mail newsletters, and blog readers, you should have a sizable base for communicating special offers, giveaways, and other app-related news.

Any online promotion, especially one that utilizes social media, should be designed to grow your audience. Don't give away free software, promo codes, or prizes without receiving a valuable connection in return. Even if people tweet about your app, there's no guarantee those tweets will turn into sales. But if people were required to follow you on Twitter or subscribe to your free e-mail newsletter in order to participate in the promotion, then regardless of the outcome, your marketing efforts would be rewarded.

That's exactly what Tap Tap Tap did with its Voices TweetBlast campaign. To get the free Voice Candy software, participants were required to first sign up for a free MacHeist account, follow @TapTapTap on Twitter, and then tweet a very specific message. Even if the promotion didn't pay off with a substantial boost in Voices sales, it added thousands of new Twitter followers and MacHeist members, enabling Tap Tap Tap to easily reach those people again in the future with special offers and new product announcements.

Timing a Good Sale to Rejuvenate App Downloads

Like freebies, sale prices are also heavily reported by many online app directories and app review sites, so the extra publicity can definitely drive more traffic to your app in the App Store. A carefully timed sale will attract new customers who ordinarily may not have purchased your app at its regular price. During a sale, you won't make as much profit per purchase, but ideally, the increase in sales volume will make up the difference.

The goal is to exceed your usual daily revenue and climb higher in the App Store charts. The higher you rank, the more visible your app is within the App Store, especially if your sale price has boosted the app into the Top 100. That visibility exposes your product to new consumers who may not have previously known about it. Seeing your app perform well in the App Store will prompt people to check it out. It's a bit of a vicious cycle. You must sell a lot of units to rank high in the App Store charts, but once you're in the Top 100, that visibility will help you sell even more. For as long as that position can be maintained, keep offering the discounted price. When your app eventually falls out of the charts, you can evaluate whether to revert to the regular price.

Some iOS developers offer a special introductory low price on a new app the moment it lands in the App Store. If it's a short-lived, hit-driven release, like a game or a novelty app that requires higher placement in the App Store charts to survive, an instant sale price can maximize its chance for success. But if you've developed a niche app that caters to a very targeted audience, offering a discount right out of the gate could prove to be a bad move.

Unlike many hit-driven games, productivity apps typically enjoy a much longer life cycle, since they satisfy a distinct need. If there's a significant demand for your app's unique features, early adopters won't hesitate to pay regular price. By offering a discount on day one, you would be selling them the app for less money than they were prepared to spend (which is great for consumers but bad for your bottom line). Since most niche apps don't rank high in the overall App Store charts anyway, an introductory sale price will only reduce the amount of revenue you could have made selling the same number of downloads at regular price.

When the initial popularity of your app starts to decline and the weekly revenue begins to slide into the "long tail" of the product's life (as discussed in Chapter 8), that's a perfect time to hold a sales event. The reduced price will help lure new customers and rejuvenate interest in the app. If you find that the discount is sustaining an acceptable level of sales, you can always decide to permanently stick with that price point for the remainder of its time in the App Store.

A well-received sale offer on one app can also positively affect the rest of your product line in the App Store. Customers who enjoy their new purchase will be curious about your other offerings. If you're effectively cross-promoting your products within each app, then a spike in downloads for the discounted app will also drive more traffic to your other apps, which often results in more purchases.

Can Advertising Sell Apps?

This is one of the most commonly asked questions by iOS developers. The answer is somewhat less definitive than you might expect. Advertising your app can result in enough sales to justify the expense if you choose the right medium and market, but that's easier said than done.

Unless you're using Apple's iAd for Developers program or a pay-per-install incentive solution like Tapjoy, it's extremely difficult to accurately track the conversion rate of your advertising campaign. Web and mobile ad networks track the click-throughs to the App Store, and Apple tracks sales of your app, but how do you tie the two reports together to pinpoint just how many of those ad clicks turned into actual app sales? One way to accomplish this is by using an iTunes Affiliate Program URL for your advertisement link. Beyond the benefit of earning a 5 percent commission on all sales derived from iTunes affiliate links (as discussed in Chapter 6), it's also a great way to track which ad click-throughs result in app sales. And if you're already using similar affiliate links on your web site, LinkShare allows you to assign a unique signature ID to the iTunes affiliate link you employ for your advertisement, so that click-throughs and sales from your ad can be easily identified in your LinkShare reports.

Advertising to a Mobile Audience

If you're going to experiment with advertising, try your hand at mobile ads first, since they are the most targeted. As I've said many times, more than 90 percent of iPhone users download apps directly from the mobile device's App Store. This is your target audience, so what better way to reach them than advertising within another iOS app or on a mobile web site?

If you've already implemented in-app advertising in your own app with AdMob (as mentioned in Chapter 7), then you'll be able to benefit from its Download Exchange program. This program enables you to advertise your apps across other apps in their network by giving up some of your app's ad inventory. Optime Software's Jon Schlegel found it be a very cost-effective way to test some initial advertising. "We typically use the AdMob Download Exchange to promote new app releases," said Jon. "The extra download volume that comes from the Download Exchange can sometimes be enough to push an app into a more favorable position in the App Store rankings."

Of course, if your app doesn't feature in-app advertising, you'll need to pay for the ad campaign. Since you're paying per click, include the price and a short descriptor to prevent the curious from tapping the ad just to find out the price or what the app does. With advertising typically being fairly expensive, if your app is priced at only 99 cents, then you'll need to be very careful not to spend more than you could possibly make in new sales.

While your ad campaign is actively running, pay close attention to your daily sales reports in iTunes Connect to see whether you can recognize sales spikes that may have been caused by the ad. If your advertisement is using an iTunes Affiliate Program link, it's much easier to track the sales performance of your ad through your LinkShare reports. If you don't see any significant sales impact, you might want to modify your ad campaign to see whether the results improve.

 Don't be afraid to continuously tweak your ad text until you find a message that proves effective. It's important to give your campaign a solid amount of time before discontinuing it. Successful advertising is all about frequency and volume. Advertising for only a couple days is not enough time to properly evaluate its effectiveness. Repetition is the name of the game. People may need to see an ad a few times before they are motivated to tap it, especially if they are immersed in the current app and have not been paying much attention to the embedded in-app ads.

Average click-throughs typically hover around 2 percent of ad views, and even then there's no guarantee those App Store visitors will purchase the app. Your ad campaign needs to be viewed by millions of iOS users for it to generate enough traffic to your App Store page. And what if that massive traffic volume still doesn't result in sales?

Many developers have found that advertising a freemium app or free lite version produces a much higher conversion rate than a paid app, since there's no risk for the consumer to download a free app. Then the freemium app or free lite version can help close the deal, acting as a much better sales tool to up-sell In-App Purchase items or a paid app. Focused Apps' Mark Johnson revealed, "We've launched a free app into the Top 100 charts on as little as $1,000 in mobile advertising and had it rise to the Top 10 in many countries. That's much harder to do with a paid app."

If you venture into web advertising, buying keywords and ads on search engines and popular portal sites is often too costly for low-priced mobile apps, not to mention that some of the people clicking your ad may not even own an iOS device. Your best bet is to focus your web advertising efforts on niche sites that specifically target your app's audience. For example, if it's a game, advertise on a popular iOS gaming site, such as TouchArcade (http://toucharcade.com).

Print advertising is difficult to justify for most mobile apps. Not only is it expensive, but it's unable to deliver instant access to your App Store page as a clickable online ad does. Your URL is listed in print, which requires interested readers to manually type the URL into their web browser the next time they are sitting at their computer or using their mobile device. By that point, they may have forgotten about your ad. If you're an independent developer on a shoestring budget, then print advertising may be out of your league—stick with web and mobile ads.

If you work for a big company with a large advertising budget, then print advertising can be very effective in reinforcing your brand identity. Print magazines usually require a three-month lead, so by the time your print ad's issue hits newsstands, your app may have already fallen into the long tail of its life cycle—an opportune stage for the ad to revive consumer interest and app downloads.

Advertising can work when aimed at the right audience. Just tread carefully to see whether it's a good fit for your iOS app before diving in with both feet. Keep in mind that no single marketing tactic will turn your app into a best seller. If you incorporate the many strategies you've learned from this book into an orchestrated marketing plan, you'll soon be on the road to achieving success in the App Store.

Taking Advantage of iAd for Developers

What sets Apple's iAd for Developers program apart from other in-app advertising options is that it seamlessly brings the App Store into the host app that's showing your iAd. When people tap an iAd for Developers banner, they see a screen that resembles an App Store product page, displaying your app's information, complete with description, customer ratings, screenshots, and even a purchase button.

Apple has deeply integrated this system with iOS and the App Store, so users can buy your app from that screen without ever leaving their host application. They can continue to use the current app while their new app purchase is being downloaded to their device in the background. There's no inconvenience to the customer, and you just gained a new sale!

Because Apple controls the entire process—from ad presentation to purchase to download—your iAd for Developers campaign reports provide a truly accurate account of the conversion rate from click-through to actual purchase. Since you're paying per click-through, this equates to your cost per acquisition—the actual cost of your new customers from this campaign based on the number of click-throughs you paid for.

Even though Apple devised the iAd for Developers program to be a cost-effective solution for independent app creators, the iAd network should still be regarded as a premium advertising platform, so the per click-through rate is higher than many other mobile ad networks. Since iAd is an Apple brand that consumers trust, that premium may just be worth the extra expense—if you have the right mix of product and price.

With a lot of iAd click-throughs and not enough actual purchases, some developers have experienced a cost per acquisition that's much higher than the actual price of the app itself. If you're selling a 99-cent app, that's a difficult advertising expense to justify. Unless you have In-App Purchase items to up-sell to these new customers, you would likely be losing money instead of making it.

But higher priced paid apps and freemium apps may be the right fit for iAd for Developers. For many developers, it produces a better cost per acquisition than other mobile ad networks. Apple has announced that 75 percent of the participants in the iAd for Developers program have renewed their ad campaigns.

Like any other advertising venture, if you feel your app would benefit from the iAd for Developers program, test the waters with a trial budget you can afford. By closely monitoring your ad campaign's performance, you'll quickly see if it's a profitable selling tool for your app. To learn more about the iAd for Developers program, check out http://advertising.apple.com/developers/.

Pay-Per-Install Incentives to Cross-Sell Apps

Another interesting advertising concept is pay-per-install *incentives*. Instead of simply advertising your app within other apps on a pay-per-install basis (hoping for a decent conversion rate), incentives are provided to help motivate more users to install the advertised app. This typically works well only in games where users are rewarded with some kind of in-game virtual currency in exchange for downloading a specific app. For example, NimbleBit's Pocket Frogs offers a free virtual frog to users who download a specified app from the App Store (see Figure 12–5).

Figure 12–5. *As an incentive to download specified apps, NimbleBit's Pocket Frogs rewards those users with a free in-game exotic frog.*

This kind of system usually requires a detection method for verifying the participating app was downloaded and run at least once. The host app needs to be notified that the task was successfully completed, and the user should be awarded the promised in-game incentive.

Some developers have created their own strategic alliances among themselves to cross-promote each other's apps with in-game rewards as download incentives. This works well for all parties involved, although results tend to be on a smaller scale.

To really take advantage of this concept and reach a much larger audience across more games, you might want to employ a third-party service, like Tapjoy (`https://www.tapjoy.com/`) or Flurry's AppCircle Rewards (`http://www.flurry.com/product/appcircle/rewards/`), that specializes in pay-per-install incentives. Pairing your app promotion with similar genre apps to reach a highly targeted audience, these programs have been known to drive hundreds of thousands of new installations a day, propelling your app into the App Store's top charts. Although these types of campaigns are often more expensive than traditional banner advertising, they can really boost app sales. This works especially well with freemium games, since there's no cost barrier to users to download, and once hooked on the game play, In-App Purchases can amortize the expense of the pay-per-install campaign.

Staying Connected with Customers

Maintaining consumer interest in your app is not just about attracting new customers; it's also about keeping your existing customers happy. Remember when I talked about loyal customers being the best customers in Chapter 8? The way to build customer loyalty is through high-quality support and delivering bug fixes and additional features/content in a timely manner.

Delivering Frequent App Updates

Don't wait months before releasing updated versions of your app. Even without any reported bugs or crashes, you should update the app periodically, providing additional polish and value. A lack of updates can negatively affect your customers' perception of your app in the App Store. If consumers notice that your app hasn't been updated in several months, they may be reluctant to purchase the app for fear that it's no longer actively supported.

By continuing to update the app, you're enhancing the user experience and keeping your app top of mind. Even if your app's overall customer usage eventually declines because of distractions from new app purchases, whenever a new version shows up in a customer's Updates list, it serves as subtle reminder of your app's value and your commitment to supporting it.

If customers remain satisfied with your app, they will be that much more motivated to buy In-App Purchase items and other new products from you. A steady stream of updates also helps sustain customer usage, which is extremely important if your primary revenue stream is in-app advertising. As long as you keep delivering a rewarding and fun experience, people will continue to talk about your app. Continuous updates and high-quality customer support are big factors in driving word-of-mouth.

Providing High-Quality Support

In previous chapters, I've discussed the importance of setting up a support site and e-mail address for customers who need assistance or have questions. How you use that communication channel will ultimately determine its effectiveness as a business tool. Customer relationship management is the most organic form of direct marketing and sales. People who feel good about your company will want to support you in return, not only by buying your apps and downloadable content, but also by becoming advocates who recommend your apps and services to friends on Twitter, Facebook, and other social media platforms. Even hackers using pirated apps have been known to later become legitimate buyers of In-App Purchase content if they appreciate the developers' efforts.

Online word-of-mouth is a double-edged sword that can cut both ways. It has the power to catapult products from obscurity to overnight success, as well as to destroy business reputations within a matter of hours. The lesson is to always treat customer inquiries with absolute respect and care.

Take the time to implement an organized customer-support system that enables you to not only respond quickly to bug reports and issues, but also effectively track customer support histories and contact information. This usually goes beyond the capabilities of most e-mail applications, requiring the use of a more feature-rich customer-management solution, such as help desk software or a web-based trouble-ticket system. Perform a search online for *customer support software*, and you'll discover that dozens of products and services are available. Many of them, such as Zendesk (http://www.zendesk.com/), offer affordable pricing tiers that cater to both solo developers and large enterprises, depending on your specific needs.

What's especially interesting about Zendesk is that it provides several appealing features for iOS developers. If you're already using GetSatisfaction (http://getsatisfaction.com/) as your online support solution, those community comments can be synchronized with Zendesk. For those of you using MailChimp to send out e-mail newsletters, that can be integrated with Zendesk for e-mail–based customer-support management. Want to access your help desk system remotely? Just download the free Zendesk app for iPhone and iPad. Zendesk even provides an open source feedback form that you can embed into your Xcode project, enabling customers to submit support requests directly to your Zendesk account from within your iOS app! You can download Zendesk's Cocoa library for iPhone at http://github.com/zendesk/zendesk-iphone-dropbox.

By tracking customer support histories, you'll be able to better serve each customer's unique needs and effectively monitor recurring issues. You should reply to every support e-mail you receive, even if it's only a feature request. A quick thank-you reply is an easy way to establish a nice rapport with your customers. People like to know their voice has been heard.

When major bugs do surface, it's important to react quickly. The first thing you should do is immediately update your app's description in the App Store, notifying consumers that you're aware of the problem. Let users know up front that the issue is being addressed and an updated version will be available soon. This should help reduce the flood of redundant support e-mail messages and—fingers crossed—help dissuade people from venting their frustrations in a public forum that can damage your app's reputation. At the very least, it should buy you enough time to investigate and resolve the showstopping bug.

If the reported issue is a severe crash affecting a large percentage of your customers, and you need to get the fixed update into the App Store as soon as possible, you may be relieved to know that Apple provides expedited reviews for special circumstances. After submitting your updated app in iTunes Connect, send an e-mail message to Apple's review team at appreview@apple.com, explaining the situation. In emergency cases, Apple can expedite the app review in a day or two, saving you several days of waiting.

Apple will perform expedited reviews for you only once or twice (and Apple does keep track), so use this "get out of jail free card" very wisely. This is yet another reason why Chapter 9 placed such a strong emphasis on extensive testing before submitting your application to the App Store. The developer community is fortunate to have this direct e-mail line into Apple, so please don't use it to communicate anything other than critical app review issues.

Additional Tips for Sustaining Momentum in the App Store

Beyond soliciting app reviews, participating in iOS-related web forums, growing your audience online via Twitter and Facebook, and the myriad of other marketing and publicity strategies already outlined in Chapter 10 and this chapter, the following sections discuss a few more important topics.

Banking on the Prestige of Awards and Endorsements

Enter your app into as many high-profile iPhone awards competitions as possible. Winning an award can do wonders for both your app and your company, providing a landslide of publicity and prestige. And with all the press that reports on the winners, being included will increase consumer awareness and boost app sales. Even if you're only a semifinalist, that extra exposure and recognition will definitely benefit your app. Here are a few to consider:

- Apple Design Awards (http://developer.apple.com/wwdc/ada/)
- 148Apps' Best App Ever Awards (http://bestappever.com/)
- Appsfire's App Star Awards (http://appsfire.com/appstar)
- App Hall of Fame (http://www.apphalloffame.com/)

Although all the awards listed here are very influential, landing a renowned Apple Design Awards (ADA) one is perceived as the highest honor an iOS developer can achieve. Submitting your app to the ADA is a great way to gain Apple's attention. Even if you don't win an award, if your app impresses Apple, it may just get selected as a featured app in the App Store. And we all know that being showcased by Apple in the App Store has the power to transform apps into best sellers.

Endorsements from respected developers and media personalities can also provide welcome sales spikes. The once little-known Simplenote was publicly endorsed online by John Gruber as his favorite notes app. Because of the large readership of Gruber's DaringFireball.net site, sales for Simplenote shot through the roof in the days that followed.

As I mentioned in Chapter 10, high-profile awards and expert testimonials should be proudly displayed on your app's web site and App Store description like merit badges. Awards and endorsements offer validation and a seal of approval that influence consumer perception of your app.

Share Your Knowledge

In Chapter 10, I discussed the value of writing blog posts and articles about your iOS app development experiences as a way to grow your online audience during the prerelease stage. Publishing your thoughts, insights, and lessons learned from the process helps bridge a connection between you and your readers. Ideally, they will have a greater appreciation for your efforts and the finished product. But don't stop once the app is available in the App Store.

iOS developers love to read about the experiences of their peers and are often quick to retweet your URL if they think the blog post would be of interest to other fellow developers. Remember that many customers follow the blogs and tweets of their favorite app creators. So, if those developers spread the word about your app, their customers could also become your customers! Other web sites and blogs may link to your articles as well. And if you're lucky enough to get some link love on Digg, Techmeme, Technorati, or even Slashdot, you could see traffic to your site rise exponentially in a matter of hours.

Streaming Colour Studios' Owen Goss saw that happen firsthand after publishing a blog article about his Dapple game's sales numbers. Slashdot posted a story about it, linking to his blog, and Owen got to witness the famous "Slashdot effect." The day of the Slashdot post, Streaming Colour Studios' site traffic increased 4,000 percent, and his Dapple sales were four times more than the usual daily sales! As you can see, publishing interesting articles of value on your blog (with links from your social media accounts) has the potential to dramatically boost both product awareness and app sales.

Participating in Interviews and Podcasts

It goes without saying that invitations by the press and the developer community to be interviewed for a story or a featured guest on a popular podcast should be accepted when your schedule permits. This can have a similar effect to publishing frequent blog articles and Twitter posts, enabling consumers and peers to learn more about you as a person and business owner. It represents yet one more valuable audience for increasing sales and awareness for your app.

Be aware of the proposed topic before agreeing to participate in an interview or podcast. If the story takes a negative angle, your involvement could ultimately tarnish your reputation.

Also be very careful what you say in an interview. When you're on the record, speaking too casually about your opinions of other products, companies, and individuals can land you in hot water. Remember that most published articles remain online indefinitely, so your words can come back to haunt you again and again.

If you're charming and don't experience difficulties speaking in public, then this additional exposure can help endear new fans to your cause. If you're shy (like most programmers) with a distinct fear of public speaking, it might be beneficial to first receive some media training. It's important that you're able to make a good impression when speaking to the press or chatting on podcasts. Sure, media-training consultants and seminars cost money, but if you blow a high-profile interview, that could cost you even more.

Looking Toward the Horizon

First, I would like to thank you for reading this book. And second, I want to congratulate you for working so diligently through every chapter. Together, we've covered a vast number of important topics. You've learned about competitive research, in-app marketing strategies, alternative business models, the App Store submission process, online promotion, and much more. There was even a chapter dedicated to harnessing the power of In-App Purchase! This book was carefully designed to provide the essential tools, resources, and knowledge needed to transform your iOS app development from a fun hobby into a successful, thriving business.

Beyond what you've read within these pages, there will always be new avenues for promoting your app. Study what other developers are doing to market their mobile products—not only what works, but also which strategies fail and why. But don't limit your scope to only the iOS community. It's important to stay well informed on current events in the entire mobile arena by reading all the latest technology news sites and blogs, such as TechCrunch, Techmeme, Daring Fireball, and Mashable (to name just a few). Even software marketing campaigns for Google Android, Windows Phone, HP webOS, and mobile web apps may inspire new ideas that would lend themselves well to your own efforts reaching iPhone, iPad, and iPod touch users. The goal is to keep an open mind and embrace new strategies that can help grow your business.

With the App Store being such a phenomenal success, the iOS platform will undoubtedly expand onto new devices. And forthcoming SDK updates will continue to roll out an endless array of innovative new features. It's a fascinating time to be in mobile software, and Apple has only just begun to tap into the possibilities. With new opportunities arising every day for iOS developers, the future promises to be an exciting journey!

Online Resources for App Research and Marketing

Throughout the app planning, development, and marketing stages, I highly recommend exploring all of the wonderful iOS-related app directories, news, and review sites available online when performing competitive research and acquiring press coverage for your app.

With new sites springing up all the time, this appendix may not represent an exhaustive list of online resources, but with more than 90 links, this collection should serve as a good starting point.

> **NOTE:** As a reminder, some app review sites may charge a fee to write an app review or to guarantee an expedited review. Tread carefully, and always read a site's app review policy before submitting your app for consideration.

iOS App Directories, News, and Review Sites

Since many of these sites (listed here in alphabetical order) offer a combination of app news, reviews, forums, and more, it's nearly impossible to separate them into distinct categories. But you should really take the time to check out each and every one of these sites anyway so that you have a good understanding of all the competitive research and promotional opportunities available online.

- 148Apps (http://www.148apps.com/)
- All About iPhone (http://www.allaboutiphone.net/)
- All iPhone Apps Review (http://www.alliphoneappsreview.com/)
- App Advice (http://appadvice.com/)
- App of the Day (http://appoftheday.com/)

- App Smile (http://www.appsmile.com/)
- App Store Apps (http://www.appstoreapps.com/)
- AppAddict (http://appaddict.net/)
- AppBoy (http://www.appboy.com/)
- AppChatter (http://www.appchatter.com/)
- AppCraver (http://www.appcraver.com/)
- AppGamer (http://appgamer.net/)
- AppStoreHQ (http://www.appstorehq.com/)
- Apple iPhone School (http://www.appleiphoneschool.com/)
- AppleTell (http://www.appletell.com/)
- Appmodo (http://appmodo.com/)
- Appolicious (http://appolicious.com/)
- AppReview (http://appreview.com/)
- AppSafari (http://www.appsafari.com/)
- AppScout (http://www.appscout.com/)
- Appsfire (http://appsfire.com/)
- AppShopper (http://appshopper.com/)
- AppSIZED (http://www.appsized.com/)
- appSpace (http://appspace.com/)
- AppStruck (http://appstruck.com/)
- Apptism (http://www.apptism.com/)
- AppVee (http://www.appvee.com/)
- AppVersity (http://www.appversity.com/)
- Ars Technica's Infinite Loop (http://arstechnica.com/apple/)
- Art of the iPhone (http://artoftheiphone.com/)
- AverageApper (http://averageapper.com/)
- Buy Me An iPhone (http://www.buymeaniphone.com/)
- Chomp (http://chomp.com/)
- Crazy Mike's Apps (http://www.crazymikesapps.com/)
- Everything iCafe (http://www.everythingicafe.com/)
- FingerGaming (http://fingergaming.com/)

- Fresh Apps (http://www.freshapps.com/)
- Fuel Your Apps (http://www.fuelyourapps.com/)
- Gamezebo (http://www.gamezebo.com/iphone-games)
- GiggleApps (http://www.giggleapps.com/)
- I Use This App (http://www.iusethisapp.com/)
- iGame Radio (http://www.igameradio.com/)
- iLounge (http://www.ilounge.com/)
- iPhone Alley (http://www.iphonealley.com/)
- iPhone and Kids (http://www.iphoneandkids.com/)
- iPhone App Index (http://www.iphoneappindex.com/)
- iPhone App Reviews (http://www.iphoneappreview.com/)
- iPhone Application List (http://iphoneapplicationlist.com/)
- iPhone Dev SDK (http://www.iphonedevsdk.com/)
- iPhone Footprint (http://www.iphonefootprint.com/)
- iPhone Freak (http://www.iphonefreak.com/)
- iPhone Gamer Blog (http://iphonegamerblog.com/)
- iPhone Life (http://www.iphonelife.com/)
- iPhone-Game-Reviews.com (http://iphone-game-reviews.com/)
- iPhone.AppStorm (http://iphone.appstorm.net/)
- iPhoneAppCafe (http://iphoneappcafe.com/)
- iPwnGames (http://www.ipwngames.com/)
- iSource (http://isource.com/)
- Just Another iPad Blog (http://www.justanotheripadblog.com/)
- Mac User (http://www.macuser.co.uk/)
- Mac|Life (http://www.maclife.com/)
- MacNews (http://www.macnews.com/)
- MacNN (http://www.macnn.com/)
- MacStories (http://www.macstories.net/)
- MacUpdate (http://www.macupdate.com/explore/iphone/)
- Macworld AppGuide (http://www.macworld.com/appguide/)
- Macworld's iOS Central (http://ios.macworld.com/)

- Modojo (http://www.modojo.com/)

- No DPad (http://nodpad.com/)

- Planet-iPhones (http://planet-iphones.com/)

- Pocket Gamer (http://www.pocketgamer.co.uk/)

- PocketFullOfApps (http://pocketfullofapps.com/)

- PocketGamer.biz (http://www.pocketgamer.biz/)

- PocketPicks (http://www.pocketpicks.co.uk/)

- RazorianFly (http://www.razorianfly.com/)

- SlapApp (http://www.slapapp.com/)

- Slide To Play (http://www.slidetoplay.com/)

- The APPera (http://theappera.com/)

- The Daily App Show (http://dailyappshow.com/)

- The iPhone App Review (http://www.theiphoneappreview.com/)

- The Mac Observer (http://www.macobserver.com/)

- The Portable Gamer (http://theportablegamer.com/)

- The Unofficial Apple Weblog (http://www.tuaw.com/)

- TheAppleBlog (http://www.theappleblog.com/)

- TiPB (http://www.tipb.com/)

- Touch Arcade (http://toucharcade.com/)

- Touch Reviews (http://touchreviews.net/)

- TouchGen (http://touchgen.com/)

- TouchMyApps (http://www.touchmyapps.com/)

- What's on iPhone? (http://www.whatsoniphone.com/)

- Yappler (http://www.yappler.com/)

Additional App Marketing Resources

Here are two additional app marketing resources:

- **Selling Your Apps Forum**
  (http://iphonedevbook.com/forum/selling-your-apps/): The popular iPhone developers' community forum, iphonedevbook.com, has a dedicated forum called Selling Your Apps, where iOS developers can share business advice and marketing strategies. Join the discussion to either contribute your own knowledge or learn from the experiences of your peers. I'll also be posting on that forum from time to time, so come say hello.

- **The Book's Official Companion Site**
  (http://www.iphonebusinessbook.com/): This is for readers of *The Business of iPhone and iPad App Development* looking for the latest book updates, blog articles, and download access to the book's example Xcode projects.

Index

N